Changing Classes

How do schools influence the kind of person a child becomes? *Changing Classes* tells the story of a small, poor, ethnically mixed school district in Michigan's rust belt, a community in turmoil over the announced closing of a nearby auto assembly plant. As teachers and administrators began to find ways to make schooling more relevant to working-class children, two large-scale school reform initiatives swept into town: the governor's "marketplace" reforms and the National Science Foundation's "State Systemic Initiative." All this is set against the backdrop of the transformation to a global, post-Fordist economy. The result is an account of the complex linkages at work as society structures the development of children to adulthood.

Martin Packer is Associate Professor of Psychology at Duquesne University.

Learning in Doing: Social, Cognitive, and Computational Perspectives

General Editors
ROY PEA, *SRI International, Center for Technology in Learning*
JOHN SEELY BROWN, *Xerox Palo Alto Research Center*
CHRISTIAN HEATH, *The Management Centre, King's College, London*

Computation and Human Experience
PHILIP E. AGRE

The Computer as Medium
PETER BOGH ANDERSEN, BERIT HOLMQVIST, and JENS F. JENSEN (eds.)

Understanding Practice: Perspectives on Activity and Context
SETH CHAIKLIN and JEAN LAVE (eds.)

Situated Cognition: On Human Knowledge and Computer Representations
WILLIAM J. CLANCEY

Cognition and Tool Use: The Blacksmith at Work
CHARLES M. KELLER and JANET DIXON KELLER

Situated Learning: Legitimate Peripheral Participation
JEAN LAVE and ETIENNE WENGER

Sociocultural Psychology: Theory and Practice of Doing and Knowing
LAURA M. W. MARTIN, KATHERINE NELSON, and
ETHEL TOBACH (eds.)

The Construction Zone: Working for Cognitive Change in School
DENIS NEWMAN, PEG GRIFFIN, and MICHAEL COLE

Street Mathematics and School Mathematics
TEREZINHA NUNES, DAVID WILLIAM CARRAHER, and
ANALUCIA DIAS SCHLIEMANN

Distributed Cognitions: Psychological and Educational Considerations
GAVRIEL SALOMON (ed.)

Plans and Situated Actions: The Problem of Human–Machine Communication
LUCY A. SUCHMAN

Continued on page following the Index

Changing Classes

School Reform and the New Economy

MARTIN PACKER
Duquesne University

CAMBRIDGE
UNIVERSITY PRESS

PUBLISHED BY THE PRESS SYNDICATE OF THE UNIVERSITY OF CAMBRIDGE
The Pitt Building, Trumpington Street, Cambridge, United Kingdom

CAMBRIDGE UNIVERSITY PRESS
The Edinburgh Building, Cambridge CB2 2RU, UK
40 West 20th Street, New York, NY 10011-4211, USA
10 Stamford Road, Oakleigh, VIC 3166, Australia
Ruiz de Alarcón 13, 28014 Madrid, Spain
Dock House, The Waterfront, Cape Town 8001, South Africa

http://www.cambridge.org

First published 2001

Printed in the United States of America

Typeface Janson Text 10.25/13 pt.   *System* QuarkXPress 4.0 [CS]

A catalog record for this book is available from the British Library.

Library of Congress Cataloging in Publication Data
Packer, Martin J.
Changing classes : school reform and the new economy / Martin Packer.
p. cm.– (Learning in doing)
Includes bibliographical references (p.) and index.
ISBN 0-521-64234-5 (hb) ISBN 0-521-64540-9 (pb)
1. Education – Economic aspects – United States – Case Studies. 2. Willow Run
Community Schools (Willow Run, Mich.) 3. Education and state – United States – Case
studies. 4. Educational change – Economic aspects – United States – Case studies. I. Title.
II. Series.

LC66 .P23 2000
379.73 – dc21

00-026199

ISBN 0 521 64234 5   hardback
ISBN 0 521 64540 9   paperback

What is at stake is our vision of the kinds of human beings we would hope Americans to be in the last years of the twentieth and the first years of the twenty-first centuries, and of the kinds of education that will help bring those human beings into existence.

Lawrence A. Cremin, *Popular Education and Its Discontents.* Quoted in the report "Research and the Renewal of Education," from the National Academy of Education, 1991.

Contents

Series Foreword	*page* xi	
Acknowledgments	xiii	
Introduction	1	
1 The Class of 2001: June 9, 1994	10	
2 Blue Monday: December 1991–February 1992	23	
3 Vehicles of Reform, Drivers of Change: March 1992–June 1993	41	
4 America's Birthday: Summer 1993	70	
5 The Last First Day? August–November 1993	78	
6 Willow Run Is America: The 1940s and 1950s	109	
7 Crossing to the New Economy: November 1993–April 1994	134	
8 End-of-Year Report Cards: May–June 1994	158	
9 Rest and Relaxation? Summer 1994	175	
10 Caught in the Middle: August–November 1994	179	
11 The Change Game: November 1994–June 1995	211	
12 The Future of the Kids Coming Behind Us: June 1995–February 1997	236	
13 Quality or Equality? The Standardization of Schooling: March 1997	243	
14 Coda – June 1999	270	
Notes	281	
Index	301	

Series Foreword

This series for Cambridge University Press is becoming widely known as an international forum for studies of situated learning and cognition.

Innovative contributions are being made by anthropology, by cognitive, developmental, and cultural psychology, by computer science, by education, and by social theory. These contributions are providing the basis for new ways of understanding the social, historical, and contextual nature of the learning, thinking, and practice that emerges from human activity. The empirical settings of these research inquiries range from the classroom to the workplace, to the high technology office, and to learning in the streets and in other communities of practice.

The situated nature of learning and remembering through activity is a central fact. It may appear obvious that human minds develop in social situations and extend their sphere of activity and communicative competencies. But cognitive theories of knowledge representation and learning alone have not provided sufficient insight into these relationships.

This series was born of the conviction that new and exciting interdisciplinary syntheses are underway as scholars and practitioners from diverse fields seek to develop theory and empirical investigations adequate for characterizing the complex relations of social and mental life, and for understanding successful learning wherever it occurs. The series invites contributions that advance our understanding of these seminal issues.

Roy Pea
John Seely Brown
Christian Heath

Acknowledgments

The good wishes, time, energy, insight, companionship, humor, and encouragement of many people made this project worth the effort, through its ups and downs. In particular I am indebted to Donna Adams, JoAnne Allen, Mel Anglin, Karen Bergstrom, Larry Berlin, Mary Brandau, Laurie Brinkerhoff, Janice Brown, Jeremy Burks, Laura Chew, Chris Coletta, Todd de Stigter, Aviva Dorfman, Liza Finkel, Scott Fletcher, Ellice Forman, Fred Goodman, Gail Green, Scott Heister, Larry Hirschfeld, Betty Hopkins, Julia Hough, Cyd Karr, Phil Kearney, Glenn Klipp, Robert Koonz, Jean Lave, Vivian Lyte, Lori MacDonald, Shirley Magnusson, Ray Melberg, John Mergendoller, Julie Nicholson, Daphna Oyserman, Joyce Page, Pandora, Sheryl Plouffe, Will Purves, Stu Rankin, Constance Reardon, Anne Reeves, John Rogers, Sharon Ryles, Shari Saunders, Aaron Schutz, Anita Smith, Paula Sutherby, Deborah VanHoewck, Jean Wolter, Youseff Yomtoob, and last – but most certainly not least – the other teachers, staff, administrators, parents, and children of Willow Run. Thanks are due to the Office of the Vice President for Research, University of Michigan, to the Spencer Foundation, and to Duquesne University for their generosity. To a host of others who helped along the way, my thanks, and to anyone whose name has become lost in my notes, my apologies.

for granting a nonexclusive license to use AP proprietary material. To the *Detroit News* for granting permission to reprint material.

Additional information on this project and related work can be found at my Web site: www.duq.edu/liberalarts/gradpsych/packer.html

Changing Classes

Introduction

The future of every society lies with its children. As each generation takes up tasks and responsibilities from the preceding one, its attitudes, expectations, and conduct shape the form society takes. Schools are, in the societies that have them, a central institution preparing young people for their future as workers and citizens. Schools, I would maintain, are more than places where young people are taught knowledge and skills; they are crucibles wherein children are transformed. In doing this schools give direction to our society – they can perpetuate the status quo or create a new future. And this means that those who can control our schools may exert a significant influence on the direction of social change.

This book is an account of struggles now taking place over public schools in the United States. It is the story of a single school district – the Willow Run Community Schools, in Michigan – but the lessons learned from this one case can, I believe, help us better understand what is happening all over the United States, and abroad as well.

At the same time the book is a reflection on the character of schooling. Schools are so familiar that we take them for granted, but the debates over schooling make it clear that there is much confusion about just how schools work. I believe we currently lack a clear understanding of the psychological and sociological character of schooling – of just how it is that attending school changes a young person's way of engaging the world, changes the kind of person they are. Here I offer the beginnings of such an account.

In the United States, public schools have become targets for increasingly strident attacks and demands for reform. In the early 1990s a striking and surprising bipartisan consensus developed that schools were failing, that as a consequence the national economy was at risk, and that a "bridge to the twenty-first century" was needed that could be erected only if schooling were reformed. In particular, public schools were accused of failing to keep pace with dramatic changes in the workplace, changes in the character of industrial production and business organization.

Over the past two decades the United States has indeed undertaken a dramatic social upheaval, as computerization, merger and divestiture, downsizing and outsourcing, globalization and the World Wide Web have brought a shift from the familiar Fordist economy – standardized, large-scale, assembly-line production with a rigid and complex top-down hierarchy – to a new post-Fordist production – flexible, small-batch manufacture with a malleable and lean horizontal team organization. The production, distribution, and consumption of goods and services have all been transformed, become global, as companies move plants in search of cheaper labor, as trade agreements ease the flow of goods across national borders, and as computerized banking and trading enable currency to circle the globe in a fraction of a second.

Today the result of these changes is generally seen as an unprecedented boom – uninterrupted years of growth, low inflation, low unemployment, and a heady rise in stock prices. It is difficult now to recall how differently our situation was viewed less than a decade ago, when Bill Clinton won the presidency in part by reminding himself, "It's the economy, stupid." But there remains today another, hidden face to "Workplace 2000" – the costs paid for the boom include an enormous dislocation in which some kinds of work, especially manufacturing, have been eliminated, and job security and benefits have been relinquished by many workers. Poverty is growing, people are working longer hours for the same pay, there is an increasing inequity of income and wealth and a hovering threat of global economic and political instability. These problems have affected not just individuals, but entire communities. Over the past decade many communities have felt the stunningly painful effects of economic transition, abandoned as industrial facilities that provided apparently well-paying and secure jobs were closed in the name of "rationalization."

Willow Run is such a community. A small, poor, ethnically mixed school district in Michigan's rust belt, near Detroit, Willow Run was the child of twentieth-century state-regulated industrial production, born of a union between the power of the federal government and the wartime demand for mass production of complex fighting machines. The community was created by and took shape around the needs of large-scale industry – industry whose needs are now dramatically different.

I was fortunate enough to witness the efforts begun by teachers and administrators of the Willow Run schools to meet the challenges posed by the downsizing, southward migration, and reorganization of the auto industry. I began to visit the schools shortly after my arrival in Ann Arbor, Michigan, in 1991, having accepted a faculty position in the University of Michigan's School of Education. I found myself drawn into a tight-knit community with a dramatic history, a striking geography, and a wealth of good feeling.

In order both to understand the local reforms and try to facilitate them, I joined the committee that was working to foster change throughout the district. I attended the meetings of this committee, school board meetings, Town Hall meetings, traveled to the state Department of Education with other committee members, visited classrooms, attended school events, and spoke with teachers, students, parents, the superintendent, and other administrators.

So I was there when the Willow Run Community Schools found themselves caught up by not just one but two major initiatives for reform of the U.S. public schools. The first, legislation begun by Michigan's new Republican governor, John Engler, designed to bring market forces to bear on the schools and improve the "quality, performance, and accountability" of education, will be more familiar to most readers – it is a prime example of the "standards-based" movement that has swept through many U.S. states in the past decade.

But the second, though less well-known, is equally significant. It was a major program by the National Science Foundation (NSF), the "Statewide Systemic Initiative," intended to promote "systemic reform" of the public schools – a major effort that played out in 25 states and the Commonwealth of Puerto Rico, each of which received up to $10 million over a five-year period.

In this book I trace the district's navigation through these reform initiatives and the changing economy, to provide an intimate look at the complexities and contradictions of public schooling, to shine a critical light on state and national initiatives for school reform, and to explore how a community like Willow Run turns to its schools in times of challenge and threat. I take the reader behind the scenes to hear teachers and administrators reflecting on the constraints and resources that influence what happens in the classroom. My story is of a community struggling to preserve its identity, of educators working to meet the needs of children in danger of being left behind by fast-paced economic change, and of the way personal change and history intertwine. The local reformers understood that if the community was to survive its children must change. The schools had to do more than teach new skills, they had to change children's attitudes toward learning, to prepare them for a new way of life as their old lifestyle vanished.

And as a reflection on the character of modern schooling this book is a study of children's development within a broad social context, a careful look at one of the social institutions that structures the development of children to adulthood. It is an interpretation of schooling not merely as cognitive change, but as transformation of the whole person.

My story begins where my visits did, at Kettering Elementary School. I describe the changes at Kettering as staff and administrators worked to explore the implications of their discovery that teaching could be "fun" for both their students and themselves. These teachers had a rich grasp of the concrete realities of classroom life and of the community the schools served. I interpret their efforts and their renunciation of many elements of the traditional classroom as an important experiment at making schooling freshly relevant to working-class kids, children whose attitudes and needs – skepticism about book learning, valuing practical labor – had their roots in the "manual/mental" division of mass production. But I also interpret these local reform efforts as grounded in practitioners' tacit appreciation of the ways teaching and learning are relational and cultural, how schooling is a matter of forging relations and building culture. The staff understood that school reform requires changes in the relationship between "teacher" and "student" and changes in the culture of the school and the classroom.

The new Willow Run Systemic Initiative committee, in its meetings and presentations, applied the "same belief system" to the learning of teachers. Again relationship and culture were central. The committee sought to foster professional development by creating a safe environment in which staff would be willing to take risks, drawing from an ethos of caring and sharing uniquely Willow Run's, eschewing "top-down" mandates – the committee insisted it wasn't imposing new solutions but was there to help teachers achieve their own goals.

And as I follow the children to Willow Run's middle school, the importance of attending to relationship and culture is further highlighted. The middle school had introduced curriculum changes but also established a climate where discipline, maintaining order, was seen as paramount. These efforts were well intentioned, but culture and curriculum clashed and students responded with growing opposition and resistance.

The middle school teachers saw this misbehavior as a sign of "attitude," and of course they were right. I want to promote the notion of *attitude* from folk term to theoretical concept and propose that schooling is *always* about children's attitude as students. Striking an attitude is a way of dealing with the contradictions of classroom life, a way of answering the question "Who am I?" Attitude is the *manner* in which children inhabit the social world of the classroom, a stance toward teacher, other students, different ways of knowing, and to self, that shows itself in posture and demeanor as well as words, but typically remains invisible unless it becomes an alignment *against* the teacher.

The large-scale reform initiatives lacked the local reformers' rich understanding of teaching and learning. Each was an attempt to rationalize schooling, in the terms of either a political or an economic logic. They reduced teaching to either a delivery system whose components require alignment or a production process whose efficiency needs improving. I describe how they clashed with one other, as well as with the local reforms. Despite its best intentions, NSF's statewide systemic initiative became a "top-down" bureaucracy at odds with Willow Run's egalitarian methods. And the governor's new high-stakes standardized testing cut deeply to the heart of the teacher–student relationship, as it judged students "proficient," "not yet proficient," and "novice." It also cut to the heart of the relationship among teachers, threatening to poison the culture of collaboration and equality the local reformers were striving to build.

A classroom's culture amounts to a new moral topography within which academic practices, especially reading, writing, and math, bring "self" and "mind" into being. "Student" and "teacher" are new social positions, from which children and adult must forge a relationship. In the traditional classroom this relationship is given official form by a "single axis of achievement" along which students are sorted, and in terms of which the teacher recognizes them. In striking an attitude children accept or reject the terms of this recognition. Because schools can't *determine* a child's attitude, but can only seek to define the culture and relationships within which it is adopted, attitude can become a major issue in the classroom. The local reformers were rejecting the "axis of achievement" and seeking to change what it meant to be "teacher" and "student"; the governor's reforms threatened to fragment their collective effort and to restore the traditional, unitary axis.

I set these reforms against the backdrop of the unfolding "new economy," using the General Motors corporation as a token for the larger economic shift taking place. The Jekyll and Hyde character of this shift became evident in the ups and downs of GM's struggle for profitability and market share. The economic transition unfolded not with inevitability or determinism, but as a bare-knuckle fight to force concessions and compliance from workers.

Employers, it turns out, now judge "attitude" the most important factor when they consider hiring a new nonsupervisory or production worker, and the attitude now most valued is *flexibility* – a willingness to accept the terms of the new workplace and demand nothing better.

Despite the pronouncements of millennialist pundits who claim to know what the twenty-first century has in store and how we must prepare for it, and despite the pronouncements of developmentalists who claim to have identified universal stages, there exist different pathways into the future, different possibilities for the future of our society as well as the development of our children. Both human development and human history are made, not caused; neither is inevitable. As teachers, parents, administrators, and politicians both collaborate and struggle to redefine the character of the Willow Run Community Schools, they seek to create the possibility for the children who attend these schools to become new kinds of people, young adults who can transform both their own community and our larger society, or who can be a flexible workforce for business as usual.

Every researcher looks at the world through lenses that are the product of his or her professional development. I view development as a complex interplay between child and culture. My interpretive framework owes its character to the fact that I began studying psychology in Britain at a time when a "new look"[1] was being fashioned, with greater attention to the social worlds in which children live and to the role of adults who "act as mediators . . . of the wider social order" for the child.[2] The work of people like Martin Richards, Judy Dunn, David Ingleby, Elena Lieven, Jerome Bruner (then in England, at Oxford), Colwyn Trevarthen, John Shotter, and others broke with the neo-behaviorist socialization theories then current, without adopting a computer-obsessed cognitivism, and focused on social interaction and social context as keys to understanding learning and development.[3]

Exposure to this new paradigm motivated me to cast around for a way to systematically investigate social interaction, a logic of inquiry that would pay appropriate attention to both the semiotic organization and the pragmatic, performative character of people's everyday interaction. This in itself became a long exploration of interpretive methods, of a "hermeneutic phenomenology," that I tested and taught in a variety of circumstances.[4] What became increasingly evident to me was the work of construction that is accomplished in social interaction, in everyday conversation, as entities are indexed, social worlds invoked, and people moved and changed. Studying this called for ways of fixing human action as a "text-analog," then carefully interpreting the language games being played.[5]

The United States imported some of the "social constructionist" paradigm[6] from the United Kingdom, but it also has a homegrown brand, going by the names of sociocultural or cultural-historical theory, situated cognition, or simply cultural psychology. Here too the concern has been to understand the role of interpersonal interaction, social practices, and cultural artifacts in children's learning and development. The pioneers in this paradigm have taught us to view culture as a medium for human activity and growth (Michael Cole);[7] in the "intentional worlds" people inhabit (Richard Shweder),[8] they have highlighted the ways cultural artifacts – tools, signs, texts – are crucial "mediational means" that shape human action and transform human agency (James Wertsch),[9] explored the notion that "children's cognitive development is an apprenticeship," occurring through "guided participation" that requires attention to "personal, interpersonal, and community processes" (Barbara Rogoff),[10] and suggested that learning always takes place in a "community of practice" where the learner is a "legitimate peripheral participant" who changes in their identity (Jean Lave).[11] As Sylvia Scribner noted, it is necessary that "an analysis of changing social practices becomes integral to – rather than merely peripheral to – an inquiry into learning and development."[12] Overall, there is consensus about the importance of looking for learning in action rather than in reflection, in relations among people rather than in the individual, and in everyday social settings rather than in the laboratory.

School is clearly one place of learning, and so researchers working within this paradigm have investigated the "activity settings"[13] of schools and their "institutional activities."[14] The influence of sociocultural concepts will be apparent in this book, and these studies have been illuminating, but their focus has still been primarily the influence of schooling on cognitive skills like memory, logical problem solving, literacy, and "schooled" or "scientific" concepts, or sometimes a criticism of the "decontextualized" knowledge taught in school.[15] The broader question of how schools change the kind of person a child is has gone unasked.

Looking at school not just as a place of cognitive change, but as a site of something broader and more profound – a site of what I've begun to call, somewhat tongue-in-cheek, the "production of persons" – requires attention to the societal context of schooling. Willow Run, a community facing historical changes, faced with the task of making history, so to speak, provided a unique opportunity to examine the social practices, cultural contexts, and interpersonal relations that together make up schooling. It offered an opportunity to contextualize children's development thoroughly in both place and time, locale and history. An opportunity to study development as a culturally and historically situated process, that is, as a process that includes not just children becoming adults, but also the reproduction and transformation (both) of the culture of a community and the appropriation and relinquishment (both) of tradition and history. I have sought, then, to articulate the connections schooling makes among children's development, political and economic systems, and historical change.

I've chosen to downplay theoretical discourse and adopt a narrative form in this book. Narrative suits both the logic of interpretive analysis and the aims of sociocultural inquiry. As Hans Joas notes:

> The story-teller tells of the knowledge and the action of other actors and objectivates this knowledge and action in so far as he places it within a context resulting from his understanding of the frames of reference within which he interprets the actions of others. He does not become an uncomprehending observer, but an interpretative reconstructor of the subjectively intended and "objective" meaning of the actions of others.[16]

Narrative is uniquely suited to a particular kind of descriptive and explanatory account, one shaped by the benefits of hindsight but capturing events unfolding in time. There is a sense of the whole, informed by an understanding, achieved in retrospect, of the larger social and historical contexts in which people acted but knew little about. A narrator can rightly employ a certain omniscience in exposition, looking back. (Not complete omniscience, of course, especially when the narrator became swept up by the events narrated – but that is quite apt.)

But narrative can also reconstruct events unfolding in time, their twists and turns, people's surprises and disappointments. Juxtaposing the partial viewpoint of the participant with larger forces not clearly visible at the time is narrative's special potency. The same twofold approach – partial understanding of actor; larger social/historical system – that a sociocultural analysis of human development seeks.

My choice of narrative is motivated too by a belief that the details are important; that while big generalizations may appear more powerful, details are more informative, especially in the long run. I've tried to convince by illustration rather than by assertion and argument. But narrative doesn't replace analysis; this narrative *is* my analysis, designed for performative effect rather than expository content. Put more simply, most academic texts gather dust on the library shelves; I hope this is more readable.

The choice of narrative has brought with it some difficult decisions, however. My understanding of the Willow Run ethos and of the effects of downsizing, for example, were augmented by personal experiences that I've felt obliged not to edit from the story nor to disguise by adopting a completely impersonal tone. I hope the reader will not judge these few passages self-indulgent.

1   The Class of 2001

June 9, 1994

> We have seen that a community or social group sustains itself through continuous self-renewal, and that this renewal takes place by means of the educational growth of the immature members of the group. By various agencies, unintentional and designed, a society transforms uninitiated and seemingly alien beings into robust trustees of its own resources and ideals. Education is thus a fostering, a nurturing, a cultivating, process. All of these words mean that it implies attention to the conditions of growth.
>
> John Dewey, *Democracy and Education*. New York: Free Press, 1916, p. 10

> We live in a time when nearly all of our institutions, including American industry, labor unions, churches, and government, are struggling to adapt to the changes of the late twentieth century. Yet in the institution where progress is arguably most critical – education – it is most lacking. Where are our passion and commitment to our most precious asset, our children? Where are our collective will and determination to give our children what they deserve and need – high-quality education?
>
> Louis V. Gerstner Jr., with D. P. Doyle and W. B. Johnston, *Reinventing Education: Entrepreneurship in America's Public Schools*. New York: Penguin, 1995, pp. x–xi

It is a rare, beautiful late-spring day in lower Michigan. It has been another hard winter, the coldest in memory, apparently the coldest on record, but spring has been kind, with sunny, dry days. The temperature today is in the low seventies, the humidity pleasant. Birds dart low across the road in front of my car, and strands of cirrus cloud line the horizon. At 9:50 I pull into the parking lot of Kettering Elementary School and join the adults carrying cakes and dress shirts past the new mural into the school. The lot is filling quickly, and people stream into the entrance of the long, single-story building.

10

Today is the last day of the school year in the Willow Run Community Schools. I'm here at Kettering for the school's graduation ceremony. The graduating class today will be, when they leave high school, the Class of 2001.

The Kettering gymnasium has been decorated with huge red and white paper mortarboards. Up on the stage is a podium with four chairs on either side for the valedictorians and salutatorians, along with potted bougainvilleas and cut flowers. On the floor of the gym are two blocks of about twenty chairs each for the other fifth-grade students. Facing these are rows of chairs for parents and siblings, arranged with a central aisle between them. I choose a spot on the margins, an aisle seat in the back row. On each of these chairs is a graduation program and a red leaflet about tomorrow's millage election. The leaflet explains why the school district wishes to raise to 18 "mills" the local property tax levied on non-homestead property and paid to the public schools.[1] The district needs the millage to qualify for the state's new "foundation" funding. I know that school staff will be handing out a second leaflet, a yellow one that contains the appeal "Vote YES!," when they stand outside the polling stations, including Kettering, next week. Teachers are not allowed to lobby citizens within a regulated hundred feet of a polling place.

The seats are filling up all around me. Looking about I notice that a large painted map of the United States has been installed high on the north wall of the gym. Students have painted a scene for each state – Alaska has snowflakes; California a desert to the south and big trees to the north; Texas a star, cacti, and settlers' covered wagons, all on a background of blue, white, and red bars. Michigan is filled with trees and lakes, with a small red star marking the location of Willow Run.

I felt tired driving to Willow Run today, even though I slept nine hours last night. I think I know what the fatigue is about: the executive committee of the University of Michigan's School of Education has just made its decisions on whether to extend the contracts of the cohort of five assistant professors of which I'm a member. But these judgments won't be announced until Friday, at individual meetings with the Dean and the chair of the Educational Studies program. My tiredness, I know, is anxiety. I expect that my contract will be renewed for another three or four years, but I've also learned to prepare for the unexpected at the School of Education.

Evaluation and departure seem to be in the air today. When I was a child, growing up in London, I was struck by the fact that my father seemed to go to work day after day, year after year, to the same job in the same way. How boring it was to be an adult and working, I had thought. Today job security is a thing of the past, in England as well as America. There's much talk of unemployment, of the frequent changes of job that young people face. Today's young graduates will be leaving behind their parents' way of life.

Kettering Elementary School is one of eight schools that make up the Willow Run school district. The 1993–1994 school year in Willow Run has been a full one, for teachers and administrators as well as students and parents, a year of adaptation to dramatic events and efforts to prepare for an uncertain future. Changes have begun at several places in the Willow Run schools, and one site is certainly Kettering. The Kettering teachers consider themselves an unusual bunch, and they are right.

The sources of change are both close to home and more distant. For the local community the schools have taken on a renewed significance. And at the state and national levels reform initiatives have begun that have caught up the schools here and form a backdrop against which to interpret local events. And behind all this is a growing awareness of profound transformations in the economy.

But this is a time of celebration not just for Kettering. The jubilant new Clinton administration – the first Democratic presidency in 12 years – is unwrapping legislation that forms the centerpiece of its efforts for education reform: the Goals 2000: Educate America Act. Clinton intends to establish a new federal partnership with the states through grants to state and local government, a plan that builds upon efforts of the outgoing Bush administration. The six "National Education Goals" will be formalized and two more added.

The secretaries of education and labor announce these plans together, symbolizing the linkage between schooling and work. Secretary of Education Richard Riley says Goals 2000 will "help create a high-skill, high-wage work force that is the best in the world."[2] It defines broad guidelines "not only on school and student performance but also on the skills that young people will need to survive in an uncertain economy." A new board with representatives from education, government, business, and labor will define standards for the occupational skills needed by non–college-bound youth. The act will provide a "national umbrella" for school reform, though states' participation will be voluntary. School improvement grants to the states are proposed, with emphasis on statewide curriculum standards, national tests, local decision making, and improved teacher training.[3]

And the Republican governor of Michigan, John Engler, is also cele-
brating – and starting his campaign for reelection. At the end of 1993
Engler pushed through major reforms of the Michigan public schools –
both finance reform (with a popular vote supporting his proposals) and,
more importantly, "quality reforms." In his January 1994 State of the
State address Engler offered his thanks "to the men and women of this
legislature who have worked together to solve problems that have
plagued Michigan for a generation – problems some said could never be
solved. . . . Our record of reform last year was truly historic."

> "The American auto industry is back. Detroit is back. My friends, Michi-
> gan is back!"
>
> Gov. John Engler, State of the State Address, Jan. 18, 1994[4]

At 10 after the hour Mary Brandau, a longtime Kettering teacher newly
promoted to principal, picks up a microphone to announce:
"The Class of 2001!"
Heads crane. The fifth graders, arranged in single file with Mrs.
Stangis at their head, are poised at the gymnasium's rear door. As the slow
march from *Pomp and Circumstance* begins on the stereo system wheeled
into the gym for this occasion they enter, stepping deliberately, arranged
from smallest, a short African American boy, to tallest, an adolescent-
looking African American boy probably six feet tall. The boys are wearing
slacks and shirts with ties and the girls formal dresses, and each clasps a
red or white carnation and wears a red paper mortarboard.
Mrs. Brandau takes the microphone again. She's a little nervous, still
adjusting to her new position. She speaks without notes, but she took
time yesterday evening to plan what she wants to say.[5]
"Ladies and gentlemen, I'm going to turn around and talk to our
graduating class. I know all of them; I know every one of them. And" –
to the students now – "I want each of you to look around, I want you to
look at the people who are with you.
"I'm going to tell you a story – you know I love to tell stories. I went
to school in Ypsilanti, and I graduated from my sixth-grade class not too
many miles from here. I remember my sixth-grade graduation, it was
the first time I had a pair of pantyhose" – there's laughter from the audience – "and my mom and dad both took off work and showed up, and
what that told me was that I was worth something. I was worth their
time. They fussed over me, and I looked good, and they cared about me
and loved me.

"The friends that I graduated high school with are all still around. One went on to be an attorney in the town, one of them works at Meijers, one of them helps me with my car. We shared something very special, we went to elementary school together.

"I hope you remember this year. I have a symbol for the year, and that symbol is the mural outside. When you think of Kettering I want you to think of that mural, because you had to plan to put that mural together, you worked together. You put it together: something magical; something special. And when we were finished working we put it up on the wall and then we celebrated. That's part of life too: you work hard and you plan, you get there, you get frustrated, and you celebrate. I want you to do that in life.

"To the parents I have a challenge. You have extremely special children. Every one of these kids has a gift. Some of the gifts are academic, some of the gifts are. . . ." She gestures to the children on the stage behind her. "I have an electrician up here, I have a cook, I have people who are good at basketball, I have a young man up here who'll run a marathon. They're all different; we value all their talents. My challenge to you is a couple of things. One is, why don't you go learn something new? Because when you learn something new you'll know what it's like for them. You learn best when you experience it, when somebody says you did a good job, when you're frustrated and you have to cope, and the kids can see you as learners. We have computers in this building and I've got a suspicion that these guys can run them a whole lot better than you!"

There's laughter at this from the parents and relatives.

"Am I right? So there's a challenge for you. The other part of that challenge is, we have to remember. . . . My father is seventy-nine years old. When he was born there were no airplanes. When I went to school, there were no computers. When these children were born, man had already walked on the moon. There's a lot of learning, and things are happening fast in the world. There is one lifetime per person. The world these children will live in is not like the world we're living in now. So the gift we can give them is to teach them to be kind, to be compassionate, and to always learn. That's what we hope we've instilled in them here. These children are special to us, they will always have a home here." She turns to the students again. "And when you get a little discouraged or you don't feel good about yourself or you don't think you can make it, come back here and we will tell you that you can."

There is applause from the audience.

Mrs. Ryles asks the fifth-grade students to rise for the class song. She turns to the parents:

"We have a dedication to the parents, the teachers, and to all the little sisters and brothers, and grandparents, neighbors, who may see your child and say, 'I think you're going in a wrong direction,' may see your child and they say, 'I'm locked out,' 'Well you can have a peanut butter sandwich,' may see your child at a store and maybe say, 'Hey, I think you need to go home, it's getting a little late.' This song is called 'You're My Hero,' and we'd like to sing it for you."

The "young ladies" begin the song, with Sharon Ryles conducting:

> There's a hero
> If you look inside your heart
> You don't have to be afraid
> Of what you are
> There's an answer
> If you reach into your soul
> And the sorrow that you know
> Will melt away.

The boys join them for the chorus:

> And then a hero comes along
> With the strength to carry on
> And you cast your fears aside
> And you know you can survive
> So when you feel like hope is gone
> Look inside you and be strong
> And you'll finally see the truth
> That a hero lies in you.

"Everyone, I need you a little louder" calls Sharon. Jamila, standing in the front row, starts to weep and Sharon draws her to her side and hugs her. The students sing the chorus again, then the last verse:

> Lord knows
> Dreams are hard to follow
> But don't let anyone
> Tear them away
> Hold on
> There will be tomorrow
> In time
> You'll find the way.[6]

Several members of the audience are wiping tears from their eyes. The chorus is sung one last time, and Sharon singles out the soloist for the last lines: ". . . that a hero lies in you!" The parents give their children a standing ovation.

"This is a very emotional time," concludes Sharon, after the applause has ended. "Any time we are embarking on a new adventure it becomes an emotional time. I'd like to present to you the Class of 2001! Would you please stand."

The fifth graders get to their feet and, at Sharon's direction and to cheers and applause, they shift the tassels of their mortarboards from right to left. To Elgar once again the students file past Mary, who shakes each of them by the hand, past Hazel Stangis, who hands each of them a diploma rolled and tied with a strand of red wool, to the rear of the gymnasium and out, past Hope, Sharon's aide, who holds a video camera on her shoulder with one hand and with the other waves a finger to her right, directing the students up the corridor toward the playing field, where refreshments are waiting.

But not all is well. For the past three years the United States has been in a severe economic recession – the worst since the Great Depression of the 1930s – and there is a deep sense of national economic crisis. A large portion of the blame is being placed at the door of public schools. There are demands for improvement in the education young people receive, especially in science and mathematics, as well as a call for new links between school and workplace. It is just a few weeks since Louis V. Gerstner Jr., the new chairman of International Business Machines, wrote an Op-Ed piece for the *New York Times*, comparing American students unfavorably with their Asian counterparts. Gerstner asserted that U.S. parents are mistaken in being happy with their children's schools and complained that industry has to "pick up the slack," paying $30 billion a year to train workers and losing an equal amount due to their "poor literacy." What's needed, he maintained, is that schools "establish clear goals and measure progress towards them," and "provide rewards and incentives." "If the goals are not met," Gerstner insisted, "we need to exact stiff penalties, changing the leadership and even dismissing staff members in schools that aren't performing."

It wasn't so long ago that American industry languished in complacency, content with outmoded practices, resistant to change. But market forces have swept the apathy away. U.S. companies have had to respond to global competition with rapid-fire changes in the way they do business. The message from our customers was simply this: change or close.

Now America's public schools are hearing a similar message. Fed up with wasteful management, falling test scores and graduation rates, and a growing number of graduates who can't perform in the workplace, more and more districts are turning over management of their schools to private companies. . . .

> This spreading rejection of the status quo should be an alarm bell for the vested interests that run our schools. But though there are some hotbeds of innovation and reform, complacency still reigns.
>
> It is a deeply dangerous situation. We cannot transform business and the economy without a labor force that is prepared to solve problems and compete on a global level. Private management may help in some districts, but the issue goes far beyond management. We need a national strategy for resurgence that reaches every school in the country. . . .
>
> If public education does not reinvent itself to meet these goals, and fast, it is the entire country that will be out of business.
>
> Louis V. Gerstner Jr., "Our Schools Are Failing. Do We Care?"
> *New York Times*, May 27, 1994, A27

The Willow Run teachers and administrators are already well aware of needs to change the way their schools operate. One afternoon the previous November a small group of us met in the classroom of Betty Hopkins, a sixth-grade teacher at Willow Run's Edmonson Middle School. Edmonson's sixth-grade wing was built as an elementary school, the rest of the building added later, and Betty's room was once a kindergarten classroom, so it has cubbies, coathooks, and a sink. There are five of us seated around a cozy low circular table, the kind young children work at, waiting for Scott Heister, who has gone off in search of the Coke machine. Edmonson is a daunting complex of identical corridors; Scott won't get lost, but he has a ways to travel. We're chatting and joking, the meeting not yet officially begun. Mary Brandau is here, along with Liza Finkel, a new assistant professor from the University of Michigan, Vivian Lyte, the district's curriculum coordinator, Betty, and me. Mary is an energetic, petite woman. She's quick to smile, and a quick thinker too; she's also quick to second-guess and criticize herself. She has worked in Willow Run for 18 years, her entire career, most recently as coordinator for Kettering's Chapter One program before being promoted to principal. As she puts it, "I have been associated with the district since before I was *born!*"

Vivian Lyte, perhaps a few years older than Mary, has also been associated with Willow Run for many years, though this is her first year as curriculum coordinator. Vivian is co-chair, along with Scott, of the newly formed "Willow Run Systemic Initiative" committee. Vivian, who is African American, was born in Detroit but moved to Willow Run in 1969. She's been principal at two of Willow Run's elementaries – Cheney and Kettering – and also director of personnel. She strikes one as astute, levelheaded, and spirited.

Liza Finkel is the University of Michigan School of Education's official representative on WRSI. She's a lively, mop-haired young woman, a new member of the faculty at the university, whose area of research is science education.

"Yesterday in our focus group," Vivian says, "one of the building principals said something that was – like, wow, she's right. She said, 'Vivian and the WRSI team are doing a great job, going about trying to make systemic change, but I wonder if they've thought about the fact that they're trying to make systemic change within the framework of a very autocratic system?'" She speaks the last words slowly and with emphasis.

Betty, a cheerful woman, who welcomes us a little nervously into her classroom, murmurs her agreement. Vivian laughs – one of her characteristic chuckles. "It's like, maybe I hadn't wanted to think about that! But you know, it's something we have to think about. We're functioning in a system. . . ."

The others nod agreement. Mary asks her, "Do you mean the total system in Michigan, or the total district?"

"Both," explains Vivian. "You can look at it from the district or you can look at it from the state. You come up with the same awesome thought."

"The same big problem," Liza adds.

Vivian continues. "And I was like, I don't know if I wanted to know that!" She laughs again.

Betty says, "Or you didn't know if you wanted to bring it to the front of the agenda!"

"Right! 'Cause I know it was there!" Vivian agrees.

Scott arrives with cans of pop. He gets out his laptop computer and we get down to business, reflecting on WRSI's visit to Cheney Elementary.

Scott Heister is perhaps 10 years younger than Mary and I. He's a compact, sandy-haired man, a science teacher at the high school, who seems to have endless reserves of energy and enthusiasm. This is his third year in the district, after a degree from the University of Michigan's Flint campus, and student teaching in Flint. He still lives there and commutes to Willow Run.

The players in the district haven't yet come together beyond a small central band. Vivian is new to her position, getting up-to-date with the staff of each school, and Scott doesn't yet know all of the school principals. For instance, he wasn't at the Cheney visit, and now he asks about Cheney's principal, Laura Chew:

"Which one is Laura?"

"Dramatic," says Mary. "She's always dramatic, in, like, swooping clothes. . . ."

"Very verbal," Vivian adds. "Late."

"Older, younger?" Scott asks, still trying to form a picture.

"Scott!" Vivian is playfully outraged. "You don't ask women that kind of a question!"

"*Our* age!" Mary asserts, to loud laughter.

"Oh, *younger?*" I add, with deliberation, to even louder laughter.

"Gray hair . . . ?" Scott asks, trying to correct his mistake, his faux pas, only digging himself deeper.

"We don't have any gray-haired principals!"

"I didn't know!" Scott says peevishly.

"That's why we love you, Scott," Mary smiles, "you just naively plunge right in!"

"I say what I think!" declares Scott, bouncing back, entering the spirit of the teasing.

"You must not have met Laura," concludes Vivian, "because you would know Laura."

Willow Run lies at the base of Michigan's thumb. Ask any native Michigander a question about the state's geography and they will hold up a hand – sometimes both. Michigan's Lower Peninsula is shaped, roughly, like a hand held vertically, thumb to the right. The thumb represents Huron County, the little finger Leelanau, the wrist corresponds to the border with Indiana and Ohio. Detroit is at the joint at the base of the thumb. Lansing, the state capital, lies on the palm. With some contortion the other hand can be turned sideways and held, thumb down, above the first to show the Upper Peninsula: the "UP." The border with Wisconsin lies part way along the upper forearm, and the fingertips stroke the Canadian border, at Sault Sainte Marie in Ontario. Where the fingers of the lower hand touch the thumb of the upper hand are the Straits of Mackinac, bounded by the six-mile-long Mackinac Bridge. Mackinac Island lies about five miles offshore.

Michigan is the only state in the contiguous United States to be made up of two land masses. It has a coastline of 3,200 miles, the longest of any state in the nation, formed by the Great Lakes, scoured out by Ice Age glaciers and Mesozoic rivers. The state's land area is 58,000 square miles, its dimensions about 400 miles north to south, 310 miles east to west. The population is 9.3 million, almost half of them – 4.4 million – in the southeastern area around Detroit. Detroit, its suburbs, and Windsor – its sister city across the Detroit River in Canada – together comprise the sixth largest metropolitan area in North America.

Michigan's geography has shaped its economy. At first what drew people was the luscious fur of hardy water creatures. The Hudson's Bay

Company traded pelts of beaver, otter, and mink and fueled conflict between English and French. Detroit, on an isthmus between Lake St. Clair and Lake Erie, was built by the French in 1701 to try to keep the company out of Michigan. The opening of the Erie Canal created an agricultural boom, more growth, and more trade; Detroit was a point where railroads, shipping lines, and merchant trade routes met. Midway between the Upper Peninsula's rich resources of timber, copper, and iron ore and the Appalachian coal fields, the city bustled by the turn of the century with brass foundries, blast furnaces, and businesses manufacturing steam engines, marine equipment, stoves, and carriages. The infant and experimental automobile industry drew on these trades.

Economies of scale consolidated auto manufacturing into a small number of growing car companies, eventually just the Big Three – Chrysler, Ford, and General Motors – and their suppliers, concentrated in southeastern Michigan. Iron founding and casting, steel milling, parts manufacture and assembly all now took place locally. Michigan's had become a "metal-bending economy," with automobile production the single export industry, and three companion industries, dealing with primary metals, fabricated metals, and nonelectrical machinery, alongside it.[7]

In World War II a national defense policy of dispersing valuable facilities took factory construction to the suburban periphery of the city, and this is how Willow Run was born. Washtenaw County, about an hour's drive from Detroit, is now in automobile country, though logging, farming, and trade with Native Americans were the activities that led to the first white settlement in the county: the city of Ypsilanti, settled in 1834. About two dozen auto plants are scattered across eastern Washtenaw County and neighboring Wayne County.

Willow Run lies on the eastern edge of Washtenaw County, immediately to the east of Ypsilanti. Ypsilanti in turn is just east of the college town of Ann Arbor, the county seat, where the University of Michigan relocated from Detroit in 1837 (the year Michigan entered the Union). Ann Arbor is the largest city in the county, with a population of around 135,000; Ypsilanti is second largest, population about 45,000. Ann Arbor, by and large, looks down on Ypsilanti, which is more working class, more black, has more crime, and contains a small state college, not a prestigious state university like the University of Michigan. Ann Arbor thinks of itself as liberal; perhaps it once was. Ypsilanti in turn looks down on Willow Run. Willow Run is literally across the tracks, the other side of the railroad line that runs through Ypsilanti.

The county is divided into 10 school districts, all under the umbrella of the Washtenaw Intermediate School District. Willow Run Community School District is the smallest in size, though not in population: it measures only 16 square miles but its population at the time of the 1990 census was 18,851, living in 7,014 residences. Seventy-four percent of the people living here are white, 24 percent African American, and there are about 300 Hispanics, 100 Asians, and fewer than 100 Native Americans. In 1990 the Community had 9,401 people in the labor force, and 853 without work – an unemployment rate of 8.3 percent.

Fifteen percent of Willow Run's population lives in poverty. Twenty-three percent of the community's children live in households where the income is below the poverty line; almost 700 households receive public assistance. Annual income per household is $31,983, the lowest of all the school districts in the county except Ypsilanti ($26,662), and just above the average for the state as a whole ($31,020). This is equivalent to an average income per person of $13,047. The average value of a house in Willow Run is $49,909 – the lowest in the county (the value in Ann Arbor is $121,057; in Ypsilanti it is $65,712).

Of those people 20 years old or older in Willow Run, 30 percent have a twelfth-grade education or less, another 30 percent are high school graduates, 27 percent have some college, and the remaining 13 percent have a bachelor's degree or higher. (The corresponding figures for Michigan as a whole are 22, 32, 29, and 16 percent respectively; for the United States, 23, 30, 27, and 19 percent.)

The community has eight schools – Thurston Early Childhood Development Center, five elementaries (Cheney, Ford, Holmes, Kaiser, and Kettering), Edmonson Middle School, and Willow Run High School. In the 1991–1992 school year, enrollment totaled 4,303 students, making the Willow Run School District third in size after Ann Arbor (14,485) and Ypsilanti (5,195). The students are about 36 percent African American, 60 percent white, roughly equal numbers of girls and boys. The graduation rate is around 77 percent – close to the average for Washtenaw County of 78 percent, below the Michigan average of 83 percent.

Another index of poverty in the district is the percentage of students eligible to participate in the free and reduced-price lunch program. (A child from a family of four qualifies for a free lunch when family income is $18,655 or less, and for reduced-price lunch if income is $26,548 or less.) In 1991–1992 the rate in Willow Run was 41.7 percent – the highest in Washtenaw County: only Ypsilanti School District came close, at 33.8 percent. The average for the 10 school districts was 15.4 percent; for the state of Michigan as a whole, it was 24.7 percent.

Willow Run *is* its school district: the community does not exist as any other political entity. It straddles, for instance, Ypsilanti and Superior

Townships. (Like every other county in Michigan, Washtenaw County is divided into 20 "Townships," blocks six miles square, laid out when the state of Michigan was originally surveyed back in 1816. Each Township is divided in turn into a grid of 36 "sections," one mile square, along the boundaries of which major roadways tend to run.) Yet the people living in Willow Run have a strong sense of their identity, of their community's unique origins, of its dramatic history. But this past couple of years Willow Run has faced a series of challenges to that identity. The community, like many others throughout Michigan, has been hard hit by changes in the automobile industry. Plant consolidations and closings have caused idlings and layoffs and undercut the standard of living enjoyed by many manual workers in the industry. Secure, well-paying jobs that required barely a high school education are now dwindling in number, and other auto-related work is affected too. These changes are not restricted to the auto industry, though it has its unique troubles: the economy of the United States is undergoing a structural transformation.

When Mary Brandau speaks of the rapid pace of change in the children's lives, and in the lives of their parents, her words must touch many in the Kettering gymnasium deeply. Although she didn't mention it – indeed she is rather circumspect about the fact – the 79-year-old father she made brief reference to was hired as a teacher when the Willow Run School District was created, back in 1943, and became one of its first superintendents. So Mary has a keen and personal sense of the history of the community in which she works and a strong sense of the threats it currently faces. The challenges she made to those at the graduation are not idle rhetorical flourishes, but are rooted in a genuine understanding of the need for the community to face up to and adapt to waves of change, to a major transformation in the conditions of its very existence.

But the traumatic event that gives deeper and poignant significance to Mary's words was not mentioned explicitly at the Kettering graduation. In 1992 the General Motors Corporation, one of the Big Three auto manufacturers whose business has dominated life in Michigan since the 1910s, dealt the Willow Run community a dramatic blow by announcing plans to close its Willow Run Auto Assembly Plant, a facility at the very heart of this community. Early this school year the assembly plant finally closed its doors. And this poses as big a challenge to Mrs. Brandau and the teachers at Kettering as the challenge she posed to the families attending today's graduation: How best to prepare Willow Run's children to face not just the pressing demands of their present way of life, but also those of an uncertain future in the new millennium?

2   Blue Monday

December 1991–February 1992

> The day a General Motors manager stood on a stage at the Willow Run assembly plant here and told 2,000 workers the line would shut down forever by the fall of 1993, Chuck Kehrer watched as the man next to him bolted for the nearest trash can and threw up.
>
> Sara Rimer, "American Dream Put on Hold at Car Plant Doomed to Shut," *New York Times*, Sept. 7, 1992, A1

"Families are going to be torn apart by this." The *Detroit News* prints these words over a banner headline in two-inch type: "BLUE MONDAY." The General Motors logo – a simple blue box containing the letters GM – is shown with a piece sliced off and falling away. The color photo below the headline shows a woman holding a young child on her hip. She looks stunned, staring into the distance with a hand pressed to her face. Her child gazes up at her with a worried expression, his mouth gaping, his hand a fist pressed to the side of his head. They are dressed in colorful winter clothes: he in a teal jacket and an olive knitted hat; she in a brightly colored print scarf and a black parka. Their bleak expressions belie the colorful photograph. "We had so many plans," the caption quotes her as saying.

When I first begin to visit Willow Run, some 18 months before the Kettering graduation, it is with some anxiety. Rumor has it that angry GM workers and their sympathizers are running Japanese cars off the road – and I've bought an old, rusty Honda Prelude. The anger begins on Blue Monday – February 24, 1992, the day General Motors Chairman Robert Stempel announces, on closed-circuit TV from GM headquarters in Detroit, that the Willow Run Auto Assembly Plant, employing some 4,000 workers, must be closed by August 1993. It is to be 1 of

23

10 plant closings, 4 in Michigan, necessitated by GM's abysmal financial situation. The company has decided to consolidate production of the vehicles assembled at Willow Run – the Buick Roadmaster, Chevrolet Caprice sedan and wagon, and Oldsmobile wagon – with production at the GM plant in Arlington, Texas. The Arlington plant has been producing other big rear-wheel-drive cars to which Willow Run's models will be added. The Hydra-matic plant at Willow Run – where automatic transmissions are manufactured – will remain open, but all jobs at the assembly plant will be lost. The plant has 4,014 workers on the books, all but 300 of whom are blue collar. One of the two shifts is currently idled, its workers laid off, supposedly temporarily, so right now 2,600 people are working. A GM spokesperson says production workers with high seniority will probably be able to transfer to other plants; for others the future is uncertain.

The fate of the Willow Run assembly plant has been in the balance since "Black December," also called the "Christmas Massacre." On Wednesday, December 18, 1991, Stempel announced a four-year plan to cut 74,000 workers and close 21 plants, including either Willow Run or Arlington. "It's obvious," he said, "we're going to have to take care of the health of the corporation for the long term."[1] Local business leaders immediately met to plan a strategy to save Willow Run, but soon afterward Arlington workers offered to add a third shift to their production schedule to increase efficiency. And the Arlington town council, meeting on New Year's Eve, voted to offer GM tax abatements worth $11 million on any expansion of their plant. Subsequently they offered an incentive package worth $30 million. On January 14, Michigan governor John Engler announced he would "match or exceed" any offer made by Texas.

That too was a bitter winter. In mid-January temperatures dropped to minus 23 degrees, the coldest ever recorded. In his State of the State address on January 21, in a speech entitled "Continuing Change to Build a Stronger Michigan," Governor Engler focused on Willow Run to illustrate his central point that change was everywhere. "What seemed certain – is now changing. What seemed impossible – is now fact." The Soviet Union had fallen; American hostages held in Lebanon had been released (one was attending the speech); and here too "Michigan is a state of change – historical change – on course for a great future." The "Taxpayers Agenda" Engler had begun the previous year – "lower taxes, more jobs, better schools and less dependence" – must continue. In Engler's view, changing the state's public schools was an important part of improving its business climate. Michigan, he noted, "became the only state in America to eliminate a massive budget deficit, increase funding for schools, and hold the line on taxes."

So far this evening, I have talked in detail about my plan to create jobs and turbocharge our economy. I can summarize the importance of my strategy – Michigan's challenge – in two words: WILLOW RUN! Sure, GM faces a tough decision. Will they make cars in Willow Run or in Arlington, Texas? Employers make choices like this every day. In fact, in the past decade, Michigan has lost the equivalent of one hundred Willow Runs. Today, we also have a choice to make. If our answer is business as usual . . . if our answer is costs that don't go down and poor schools that don't get better . . . if our answer is tax shifts and tax hikes . . . it's a done deal. Our jobs will take a hike – to Texas. I fight for what I believe in. I believe these jobs belong in Michigan. And I will fight to keep them here – each and every one! . . .

Tonight, I've got a message for the Japanese Speaker of the House of Representatives: Our cars are second to none. Our autoworkers are second to none. Michigan is second to none. Something else that has to be second to none is the education of our children. We can't compete for jobs unless our kids have the skills to fill them. I would again urge this Legislature to enact the reforms I proposed last September in the Michigan 2000 strategy to improve our schools. Ladies and Gentlemen, I am not satisfied with the state of our schools. And I know you're not, either. That's why initiatives like the Michigan Education Warranty are so important. It is time our schools stood behind their students the way we expect our automakers to stand behind their cars.

Gov. John Engler, State of the State Address, Jan. 21, 1992[2]

Stempel insisted early in February that GM's choice between Arlington and Willow Run would be based entirely on cost and that the company had no wish to initiate a bidding war between the two communities. Hopes in Michigan remained high, especially after a report published on February 21 claimed that GM had reached a decision to close Arlington. The Willow Run plant was reported to have a $500 to $1,000 cost advantage per car; it is also closer to parts suppliers. On the other hand the plants operate under different work rules. The Arlington labor-management team is reputed to be more innovative and flexible.

Willow Run is a traditional plant with a full complement of line supervisors, plus many job classifications for skilled trades and production workers. Work rules prohibit skilled trades workers from performing jobs outside their classification. Some traditional plants have as many as 25 categories for production workers.

> But Arlington has only two production classifications – team member and team leader – and eight skilled trades. That is similar to streamlined work rules at Japanese assembly plants. GM has stressed it wants other plants to form work teams and agree to fewer job classifications.
>
> David Sedgwick and Helen Fogel, "GM Forcing Shutdown on Work Rules?" *Detroit News*, Feb. 25, 1992, 1A, 7A

The Big Three simply aren't selling enough cars and trucks. GM was prosperous in the postwar years; chairman Alfred Sloan created upmarket products to compete with Ford's cheap commodity automobile. GM cars were big and flashy. Sloan created autos that were status symbols, emphasizing styling over engineering, introducing the annual model change. Chevrolet – built at Willow Run, and other plants – was the company's centerpiece, generating three-quarters of GM's profits. The middle-class market was captured, and blue-collar workers shared in the prosperity, coming to enjoy a middle-class lifestyle.

But the auto industry faced a series of problems in the 1970s. Oil embargoes in the Middle East caused gasoline shortages in 1973 and 1979. Customers started to purchase smaller, more fuel-efficient cars, and imports, particularly those from Japan, gained an increasing share of the U.S. market. The Japanese cars were also cheaper, due to much more efficient production techniques. General Motors was too big and too complacent to respond adequately to these changes – what was needed was not just new models to attract back customers, but a whole new way of organizing the process of automobile production. The Japanese were reaping the benefits of a postwar reorganization of their industrial production – guided, ironically, by an American, William Edwards Deming, who designed new forms of statistical quality control: "Total Quality Management."

The Big Three first tried a "Southern" strategy to trim costs by shifting production to nonunionized plants in the U.S. sun belt and Mexico. Then in the 1980s a new chairman, Roger Smith, spent $40 billion – enough to have bought Honda and Toyota outright – on new plants with advanced technology and automation. The results were farcical: robots smashed lights and painted each other. And although the cars were cheaper, this was mainly because they were cheap. GM's share of the U.S. auto market fell from 47 percent to 35 percent during the 1980s. But according to a 1980 survey in *Fortune* magazine, GM was still the largest corporation of any kind in the world, with sales totaling over $96 billion.

A "global car" strategy was tried next, dispersing production geographically, mostly to limit union power, with parts produced by foreign subsidiaries. The Big Three closed 66 plants in the United States between 1979 and 1991. In 1986, GM announced a $1.23 billion cost for closing 11 assembly and components plants; between 1987 and 1988 it eliminated 25 percent of all white-collar jobs, 40,000 in total. A former GM executive vice president looking back on those years said: "We just weren't humble and modest enough to say, it starts with people, getting the right people. If you have an authoritarian plant manager running each of our existing plants, you can't put in the new team concepts that Toyota taught us is the way to do things now. So we didn't do it the right way. We had the knowledge, but we didn't have the will."[3]

In 1990 Smith retired – with an annual pension of $1 million – and Roger Stempel took over. Stempel immediately announced that job security could be ensured only if GM became a low-cost producer, focused on quality. In November 1990, GM announced a plan to close another 7 of its 36 assembly plants in the United States and Canada, taking a $2.1 billion charge for the restructuring. But sales were still down 12.5 percent the next year – net losses for 1991 were $4.5 billion, the largest annual loss ever for any American company. Hence the further cuts announced on Blue Monday.

How much is $4.5 billion? If you could spend it, you could buy 562 Drummond Islands (asking price $8 million), pay outfielder Cecil Fielder's salary for 1,000 years or buy 201,793 fully loaded 1992 Chevrolet Caprices (at $22,300 apiece, and manufactured at the doomed Willow Run plant). If you want to see $4.5 billion, count the squares. Each square represents $10 million.

[Little squares run across the top of four of the newspaper's pages and end with a note saying it would take eight pages more to represent the $4.5 billion GM loss.]

Editor's note, *Detroit News*, Feb. 25, 1992, 4A

The problem is not General Motors' alone; Ford and Chrysler have also posted record losses. In 1991, the worst year in the history of automobile manufacturing, the Big Three together lost $7.6 billion. Robert Stempel acknowledged, "In 1991, the North American automobile industry sustained losses unparalleled in its history." In the first quarter combined annual sales for the Big Three fell to only 11.9 million units, 21 percent below 1986 levels.[4]

But GM is faring worst: its sales dropped 7.1 percent in the year ending August 1992, while Ford's sales increased 8.1 percent and Chrysler's increased 7.7 percent. GM has lagged behind in reorganizing production:

it has more wasted plant space, makes more of its own parts, and has the most complex product line. GM's cost for producing a car is estimated at $7,205, compared with $5,415 for Ford, and $5,841 for Chrysler – an American average of $6,395, compared with $6,644 average for Japanese manufacturers.[5] In January 1992, Wall Street, critical of the Black December plans, downgraded the status of General Motors' debt, saying "The proposed realignment program will be insufficient to make GM fully cost competitive in the global industry."[6] Forecasters see none of the Big Three making any profit until the fourth quarter of 1992 – and even this slight degree of optimism causes stock prices to jump. Nonetheless, General Motors is still the largest auto manufacturer in the world, with worldwide sales of $123.1 billion – 7.2 million cars and trucks – in 1991.

The *Ypsilanti Press* understandably covers the closing announcement intensively. The headlines tell the story – "Willow Run to Be Closed" in large type. "Meddling by Bush Blamed." "Local Leaders Shocked." "Engler Accused of Failing to Help . . . . " "Union Members Stunned . . . . " "Dazed and Confused." "Union Members Gather, Say They Won't Abandon Hope." The editorial the next day declares that "Ypsilanti is down – but not out." Although workers are faced, at best, with a choice between their jobs and their community and roots, and while accusations that Bush gave special treatment to Texas are plausible, nonetheless "We must strive to maintain . . . optimism and direct it toward keeping our community viable."

Detroit's two metropolitan newspapers each find a message in the announced closing of Willow Run. Sympathetic to industry, the *Detroit News* devotes five of the eight pages in its main section to the story. The editorial asks: "Who's to Blame for Willow Run?" Its answer: the United Auto Workers' "friends in Congress" have crippled industry by growing the national deficit and imposing clean air regulations that have produced an economic stagnation that "drove auto sales down and exposed GM's inefficiencies." The Willow Run union-management team "refused to budge" when flexible work arrangements were sought. And the UAW and state Democrats have contributed to the poor character of Michigan's "business climate." Health care costs are high in Michigan; average property tax is 40 to 50 percent higher than the national average; and court costs are higher and workers' compensation laws more stringent in this state, the editorial concludes.[7]

Next day the *Detroit Free Press*, generally more sympathetic to the interests of labor, responds with an editorial of its own: "GM Closings: The Search for Scapegoats Won't Help Save Jobs." The *Free Press* declares that "the quest for external scapegoats can only obscure the real, urgent meaning of GM's self-surgery. And to the extent that such behavior is aimed at gaining momentary political advantage, it is a disservice to the families and communities affected by the cuts. . . . The GM closings also baldly expose the limitations of Gov. Engler's simplistic economic development strategy, based on little more than undifferentiated tax cuts, deregulation and other corporate water-carrying." Engler is accused of "standing on the sidelines" while GM made up its mind which plant to close. The editorial ends with the suggestion that there is no reason not to take GM at their word – "the solutions to GM's problems are essentially internal, especially in labor relations" – or to disbelieve chairman Robert Stempel's statement that the decision was based on economic, not political, considerations.[8]

> In school districts affected by GM plant closings, educators spent Tuesday assessing the potential damage caused by the loss of GM tax dollars. They also tried to calm students' fears, and their own.
> Maryanne George, "Closings Could Mean Trouble for School Districts,"
> *Detroit Free Press*, Feb. 26, 1992, 9A

The *Ypsilanti Press* reports the principal of Kaiser Elementary School – Laura Chew – describing how the news has upset her students. "Many, many are expressing anger at President Bush. One said if he could get his hands on the president, he'd give him two black eyes."[9]

Aides to Governor Engler describe him too as "bitterly disappointed" by the news. The governor – who says he received only 15 minutes warning of the announcement – and Michigan members of the U.S. Senate and House of Representatives ask GM to explain the choice of Arlington, but a spokesperson responds that all considerations are confidential. Engler continues to insist that the state's poor business climate and high taxes are the problem – "Business as usual is not good enough."

And Jesse Jackson announces he will lead a rally at the Willow Run plant. "The issue is not shifting furniture around in a collapsing industrial house," Jackson insists. "GM and Ford and Chrysler's losses are evidence of a major economic depression on the horizon."[10]

"UAW Draws Battle Line," reads the *Detroit Free Press*'s front page headline the next day. Stephen Yokich, United Auto Workers vice president, is pictured with his hand raised in warning and remonstration. Accusing GM of fostering competition between workers at the two plants – "whipsawing" – Yokich declares that the UAW's 1990 contract with GM will not be opened for renegotiation, nor will the union approve the

Arlington plant's introduction of a third shift. "Stempel and his corporation are playing with fire if they encourage plant-against-plant competition over work rules in efforts to pressure the UAW into eroding the
contract. . . . We plan to enforce that agreement vigorously." Since GM is
apparently seeking concessions from labor as it decides on 10 additional
plant closings – Stempel has said, ominously, that future shutdowns will
depend in part on workers' willingness to improve productivity – this
amounts to a showdown. General Motors' vice president of industrial relations responds, "We continue to believe that we have more in common
than in conflict with the UAW and intend to work with the union in taking a common approach to beating the competition."[11]

And another asset, perhaps our biggest, is the people who make up our community. We have learned to be scrappy, to fight, to dig in our heels when
outside forces – be they economic turmoil, political maneuvering, or anything else – threaten us.

It is that fighting spirit that will keep Ypsilanti on its feet, and it is such
strength that will not buckle in the face of betrayal by a giant company that
turned its back on this community's loyalty.

[Editorial] "The Battle Begins," *Ypsilanti Press*, Feb. 25, 1992, 6A

So very sad about Monday's announcement is the fact that the Ypsilanti area
has made such giant strides recently, especially in the way it is perceived.

This is notably true in Willow Run, particularly in the schools. Under the
spirited leadership of Superintendent Youssef Yomtoob, Willow Run Community Schools has made such a turnaround that the question long ago
ceased to be "why would you send your children to Willow Run?" and became "why wouldn't you send your children to Willow Run?"

The same can be said of our community as a whole. People who don't
know any better ask, "Why do you stay in Ypsilanti?" and we've been confi-
dently able to reply "why not?". . . .

The reality is that we've been hurt and hurt badly. And working to make
sure the blow isn't fatal is perhaps the biggest challenge we've ever faced.

Steve Repko, "Once Again We Face Major Challenge," *Ypsilanti Press*,
Feb. 25, 1992, 6A

Repercussions from the plant closing will ripple through the surround-
ing communities. Unemployment is anticipated in a variety of associated
businesses: the Institute for Community and Regional Development
(ICARD) at Eastern Michigan University in Ypsilanti predicts the loss of
Willow Run's 4,000 jobs will lead within three years to 7,730 jobs lost in
Washtenaw County alone: a drop of 22.2 percent in motor vehicle em-

ployment and of 3.8 percent in total county employment. The estimated total job loss throughout the state of Michigan is 18,100 – 0.4 percent of the state's total employment. The other cuts planned by GM are likely to push these figures to 9,340 jobs lost in the county and 80,000 in the state. About half GM's reductions in blue-collar jobs will occur in Michigan, and perhaps 80 percent of white-collar jobs.[12] There are no clear figures available to show how many of the workers who will lose their jobs live in the Willow Run community. (The city of Ypsilanti houses 708 employees.) But Willow Run will be affected both directly and indirectly.

Several local communities have high proportions of Willow Run employees, and these communities will bear a disproportionate share of the income and property value changes that result from the Willow Run closing. These communities will face lost tax revenues from declining property values and incomes, and will face additional trouble in school funding if families are forced to move from their current districts as a result of job losses at the Willow Run plant or through the multiplier process through which jobs in other sectors of the economy will be lost.

In addition to declining property values and property tax revenues from job and income losses, Ypsilanti Township, Washtenaw County and two school districts will suffer direct property tax losses as the state equalized value of the Willow Run plant is lowered, if it remains unused or is dismantled. For example, Van Buren School District with 6,300 students, and the Willow Run School District of 3,200 students currently receive $2.1 million and $0.8 million per year, respectively, from the Willow Run assembly plant. Both districts are "in-formula," meaning that each district's relatively low tax base results in State of Michigan funding on a per-pupil basis, so they will also suffer a partial loss of state funding if their enrollments decline.

D. B. Crary and C. Hogan, *Willow Run and Related Plant Closings: Causes and Impacts*. Institute for Contemporary and Regional Development, Eastern Michigan University, 1992, p. 44

If the effect on the surrounding community of closing the Willow Run assembly plant is grasped largely in economic terms, the effects on the individual workers who will lose their jobs when the assembly plant closes are more visceral. A local social worker describes the stress from the plant closing as "like a brick hitting you in the face. You're so stunned you don't even know you're bleeding." In May and June, three men from the plant, all in their forties, die from heart attacks. Workers attempt suicide, substance abuse increases, as do reports of domestic violence. Local mental health workers anticipate denial, followed by depression.[13]

The reaction in the community is one of shock, anger, and bitterness. This turn of events is completely unexpected; although there had been gnawing uncertainty for some time, there were also many indications that GM's decision would go their way. Workers and their families express their sense of unfairness; their feeling that they have been duped, ripped off, betrayed. They have worked hard; they have built cars of high quality more cheaply than the Arlington plant, but they have still come out the losers. The feeling of unfair treatment is fueled by the fact that Stempel has not said what his decision is based on. This feeds anger: at General Motors, at George Bush, at John Engler, who are splitting families apart, dividing the community, creating yet more "GM gypsies." Workers and their families face uncertainty about the future, about what to do next. They must confront practical problems: Should the house be put up for sale? Can they manage the mortgage payments? Should they hold onto an old car? Cherished plans must be abandoned – to send a child to college; to fix up the house; to buy a new car – and this fuels bitterness. There's a growing sense they can't depend on anything; they have to fight just to stay alive, let alone get ahead.

These psychological sequelae are the focus of a series of special reports in the *Ann Arbor News*, titled "Lives on the Line." An editor's note sets the tone: "The Willow Run assembly plant will send an economic shock through the area when it closes next summer. But the reverberations will be felt one family at a time."[14]

The headlines again tell the story: "They Feel As If They've Been Sucker-Punched by Plant's Closing." "There's a Lot of Broken Dreams." "Depression: 1st Hurdle for Targeted Workers." "Feelings of Anger, Betrayal Expressed." "Future: What Happens Next?"

All this is news for the national press too, which follows the story over the next several months. The *New York Times* publishes a series of six front-page articles on the Willow Run plant closing. The first, published on Labor Day, September 7, 1992, headlined "American Dream Put on Hold at Car Plant Doomed to Shut," begins: "The planned plant closing has brought significant stress to the lives of the plant workers and their families, and to their friends and neighbors throughout Willow Run and the surrounding communities." The *Times*'s article highlights these effects on the lives of the workers: "The cars can be produced somewhere else. But what the workers fear cannot be transplanted is the way of life that has been built around their plant in Ypsilanti. Willow Run means picnics, Christmas parties, bowling leagues and the union."[15] Chuck Kehrer, a worker profiled in the *New York Times* article, describes his co-workers' reactions to the announcement. "People were crying and running out. I felt very, very sad. I felt as if the Titanic was going down, and everyone was running for the lifeboats, and the lifeboats had holes."

Wesley Prater, supervisor of Ypsilanti Township (a position like that of city mayor) put it this way: "GM has some responsibility to our community. Whether they admit it is another matter."

The national business community, on the other hand, is pleased to see Stempel taking a decisive stance after years of complacency and indecision at General Motors. There's truth to the slogan that GM is "The Heartbeat of America." Stempel, considered slow but surefooted, has also unveiled plans to merge GM's three vehicle groups – Buick-Oldsmobile-Cadillac, Chevrolet-Pontiac-GM of Canada, and Truck & Bus – into a single structure, North American Operations, to encourage teamwork among designers, engineers, and manufacturing specialists. And the 19 separate families of car and truck will share fewer combinations of chassis and powertrain (engine and transmission). Stempel sounds aggressive and determined: "It's clear that we're not going to get help from the government. It's clear we're not going to put restrictions on this market. By God, we're going to have to compete. And that means you have to be lean. You've got to have costs down." And in this manner GM is caught up in a national, indeed international, transformation of the organization of economic production.

[Jerry Clifton, bargaining chairman of UAW Local 176 at the Willow Run assembly plant, says] "We're not smart enough to see what's happening to us. It's bigger than Willow Run. It's Willow Run first, then the state of Michigan second, and then the United States. We've got to say enough is enough."
Russell Grantham, "Special Report. Lives on the Line. Union Leader Battles Odds," *Ann Arbor News*, May 13, 1992, C1, 6

The day after the closing is announced *Detroit News* columnist James Higgins articulates this transformation.

We've arrived at a peculiar stage of the auto industry worldwide – a new age of manufacturing is beginning to ripen. This hasn't happened since early in the 20th century, when supervisors at the Ford plant in Highland Park found that machine and materials technology had progressed to a stage where something entirely new was possible – mass production.

Lately, automakers have been refining mass production into "lean" production, a buzzword of the 1980s. Mass production reached its highest level when it got lean, with reduction in inventory, scrap and labor effort.

> Today, computer and information processing technology is paving the
> way for another dramatic step – agile production.
> James Higgins, "It's New Age of Manufacturing for Auto Firms: Higher
> Output, Fewer Workers," *Detroit News*, Feb. 25, 1992, 7A

Higgins says, "If you think this is pie-in-the-sky, here is GM's own internal assessment of what an agile production assembly plant might look like in the 21st century." He describes a plant that would assemble the same number of cars per hour as today – 66 – but in a space 70 percent smaller, using one-fifth the number of parts, with even fewer of these unique to each model, in four times as many different styles, with one-third the number of labor hours. Clearly, employment in such a plant would be far less than it is today. As manufacturing executives view this future, the needed agility will be achieved through an integration of the resources of technology, management, and labor into a "coordinated, interdependent system" working together with an ethics of "mutual trust." Trust, that is, both of workers and of computer design-and-test systems. As Higgins sees it, the bottom line is that unless everyone pulls together to help U.S. industry through this transition, "the standard of living Americans enjoy today is at risk."[16]

Capitalism has long been appreciated to be a form of economic organization prone to periods of crisis. As economist Joseph Schumpeter saw, writing in the 1930s, capitalism is a system of "creative destruction"[17] that depends upon continuous innovation to maintain profits, and, as David Harvey puts it, "innovation exacerbates instability, insecurity, and in the end, becomes the prime force pushing capitalism into periodic paroxysms of crisis"[18] – what Schumpeter called capitalism's "long wave swings." One such crisis has been mounting during the past 20 years, with a shift in the way capitalism operates that amounts to "a transition in the regime of accumulation and its associated mode of social and political regulation."[19]

Novelty is the norm in a capitalist economy; capitalism is a system of self-generated metamorphosis. The source of energy in this system is the drive to get ahead, the impulse to make money, to accumulate capital. And capital is not simply wealth, it is wealth reinvested in the system that produced it. Capital, converted into raw materials, allows the production of goods which, sold on the market for a profit, generate still more capital.[20]

Capital also provides command over labor; a capitalist economy presupposes a fundamental social and economic inequality. Karl Marx is famous for placing this at the center of his analysis of capitalism, but Adam

Smith noticed it too.[21] The basis of capitalism is the distinction between those who own the means of production – equipment, plant, the credit to purchase raw materials – and those who sell their labor power for a wage. In a capitalist economy, labor power has itself become a commodity to be bought and sold in the marketplace. The laborer, robbed of the opportunity to support self and family on communal land, is forced to earn a living by selling his or her capacity for physical labor by the hour, for a wage. Once sold, that capacity for labor becomes the property of the employer, to be applied as they see fit, and the products of labor are also the property of the employer rather than the laborer, even though it is the latter whose activity produced them. When the value of the goods produced exceeds the cost of their production the goods can be sold at a profit, and this too is taken to be the property of the employer. To ensure profit, employers have an incentive to keep prices high and costs, including the cost of labor – wages – low. There is economic inequity and moral injustice at the heart of any capitalist economy.

The need to increase or at least maintain profitability through competition and squeezing labor motivates the search for new technology and new ways to organize production. Productivity can be multiplied by expanding the division of labor so that people perform increasingly specialized tasks with progressively more advanced equipment. Competition can be enhanced by innovating new products and abandoning old ones as outmoded and obsolete. This dynamic growth has contributed to an elevation of living standards – eight times over in America between the 1750s and the 1930s, for example. But, as many have documented, it has also generated great misery in the form of low wages, the loss of communal land, the periodic depressions of the so-called business cycle, deskilled and numbing jobs, and environmental damage. In a capitalist economy the very conditions of existence become unstable and uncertain.

This dynamism can also be seen in the waves of technological innovation that have changed the way we do business and the way we live. In the first industrial revolution of the late eighteenth and early nineteenth centuries the steam engine was used to drive manufactures like the cotton mill and to power innovations in transportation such as the locomotive and steamship. A second revolution at the end of the nineteenth century and the beginning of this one harnessed oil and electricity for lighting, communication, and the new automobile. A "Third Industrial Revolution" now builds upon electronics and computers. Each of these has radically altered the face and body of society.[22]

The last significant shift in the way the American economy operates took place first in Michigan, and in the auto industry. The innovation of standardized, factory-based, assembly-line production was first fully implemented in 1914 at the Ford Motor Company's Highland Park plant in Dearborn, for manufacture of the Model T. Influenced by the time-and-motion studies of Frederick Taylor, Charles Sorensen ("Cast Iron Charlie") created a continuously moving line with overhead belt conveyors bringing parts to workers at their stations and carrying the finished product away. Ford (who later claimed the concept was his own) described the assembly line as "the focusing upon a manufacturing process of the principles of power, accuracy, economy, system, continuity, speed and repetition."[23] The result was that a Model T Ford no longer took an average of 12½ man hours to build; it now took only 1½ hours. The assembly line enabled production to be speeded while prices were cut, thereby greatly increasing demand. It enabled Ford to turn the automobile into a commodity and made him a very wealthy man. But what was progress for Ford and his company was not immediately an improvement for his employees.

> If unrest and agitation had not yet become labor issues, demoralization and transience were. Employees saw themselves as robot laborers; those with skills found that they were of little use on the assembly line with its endlessly repetitive activities. Anyone who outproduced another worker had to wait for him to catch up; the only virtue was monotonous efficiency. That there was practically no identification with or loyalty to employers was shown by the help-wanted advertisements swelling the Sunday newspapers. So great was the alienation that in 1913 the Ford Motor company had to hire 963 workers for every 100 it wanted to remain permanently on the payroll. Accountants pointed out that it took $100 to train each one, and that the company was thus losing $3 million a year solely because of worker defections.
> Peter Collier and David Horowitz, *The Fords: An American Epic.* New York: Summit Books, 1987, p. 65

Ford reluctantly raised the wage for his workers from $2.50 to $5 a day. Other automobile manufacturers told Ford he was wrecking their industry and was a traitor to his class. But absenteeism dropped dramatically, and Ford workers began wearing their identification badges when off duty, to show their company affiliation and indicate their wealth. Furthermore, better wages offered Ford's workers a middle-class lifestyle and created a whole new group of consumers. The automobiles that hitherto only the prosperous few could afford were now within the grasp of blue-collar workers. "What was special about Ford . . . was his vision, his explicit recognition that mass production meant mass consumption, a new system of the reproduction of labour power, a new politics of labour control and management, a new aesthetics and psychology, in short, a new kind of rationalized, modernist, and populist democratic society."[24]

Fordist production had impacts outside the workplace. The Great Depression of the 1930s, when supply greatly outstripped demand, showed that Fordism required the government to develop fiscal and monetary policies that would restrain the economy by curbing business cycles, foster it by developing infrastructure, and provide basic social services, including greater expenditure on education. Capitalist economy and democratic state must work in tandem.

But a sharp recession in the 1970s marked the end of the triumph of the Fordist mode of economic organization. Economic restructuring and social and political readjustment have followed. The U.S. consumer market had become saturated: corporate profits began to shrink. In the 1970s and 1980s slumps in productivity were countered with layoffs and dismissals, which in turn led to decreased consumption and lower demand for goods, in a vicious cycle. Conversely, upturns caused a tightening of the labor market, rising wages, inflationary pressures, and a squeeze on profits. Many contrasted this with the Japanese system, where long-term employment guarantees and an export orientation appeared to give stability, and education provided a skilled and remarkably adaptable workforce across all segments of society.[25]

U.S. businesses struggled to cut costs and improve efficiency by investing in the new information technology, and discovered that new kinds of organizational structure were needed to use it effectively and adapt to the complex global financial system it made possible. The traditional corporate hierarchy – with blue-collar workers at the bottom of the heap, their tasks prescribed, their voices ignored – was too rigid and bloated to adjust to sudden market fluctuations. Now standardized mass production is being replaced with "lean" and "flexible" production. In this post-Fordist approach, costs are kept low and agility high by the use of "just-in-time" production, where stockpiling is avoided and parts and products are kept at minimal levels. Teams of workers from various departments work together, mental and manual labor no longer separated. Quality is ensured by processes of continual improvement – called *kaizin* by the Japanese – that draw upon all workers' experience in collective problem solving. Companies are getting flatter, smaller, and nimbler, demanding from their workers speed, innovation, quality, service to customers, and "making do with less of everything."[26]

---

1. a transition from physical skill and manual labor to intellectual capabilities or mental labor,
2. the increasing importance of social and collective intelligence as opposed to individual knowledge and skill,
3. an acceleration of the pace of technological innovation,
4. the increasing importance of continuous process improvement on the factory floor and constant revolutions in production, and
5. the blurring of the lines between the R&D lab and the factory.
   Martin Kenney and Richard Florida, *Beyond Mass Production: The Japanese System and Its Transfer to the U.S.* New York: Oxford University Press, 1993, p. 14

If this general picture is evident, the details are by no means clear. Economic transformation is neither preordained nor smooth; it results from individual choices and conflicts as much as broader systemic tendencies. In 1992 the U.S. national economy was still in dire straits. The announcement of Willow Run's closing came at a time that the National Association of Business Economists called "the worst three-year interval centered on a depression since the Great Depression." A government study showed that the number of workers earning under $12,195 annually had doubled in the past decade. Economists said this increase was due not to the business cycle but to "structural or long-term factors," as service jobs replaced jobs in manufacturing. Other reports showed that disposable income hadn't grown since President Bush took office. In 1992 a 30-year-old worker with a high school degree earned $3,500 less than he or she would have in 1979, and median household income had fallen 5.1 percent since 1989. Americans were working on average 158 more hours each year than they had 20 years before. The number of people living in poverty grew in 1991 by 2.1 million, to 35.7 million – 14.2 percent of the population. Although the worst was seen as past, and some growth was now expected, it was projected at only a sluggish 2.3 percent.[27]

Furthermore, the gap between rich and poor was growing wider. The pretax income of the top 1 percent of salary earners grew (after adjusting for inflation) by 77 percent from 1977 to 1989, to an average income of $559,800, while that of the bottom fifth dropped by 9 percent, to an average of $8,400. The richest 1 percent of families received 60 percent of the after-tax income gain.

Not surprisingly, bankruptcies, both personal and business, were rising dramatically nationwide. In eastern Michigan they had increased for seven years in a row; 1991's increase was a startling 27 percent, with 17,941 bankruptcies declared during the year. People were trying to pursue a lifestyle that was no longer affordable. A local attorney explained, "Nowadays, our typical client works either for Ford or GM or for a small machine shop, secondary to the automakers, and they've had significant job cutbacks, either layoff or loss of overtime."[28]

Joseph Schumpeter saw the "perennial gale of creative destruction"[29] forever opening up fresh vistas for capitalist ventures, but he also believed that capitalism destroys the moral authority of all institutions, including its own. Its instrumental rationality eventually attacks private property and middle-class values, and this will lead, Schumpeter maintained, to an elite group of managers who will regulate the lives of members of the middle and working classes so inured in habit and routine that their fates will be unnoticed.

Arguably, capitalism's unique and characteristic dynamism is its own worst enemy. It is tough to maintain order, both micro and macro, in the face of the problems a capitalist economy generates. Markets both thrive on and are destabilized by irrational expectations, and the marketplace turns its back on "externalities" such as pollution and unemployment. Capital accumulation is always threatened by the potential saturation of demand. The relation between government and business is a source of friction, and a constant balancing act between overregulation and failure of government oversight.

And the tension between capital and labor is a constant source of strife. The ills of the system tend to be laid at the doors of its victims – those least able to defend themselves find their skills rendered obsolete, their jobs eliminated, their communities fragmented, their children hungry.

How can these consequences of economic dynamism be justified? The moral legitimacy of a social contract in which labor is purchased, squeezed, and discarded is questionable at best. Other nations are exploring different solutions to this practical and ethical problem, but in the United States layoffs occur as the safety net of welfare, built after the Great Depression, is being dismantled. A new social contract is being shaped, a new definition of the relation between government and citizen, between employment and well-being.

It is clear that a major transformation is under way, but in 1992 there was palpable uncertainty about the outcome. Would a new legion of jobs be created that require intelligence, planning, the ability to work collaboratively, to identify and solve problems, to innovate? Or would the new jobs be largely in the service sector – hamburger-flipping McJobs with few benefits and little security? Or would many jobs be lost completely, moving south of the border or overseas? The outcome was not predetermined; it would depend on the insight, leadership, and humanity of many people. This much was clear – the relationship had changed between the Willow Run community and the industrial giant it had served for so long. The next year would demonstrate this changed attitude – as the local community, struggling to retain its pride and position, took GM to court, and as the presidential election campaign brought national politics to town. And as the Willow Run schools were caught up in major initiatives seeking the reform of public education. The conjunction of all these elements would highlight the way schools must function within complex webs of political and economic influence: direct "vehicles of reform" and indirect "drivers of change." The next year would offer an opportunity to study the connections between school, the economy, and the state.

3   Vehicles of Reform, Drivers of Change

March 1992–June 1993

The 1983 document titled *A Nation at Risk* was the earliest of a series of reports blaming U.S. schools for the country's economic troubles. Famously, the authors of that report, commissioned by the secretary of education for President Reagan, T. H. Bell, fancied that "if an unfriendly foreign power had attempted to impose on America the mediocre educational performance that exists today, we might well have viewed it as an act of war." They suggested that what amounted to "an act of unthinking, unilateral educational disarmament" has left the nation's schools lacking solid content to curriculum and with low expectations of student performance. Students spend less time in school than in other countries, and that time is used poorly. The profession of teaching pays badly, attracts less-qualified people than it might, and trains them insufficiently in the subject matter they will teach.

Citing "a steady 15-year decline in industrial productivity," a situation in which "one great American industry after another falls to world competition," *A Nation at Risk* declared that "the risk is not only that the Japanese make automobiles more efficiently than Americans and have government subsidies for development and export," but more broadly that we are entering an information age, a global village, where the "new raw materials" are "knowledge, learning, information, and skilled intelligence." To compete in world markets for industry and commerce, the nation's educational system needs reform. We are in "a world of ever-accelerating competition and change in the conditions of the workplace, of ever greater danger, and of ever-larger opportunities for those prepared to meet them." Traditional jobs shrink in number, replaced by work requiring more "sophistication and preparation." But beyond this economic concern, "the very fabric of our society" is at risk.

41

A "common culture" must be fostered, the writers of the report insisted, and education plays a critical role here.

Evidence for this diagnosis? The authors acknowledged that "the average citizen today is better educated and more knowledgeable than the average citizen of a generation ago," but at the same time "the average graduate of our schools and colleges today is not as well-educated as the average graduate of 25 or 35 years ago, when a much smaller proportion of our population completed high school and college." This, they insisted, has a major negative impact. The problem is caused by "weakness of purpose, confusion of vision, underuse of talent, and lack of leadership." Needed is "life-long learning," the creation of a "learning society."[1]

In 1988 George Bush – keen to be "the education President" – met with the 50 governors at an Education Summit in Charlottesville, Virginia – only the third such meeting to address a national issue in U.S. history. The National Governors Association had for several years been drawing up recommendations for improving public education, mainly by defining standards. In what was described as a "remarkable consensus"[2] about the state of public schooling and the need for a national strategy, the bipartisan task force – led by Bill Clinton, then governor of Arkansas – announced six "National Education Goals" to guide school reform at all levels.

By the year 2000:
1. All children in America will start school ready to learn.
2. The high school graduation rate will increase to at least 90 percent.
3. All students will leave grades 4, 8, and 12 having demonstrated competency over challenging subject matter . . . and every school in America will ensure that all students learn to use their minds well, so they may be prepared for responsible citizenship, further learning, and productive employment in our Nation's modern economy.
4. The Nation's teaching force will have access to programs for the continued improvement of their professional skills and the opportunity to acquire the knowledge and skills needed to instruct and prepare all American students for the next century.
5. United States students will be first in the world in mathematics and science achievement.
6. Every adult American will be literate and will possess the knowledge and skills necessary to compete in a global economy and exercise the rights and responsibilities of citizenship.

Progress of Education in the United States of America – 1990 through 1994,
U.S. Department of Education[3]

The Bush administration soon proposed "The AMERICA 2000 Excellence in Education Bill" with a variety of specific recommendations for reform of public schools. The proposed bill was essentially intended to bring the principles of a market economy to schooling, rewarding excellence and introducing freedom of choice – but Congress didn't pass it.

Despite this setback, Bush created the National Education Goals Panel, in July 1990. A bipartisan association of governors, senior administration officials, and congressional representatives, the panel was to chart progress toward the national goals. Citing a need for new standards for educational achievement, the panel adopted a charter for a National Education Standards and Assessment Council (NESAC), with the mission to coordinate various standard-setting activities. Its goal was to have a system of voluntary academic standards in place by 1994–1995. NESAC asked professional organizations to develop voluntary standards in their fields – mathematics, science, history, arts, civics, geography, and English – and the U.S. Department of Education awarded grants to help them do it. Fear was expressed in some quarters that standardized national testing might lead to a standard national curriculum, but the panel insisted that national standards did not mean federal standards, that the federal government was not developing these standards, and that, anyway, states were free to adopt or reject them. The NESAC disbanded in 1992, its initial task completed.

At President Bush's specific request business leaders formed the New American Schools Development Corporation (NASDC), with the mission "to support the design and establishment of new high-performance learning environments that communities across the country can use to transform their schools for the next generation of American children." The NASDC was analogous to a research and development department in business or industry; its objective was to raise $200 million to support "design teams," each of which would provide the blueprint for a "New American School."

Bush issued a call to arms: "For the sake of the future – of our children and the nation – we must transform America's schools." He called on every community to become an "AMERICA 2000 community" by adopting the six goals, developing a community-wide strategy to achieve them, designing a report card to measure success, and planning for and supporting a "New American School." The central notion was that the best solutions for school reform would be local ones. The proposal met with much criticism from unions (opposed to school choice) and conservatives (who saw threats to local autonomy), but by the end of 1992, 48 states and 2,000 communities had signed up.

Michigan's Governor John Engler is one of the eight members of the National Educational Goals Panel. Not surprisingly, he supports the Bush administration's calls for school reform. When Engler took office in January 1991, beating the two-term Democratic incumbent by just 17,000 votes, the state of Michigan had a $1.8 billion budget deficit, unusually high property and business taxes, and unemployment above the national average since 1966. Engler is ambitious and energetic, the oldest of seven children raised on a beef cattle farm in Beal City, Michigan. President of his dormitory at Michigan State University, he helped his father run for state representative while majoring in agricultural economics. In 1970, two years later, aged 22, he won a seat himself in the Michigan House of Representatives by 162 votes. As governor, Engler immediately took steps to cut taxes and "improve the state's business climate" – words interpreted by many to mean reducing union power – in part by reforming Michigan's public schools.

The previous administration had drawn up a "blueprint for action" in the state's schools, based on reports like *A Nation at Risk*, stressing improved equity and opportunity. Public Act 25, adopted in 1990, called for "quality education reform" by providing financial incentives for school improvement plans, a yearly status report from each district, and the design of a core curriculum to serve as a "model" for all K–12 teaching. Unusually, this model core curriculum, the "Michigan K–12 Program Standards of Quality," defined expectations of "student outcome" rather than listing courses or programs of study.

To that point, accreditation of Michigan's public schools had been entirely voluntary and based on "input" criteria such as levels of staffing and other resources, the existence of required policies and procedures, and so on. PA 25 proposed new standards (though these were not immediately approved) that focused not on input but on a school's ability to demonstrate improvement in student achievement and other student "outcome" data. Engler's reforms started from there.

In his January 1993 State of the State address Engler focuses on his plans for creating a "new generation of jobs." To ensure that industry will get the highly trained workers it needs he will "cut red tape" for business and industry in the state "and roll out the red carpet." Engler has placed school reform high on his "Taxpayer's Agenda." Emphasizing that the state's job growth is now "more than triple the national average," Engler acknowledges he's "also seen faces of despair." "To succeed, Michigan needs both highly trained workers and an entrepreneurial climate that invites investment and rewards risk-taking, because one without the other is not enough." He announces plans to reorganize and consolidate the state's job training programs, combine the roles of the departments of Labor and Social Services, build partnerships with business, and cut property taxes. And he will increase school spending, but "we must get more for our money."

Our universities are helping Michigan move from the Industrial Age to the Information Age – a new era in which knowledge and the ability to transmit that knowledge quickly across cities, counties, countries and continents will determine economic prosperity and the quality of life for our people. Knowledge opens the door to success, and I want every Michigan citizen to have the key. No one should be left behind. Helping people through education is a vital part of my vision for a new generation of jobs.

Our children's schools must be the very best. If our schools fail, the cost will be staggering – more crime, dependence, broken families and shattered dreams. My friends, we cannot tolerate the loss of even one child. That's why, despite tight budgets, I have fought to increase school funding. Over the past two years, while overall state general fund spending remained constant, we have increased spending on public schools by 48 percent – $352 million. This school year, Michigan taxpayers will spend more than $9 billion to support the education of kids from kindergarten through high school – that's more than $5,300 per child; or to put it another way, more than $130,000 per classroom.

I recognize there are those who say schools cannot get better without more money, and that current inequities in funding make it impossible to improve outcomes. I disagree. The facts simply do not support the argument. Clearly, there are inequities. And I will again, as I did last year and the year before, offer recommendations to reduce those inequities when I present my budget.

Regardless of our differences, we all agree on one thing: We must get more for our money. For all we spend, our schools must do better. I believe every parent has a right to know how their school is doing. To inform parents, I will initiate a Governor's School Report Card. This building-by-building report on all 3176 Michigan schools will detail performance and spending – allowing comparisons with schools across town and across the state.

Tonight, I also renew my commitment to expanding options and fostering excellence in our schools. I applaud President David Adamany and Wayne State University's College of Education for their effort to break the mold and establish Michigan's first charter public school in Detroit this September.

I also urge this Legislature to move swiftly to enact teacher tenure reforms to insure that good teachers move up and bad teachers move out, as well as the Michigan Education Warranty to insure that our schools stand behind their students the way our automakers stand behind their cars.

Gov. John Engler, State of the State Address, Jan. 26, 1993[4]

Several organizations within Washtenaw County have put out a similar call for what one of them describes as "crossing to the new economy." Michigan Future, Inc. – a "non-profit, non-partisan citizens group" supported by contributors that include Chrysler and foundations such as Detroit Edison, Dow, Kellogg and Mott – has undertaken the strategic task of publicizing the need to "provide the new learning demanded by the New Economy in our schools and adult training programs."[5]

Michigan schools did an excellent job of preparing us for the mostly unskilled, mass production factory and office jobs of the Old Economy. The classrooms we attended looked like Old Economy workplaces. We sat in industrial rows, moved to bells, and learned mainly by memorizing. We were trained to take orders.

But as we've seen, the emerging New Economy demands employees who can solve problems with fellow employees without being told what to do by a supervisor or foreman. It demands employees who can keep learning new skills and master sophisticated technologies. The new economy requires very different schools and ways of learning – schools where students learn by working together, and where teachers coach students instead of telling them what to do.

Michigan Future, Inc., *Crossing to the New Economy: A Citizen Vision for a Prosperous Michigan and a Strategy for Getting There*. Michigan Future, Inc., 1992, p. 17

In February, Michigan Future, Inc. holds a Washtenaw County Area Town Meeting to discuss how local schools could help create a flexible local marketplace of customized goods and services, preparing a workforce that is more responsible and consequently is awarded a larger stake in companies' success.

But at this meeting the Superintendent of Washtenaw County Intermediate School District, Michael Emlaw, presents survey data that paint a very different picture of what Michigan employers look for in a worker. The data show that most employers value not academic skills but character and attitude: the absence of substance abuse, honesty and integrity, ability to follow directions, respect for others, and punctuality. The *bottom* five items are achievement in academic subjects such as math, social science, natural science, computer programming, and foreign languages.

There is a second national impetus to school reform. Early in 1990 the National Science Foundation launched its "Statewide Systemic Initiative" program – the first time NSF had provided major funding for efforts to transform the states' educational systems. The architects of "systemic reform" were Marshall Smith, then dean of Stanford University's School of Education, and Jennifer O'Day, then a Stanford graduate student.[6] In 1988 Smith, at NSF's request, wrote a position paper sketching a way to organize statewide reform of math and science teaching. The concern he articulated was that new emphases on teaching children "higher order thinking skills" – solving complex problems and applying knowledge to novel situations – threaten to leave minority and poor children behind, because the schools serving these groups often lack the trained teachers and other resources for such teaching.[7]

Smith and O'Day were convinced that an "equality of educational opportunity" is "*necessary* for responsible citizenship in our diverse modern society."[8] An ability to grasp "differing perspectives and novel approaches"[9] is needed in our modern democracy and complex world. Their concern was moral and political, not economic (they added, almost parenthetically, that economic improvement might occur too), and their focus was on equity. "Simple justice dictates that skills and knowledge deemed *necessary* for basic citizenship and economic opportunity be available to *all* future citizens."[10]

They elaborated the view that get-tough, "top-down" school reform mandates of the early 1980s had not worked, and neither had more recent, scattered, "bottom-up," site-based reforms. The crucial issue is how to "deliver" the new higher-order knowledge and skills fairly, without regard to race, class, gender, or language, and to do so in a way that still allows diversity among local school districts in their choice of curriculum, instructional strategies, topics emphasized, and language of instruction.[11] Systemic reform would seek to "align" all the components of public schooling – legislation, curriculum materials, teacher training and certification, in-service training, and student assessment – and provide direction through a "common content" – the curriculum frameworks many states have developed to define expectations for what children should know and be able to do at different grades. The focus would be math and science education, both K–12 and postsecondary.

To avoid the problems previous reform efforts ran into, such an approach should "marry" the "vision and guidance" of government policy to the U.S. tradition of local responsibility and control. Systemic reform would require only a loose coupling of national and local activities, with the state as the crucial intermediary. The state would act as "stimulant" for local reform, providing direction and vision through clear standards for what students should learn, ensuring that state policies coherently support local districts, and seeking to reform legislation to give teachers the resources and flexibility to get on with the job. Individual schools should remain free "to choose the instructional strategies, language of instruction, use of curriculum materials, and topics to be emphasized."

Now NSF is awarding competitive grants to states with proposals for such systemic reform, up to $10 million over 5 years. State projects must aim to broaden the impact, accelerate the pace, and increase the effectiveness of improvements in math and science education, though they can tackle this task whatever way they consider best. In October 1991, Michigan submitted a proposal requesting Statewide Systemic Initiative funding. The proposal promised a review of existing state, local, and professional association policies, programs, and activities to see how they are or could be better "aligned," and a competitive grant program to provide funding and technical assistance to several urban and extreme rural "target" school districts. These districts would be expected, with technical assistance and guidance from the state, to design local "Models of Effective Learning." In addition, a "framework" would be created to redesign the education of new teachers in Michigan universities and colleges. Among the Project Steering Committee are a principal investigator from the Michigan Department of Education and three co-principal investigators, from the Detroit Public Schools, the Michigan Partnership for New Education, and General Motors.

Located in the Michigan Department of Education Bureau of Instructional Services, MSSI operates within the Office of Quality School Programs. The goals of MSSI are to communicate the Vision for high quality science and mathematics education; align curriculum, instruction, and assessment; review educational policies and programs for coherence; create, in selected school districts, models of effective learning; redesign teacher education and professional development; provide leadership for and empower stakeholders; and ensure accountability and continuous quality improvement.

Zoe Barley, Mark Jenness, Sharon Dodson, and Rebecca Thomas,
MSSI: Evaluation Report for Year 04, 1995–1996.
College of Education, Western Michigan University, April 1997

The award of NSF funding for Michigan's Statewide Systemic Initiative (MSSI) is announced in October 1992. In spring 1993 MSSI sends a first draft of the "Vision" that will guide its efforts to all public and private school principals and superintendents, as well as to business and community organizations, to initiate a discussion among these "stakeholders." MSSI's Vision will be the "measuring stick" for reform; a final version will be written by the start of 1994. The draft suggests that the emphasis of systemic reform has shifted, reaching Michigan, from educating citizens to preparing workers.

> Success in today's global economy depends on scientific and technological strength which is built on the foundation of mathematics and science education. The Michigan educational system must accommodate the changing needs of our society in general and the workplace in particular. Our schools must graduate students who are mathematically and scientifically literate and motivated to pursue further education and careers in science, mathematics, engineering and technology. Our state and national economic growth and their place in world markets are determined, in part, by our ability to provide scientifically, mathematically and technologically literate workers and life-long learners.
>
> *The Vision: New Directions in Mathematics and Science Education.*
> Michigan Statewide Systemic Initiative, 1993, 5

> The educational system in the United States is highly decentralized. According to the Tenth Amendment to the U.S. Constitution: "The powers not delegated to the United States by the Constitution, nor prohibited by it to the States, are reserved to the States." In accordance with this Amendment, the federal government has no authority to establish a national education system, nor do Federal agencies ordinarily prescribe policy or curriculum for local schools. Such decisions are made at the State or district level.
>
> *Progress of Education in the United States of America – 1990 through 1994.*
> U.S. Department of Education.[12]

The 15,000 local school districts in the United States have traditionally exercised considerable autonomy. The system of public schooling in the United States, unlike that of many nations, has been designed specifically to avoid centralized authority. Each school district has its local school board, and each district is typically funded mainly by local property taxes. This means that efforts at the state and national levels to change what and how schools teach are confronted with what can seem like inconsistencies, fragmentation, and diffusion. In particular, any approach to reform that mandates a standard national curriculum flies in the face of long-standing and fundamental assumptions about the function and role of public schooling in this country.

But these assumptions have come under attack. Local property tax financing creates financial inequities, say many – and efforts are under way in several states to identify alternative approaches to school funding. Local control makes large-scale reforms overly difficult to implement, say others – and the independence of local school districts is challenged by efforts to merge them into larger units or to permit children to attend schools outside the district they live in. To many people the notion of a "systemic" approach to educational reform is very appealing.

> Willow Run today is a place where nearly 15,000 people live. It is not a city or an incorporated village. We have no Service Club or Chamber of Commerce; no Department of Parks and Recreation; no Local Unit of Government except the Township. As a result our schools perform many functions.
> *Handbook of General Information for Willow Run Teachers*, 1951.
> Cited in Roxanne Jayne and Susan Sachs,
> *Southern White Migration to the North: From Willow Run to Today.*
> University of Michigan, American Studies class 498, Apr. 25, 1973

But the Willow Run Community Schools have already begun to change. Willow Run's schools have always played a central role sustaining the community in the face of the stresses of work at the plant and the antipathy, even scorn, of the rest of Washtenaw County. Superintendent Dr. Youssef Yomtoob – known affectionately to staff and students as "Dr. Joe" – takes an active role as soon as the plant closing is announced. On Blue Monday the *Ann Arbor News* quotes on its front page his immediate reaction: "We were getting encouraging news, so we were feeling good about it. It's very bad, very, very bad. . . . I don't know what else we can do . . . just keep supporting our people."[13] Yomtoob describes the closing as devastating to the school system, the community, and the surrounding area, tearing the social fabric and undermining school finances. A more sanguine "superintendent's message" appears in the spring issue of the *Report Card*, the schools' community newsletter:

> On Monday, February 24, 1992, our community was hit with the devastating news that General Motors was going to close the Willow Run CPC assembly plant. . . .
> Without question, this decision will have an impact on the Willow Run Community, Washtenaw county and the entire state of Michigan. We will lose good people to other communities, cities, and states. In no way do I want to minimize the negative effects. However, we must all now turn to the future and do everything we can to lessen the toll the plant closing will take. . . .
> There are two strong messages that have been sent by the plant closing. First, as a District and a community, we have to do everything in our power

to present Willow Run as a good place to live and to learn. The schools have to recommit themselves to providing education of the highest quality to entice young families to move into our community. Eastern Washtenaw County is still the best housing bargain available and we have to make sure that this fact is widely known. Second, there is a painful but important lesson for our kids. The opportunities that were available for their parents may not be available to them in the future. We have to instill in them a strong value and thirst for education, an education that will position them to take full advantage of the opportunities waiting for them in the 21st century. They must be fully prepared to respond in a rapidly changing world. Only with the help and guidance of their families and the schools will they achieve that goal.

Willow Run is a caring, concerned and strong community. Together we will weather this latest storm and I have faith that we have the power to emerge even stronger in the future.

Youssef Yomtoob, "Superintendent's Message,"
Report Card, Willow Run Community Schools, Spring 1992.

Superintendent Yomtoob, hired in 1988, is widely credited with boosting morale and improving the district's image. He pushed for refinancing the bond issued to rebuild Willow Run High School in 1985, and $1.3 million of this money is for technology improvement – computer labs in all the schools, libraries turned into media centers, computers in the classroom. The middle school will get a new technology lab with robotics, a wind tunnel for testing model cars, and computer-aided design and machining. Willow Run High School will get a lab for computerized architectural design and urban planning. Multimedia production equipment will be added at all levels, and there will be a districtwide electronic media center. The final phases of the plan involve more networking, a satellite link for distance learning, more classroom computers, and telephones in each classroom.

Yomtoob has been passing out little red bear stickers with the slogan "I ♥ Willow Run" – a small, playful gesture, but an important corrective to the negative image the community's history has given it in the eyes of the rest of the country.

Some say image is everything.

For several years, Willow Run Community Schools suffered from a negative image due to financial difficulties, aging facilities, and its curriculum.

But changes instituted during the tenure of Superintendent Youssef Yomtoob have moved Willow Run in a different direction.

"When I came here (to Willow Run), we set three goals for ourselves. The goals were higher achievement, financial stability, and positive image," Yomtoob said.

"And during those five years, that is where we have concentrated our efforts. In terms of reaching those goals we have come a long, long way," Yomtoob said.

Willow Run's negative image posed a problem attracting families and encouraging growth in the community, Board of Education Trustee Clifford Smith said.

For the past five years, red bear stickers bearing "I Love Willow Run" have become Yomtoob's trademark. His style and openness is credited with some of the success of the school district.

Raymond McMillan, "Willow Run Crafts New Image," *Ypsilanti Press*, June 14, 1993, 1A, 4A

In his office in the old Spencer School building, Yomtoob muses on his decision to come to Willow Run. "I think it was love at first sight. . . . I like challenges. All my life I've believed that there are certain parts of the population which are underdog for one reason or another, and it is up to all of us to work with them, and they should succeed. I did not come here in terms of charity, that I'm doing a favor. They did me a favor to hire me; I appreciate that. But I think I understand where they're coming from, and I know where we want to go. They have to have the same chance as anybody else, maybe more because they come from underprivileged homes which is a disadvantage for them when they get to school."[14]

Now Yomtoob must guide the district's response to the plant closing – the local manifestation of a much vaster economic transformation.

The reform efforts in the Willow Run Community Schools are guided not by large conceptions of public schooling as a system, or even by a sense of its failure to keep pace with economic change, but by the expert know-how of skilled practitioners with a keen understanding of the community and its children. As Mary Brandau describes it, the changes at Kettering began seven years ago when it was the school's turn to host the district's Ethnic Fair.

"It was *wonderful;* we had such a good time with it. It was so much fun, and it was a lot of learning, and so much community support and involvement." This was what sparked the staff's interest in changing what happens in the classroom, though they hadn't figured out explicitly what they wanted to do. "When we did it, we didn't have any idea, except we knew it made *us* excited about teaching, it was fun, it was fun for the kids."[15]

Mary chaired the arrangements. "It was a year-long look at cultures. Every classroom became a continent, and then took one country in that continent. We had graphs comparing countries all over the building, we had maps all over the building. We invited people from the different countries to come and speak to different classes, and kids ate with chopsticks, and they took their shoes off outside the classroom. We talked about how they do that in Japan, and how they clean their own buildings, and what schools look like in different countries. We had missionaries come in, and the kids were really fascinated with different languages. Fifth graders assumed that if you came over on an airplane then you knew how to speak English. And I thought, oh my goodness, where did you get that? 'Well, they're here, they should speak English.' It was fascinating; I can still remember thinking, if you don't let kids talk, you have no idea what their misconceptions are."

Excited by the sense that there was a way of teaching that both they and the children found fun, the Kettering staff started working as a team on innovations like integrating instruction across the curriculum. For example, "We talked a lot about doing math. We would find out how money was done in another country, and how you would do conversions. Teachers got into it, it was a lot of fun." Kettering developed a five-year plan with the goal "to maintain high standards while integrating subject areas and increasing hands-on, minds-on activities." Vivian Lyte was Kettering's principal then, and that helped. Her attitude, Mary recalls, "was, 'If you need something I will get it for you. You figure out what you need to do to teach, and I'll get you what you need.' Instead of this feeling, 'I have to own what I have, because if I don't protect what I own, if I let my resources out of my sight, then I will be deprived.' I have to keep that up," Mary reminds herself, " 'cause it's real true."

Many of Kettering's children belong to families over the edge of poverty, struggling and stressed. The students here are among the poorest in the district. Some are children of single parents who moved into subsidized apartments near Kettering; others have young parents just starting out, working long hours in jobs that don't pay much, working overtime whenever they can, without the time or patience to give their children much attention. Some come from broken homes. I hear of grandparents raising several sets of grandchildren in tiny apartments, some sleeping on the living room couch, and of women who got pregnant very young and are still living with their own parents, lacking job skills, lacking the schooling to help their children study. Each day, some children come to Kettering hungry, tired, lonely, scared, even angry.

Many are hungry for adult attention, with little experience of reading or being read to, expecting to fail. Teachers speak of a child who pooped in his pants because he'd been sexually abused and who couldn't work sitting down, instead perching on the table's edge. One little boy I speak to when he drops by Mrs. Brandau's office tells me casually that his father and the fathers of both his stepbrother and stepsister are all in jail, and his mother is considering leaving the area before any of them is released. Mary believes her school is one of the few places some children experience that is clean and hygienic, where people smell good.

At the same time, people in this community take care of one another. Vivian recalls her arrival at Kettering as a new principal.

"I was real nervous about being over there, [but] the parents would do anything for me. I remember the first time I needed something; something I needed for an assembly, and this parent was standing there – you know how you talk to yourself out loud? – 'Oh gosh, I forgot something.' She says, 'I'll go get it,' and she took off and got it! She went and bought it, and that is how they were. That is sort of how the community is. 'You need that? Okay, I'll go and get it.' It doesn't matter whether I have the money, whether it is my last dime, but you need that and if you don't have it, I will go and get it. I guess that is what I mean about the connectiveness; that is what I'm talking about – the Willow Run story; and it goes way back. Even when there was a separate black and white community, they were separate and they argued and fought with each other, but when they came together it was, 'We are a community. We are Willow Run.'"

So when Mary talks of making learning fun, of engaging children in a way that was missing before, and of involving parents, she's speaking of the particular needs, attitudes, and strengths of the children of this community. And these needs and attitudes stem from the fundamental organization of working-class life under Fordism. At the same time, the strengths of Willow Run arose from the circumstances of the community's birth at the hands of Ford's company.

The division of labor in Fordist production – mental labor, manual labor – has shaped the lives and lifestyles, the tastes and attitudes, of the two social classes of capitalist society, including the different attitudes the working class and middle class have to work, to knowledge, and to schooling. Fordism required an "indirect, cognitive and symbolic relation"[16] on the part of white-collar workers – managers, accountants, engineers, designers – but of blue-collar workers it demanded obedience, punctuality, a strong body, and tolerance of monotony. Working-class culture consequently adopts a skeptical attitude toward theoretical knowledge and book learning. Paul Willis noted among manual workers in the English midlands

a massive feeling on the shopfloor, and in the working class generally, that practice is more important than theory. . . . The shopfloor abounds with apocryphal stories about the idiocy of purely theoretical knowledge. Practical ability always comes first and is a *condition* of other kinds of knowledge. Whereas in middle class culture knowledge and qualifications are seen as a way of shifting upwards the whole mode of practical alternatives open to an individual, in working class eyes theory is riveted to particular productive practices. If it cannot earn its keep there, it is to be rejected.[17]

Willis adds that "The working class view would be the rational one were it not located in class society" where theory has taken on a social guise that makes it the hollow currency of social advancement and cuts its close ties to material reality. For the middle class, theoretical knowledge confers choice and mobility. For the working class it has no such utility.

The economic circumstances of the classes reinforce these differences. Along with its division of labor, Fordist production, like earlier versions of capitalism, entailed the exploitation of members of the working class: the profit squeezed from the products of their labor flows to the owners of plant and equipment, not to the workers. The middle class consequently enjoys a "distance from necessity," an "indirect" relation to the world, that the working class does not experience. The former can cultivate detachment, indifference, and a separation of form from function, while the working class find themselves pressured to adopt a pragmatic, functional, and matter-of-fact attitude to their circumstances.[18]

Kettering's students are the fruit of this lifestyle, born into a culture that values manual labor and practical reasoning. Consequently the hands-on student-centered pedagogy catches their attention. Traditional schooling – sitting silently at a desk, filling out worksheets – might keep such kids in line, but at the cost of losing their allegiance. This is schooling more attuned to where the children are coming from, and where they could – should? – be going.

A parent, a tractor-trailer mechanic in Detroit who left the Willow Run schools in 1982, tells me what school was like then. "School was alright, you just had to go there. All you had to do was be there, and you'd pass. You didn't have to do nothing. I was a hard-headed kid, thought I knew everything. I had classes that I went to and I never did nothing. I never lifted a pencil off the table and passed with a D. Well, I just wanted to get out of school." He laughs. Of his son, in fourth grade, he says, "I'd like to see him go to college and not have to go to work and do manual labor like I do. You know, I'd like to see him wear a suit and tie to work." His wife adds, "Not have to come home all dirty."

One morning in third grade illustrates children's attitudes toward traditional academic tasks. Their teacher has just assigned seatwork from the math textbook dealing with "fact families." The task is to work on problems like 7 + ___ = 14 with multiple choice answers.

As the children start to work (or at least as the teacher finishes her explanation of the task and hands over responsibility to them) I pull my chair up to a group of four girls and ask them what they are doing. Tabatha says she doesn't know. She hates math. She flops back in her seat. I say maybe we can figure how to solve the problem, even if she doesn't know the answer right now. She looks bored and uninspired. Lesley says they had four pages of math for homework just the previous evening. She pulls her work out of her desk to show me. She goes through the first problem for me, but she solves it by drawing on the fact that 7 + 5 = 12, 12 + 2 = 14, 5 + 2 = 7, so the "added" is 7. This approach isn't going to help Tabatha, whose eyes are still glazed. "Did you find out how to do it?" she asks me. "Yes," I say, "hold on," because Jessica is leaning over from the far side of the table to tell me that she has done all the homework and she is going to get all this work done quickly too. Goody-two-shoes, I think, but ask her if she can tell me how she solved the problems. She pulls her paper back toward her chest. "I do my own work," she says scornfully.

At that point the teacher interrupts to make an announcement, and Tabatha takes advantage of this to engage me in small talk. "There's pizza for lunch," she says with a smile of anticipation. "Really," I reply politely. Then a little touch of inspiration hits me. "How much pizza do you eat?" I ask. "Just one." "What if you ate five pizzas?" I say. She grins; "That would be five dollars!" "What if you ate seven pizzas?" I persist. "That would be seven dollars!" "What if you ate seven more pizzas?" She pauses to think, then: "Fourteen dollars." "Fourteen dollars," I repeat. "You just solved the first problem: seven plus seven is fourteen." Her eyes widen and she starts to smile.

Mary explains that Kettering's first efforts were a good beginning but they want to go further. "There was no 'essential question,' and no level of higher-order thinking. Our problem is, we can do *that* kind of stuff. *Now* the test is, are we still pushing the kids to the higher levels of thinking? Not 'This is the flag of the country and draw the flag of the country,' but, the next time we do it, what is the level of learning going to be?"

The Kettering teachers spend much of the 1992–1993 school year testing out the next step. With the guidance of Professor Shirley Magnusson from the University of Michigan, teachers in third through fifth grades work to coordinate their instruction, collaborating on "project-driven inquiry." Students design and assemble a variety of scale-model buildings – a mall, houses, a zoo, Kettering School itself – and wire them with batteries-and-bulbs lighting. The children are given opportunities to work in small groups and find they have to learn to cooperate, respect differences, and organize their activity. Children sometimes become angry with one another, and some of the buildings get trashed several times over in frustration. But they are rebuilt, and some children build houses at home, without the teachers' assistance, while others discover the concept of π as they measure the circumference of the school's pillars and try to figure out the radius for their scale model.

Parents become involved, too, and those I speak with are pleased with what is happening at the school. Some of them come to cut foam-core board in the art room, when the knives are too sharp for the children to use safely. Cyd Karr, the district's roving art teacher, describes how parents come in to help their children work in the artroom and end up playing with the paints themselves. Cyd has to tell them, "No you don't, this is your daughter's painting." Janice Brown, principal for the year following Vivian's promotion, calls it "Copping a paint." And Hazel Stangis talks of the parent trying to help her child make measurements, who says, "The kids know more about measuring than I do!" "But we didn't scare her away!" says Hazel. "And she still helped the child," she adds in a tone of wonder.

And in what is called "process writing" the children articulate what they have learned about electricity, going through as many as six or seven drafts – an interdisciplinary use of language arts skills to discuss and describe electricity, a scientific concept. Much of the composition uses the new computers for word processing. This kind of writing calls for a good deal of intense individual attention from a teacher, working on spelling, sentence structure, paragraph development, and so on. The children draft, type, then they read to each other ("What are you saying?"), then more editing before the final draft is ready. Their reports include reactions to how they've worked together – some now refuse to sit together, others have developed close relations with their peers.

For the staff this project is not all plain sailing. It really tests their commitment, and they hit difficulties and contradictions. Constructing the buildings takes far more time and effort than anticipated, "running ahead" of them. Concern develops over "ownership" of the project – much of the students' creative work happens in the art class, and some teachers feel Cyd has the best job.

At one staff meeting Mary admits, "I was very disappointed in their report writing, some of the students aren't making any sense. 'I learned how to diffuse a battery. . . .' It's a lot of conversation and sometimes they're getting it; they know their actions, they know what they have done, but they don't know how to take what they have done and have it make any sense. They know they built the building, they know they put the wires and batteries and light bulbs together, but they really don't understand, some of them, 'circuit' or those keywords. They can't answer the questions." The Kettering staff begin to talk about how to make the connection between discovery learning and more direct instruction. "How much direct teaching is it going to take, to be more of a coach, for the kids? I dance, but I know that I don't do it by trial and error. I can't learn that way. So maybe we need to learn more about how kids learn. It concerned me – all this work, all this energy, and kids not answering these questions."

Traditional classrooms foster an annunciatory conception of truth, where the child falls in with the opinions of the teacher, and validity is based on conformism with authority.[19] The Kettering staff, along with others in Willow Run, want to escape from this model of learning. But what is the alternative? The louder calls for school reform are often linked with proposals for "constructivist" pedagogy, like that in 1989 from the National Council for Teachers of Mathematics (NCTM),[20] which called for teaching for understanding rather than memorization, fostering application of knowledge to new settings through discovery and hands-on investigation. Such proposals have met with a host of criticism because they are seen as replacing instruction with appeal to children's intuitions. This is "fuzzy math," the critics say. After all, they point out, mathematics is not natural, it is a highly complex acquired skill. Children won't spontaneously rediscover mathematical and scientific concepts on their own. Critics have demanded a return to the traditional model where the teacher instructs children in "correct" reasoning.[21]

NCTM has probably been misinterpreted; the intention was not to suggest teachers leave the classroom altogether, but once direct instruction is relinquished, finding the right balance is tricky. Student-centered reform seeks to lead children to an understanding that knowledge is a human product, constructed, always fallible and incomplete. The American Association for the Advancement of Science (AAAS) explains:

It is appropriate in science, as elsewhere, to turn to knowledgeable sources of information and opinion, usually people who specialize in relevant disciplines. But esteemed authorities have been wrong many times in the history of science. In the long run, no scientist, however famous or highly placed, is empowered to decide for other scientists what is true, for none are believed by other scientists to have special access to the truth.[22]

The AAAS recommends that even in kindergarten, children should be asking and investigating their own questions, and that before they graduate high school they should design and conduct a major investigation in which they "frame the question, design the approach, estimate the time and costs involved, calibrate the instruments, conduct trial runs, write a report, and finally, respond to criticism."[23] In such an approach, comprehension is emphasized, rather than coverage of academic content.

But these new math and science standards and frameworks make only broad and general suggestions about *how* to teach, leaving teachers to figure out most of the details. The NCTM *New Standards* make minimal suggestions about pedagogy beyond "actively involving students individually and in groups in exploring, conjecturing, analyzing, and applying mathematics in both a mathematical and a real-world context. . . . Being a facilitator of learning."[24] The *Michigan Essential Goals and Objectives for Science Education* clearly states its aim to "provide suggestions about what to teach, but *not* how to teach or how to assess student learning."[25] And nowhere is there discussion of children's different attitudes. Teachers and administrators like those at Kettering must learn how to make this new pedagogy work.

And so, Mary insists, the main issue is, "what are *we* learning from this? What are we learning about how we coordinate and integrate instruction, and what are we going to do to prevent this in the future, so that *you're* not saddened, and *your* class isn't out for a part of it. I'm saddened personally because I miss it, but *they're* not saddened because they've got the greatest over there. What they're learning is wonderful."

The Kettering teachers are searching for ways to satisfy their students' needs for attention and support, for food and rest, and they are finding ways to work with, rather than against, the children's skepticism about book learning and negative expectations of schooling. I come to see this search as an important experiment – an attempt to make schooling relevant to working-class children; one that amounts to an effort to change the kind of person these children can become, to counter the costs and consequences of Fordist capitalism. But it remains to be seen how this vision of the future, in which local children acquire a "thirst for education" and Willow Run is appreciated as "a good place to live and learn," will mesh with the Governor's vision of a freshly trained and flexible workforce that will entice new industry to Michigan.

> In recent years, the Willow Run schools have undergone a rebirth. The pride in the schools is increasing; parents are becoming more involved, and community support for the schools and the programs is increasing. That is not to say that Willow Run does not face issues. It has the same problems as other schools. While it is solid right now, finances are tight; there is concern about the achievement levels of the students; there is need for more parent participation. But overall, there is no doubt that Willow Run's fortunes are rising, and the current board deserves a share of the credit for that.
>
> Editorial, "Willow Run," *Ypsilanti Press,* June 7, 1993, 6A

An open house is held at the end of the year. The local press, the superintendent, and members of the school board are here, along with all the students and their parents, and the mood is one of celebration and shared accomplishment. In the gymnasium are arranged the scale models of the school, the mall with its Sears, the working-class bungalows, ranch-style houses, and elaborately architectured houses Cyd helped design. "Oh, I wouldn't mind living in one of those myself," Cyd says, and I find myself echoing her. Custom designs, cathedral ceilings, skylights – each angled differently to the road, with orange paper driveways to a car porch. The bungalows sit more modestly, squarely facing the road, with no off-street parking.

The parents here appreciate the project; to them it makes sense that their kids have made something concrete. Mr. Maylone is an auto engineer with two kids in second grade, another in middle school, and a fourth at college studying engineering. "He's following in your footsteps," I say. He hesitates, as though considering that I might be mocking him, then says, "Well, I think he'll do better than me."

Progress is not simply change in a valued, an envisioned, direction; it is change that can be sustained. The Willow Run teachers must find ways not only to transform their classrooms, but to sustain these changes, as the ground shifts under them and they face a variety of obstacles. Janice speaks of "the whole group dynamics and problem solving and confrontational issues" among staff, as well as "the acceptance or rejection or struggle with project-based science."

There is a variety of teaching skills and personal styles in the building. An approach like project-driven inquiry appeals more to teachers who see students as engaged learners, who try to get their students involved and don't necessarily follow the textbook. Other teachers follow the book more closely and struggle with an inquiry approach.

Mary observes, "Unfortunately – and I mean very unfortunately, because we have learned so much from each other this year – teachers are really used to working in isolation. And old tricks die hard. It was very clear to me that once we got our heads together we collectively knew a lot more about electricity than any single individual did."

Janice tells me, "Another example is the schedules, and bells, and all of the false, system, bureaucratic kinds of things that we create, which have nothing to do with children. They're for our own organizational purposes, and I see a lot of conflicts with that."

"How easy is that to change?" I ask.

"*Oh, Martin*, it's the hardest thing in the world to change. You have the parents who believe in a certain tradition of schooling. You have the administration that tells you to go ahead until you go too far. Then you have the teachers that *must* have, and should have, certain rights protected. You have all of those things. And then you have a single administrator that, no matter how good he or she is, cannot manage two hundred and fifty children at one time. That's the reality of it."

The Kettering staff appreciate the need to be sensitive to parents' views of schooling. Many parents are proud of Kettering; they tell me the school is "closely knit." "If you could get a view from the top, you'd see a big light here. The school is the hub, playing a vital part in the community. And kids are the biggest vehicle of change." But Janice Brown explains to me, "This is a working-class community – working-class or non-job, that type of community. And there's reason for the people in this community to be suspicious of the educators.

"Some of them have gone through this system and not been successful, and they base their experiences on their own successes, so we have to prove to them that that kind of thing is not gonna happen with their child. *Many* of the parents have been in and said they have seen great improvements, so I *know* that we're working hard to improve things. But, also, their aspirations for their children may be that they just go to high school and get a job, and our aspirations, professionally, may be much greater than that. So we have to make sure we're always in tune, and sensitive to aspirations and so on."

As a child Vivian Lyte worked in her father's grocery store, and he tried to keep her away from the cash register, for fear she wouldn't learn how to count if she used the machine. She feels parents in Willow Run resisted the introduction of calculators into the classroom for the same reason. Vivian tells this story to illustrate how the parents need educating too. Their attitude to kids is that they'll do wrong unless they are prevented. And you can best change parents by drawing them into the decision-making process in the schools. Every school is supposed to have a group with parents as members; not so many that they form a majority. And these representatives will talk to other parents in the community so word gets around.

Some parents may share the educators' aspirations for their children but disagree on the means being employed. The notion of kids "teaching themselves" may be going too far. Janice explains, "We do a lot with our parents here, so they're getting a more intuitive view about what education should be about. The traditional view of course is that education is based on facts and figures, one correct answer, textbook approach, and so on, and we've spent a lot of time with our parents saying, 'That is a tool, but it is not the product.' It is *not* the product. And we've given them examples of the kinds of things that are different."

Janice adds, "In fact I know a high school principal that literally lost his job – he got it back again, but he lost his job because he worked in a working-class community. When he started there about twelve percent of the students went to college and now seventy-some percent do. And he didn't do a very good job of preparing his community for that."

"What was their objection?"

"Well, they knew the children would grow up and leave the community then."

"So you're getting a sense that there are some boundaries that you may not want to cross?"

"Well there's some boundaries I will cross, and then we'll see what happens. I say that, but there's never been a time here when I haven't felt the support of the community. I have a tremendous community. I don't know how far they want to go though. We'll just see. And maybe, maybe I'm going too far; I don't know."

> [T]he changes since 1987 have come so fast as to seem almost magical: distributed data processing, interactive telecommunications, computer-integrated manufacturing and control systems, shared-database marketing alliances, supplier and customer networking, real-time order entry and control systems, robotization, customization, disaggregation, globalization. Increasingly, the mindless work of our civil society is accomplished by mindless things: machines and software. In short, there is hardly a job left in our own society that does not require a talent for integration. . . .
>
> In this world, employees . . . will need the very qualities of mind advocated by democratic pamphleteers long ago. These include the capacity for grace under pressure, creative poise, abstract thinking, technical problem solving, cogent speech, and conflict resolution. . . .
>
> What is "best" for companies is also, more and more, "right" for people. Not that businesses have suddenly become citizens. But for the first time in the history of industrial capitalism, the interests of businesses are consistent with those of citizens, consistent with the yearning for intellectual cultivation, self-direction, uniqueness, and zest in work. . . .
>
> [And this] requires us to think about business's obligation to support the reshaping of public education.
>
> Bernard Avishai, "What Is Business's Social Contract?"
> *Harvard Business Review*, Jan.–Feb. 1994, pp. 44–46

Is it really conceivable that "for the first time in the history of industrial capitalism, the interests of businesses are consistent with those of citizens"? The relationship between GM and Ypsilanti Township hardly demonstrates such shared interests. Perhaps it was the last straw in a bleak time, perhaps GM finally went too far, perhaps it is the symbolism of Willow Run's plant – the local community is going to fight. In early March 1992, the Ypsilanti Township Board of Trustees takes an unprecedented step, voting, with UAW local support, to claim breach of contract against GM and try to force the company to keep the Willow Run plant open. When the company received $250 million in tax abatements in 1984 and 1989, saving it about $14 million, GM said jobs would be kept at the plant. Now township attorney Doug Winters says, "It's time to find out what a community's rights are. . . . They make the same promises everywhere. They should have some kind of corporate conscience, not to make promises they're not going to keep. It's binding on us for twelve years. It should be binding on them for twelve years."[26]

A trial for Ypsilanti Township's suit against GM is scheduled for next January. Governor Engler is trying to stay out of the suit, appealing an order from County Court judge Donald Shelton that the state take a position – the attorney general's office tells the Court of Appeals that doing so would damage the state's relationship with local governments and businesses.

The government released a report Monday showing that the percentage of full-time workers who earn less than $12,195 annually grew sharply in the past decade, a period of economic expansion that brought new prosperity to the affluent. . . .

The report was finished months ago but delayed while Census officials fought over how much attention to draw to it.

New York Times and Associated Press, "More Fall Into Low-Wage Jobs: Number Grows Despite Boom," *Ann Arbor News*, May 12, 1992, 1A

This is a presidential election year, and here too a sharp clash between the interests of workers and those of business is evident. Blue Monday was the day after the Democratic primary in Maine, and the race is being described as topsy-turvy, a lively free-for-all. Paul Tsongas and Gerry Brown tied with just under 30 percent of the votes each, 16 percent of voters remain uncommitted, and Bill Clinton – considered the front-runner just a month before – received only 15 percent of the vote. When the candidates for the Democratic Party nomination reach Michigan, they find an angry electorate. A Willow Run worker is quoted in the *New York Times:* "The politicians say, 'I'll do this, I'll do that.' Yeah, right. Then they get elected and do nothing. If I had my way, I'd throw out every politician. I would." Another worker yells "The system don't work," then stomps off.[27]

Iowa senator Tom Harkin, popular with midwestern blue-collar workers, withdraws from the race in March, leaving many wondering where to turn next. National union leaders decide not to endorse any of the remaining candidates for the present.[28] Clinton and Tsongas are seen as candidates of business and the rich – both support free trade with Mexico, and Tsongas has opposed legislation to prevent companies hiring replacement workers during a strike. Gerry Brown has taken to wearing a UAW jacket and makes Michigan a major focus of his campaign.

Political activity in and around the Willow Run plant greatly increases in the months before the election. The union local had endorsed Tom Harkin, then Gerry Brown, and finally Clinton, and voter registration is high, motivated by a desire "to make sure George hits the unemployment line before I do."[29] Pundits declare Michigan a swing state vital to George Bush's reelection prospects, but Bush is detested here, even though "Reagan Democrats" in Michigan supported him four years ago, when he won the state with 53.6 percent of the vote, and although the Bush campaign is being helped by strong Republican organizational support from Governor Engler.[30] "Bush has lied to us for so long," says one auto worker. "I'll never vote for him again. God, nobody's got a job. You practically trip on the homeless." The *Detroit News* explains: "Most workers expressed anger and disgust, particularly at President George Bush. They figure he played a part in steering work to his home state of Texas because it will play into NAFTA – the North American Free Trade Agreement now being negotiated, which would remove tariffs and other barriers to the movement of goods, services and investments among Canada, the U.S., and Mexico – and because Texas offers a lot more electoral college votes than Michigan."[31] A Washtenaw County commissioner is reported saying, "This is hardball politics on a national level." Some workers have taken to wearing buttons that read, "George Bush: the best president that Japan ever had." Clinton is increasing his attacks on Bush, saying in a speech in Detroit that Reagan and Bush have "driven the American dream into the dirt for millions of Americans. This country is an open wound tonight."[32]

Labor Secretary Lynn Martin conceded that the North American Free Trade Agreement could put up to 150,000 Americans out of work, while Democrats asserted that the President's plan to help them was inadequate.

Keith Bradsher, "Democrats Call Plan for Help Insufficient. Trade Pact Could Cost Up to 150,000 U.S. Jobs," *New York Times*, Sept. 11, 1992, C1

Josh, a sixth-grader at Edmonson Middle School and a student of American karate, has recently become interested in union activities. After the Willow Run announcement, he accompanied his parents to a UAW-backed rally at Willow Run High School that featured Jesse Jackson. He also has spent some time picketing local Kroger supermarkets in support of striking workers there. "I'm worried that [there] won't be any more unions in America in the future," he says.

Owen Eshenroder, "Waiting in a Shadow: Sleep's Not Easy as Couple Ponders Life Beyond Willow Run," *Ann Arbor News*, May 11, 1992, C1, C4

But voters across Michigan are "turned off and didn't turn out" in the primaries, as the *Press* puts it. In Ypsilanti Township only 5,000 people go to the polls – 18 percent of registered voters, equal to the percentage statewide. Clinton and Bush win their respective primaries at both state and local levels; Clinton is now considered to have virtually clinched his nomination as Democratic candidate.[33]

When Bush's presidential campaign comes to Michigan in October, Bush tries to argue that higher gas-mileage requirements Clinton has proposed will eliminate auto industry jobs, but UAW officials counter that they will stimulate new technologies and create jobs. The economy is starting to show some slight signs of recovery – a survey of executives shows 47 percent are optimistic, and retail sales are up slightly[34] – but this is too little and too late to help Bush. National opinion polls show 78 percent of people judge the economy "fairly bad" or "very bad," and 80 percent disapprove of the way Bush is handling the situation. Bush's approval rating has eroded rapidly as he continues to insist that things aren't as bad as they look and tries to shift the election debate to social issues and "family values." Throughout the Midwest, the economy and jobs are the issues that voters are concerned about. When Clinton wins the presidency, in November 1992, Bush's loss is attributed to the hard economic statistics, but also to a palpable and pervasive "sense of economic foreboding, a fear that the United States [is] losing its manufacturing base and economic leadership to Germany and Japan."[35]

Several new economic reports demonstrate starkly the extent to which Americans' incomes have stalled, painting a depressing picture of workers struggling to crawl up a down escalator.

Steven Greenhouse, "Income Data Show Years of Erosion for U.S. Workers. A Decline in Expectations: Democrats See an Opportunity to Stress Voters' Perception of Flaws in the Economy," *New York Times*, Sept. 7, 1992, A1

Suddenly, Robert Stempel resigns as chairman and chief executive of GM, apparently forced out by the board of directors, a week after collapsing at a meeting and being hospitalized for high blood pressure. When the *New York Times* publishes the sixth in its series of articles on the closing of Willow Run, it focuses on the news about Stempel: "Just when the workers thought things couldn't get worse, they did."[36] The board apparently feels that GM is not changing quickly enough, that Stempel, a 34-year veteran, an engineer who made it to the top, a "car guy" who workers feel knows the industry in a way the "finance people" do not, is too steeped in the old GM culture. A dollar of GM stock bought ten years ago has earned only 10 cents profit, compared to $2.42 profit from Chrysler and $3.66 from Ford.

The UAW issues a statement calling Stempel a "victim" of "White House policies that have relentlessly tightened a noose around our nation's domestic auto producers." Others say that Stempel should have better understood GM's problems.[37] One worker says, "The first thing I did was just laugh. I thought, 'Well, he's expendable too. He's finding out how it feels.'"[38]

GM's current president – John F. ("Jack") Smith Jr. – is named new chief executive, and the board says they'll give him six months to turn the company around. Smith, who has been highly successful cutting costs in GM's international operations, speaks in New York of the need for help from the UAW, and talks of a "common ground" of understanding emerging between GM and the union. He says he will announce four more plant closings by the end of the year, and he predicts GM will return to profitability by next year. White-collar jobs will have been reduced to 79,000 by the end of 1992 from 91,000 at the start of the year, with a goal of 60,000, while hourly jobs will have been cut to 288,000 from 304,000.

In December, confidential GM papers unsealed in the Washtenaw County Circuit Court suggest that union relations did indeed play a key part in the decision to close Willow Run. They show that consolidating production at Arlington will save $197.9 million each year, but consolidating at Willow Run would have saved $271.7 million. It would have been cheaper to upgrade the Willow Run plant than the Arlington plant, and will cost more to close it. In addition, worker absenteeism was lower at Willow Run. But Arlington was apparently judged by GM to have "progressive union-management relations," including a UAW local that is more flexible on job classification, files fewer grievances, and has settled contracts before deadline. Local 276 at Arlington has "been more receptive to taking more innovative approaches to bargaining" and "more flexible" about GM shipping work to outside contractors.[39] An unnamed GM administrator says Arlington offered a union contract with streamlined terms that would significantly reduce labor costs, allowing GM to run the plant 24 hours a day.

Regional UAW director Bob King says "It's what we've said all along. They lied to the local union. They lied to township and county officials. They lied to state legislators. I hope Michigan's congressmen and senators take this up with them. They owe Ypsilanti workers a new product. With GM in such bad financial shape, it's crazy to make the decision on anything except finances."[40] Doug Winters, Ypsilanti Township attorney, says "When this plant has a lower unit cost and GM says it will have trouble securing a work force down there, it tells you they've got their eye on the border. They're not getting out of the car business, they're getting out of the state and busting the union."[41]

February 1993 brings unexpected and exhilarating news. After a nine-day trial, Judge Shelton rules in Washtenaw County Circuit Court that GM may not close the Willow Run plant! "The local governments of this state are placed in a position where they have no choice but to give taxpayers' resources away under a statement that does not mandate that they receive anything in return," Shelton reads from his judgment. "There would be a gross inequity and patent unfairness if General Motors . . . is allowed to simply decide that it will desert 4,500 workers and their families because it thinks it can make these same cars a little cheaper somewhere else. . . . My conscience will not allow this injustice to happen." He is interrupted by loud applause. GM has "lulled the people of the Ypsilanti area into giving up millions of tax dollars which they so desperately need to educate their children and provide basic governmental services." He issues a "promissory estoppel," which provides compensation for a broken promise or quid pro quo. "GM is hearby enjoined from transferring the production of its Caprice Sedan and Buick Integ . . ." He is interrupted again by applause and cheers from overjoyed workers in the courtroom.

The judge rejects Ypsilanti Township's claim that the tax breaks accepted by General Motors amounted to a contract, but he does accept that the company had promised continual employment at the Willow Run plant until 2003.[42] Jerry Clifton says, "It brings tears to your eyes. It looks like America again." A plant worker says, "Throughout the Reagan era, big business got their way. Now maybe it's time for the working man to get his way."[43] But a GM lawyer calls the judge's ruling "ridiculous" and says the company will appeal.

The *MacNeil-Lehrer News Hour* covers this development. In an interview, Township Supervisor Prater calls the tax abatements a "nice form of blackmail: the company is essentially saying if we don't get the abatement we'll leave your community." He says, "we had two choices – either to be a willing victim, or an unwilling victim. The moment that Judge Shelton said 'I hearby enjoin General Motors,' it was a surprise, it was a very pleasant surprise but, you know, we had achieved our goal, what we wanted to do." But the *News Hour* report notes that an auto industry analyst describes the attitude of company decision makers to "a township that will take a company to court when the company is trying to survive" as "extraordinarily negative." GM could become embittered, feeling kicked when it is down. It could even respond by closing the Hydra-matic plant. *News Hour* reporter Fred de Sam Lazaro notes, "GM seems determined to fight for what it sees as its right to make and act on business decisions. GM has already served layoff notices."

Prater replies: "Well we're not really trying to tell them how they conduct their commerce. . . . It *is* very competitive out there, but it's not like they haven't been made aware in advance that we can't continue to export *all* of the jobs out of this country and expect us to be healthy as a society. These companies such as General Motors, Ford, they're all profit-driven, and at some point in time I think the *social* responsibility as well as profit has got to come into bearing."

4   America's Birthday

Summer 1993

> It's America's birthday, and everyone should take some time to pause and have a little fun.
>
> It's been a tough couple of years. The economy hasn't been great, and we've had our problems locally too, but this is a time to stop and consider that America, now pushing 220 years of age, remains the best country in the world.
>
> And with a little work, it will be better still as it grows older.
>
> Editorial, "July 4," *Ypsilanti Press*, July 4, 1993, 6A

The assembly plant's regular summer shutdown, the end of the 1993 model year, leaves only a few workers cleaning equipment for possible shipment elsewhere. In May the township asked the Michigan Court of Appeals to uphold Judge Shelton's order that GM continue to operate the plant – at the same time, General Motors served a federally required notice of its intention to close it between July 2 and July 9. Local union officials say that if Judge Shelton's injunction holds, GM will soon have to start retooling for 1994 models, and the township's attorney accuses GM of "trying to wear on the psyche and morale of the people." The local plans its summer picnic, uncertain whether it's an occasion for celebration or mourning.

Then, on August 4, the Michigan Court of Appeals issues an order reversing Judge Shelton's ruling.[1] "Willow Run Falls in Court; Ruling Stuns Workers" is the *Ypsilanti Press* headline.[2] The court finds Shelton's decision "clearly erroneous," adding that "the fact that a manufacturer uses hyperbole and puffery in seeking an advantage or concession does not necessarily create a promise." GM petitions the court to make the decision effective immediately.

The president of the Ypsilanti Area Chamber of Commerce suggests the community move away from the dispute, saying the media has overstated the likely effects of the plant closing. And the township's state representative suggests renegotiating use of the plant with GM. But on August 18, Ypsilanti Township files an emergency request with the Michigan Supreme Court seeking to reinstate Judge Shelton's verdict. The UAW is rooting for the township. "We're in the ninth inning, and I think we should finish the ball game," the financial officer for the plant local is reported as saying. Even so, production has begun at GM's Arlington plant of models like the Chevrolet Caprice, which was made at Willow Run. About 250 workers have already transferred to Arlington, with another 100 moving soon. The *Ypsilanti Press* reports these workers unimpressed by the team approach to production GM has implemented there, finding the pace of work busier but overall production lower than at Willow Run, and surprised to be using technology 15 years behind what they are used to.[3]

The U.S. economy is still roiling. Figures released in the spring of 1993 suggest that the U.S. deficit will grow to 22.2 percent of total spending, up for the fifth year in a row. In January the *New York Times* described "big business in turmoil" – large companies such as Sears, IBM, Westinghouse, Boeing, and McDonnell Douglas are shrinking, trying to become "small and nimble," in a trend the report described as extending well beyond the current business cycle. They are facing tough competition now not just from foreign competitors but also from emerging or restructured American rivals. One consequence is that secure, long-term stable employment in exchange for loyalty to the company is becoming a thing of the past. President Clinton's new secretary of labor, Robert Reich, notes some hopeful signs but acknowledges that "the employment picture is still very, very bad."[4]

Nonetheless, GM reported first-quarter profits of $513.3 million, a big improvement on the losses of the previous year, though its market share has dropped a little further. The Big Three's sales rose nearly 10 percent in June, and then 14.6 percent in early July. The average car is over eight years old and replacements are creating a "pot of gold" estimated at between 2.5 and 6.6 million vehicles. GM has increased car and truck prices. Secretary Reich criticizes "some American companies" for raising prices, as favorable currency exchange rates make imports more expensive, but will not confirm he is speaking of the auto industry.

GM workers recently struck at a parts plant in Lordstown, where GM had issued parts makers an ultimatum to cut costs. This was an "Apache raid" – a strike at a small plant intended to cause larger problems; it quickly grew to involve more than 30,000 workers in nine assembly plants, which could not operate without the parts, and threatened to affect twice as many. The six-year contracts between the UAW and the Big Three will expire later this year, and the strike is considered a dress rehearsal for negotiations. The auto manufacturers are keen to trim the indirect costs of labor, especially benefits such as health care, pension contributions, and guaranteed pay during layoffs. The union, on the other hand, is concerned to curtail layoffs, which cut into union membership and reduce its clout. The union is placing newspaper and TV ads – "The men and women of the UAW, building great cars and a stronger America."

Together the Big Three have 400,000 active workers and 390,000 retirees and surviving spouses, and payments for pensions and health care have become a significant portion of their costs.[5] The auto manufacturers can't plead their need for desperate measures as convincingly as they could a couple of years ago, with second-quarter profits totaling $2.34 billion, but they try. "How can you tell one story to Wall Street and another to the union," asks a labor economist interviewed by the *New York Times*. "They look like they're talking out of both sides of their mouth, and they are."[6]

The UAW always picks one company as its initial target for contract renegotiation, and each of the three says it would like to be that target. The company that is picked has the advantage of tailoring the contract to its own situation, and that contract becomes the model for the two others, but if negotiations fail the union will strike the target company. GM has hinted at reduced job cuts if it is named target, but Ford is first to offer a contract proposal and is picked as target at the end of August. Ford is the healthiest of the Big Three and has agreed to increase contributions to long-term layoff funds; since it has already laid off all the workers it plans to, and recently began hiring again, this won't cost anything, but for the other auto manufacturers, especially GM, it will be a costly model.[7]

NAFTA is a cloud looming on the horizon, yet another sign that the way of life of places like Willow Run is a thing of the past. The administration hopes for implementation by 1994. An *Ypsilanti Press* editorial explains that "the big fear around here is, of course, that even more good-paying jobs will be exported to Mexico from the United States if NAFTA goes into effect."[8] Ross Perot visits Flint in June and warns that NAFTA would ship good jobs out of the country at a time when it is $4 trillion in debt. Perot tells the capacity crowd, which gives him two standing ovations, "You are like straws in the wind in this big game, people." One Flint resident, laid off by GM in 1986, tells reporters, "I think if his message doesn't get through, this country's in big trouble." But the Michigan International Trade Coalition denies Perot's charges, saying that NAFTA would, by reducing tariffs, make Michigan autos cheaper in Mexico and so increase sales.[9]

A dramatic development for Michigan schools comes in July, when the Michigan House of Representatives and Senate vote to ban the use of property taxes for the support of public education and thus wipe out $6.5 billion – two-thirds of the funding for public schools in Michigan.

Governor Engler has been committed to reducing the state's property tax since he took office, but each proposal has been rejected by the voters. Earlier administrations' efforts to reform school finance failed too; voters rejected nine such measures between 1972 and 1989.[10] Michigan has higher property and income taxes than many states and a lower sales tax.

Early this year Engler tried again, offering a bill to the Republican Michigan Senate and the House of Representatives (which, after the November 1992 election upsets, no longer has a Democrat majority but is equally split Democrat/Republican). House legislators were studying a reform of property taxes linked to school reform so, recognizing the tide of sentiment, Engler offered a constitutional amendment – Proposal A – that would both cut taxes and reform school financing. The reliance on local property tax millage to fund Michigan's schools has produced vast inequities; although the state guarantees a minimum level of spending per pupil, in 1989–1990, for example, Willow Run raised only $1,752 per pupil from local tax dollars while Ann Arbor raised $5,761. The state provided an additional $2,004 per pupil for Willow Run, but this still left a difference of $2,000 between the two districts. This despite the fact that the local millage was 10 points higher in Willow Run than in Ann Arbor.[11]

A June *Ypsilanti Press* editorial explains that Willow Run will be forced to seek a millage increase because of "the absurdity of the Michigan school finance system" and the failure of Proposal A, and blasts the "flim-flam" of state officials who talk about bringing more equity to school finance and then shift the cost of education onto local districts. "These con artists use complicated formulas and fast talk, but the final result is this: The state is diverting more of the money it controls away from education into other activities, and it is doing that on the backs of the property taxpayers that state officials say they desperately want to help."[12]

And in June, Engler's Proposal A is rejected too. A joint House-Senate conference committee continues to review cuts in property tax financing for schools but becomes bogged down in disagreements over what would replace this revenue. Democrat leaders call for tax increases, but Republican leaders want nothing of the sort. In an evening Senate session, Senator Debbie Stabenow, a front-running Democratic candidate for governor, challenges the Republicans by introducing an amendment to entirely eliminate local property tax funds as revenue for public schools.

Stabenow later describes her action as a bold stroke to end the log-jam; others see it as foolhardy. Majority Republicans quickly accept her proposal – on July 20 the Senate votes 33 to 4 to repeal property tax funding, and the House approves the repeal by a vote of 69 to 35 less than 24 hours later, in an unusual evening session. The Senate sends the bill – Public Act 145 – to the governor for his signature. The repeal is to take effect on December 31, 1993, so the legislature has set itself a three-month deadline to revamp the state's entire school finance system.

Engler calls the plan a landmark action, "an historic step forward to make Michigan competitive and help create jobs. . . . Michigan's over-burdened taxpayers will get substantial tax relief, job providers will gain a competitive edge, and the people of our state will have an unprecedented opportunity to reform our schools."[13]

Stabenow calls for an "education summit" to restructure school financing. But as one analysis later put it, "Act 145 put the Governor back in the driver's seat. He was to have first crack at providing answers to the three key issues facing the legislature, namely, how to replace the lost revenues, how to allocate those funds to schools, and how to bring about quality reforms."[14]

Local education administrators are less than enthusiastic. One superintendent interviewed by the *Ypsilanti Press* says, "They've taken away the support for schools and they haven't replaced it with anything. It's like sawing somebody in half, only I'm afraid this time they forgot where they put the other half." Youssef Yomtoob makes a similar point.

> "Where are we going to get the money to replace it?" Yomtoob asked.
>
> "I like the concept of not relying on property tax but I'd like to know the solution before we get rid of what we have."
>
> Willow Run voters will be asked to approve a 2.6-mill increase on Aug. 21. The Board of Education opted to ask for only a one-year renewal in anticipation of tax reform legislation, but they hadn't expected that reform to come so soon.
>
> "It doesn't really change anything for this year," said Yomtoob. "Since our millage is only for one year . . . it's good timing on our part."
>
> Juanita C. Smith and John Mulcahy, "School Officials Wary of Change,"
> *Ypsilanti Press,* July 22, 1993, 1A, 5A

Many interpret the move as a threat to local community control of schooling. As Senator Lana Pollack, D-Ann Arbor, puts it, "If you take away all of the property tax, you take away the underpinnings of locally based education."

> "We can't afford to play Russian roulette with the education of our children. There must be replacement dollars for public education," said Julius Maddox, president of the Michigan Education Association.
>
> Associated Press, "Legislature Passes Radical Property Tax Plan,"
> *Ypsilanti Press,* July 22, 1993, 1A, 5A

During July, Engler gives a series of public presentations and issues statements insisting that restructuring the Michigan school system takes a higher priority than simply revamping financing. He proposes several possibilities, including school vouchers, schools of choice, and school district consolidation. The next month, proponents of school choice prepare a petition drive to put a voucher plan on the 1994 ballot. Meanwhile, house Democrats and senate Republicans both announce statewide hearings on revamping the school system. A bipartisan group, the Citizen's Alliance for Rescuing Education, announces a petition drive to seek reinstatement of the property tax.

The proposed millage increase for the Willow Run schools is rejected by local voters. Only three of the district's seven precincts pass the proposal, with fewer than 1,000 voters turning out. The final vote is 538 against, 451 in favor. The managing editor of the *Ypsilanti Press* pens a column in which he predicts that, despite voter appeals for school finance reform, "legislators don't and won't do anything because what average people want is of no concern to the state legislature."[15]

> We are urged to vote so we have a voice, but who heard our voice? The people protested to show their disappointment, their anger, their sadness; some even begged don't take our baby, don't close our plant, don't close our school. And their pleas fell on deaf ears. So to these people that sit on benches and boards, something may touch your lives some day to cause you great sadness, something that perhaps could have been prevented had some one listened. Should it happen to you I hope you remember Willow Run, Baby Jessica and Fletcher School kids.
> We the people, ha!
>   John Megehee, Augusta Township, Letter to the Editor, *Ypsilanti Press*,
>   Aug. 12, 1993, 6A.

Engler signs the bill into law on August 19 at the State Fair Grounds and renews his pledge to offer a plan to completely restructure the state's school system. The next day the Michigan Federation of Teachers files suit in Wayne County Circuit Court, asking the court to "take charge of the dispute and order the state to find a way to fund schools."

> Something is missing in this year's round of contract talks between school districts and teachers.
> The money.
> "No one is really sure how much money is there," said Paul Ollila, superintendent of the Copper County Intermediate School District in Hancock.
>   Associated Press, "Uncertainty Slows School Contract Talks,"
>   *Ypsilanti Press*, Aug. 22, 1993

Meanwhile, Michigan's Statewide Systemic Initiative program is revving up. MSSI is inaugurating the "Models of Effective Learning" component of its plans. It intends to identify 24 "focus districts." Of these, 11 will be "target districts," urban or extreme rural districts with low student achievement in math or science, which will be offered technical assistance and financial support of $25,000 to $65,000 annually for four years. The remaining 13 will be "affiliate districts," more wealthy, already undertaking reform. The focus districts will be "learning laboratories," from whose experiences MSSI will be able to recommend programs and policies to facilitate local change statewide.[16]

> The Willow Run community provides a classic example of why things need to change in our schools. Many of the parents of Willow Run students have been employed in the local auto plants or with auto suppliers. Many have

little more than a high school education but have been able to support their families well with good paying jobs that required relatively low technical skills. These former jobs are disappearing, and Willow Run graduates face a difficult path to employment unless new approaches resulting in higher technical skills for students are undertaken. The student population consists of capable students who need to realize their own capacity for high level technical, mathematical and scientific understanding. To date, students have not realized their potential in these areas.

Competitive Grant Application for 1992–93 Models of Effective Learning Grants:
Mathematics and Science Initiative, May 26, 1993

The Willow Run Community Schools respond to the request for proposals from MSSI,[17] and late in the summer, Willow Run receives notice it will be awarded funding as a focus district.[18] So it is that in October 1993 I introduce myself to the new Willow Run Systemic Initiative – "WRSI" – committee. How will the new committee steer a route through Engler's new marketplace reforms and Michigan's Statewide Systemic Initiative? Can the local reformers continue to find ways to meet the needs of the children and the attitudes of their parents while coping with the fallout of the plant closing, the shifting fortunes of Ypsilanti Township's legal battle with General Motors, the elimination of all public school financing, and at the same time handle the demands of being a focus district?

5   The Last First Day?

August–November 1993

Emotions among parents, educators and some students are running high as Michigan's 1.5 million public school students began heading back to classes this week with no guarantee that their schools will even exist next September because of a new state law that lops off two-thirds of the funding for schools.

"I'm really not confident that we will even have public schools after this year," said Donna Evans, 32, whose three sons head back to Detroit Public Schools Tuesday. "It seems that the harder they push kids to get a good education, the more barriers that get in the kids' way." . . .

"Everyone is sort of stupefied," said Rollie Hopgood, spokesperson for the 26,000-member Michigan Federation of Teachers. "They're saying, 'Holy smokes, what do we do?' " . . .

"The Legislature has cast a cloud over the start of school," said Kim Brennen Root, spokeswoman for the 123,000-member MEA. "We're seeing that in bargaining; we're seeing that in the enthusiasm of people going back to school."

Margaret Trimer-Hartley, "The Last First Day? Future School Funding Uncertain," *Detroit Free Press*, Aug. 27, 1993, 1A, 10A

T.E.A.M. = Together Everyone Achieves More

Teamwork is the ability to work together toward a common vision, the ability to direct individual accomplishment toward organizational objectives. It is the fuel that allows common people to achieve uncommon results.

Poster, Kettering staff room

The last day of August 1993 is the first day of a new school year: a day of promise and anxiety. At Kettering Elementary School children and parents cluster at the entrance waiting for school to open. Located at the south end of the district, named after Charles F. Kettering, a Ford engineer who invented the electric self-starter first used in the 1912 Cadillac, and who later became vice president for research at GM (teachers occasionally joke they're still in the business of producing self-starters), Kettering this year has a teaching staff of 15 and an enrollment of 221. Enrollment has slowly decreased from around 380 twenty years ago; over the same period the proportion of African American students to white students has increased from one in five to one in two.

Around Kettering the houses are detached one-story wooden constructions, well kept, with trimmed lawns and occasional garden ornaments. A lot of homes are for sale, but young families are moving into the area – there are affordable homes here, unlike in Ann Arbor. In the afternoons young children can be seen playing on the lawns and driveways; it feels like a neighborhood.

Kettering is laid out as two corridors in an L-shape, extending from the main entrance where they meet. The "lower hall" houses the classrooms of grades one through three, the Special Education room, and the staff room. The "upper hall" stretches to the right, with classrooms for grades four and five, the gymnasium, art room, and library. The school has been refurbished, and a new media center added that has computer facilities for small group, whole class, and individual work.

There's bustle in the hallways and the high-pitched noise of many young children talking excitedly. The occasional adult voice cuts through the chatter. At Mrs. Page's classroom, Room 2, the children enter slowly and shyly, most of them accompanied by an adult female, a mother or grandma. The children look bashful, the adults formal and awkward. Joyce Page has taught first grade at Kettering for many years. She was hard at work yesterday preparing the room, with her husband's help, and each desk has a folded card with the name of the student who will occupy it, and a name tag to hang around his or her neck. The first graders' desks are arranged in small clusters with seating by alphabetical order, though Joyce will be changing the organization in a few weeks once she knows the children better. She greets arrivals at the door, then helps the children find their seats. "This is your chair. This is where you sit." Some of the children help others ("Where's your name?", "Sit down, right there!"; "Sit where your name is, there!"), and some help the adults too ("Right here, nanny!").

The background noise is diminishing as children around the school find their new classrooms. At 9:10 A.M. there's a long ring on the school bell.

"Anyone not find a seat yet?" Joyce chats pleasantly with several of the parents, then turns to her assembled class. "Morning everybody."

Some, but not all, of the children return her greeting. "Good morning." They don't reply in unison the way they will within a few weeks, nor do they add "Mrs. Page" as they will learn to.

If the changing economy is unfamiliar terrain to most of us, the routines of the school classroom are so familiar that we don't notice them anymore, let alone pause to consider their functions and consequences. But to understand what's being attempted in Willow Run we need to appreciate how school works – how a vision of the kinds of human beings young children will become plays out in practice. The first day of school offers an opportunity to see firsthand how schooling is not just about teaching knowledge and skills, but about preparing the kind of human being a child grows up to be. The first graders in Joyce Page's class are novices and her classroom their novitiate – their relationship with her, and the routines of Room 2, will exercise a powerful influence on them.

School takes over from the family the task of transforming children into adult members of society. In the terminology of sociologists, schools are institutions of "secondary socialization," taking over from the "primary socialization" of the family. While children leave home to attend school, they typically return home at the end of each day, and this means the school must coordinate its socialization with that of the family, or at least reach a compromise, sometimes uneasy. As one Kettering parent put it, "We're all teachers; the pendulum swings between home and school." But at school children meet adult figures who are not their parents or relatives. Children enter the impersonal relationship of "student" and "teacher." Each child's "mommy" is a unique, particular person, but in school there are many people who will be their "teacher."[1]

We seldom pause to consider what it means to be a student, or how a child becomes one. "Teacher" and "student" are social positions within the world of the school and classroom, positions that adult and child must adopt. Children must make sense of their new position in one way or another, and in doing so they will be transformed, altered in their knowledge and skills, but altered also in their identity, their sense of who they are and what is possible and impossible for them.

While the influence of a parent is grounded in an intimate personal relationship, that of a teacher rests on an institutional status that young children know little about. A teacher must establish her position in the eyes of her students – whether it is as an authority figure or someone more like a coach. When Joyce Page does this she is not starting from scratch – many of her students attended kindergarten classes at Willow Run's Early Childhood Development Center, Thurston School – but she still needs to establish who she is – as when she refers to herself in the third person and tells the children what "Mrs. Page" likes and dislikes. Today, and for a while, Joyce maintains an element of the personal alongside the impersonal to soften the transition. And, today, once she steps into her position as teacher she doesn't speak directly to the parents any longer, she talks to them *through* the children, instructing them to tell their caregiver they will see them later. The adults take this as their cue and bid the kids good-bye, and Joyce has established the priority of a line of communication that goes from her to the students, and then to the parents. The children find themselves transferred from one guardian to another: their mothers and grammas may bring them to school but the responsibility for their care has been taken over by Mrs. Page. The bond between child and family is now mediated by the teacher and school. The impersonal relationship between student and teacher has begun.

"Are we all set for a good year?" There are various uncertain and subdued responses. Joyce is upbeat and energetic. "Great! Okay, what you need to do is give mom or dad or whoever else is with you a great big hug and tell 'em you'll see 'em at eleven fifty-five. Okay?" The children bid farewell to their family members, who leave the room.

Joyce gets down to business. Mrs. Page is a tall woman with wavy blonde hair and a cheerful expression. She is energetic, disciplined, and discerning. Her room is organized and colorful, though she apologizes for the clutter on her desk. Her manner with the children is sensitive and friendly, but firm and authoritative.

"Okay. One of the first things we learn in Room 2 is that when we get out of our chairs we put them right back under our desks, and the reason we do that is because we don't want anybody to get hurt when they trip over them. So let's practice doing that right now: let's get up, let's put our chairs back under our desk. . . ." The children do as she asks and she voices her approval. "Wow, you did that job very well. Okay, now if you don't have your name tag on yet would you please just carry it with you. Okay, I'd like you to come on up here and sit on the rug by my chair." Joyce and one of the children move some of the desks to one side to create space by her chair. The children cluster around her, sitting on the floor. "Boy, I surely do like the way you came up on that rug."

Instruction slips into the morning's administrative tasks. Joyce asks one of the students – a little African American girl – to count the number of children in the room. The girl looks around and announces a total of twenty. "How many did you get?" Joyce asks. "Twenty? Okay, would someone else like to try?" Another African American girl volunteers and counts to thirty-three. Joyce expresses polite and nonjudgmental surprise: "Thirty-three! Oh my goodness that's a big difference, between twenty and thirty-three, isn't it? Okay, do you want to try it? This is the last one." She picks another volunteer and suggests some strategies to him. "And this time, let's hear you count out loud, and put your hand on everybody so that you can say their name." The boy counts slowly. "Nineteen, now that's closer to what Yolanda got." The little boy corrects his total to twenty. "Twenty, cause you forgot to count yourself, right? Okay, let Mrs. Page count and let's see how many we have." She counts slowly to twenty-two. Some of the children call out the total with her as she reaches it.

Schooling has always been about training in the skills of literacy – reading, writing, arithmetic. The first schools trained scribes to record business transactions. Modern elementary schooling in particular is concerned with introducing children to the worlds of text and of number – the "magnificent conceptual systems that lie at the base of all human culture."[2] Used to transform nature, they transform mind too – indeed, they help create "mind" as we usually understand it: something disembodied and cerebral, quietly reflective, dispassionate, and deliberate. Mrs. Page casually introduces both these symbol systems this morning; in this simple exercise she has an opportunity to assess the children's facility with counting and to give them some instruction in technique. Putting a hand on each child provides a way to keep track of who has been counted so far; counting out loud helps keep track of the sequential ordering of numbers. She also shows them that different people get different answers to the same question, that she will evaluate these answers, and that she will generally provide the correct answer. An arithmetic task has been structured as an activity both practical and social.

Next Mrs. Page draws the children into a familiar and comforting activity, reading a text that acknowledges the stresses of their new relationship.

"Alright, I would like to begin the morning by reading you a book, because this is not *exactly* what you're going through today, but I'm sure it feels this way. You're all pretty familiar with your kindergarten teachers and I'm sure if you're anything like my now-second graders, you're missing your kindergarten teacher today, and it seems a little strange to have this person sitting in this chair being your teacher. The name of this book is called *The New Teacher*, and all of you sitting here have a new teacher today."

Joyce reads the story of a girl, Tiggy, who likes her teacher very much, but she leaves and Mrs. Prickles takes her place. Tiggy is upset and makes up her mind not to like the new teacher. She paints a messy picture and is so careless that she spills the paint and splashes Mrs. Prickles's apron. Mrs. Prickles turns out, of course, to be a nice person, and she asks Tiggy to play the part of princess in the school play. A new costume must be made: "'You will have to work hard; can you do it?' 'Oh, yes!' said Tiggy happily, 'I'll try hard.' Where do you think Tiggy is in this picture?" "The pink one!" the children call out. "Why do you think that?" "Because she's the one getting the crown." "That's right. She's the one getting the crown. Boy, what good listeners you are." Tiggy is very good in the play, and Mrs. Prickles says she looks like a real princess in the costume her mother made for her. " 'You have done very well,' said the new teacher, 'and I'm very proud of you.' " At the end of the play – as the handsome prince rescues the lovely princess from wicked pirates – all the parents clap, Tiggy's parents the loudest.

The children seem satisfied by the story.

Becoming an able reader, writer, and calculator is not just a matter of new skills. These symbolic media, these "cultural amplifiers,"[3] inaugurate changes in the child's relationship to the world. The traditional view of literacy in text and number is that it is "a torch that will illuminate the world,"[4] fostering "an abstract, self-conscious and controlled level of thinking."[5] To read or to write about some element of one's experience makes one an observer of it, able to stand at a distance. The words permit, then demand, a reflexive stance on the writer's part.

It is easy to think of this as a move to a higher plane, to higher levels of thinking. But the torch's light can be blinding, hiding important things from sight. To write about one's family and home life, especially, can introduce a fissure between child and family. The child first lives the life of the family as natural necessity;[6] if this life is examined through the mediation of written language it may no longer be lived so immediately and so directly, but seen instead with a mediated, objectifying attitude. Thus the child is introduced to a world of abstractions like "shape," "size," "quantity," "number." But this is not the only way to use text and number, or the only mode of engagement they can foster. For "literacy . . . is always profoundly and pervasively social in nature. . . . Literacy activities come into being (acquire 'motivational' power) through larger political, economic and cultural forces in a given society; neither their structure or function can be understood outside their societal context."[7] It is not writing per se that objectifies and sometimes alienates, but specific genres of writing. The project-driven inquiry that Kettering has been experimenting with introduces new, different reading and writing activities, less likely to abstract things from their practical relevance, more "riveted to practical productive activity," offering different kinds of satisfaction.

The classroom is a place for reading, writing, and arithmetic, but it is more than this – it is a small community. Institutions such as school transform the people who participate in them by creating such communities – establishing a tone to daily life, delineating space and time, defining positions and relations. Building the order of Room 2 starts today. It is a community whose members are governed by shared classroom rules, as well as by customs and routines.

"Okay," says Joyce. "I think most of you already know, but if you don't know, I'm Mrs. Page. We have a guest in our room already this morning, back there in the corner is Dr. Packer, can you say good morning to him? He's just visiting to see how first graders start the year. And I know one thing they start with, and I don't see them, but in Mrs. Page's room everybody starts the day with a? . . ."

"Smile," calls one of the children.

"A smile! Can I see a smile? What a nice smile, Timothy. Great, that's what I like to see. We have a really special rule here in Room 2, you have to have a smile to come in the door, and you have to have a smile to go out of the door. So everyday I want you to come in with a smile on your face, and I want you to leave with a smile on your face. And I want you *always, always,* to have a smile in your heart. Can you do that?"

Joyce is interrupted by the arrival at the classroom door of Mary Brandau.

Joyce turns to address the children. "Boys and girls, can anybody guess who this is over here, who just walked in?"

"Mrs. Brandau," they chant.

"Mrs. Brandau, that's right. Boys and girls, this is our new principal, this is Mrs. Brandau. And she's just like you, she's got a new job this year too, just like you. You're new first graders." She turns to Mary: "We practiced saying your name a little bit ago." To the students: "Can you show her how good we are at it? Mrs. – ?"

"Brandau."

"Mrs. Brandau, that's right."

Mary says, half to the children and half to Joyce, "I saw a lot of you outside this morning, before they came in to school. They knew just what to do. Kinda lined up, didn't run into school." She asks Joyce, "Can I tell them something about the Kettering Creed?"

"Yeah, go ahead," Joyce replies. "I mean that's fine."

On the wall is a poster showing the Kettering Creed – the product of much debate among the Kettering teachers. Mary points to it and says, "We have something at Kettering that we all believe in, and we have to believe in it, and this is how we *act*. This is how we make decisions about how we act. The first one says, 'Exercise self-discipline and self-control.' Does anybody have any idea what that might mean? It's kinda a funny saying."

Exercise self-discipline and self-control
Show respect for other people's feelings, ideas, space and property
Use problem solving methods when conflicts occur
Listen carefully while others are speaking
                    "The Kettering Creed," Kettering Elementary School

---

"And it's *awfully* big words for first graders," Joyce adds.

"Self-discipline," repeats Mary. "Self-control." But she's interrupted by the appearance in the doorway of a tall male figure dressed in a dark suit. He seems to loom over the little children seated on the rug around Mrs. Page's chair. It is Superintendent Yomtoob.

"Boys and girls," announces Joyce, "that's Dr. Joe."

"Morning," Dr. Joe says to the children. "Can you say good morning?"

"Good morning," the children reply, uncertainly.

"And my name is Dr. Joe, so can you say good morning, Dr. Joe?"

"Good morning, Dr. Joe," the children call out, in unison now.

"I can see you've got a bright classroom here," Dr. Joe remarks to Joyce.

"Already, they certainly are," she agrees.

"Alright. Expecting high things from them. You have a good year, you hear?" Dr. Joe tells the children.

"Yeah."

"You have a good year, *okay!*" he repeats, working the crowd.

"*Okay!*" they call back.

"Alright," he says with satisfaction, nods good-bye to the adults, and leaves as gracefully as he arrived.

Joyce tells the children, "Dr. Joe's our superintendent of schools. He works over at central office, and it's very nice of him to come visit us here at Kettering." She turns back to Mrs. Brandau. "Okay. Self-discipline and self-control."

Mary has taken the opportunity provided by Dr. Joe's short visit to think through what she wants to say about these abstract terms. She speaks without hesitation. "That means you have to be in control of your own body, and what you do, and what you say. Maybe you're kinda angry and you're thinking angry things, but you think, that wouldn't be a very nice thing to say, that wouldn't help, that would make things worse. Well, if I can control it, I'm not going to say it. But I'm not going to lay on the floor, because that doesn't make any sense. I'm going to control my body, and I'm going to sit in my chair. And that means I'm in control. Let me see if you can show me that you're in control of your body right now." She waits until they are still and silent. "That's perfect control of your body. Are you in control of your mouths, or are your mouths just talking and saying things?"

"Unhhh uh!"

"No," Mary continues, "You're in *control* of that, and that's what that means, that you have control over your body and what you say. The second thing is, 'Show respect for people's feelings, ideas, space and property.' I think that is extremely important too – I think they're all important, but I think that respect thing is kind of important. That means I won't say anything bad about anybody, it means I'll say good things, and that I care about you, and I care about what happens to you. And that, if you have an idea, maybe it's a different idea than I have, I'll say, 'I'll think about that.' Help me out here Mrs. Page, if you have any ideas." She laughs. "The third one is problem solving."

Joyce helps out. "We're going to do a *lot* of work this year on problem solving. That just means if somebody's not getting along or whatever, we're going to teach you ways to figure out how to handle that *all* by yourself. So that you don't need a teacher to do it. That goes back up here," she points at the poster, "with self-discipline and self-control. You know, if you can take care of yourself that's where self comes from. Point to yourself; where's your self? This is your self." She points a finger at her chest. "So when your self takes care of keeping you to follow the rules that we were talking about, or keeping you from doing things that might get you in trouble, or might get somebody else in trouble, then you're doing them. Sometimes boys and girls can be mighty mean to other children, and they say some pretty mean things. But if you're

following the Kettering Creed," – she speaks slowly and clearly to highlight these last two words – "you won't do that. Okay? And the last one,
Mrs. Brandau?"

Mary takes over. "The last one is listening carefully, and I noticed
that you are *all* listening very carefully. So obviously that rule – listen
carefully when other people are speaking. . . . And you're doing a wonderful job listening to me. But I distracted you from Mrs. Page a little
bit. Can I do one more thing?" she asks Joyce.

"Sure!" Joyce agrees.

"I want to ask you to wiggle your fingers. I bet you did this in
preschool and kindergarten. Wiggle your toes. Inside your shoes. Wiggle your shoulders. Wiggle your nose!" The children squirm on the rug.
Some use a finger to move their nose from side to side.

"Woh!" exclaims Joyce. "Shoshanna can do it *without* her fingers!
That was good!"

The children giggle.

"I wish I could," says Mary. "Now, I feel more wiggles inside of me,
and I'm as still, as still, as I can be." The last is said very quietly.

"Thank you for letting me talk to you," says Mary to the students. "I
will be in to see you a lot, and I hope maybe I can come in and read and
stuff to your class? I *love* to read." Now that she's principal, Mary will be
spending much less time in the classroom with young students, something she loves to do.

"Oh certainly," says Joyce. "Certainly." She turns to the children. "So
we're going to say good-bye to –"

"Bye, Mrs. Brandau," call the children.

Learning to follow the rules of Room 2 and the Kettering Creed will require from the children a new quality of personal control, a new kind of
agency. In an important sense "self" – the personal locus of intention,
desire, and will whose cultivation yields self-mastery, a "private, psychic
consciousness"[8] – is formed in the child's encounters with the classroom's apparently objective order. We aren't born with selves the way
we have arms or legs; the self is formed in relation and in culture. When
Mrs. Brandau and Mrs. Page speak to the children of self-discipline, of
control of one's body, of one's actions and words, of curbing "impulse,"
they are defining the moral topography of the classroom community
within which "self" and "mind" can appear.[9]

The aim is not blind obedience to the school and classroom rules. As
Mary describes it, Kettering is trying to instill in the children a capacity

for responsibility and respect. The ability to choose between right and wrong and the consideration of others as people in their own right – these are the antithesis of the obedience and conformism of work on the assembly line. The staff know this capacity doesn't arise spontaneously, nor can it be coerced. There's a complex dialectic in which control by others can, in an apparent paradox, foster self-discipline, self-control, and independence – reminiscent of the graduation song: "Look inside you and be strong . . . a hero lies in you." One morning Mary Brandau has in her office four boys caught fighting. Mary reprimands them, then picks up the phone to call their parents. One of the boys complains, "This is the third time my mother's been called!"

"Whose problem is that, though?" Mary asks him.

"Mine," he concedes. "But Tommy made me do it."

"What do you mean, he *made* you do it?" replies Mary, with an astonishment that's half assumed and half genuine. "He picked up your arm and moved it?"

"No," the boy acknowledges.

Later, Mary and I talk over lunch, at the Burger King that is her regular spot when she has time for lunch at all. I ask what responsibility means to these children.

"Last year," Mary says, "my word for the year was 'respect,' and I really focused on that. This year my word is 'responsibility.' In the Kettering Capers" – the school's newsletter – "you're supposed to find the word 'responsibility' and turn in your little slip and I draw for the prizes. What I am noticing is nobody is responsible for their own behavior. If I hit somebody, if I hit you, it's because you did something to make me hit you, to make me do that."

A dance has been organized as reward for the children who participated in the Science Fair. Some children are very angry; they didn't do a project for the fair, or didn't get it completed on time, but they still want to go to the party. One of them told Mary, "You didn't give me the materials, so I didn't do it." "So we talked about that," she says. "If you didn't ask for them, it's not my responsibility, that's your responsibility. 'You didn't give us enough *time*.' I said, 'So you planned your time poorly. It's *my* fault that you planned your time poorly?' It was just fascinating."

A key driver of these transformations in the school classroom is the child's desire for recognition from their teacher, the new adult in their lives. Children are not empty vessels, passive recipients of knowledge, they are active and involved from the outset, keen to speak up and get noticed. Their relationship with the teacher provokes the changes we call learning. Today they bid keenly for Mrs. Page's attention.

Joyce turns back to the poster of rules. "These rules very much go along with the Kettering Creed. Okay. 'No running' is very important to Mrs. Page. This is the one that I might get kind of mean with, because I do not want to see any of your beautiful faces hurt. And I don't want to see blood running down your faces. There is a place where you can run; does anybody know where that is?"

"Outside," they chorus together, with enthusiasm.

"Outside, you bet. Once you are outside the door, you can run, because that's a safe place to run. You may also run on Thursday in gym."

"In gym," David starts to say. "We only . . ."

"In the gym," Joyce repeats, raising her voice over his. "David, just wait a minute, okay? If you have something to say you need to raise your hand. Okay. You know what? The other place that you can run is at home. But you may *not* run in Kettering halls, ever, ever, ever, ever, ever."

"I can't run at home," says a child.

"And I don't want you running around the desks. I mean at home outside," she adds, replying to this comment. "It's not safe, boys and girls. We have a lot of desks in here, it's just not safe to run in here. Can you all promise me that you won't run? Say, 'I promise not to run.' "

"I promise not to run." They chant this together in the appropriate manner.

". . . in the wrong places. 'Cause outside I *want* you to run, I want you to run long and hard and fast, okay?"

" 'Kay!" yells one boy, with gusto.

" 'Cause here at Kettering we have a mileage club and you get to run, run, run, run, run, at lunch time. And so we'll talk more about that later on. That's a *good* time to run. 'Cause it gets all that energy out. Emily? Do you have a question?"

"Yeah. I can't run out back in my yard because my dog runs after me sometimes," offers Emily, keen to share something about her family that makes her special.

"Oh, well then it might not be a good idea," Joyce replies, allowing the conversation to take this new turn.

"My dog – when I run –" another child pipes up.

"My dog always runs *after* me," calls another.

"He's *my* dog, and he runs real fast."

"I have a dog," calls another.

"I have a dog too," and another.

"We have *three* dogs, *three* dogs." They are boasting, bragging, bidding for her attention.

"Four. Five."

"When I go in the yard my dogs come after me and bite me!"

"Oh boy," says Joyce patiently. The children have breached the order Mrs. Page has been working to establish in Room 2. They've done this not to misbehave, but to connect with her. "Okay, just let me ask Regina what she wants and then . . . David, you need to listen, sweetie. Regina?"

"I have a dog at my house," says Regina very softly.

Joyce sssshs the other children, and draws them gently back to a conversation that is more appropriate. "You know what," Joyce says, "when I hear all these 'I've got dogs' stories I bet you're really going to be excited to learn some of the things we're going to do this year, to learn about animals. We're going to learn *all* about animals, so we'll be able to talk about our pets later on."

"Teacher?" calls a boy, but Mrs. Page moves on.

"Let's go back now to the other two rules that we had . . ."

But the boy persists, interrupting her. "She got, she got a lot of pets."

"Okay," says Joyce, gently but firmly. "We'll talk about that later; did you hear what I said? We'll talk about our pets later. For a long time." And work has been done transforming the children from member-of-a-family to student-in-a-classroom.[10]

The classroom, then, is a new community in which children enter a new impersonal form of relationship and, seeking recognition from their teacher, start to use the symbol systems of number and text to master the world around them. What we call learning is this growing facility with writing and arithmetic; at the same time, "mind" and "self" take form. What motivates this is the relationship between children and adult, now, in the community of the classroom, acting as "students" and "teacher." If one wishes to improve children's learning, let alone change who they are going to be, it makes sense to focus on changing this relationship.

Joyce has begun to change the way her classroom runs, though it still has several traditional elements. Although Joyce's first graders were not part of last year's "Lighting a Building" project, she strongly supports these efforts. This year, first grade is part of a whole-school focus on communication, one part of which is the design and construction of a tile mural to be installed at the school entrance. Joyce is using a combination of traditional worksheets, hands-on activities, and team projects. But it's not easy to make the changes; Joyce was trained as a traditional teacher, and she's quick to acknowledge that adjustment has been slow and at times painful. The traditional elementary classroom has an easily recognizable character – the teacher is the authority, controlling student conduct, assigning academic tasks (typically, individual seatwork), and evaluating student performance. The teaching techniques of choice are direct instruction, exposition, drill, and memorization. Joyce sighs. "The thing that's so very difficult for me is that I was very successful at being a structured classroom teacher. I knew how to do it, I knew how to do it well, I got very excellent test results, probably as good if not better than most of the other rooms in the school, or the district, *but* we didn't have a whole lot of fun all the time, you know, we really didn't. It was very structured."

Now she has the students working in collaboration. "It's taken me a long time to get to there. A *long* time to get to there. There was a time when any kind of noise like that" – referring to the period I've just seen – "would just drive me crazy. I was brought up that schools are rigid and you know, da da, da da, no noise is good. But I have been taught by the last three administrators" – Vivian, Janice, and Mary – "that noise can be good, and it can be constructive, as long as they're staying on task. So does the fact that I feel a headache in the back of my head have any indication of that? Yeah, probably, but I am working on it, I am working on it.

"I do hear good noise, where they're actually arguing back and forth about what it's supposed to be or how it's supposed to be, and for the most part they do stay on task. Now there's a few that can't stay focused for longer than thirty seconds, and I'm aware of that, but . . . I've had pretty, um, directive type administrators who know not to push, and not to force, and not to demand, it's just 'Why don't you try this? . . .' and it just kind of leads you through the little golden path, you know? You do this and it's successful."[11]

Forty years ago, sociologist Talcott Parsons recognized how the arrangements of a traditional elementary classroom support a "single axis of achievement" along which children are sorted – "good students" at one end, "bad" at the other.[12] Especially in the early grades, intellectual and moral aspects of classroom tasks aren't distinguished: a "good student" is one who gets the right answers or just works hard. "Achievement-motivation" – willingness to work – is the standard, on the assumption that children naturally differ in their aptitude for academic work. Individual, competitive effort on identical tasks sorts out who's capable and who's not. This axis of achievement gives institutional form to a teacher's recognition of her students.

There are lots of problems with this kind of arrangement, not least that children fail to achieve for all sorts of reasons other than lack of aptitude. For example, many researchers have noted that families with different class and ethnic backgrounds use language in different ways. Different families have different "ways with words."[13] For instance, Shirley Brice Heath noted differences in the kind of talk that middle- and working-class children experience at home. She found middle-class families providing their children with decontextualized labels that prepared them well for the simple academic exercises of the primary grades. "It is as though in the drama of life, [these parents] freeze scenes" for examination and direct the child's attention to objects and events to be named and described. They encourage imaginative manipulation of events and context.

The white working-class families Brice Heath visited gave few opportunities for narrative, for creatively varying elements of an event or item, or for grasping how the outcome or identity of a whole depends on its parts. Instead, mastery of written language demonstrated that one recognized one's place in a clear hierarchy where literal interpretation of texts, especially the Bible, was valued. And in the black working-class community, language was used in ways that demonstrated a creative approach to life in general – since few things were predictable, one had to be flexible and "quick on your feet" – but "neither talk, time, nor space is set aside especially" for children. Caught up in a "fast-moving drama" with "few predictable outcomes," these children were not encouraged to explicate features or apply labels. Their language was both logical and poetical in its own way, but the children were ill-prepared for the abstract tasks of the early school years and seldom encouraged to hold onto their skills at contextualization until the upper grades, where more complex academic tasks would require them. So "they fail in the initial sequences of the school-defined hierarchy of skills."[14]

For these and other reasons, children from working-class families tend to do less well in school, and often end up convinced they lack academic ability. Schools confer "badges of ability" on their successful students, and working-class children often receive the "hidden injuries of class," quitting school with a lack of self-worth. They come to feel they lack control of their lives, unlike white-collar workers they see, and while they consider their own work more moral and meaningful, they come to envy the degree of self-determination they perceive the middle class to have.[15]

The Kettering staff are keen to avoid this kind of outcome for their children. The unspoken tenet of their efforts is that children will learn more if they believe in themselves, if they feel that everyone can learn, if all talents are valued. The Kettering teachers maintain that fostering this kind of attitude requires that they establish a new kind of relationship with the children. They know that children respond unthinkingly to the expectations of teachers – the Pygmalion effect first discussed thirty years ago.[16]

Getting rid of the single axis of achievement is a necessary step, one that requires putting into practice the belief that all children can and will learn, given the right conditions, albeit at different speeds and in different ways. Joyce has witnessed this. For example, she used to separate children into "ability groups" for reading – the Robins, the Bluejays, and the Buzzards – but the children always knew "who could and who couldn't, who the haves were and who the have nots were." Vivian was principal then and she tried to talk Joyce out of this grouping. "She said, 'Try whole-group instruction.' 'Vivian you're crazy! There are children in my room not ready to read yet, they're not ready . . .' She said, 'Just try it.' Every week for the first twelve weeks of school I went in there and said 'I'm not going to do this anymore, these kids are not learning how to read. I blahblahblahblah . . .' You know, the whole argument. 'One more week,' she'd say, 'just try it one more week.' Got to be a game with us, you know, but eventually, it was right after Christmas, I started seeing the would-be Buzzards starting to pick it up! And lo and behold it didn't matter that they couldn't read the first three books, all of a sudden they were reading the fourth book. Learning through osmosis or whatever, they had picked up all the way, and they hadn't been alienated, they hadn't been earmarked – 'You're a dummy, you can't read, this is what you're going to do for the next twelve years.' They just blended right in. Every day there's another one that's jumping on the reading train, that's the way I look at it, and it's really amazing."

Joyce literally has a Reading Train on her classroom wall: the cutout caboose pulls wagons along the tracks, and paper bears with the name of each child sit in the wagon that corresponds to the book they're reading.

Next she tried children working at different Learning Centers around the room. "Vivian came in and I said 'I can't believe how noisy this is' and she said 'Come with me.' She walked me around to each of the groups, and she said 'What's the noise from?' and when you listen to it, it *is* engaged learning; they're talking about what they're doing. So I'm learning, I'm learning daily, what to do. And now I'm getting so that

I'm not so much the *learner* as the *teacher* to the other people in the building – if I can do it, you can do it; so I've taken on a different role. But it's been very gradual, I would say that I started doing this probably five years ago. And every year it's a little bit, you know?"

At Kettering the search for a new kind of relationship in the classroom is viewed not as an individual effort but as a collective one: the whole school staff comes together to craft a new culture in the school. They have changed the daily schedule to permit common planning time, so staff can work together in teams, reaching decisions that are consensus driven rather than following the dictates of a principal – Mary Brandau considers herself a "teacher-leader." At meetings the Kettering teachers maintain an ongoing banter that serves to air different opinions and perspectives. At one meeting Joyce Page says, to no one in particular, "Consensus is a touchy area on our staff!" And third-grade teacher Anita Smith replies softly, "Yet we generally reach it."

A sad end comes to the 16-month struggle between Ypsilanti Township and General Motors a month after school begins. Michigan's Supreme Court refuses to hear the township's appeal and lifts the order imposed by Judge Shelton preventing GM's moving production from the plant. The company announces an immediate start to the move. But the *Ypsilanti Press* judges the $600,000 the township spent on the suit money well spent. (GM paid taxes of $450,000 a year for the plant.)[17]

It was an eerie, diminished scene in the quiet of Clifton's office late in the day Friday when he, Harlow, and Ypsilanti Township Attorney Douglas Winters talked with the Japanese television crew [which had waited two days for the story to break].

"Nobody will ever say they shut it down because the people stepped aside and did nothing," Winters said. Harlow, Clifton and Winters suddenly joined in a three-way handshake, smiling for the first time since the interview began.

"We put up a hell of a fight," Harlow said.

And that was it. There are still some remedies the township can seek, but everyone knows they lost the main battle.

John Mulcahy, "A Furious Battle Ends Up With Barely a Whimper,"
Ypsilanti Press, Sept. 4, 1993, 1A, 4A

"The high court's heart is in the same place that GM's is: in their wallet," concludes one longtime plant employee.

Another is equally blunt. "We got screwed, more or less," he says. GM "knows they can walk all over the township. I guess I'll just keep going on with my life."[18]

> What Ypsilanti Township officials and their attorney tried to do was change how people look at the relationship between a large corporation and a community that did a lot to help it become that large corporation.
>
> In their suit, they tried to say that communities – employees and business people and governments – that have worked with companies and come to depend on those companies for their livelihoods have a right to expect a commodity that is becoming ever so rare in America: Loyalty.
>
> I'm glad they did it. Somebody needed to.
> Dave Melchior, "Opinion. The Passing of the Willow Run Plant,"
> *Ypsilanti Press*, Sept. 12, 1993, 6A

Throughout the fall the heated debates over school funding and school quality continue. Senator Stabenow releases a "Framework for Education Reform in Michigan," based on "The Three Rs for Michigan Education: Revitalize Local Schools, Reduce Bureaucracy, and Require Basics." She proposes offering parents a choice of school within each district, charter schools, and a mandatory core curriculum.[19] Governor Engler delivers a "special message" to a joint session of the legislature (October 5, 1993), speaking of "evidence of a mounting crisis" in public education – nothing's changed in a quarter of a century, yet "the system's broken! It needs fixing. And it needs fixing now!"

Engler lays down four "fundamental principles" to fix schools. First, to "empower kids" with a "world-class education" by raising expectations and setting higher standards – "world-class standards." In order to meet the National Education Goals a "world-class core curriculum" must be developed, along with evaluation of student progress "with tests that measure us against the best in the world," and use of technology "to bring the world's best libraries" into the classroom. He calls on the state of Michigan to "put its reputation on the line with endorsed diplomas, and exams that indicate those subjects in which a student has achieved mastery, and the Michigan Education Warranty."

"I've said it before, and I'll say it again: It's time our schools stood behind our graduates the way we expect our automakers to stand behind their cars! We can no longer accept diplomas that merely measure attendance."

Second, to empower families by providing choice. "Public education is a monopoly, and monopolies don't work. Why? Because in a monopoly, customers don't come first." Districts will have the option of accepting students from outside their boundaries – "my plan strengthens local control by putting parents in control." Charter schools, freed from "unnecessary restrictions" like teacher certification, will permit further choice. Annual financial reports from the state on public school spending, and a report card from each building, will provide parents with the "consumer information" on which to base their choices. A foundation grant of at least $4,500 that will follow a child to whatever school the family chooses will ensure that "the state fund not 'the system' but the students. . . . The customer decides. That's the American way. And that will be the Michigan way!"

Third, to empower teachers – who, due to charter schools, will no longer be compelled to join the union, and for whom "tough-love legislation" will provide a "drug-free, gun-free environment." The governor holds up a sawed-off shotgun taken from a 16-year-old.

And, fourth, to empower taxpayers. Engler lays out his proposed replacement revenue package, centered around an increased sales tax. Because this would raise the ceiling on state spending it requires a constitutional amendment, and so must be put to a popular vote next year.

Quality, performance, accountability – these will be the prized attributes of successful schools, because parents will be looking to do what is right by their children. The total funding level of schools will be determined by how many students they can retain or attract. The schools that deliver will succeed. The schools that don't will not. No longer will there be a monopoly of mediocrity in this state. No longer will there be exclusive franchises over education. No longer will there be a company store holding our families hostage. Because our kids deserve better!

Gov. John Engler, Special Message to a Joint Session, Oct. 5, 1993

The rancorous debate that erupted this week in the Legislature over charter schools is one more piece of evidence that lawmakers have to remain focused on school finance this fall. . . .

Creeping into the debate about school finance are proposals to revamp schools, such as creating charter schools and schools of choice.

This week, an official of the In-Formula School District caucus had harsh words for the charter school idea, which prompted a harsh response from lawmakers.

Such debate on school reform is healthy and should come, but not in the short time between now and the end of the year.

There are two distinct issues involved in this debate: Finance and school reform. Right now, the debate needs to remain focused on the issue of finance . . .

Editorial, "School Changes," *Ypsilanti Press*, Oct. 17, 1993, 6A

MSSI's second year (WRSI's first), starting now, is to be one of "communication initiatives, . . . coordination of efforts within the Michigan Department of Education, and initial action recommendations." MSSI intends to bring together major stakeholders – "partners in action" – and catalyze change.

MSSI documents are careful not to dictate particular kinds of curriculum and instruction, because this is where local districts are to have choice. Instead, the approach is to define outcomes: first, formation of a "community coalition"; a three- to five-year strategic plan for reform; "evidence of continued improvement in student achievement"; "involved" district staff; and "evidence of a restructured math and science program." How the districts achieve these outcomes is up to them; the supposition is that the local community coalition, guided by the strategic plan, will make decisions about curriculum and pedagogy that will lead to the desired achievement gains. Even the last outcome – restructured math and science programs – is to be evidenced not by adopting specific curriculum materials or teaching techniques, but by *alignment* of assessment, pedagogy, and materials with national standards. MSSI is walking a fine line trying to encourage change toward a common goal without dictating how to achieve it.[20]

The first issue of a newsletter – the *MSSI Exchange* – describes the focus districts as "pioneers of systemic change," collaborating to achieve a shared goal in a variety of ways. "They understand the link between education and employment." The quote for the quarter is, "Change is inevitable, growth is optional." MSSI is described as "an audacious initiative with an audacious task . . . *systemic change*. Change isn't easy and it's scary, but necessary for growth." And if the "mission" of MSSI is "mathematics and science success for all" then it must reach "the low achieving and historically underrepresented student populations (minorities, women, the handicapped)."[21]

The 21st century economy will require people who can think and solve problems, who can communicate both orally and in writing, who can work

> on a team with peoples of diverse cultures and understand the basic mathe-
> matics and science ideas underlying complex systems.
>
> *MSSI Exchange*, Vol. 1, No. 1, Autumn 1993, p. 1

MSSI holds an orientation meeting in early October at which each focus district team is guided through "planning for planning" – formulating their first-year goals. "The intent is to enable the core team to do some background *reflecting* and *preparation* for the process of strategic planning."

Each district drafts its "intended outcomes" and the organizers collate these to draw up "a set of common outcomes/results" which are supposed to facilitate networking, planning of technical assistance, and evaluating everyone's progress.[22] Working with these common outcomes, each district starts to identify specific objectives for the first year. "As you begin the planning process you will need to articulate the *needs* which undergird your planning as well as *objectives for the first year.* You are then to delineate *activities* and *timeframes,* and assign *responsibilities.* In succeeding years we may refine and modify the intended outcomes but will not need to recreate them."[23] MSSI's Evaluation Team – from Western Michigan University – will review these plans to help develop evaluation questions and suggest indicators. "As approved or modified by the district design team," this becomes the evaluation section of the strategic plan.

The WRSI team decides our first-year objectives are to build a system for communication, forge a coalition, form support groups for those involved in project-driven inquiry, assess the current state of instruction in the district, and have each building play the Change Game.[24] We'll begin by visiting each school to introduce ourselves. Vivian provides a description of the Willow Run Community Schools for a booklet cataloging the focus districts. After describing the district's location, its size, the eligibility for free or reduced-price lunch, and the schools, she writes three sentences that MSSI later edits out: ". . . a cutting-edge school system widely known for innovative approaches to teaching and learning since the early 1970's. Always at the forefront of developing and implementing curricula that challenges all learners to their maximum potential. The student body is representative of the cultural diversity within the Willow Run Community."

On a crisp, bright afternoon, after an overcast weekend on which the first snow fell, I drive out to Kaiser Elementary for the Willow Run

Systemic Initiative Committee's first presentation to a school staff. Railroad, highway, and freeway, the major arteries of the circulatory system feeding raw materials and workers into the Willow Run plant, conspire to divide the Willow Run school district into distinct regions. Michigan Avenue, the old route between Chicago and Detroit before Interstate 94 was built, runs through the center of Willow Run, though not through its heart. At this point it's a four-lane highway paralleling the railroad with businesses on both sides: auto dealerships, fast-food restaurants, a Kroger's supermarket. But it's possible to spend a day in the community and not set foot or tire on this main road. What makes this possible is Ford Boulevard, a sweeping four-lane stretch of concrete running from Clark Road in the north to Ecorse Road in the south, spanning Michigan Avenue with an overpass. Driving along it one gets no hint of the commercial bustle below. Ford Boulevard connects what are now north and south Willow Run – the only way across the railroad tracks. This connection isn't simply an aesthetic escape from Michigan Avenue, though; the road was built during the war to convey workers efficiently to the plant.

Interstate 94, after running due east from Ann Arbor and past Ypsilanti, turns southeast in the center of south Willow Run, splitting into two arms that stretch along the south and north sides of the plant. These stretches sweep and turn with an impressive grandeur and self-confidence, defining the scope and scale of the plant both on the map and on the geography of the area. But in connecting the plant to the outside world they cut through and carve up the portion of Willow Run below Michigan Avenue. Crossed or burrowed under at only a few places, they create triangles of land into which the growing Willow Run community gradually extended.

Kaiser Elementary is in that triangle known as West Willow, misleadingly since this is the east side of Willow Run, but it was west of the stream that gave the plant and the community its name. Bounded by freeways on all three sides, West Willow is an isolated residential area, with no stores, no restaurants, no bars – just three Baptist churches. Its only recreational feature is West Willow Park; graffiti scrawled on the park's wooden sign is the only visible indication of the gang activity that West Willow has become known for.

Most of the houses on this island are single-story, two-bedroom bungalows with one basic floor plan. Behind most houses is a two-car garage half the size of the house. Chain-link fences contain large well-kept lawns. On many there are plastic swans, pelicans, deer, Dalmatians.

A few pumpkins are visible: this is November 1, the Monday after Halloween. Large, mature trees line the streets.

Named after Henry Kaiser, owner of the plant after the war, the school sits among a cluster of streets named after the auto industry – Desoto, Olds, and Hudson Avenues; Dodge Court; Zepher, Studebaker, Chevrolet, and Buick Avenues. Kaiser is laid out along a single extended corridor with the entrance at the center. The school is colorful, with paintings, drawings, and photos of school events on the walls. The bright late-autumn sunshine spilling through the windows gives a spacious and airy feel.

There are about 15 teachers in the room, about half African American, half white. Only principal Ray Melberg and Craig, the teacher advisor, are male. The first few minutes of the meeting are school business, then Vivian begins our presentation.

"In spite of the fact that Mr. Melberg said we were going to present our plan, that's not what we're going to do. We have three sets of questions that we'd like to ask you to be involved with, and then we're going to share some information with you about where we are in terms of systemic change.

"I want you to get a picture of someone in your mind, either your own child, grandchild, a little brother or sister, or a niece or nephew, someone in your family that is in school or will be going to school within let's say the next three to five years. And I want you to think about the kind of learning environment that you would like for that loved one to be involved with.

"That's what our systemic initiative team is all about – learning environments, and particularly we're thinking of course about Willow Run. We've had the opportunity to go to several workshops, and recently we attended a workshop at which we saw a video that was really outstanding. I'm going to share with you a story about the Japanese. Joe Barker, the person who did the video, describes how the Japanese continue to outstride other countries. They have one word that they try to live by, and it's *kaizin*. *Kaizin* for the Japanese means that every single day that you do something, you try to do it better than you did the day before. I'm sure you've heard of Total Quality Management; that's what that came out of. There is a belief that if you try to do something better than you did it before, it doesn't mean you didn't do it right, it just means you're continuing on improvement. And that's what we're all about."

Scott divides the teachers into small groups with sheets of newsprint and markers. "Okay, what I want you to do is think about the learning environments that Vivian was just speaking about. I want you to come up with a *vehicle* that can drive education in the future. How can we create a learning environment which will achieve the Willow Run Community Schools' vision statement, that you all have a copy of? How can we create some kind of a vehicle that could drive that vision statement? It's very open-ended."

"Let the creative juices flow," adds Vivian. "Now I want you to remember, you have a perfect world. So don't get hung up on how you're going to do it, just make the vehicle. Okay? I think I hear some people hung up on *how* they're going to do it. You've got a perfect world; just make the vehicle."

These are the committee's first efforts; we'll fine-tune our presentation over the next few weeks. Scott moves around from group to group, answering questions. There's lots of earnest talk. He asks for a volunteer to present. "Order, order!"

"Okay. This is the perfect school, right? Perfect people, perfect teachers, everything. We said all high school students should be required a minimum of two years of child development or parenting. Students will be grouped by their talents, part of the day. In other words if she's real good at art, she'll be grouped with an art teacher part of the day. Or if she's good with music, or physics, or calculus, then group them with that particular teacher. There will only be school for four days a week."

"Why?" asks Scott.

"Because the fifth day will be concrete experiences. For example, this child would go to a museum. Maybe another country. Or if you're in physics you might go to U of M and have a little mini course. Individual instruction, for each child. Each child would have their own computer with their own interests plugged in."

There's applause, then the next group. "We had a variety of different ideas, some are usable, some are just extreme but wouldn't it be nice if they really came to be. We felt that certainly technology was a real important component of this, and we felt that the teachers not only needed to have that technology but they needed to be well-trained and real comfortable with the use of this. We would also like each child to have a computer, not only in the classroom but one in their home, so that we could use this as a way of working with the parents, so the parents are aware of what is going on, and they also had some control of the computer and had an understanding of it. It could be used for communication, for homework, for a school-home bulletin of some kind.

"We really felt that, in this perfect world, kids needed to come from families that are intact and cohesive and peaceful, so that when they came to school they were ready to learn. We have all these wonderful ideas but before we can do anything we have to have these kids' attention and that they were here so that they *could* learn. In this perfect world we're only going to have fifteen kids in a classroom with one teacher, so that we can give them the best that we possibly can.

"We also know that not all kids are academically talented. We need to explore every child's gift, so we want to have more vocational programs for the kids that *aren't* college-bound, or even the kids that aren't going to have a real technical job. We want them to feel good about themselves, and we want to have lots of options for these children."

The next representative rustles sheets of notes.

"In our perfect world, we want to have parents, teachers, and the community working together. 'Cause you know if they don't it doesn't work. We want to see a longer school year, so we have shorter breaks away from school so our children don't forget as much as they do. But we want to have these breaks more frequent. We want to see team-based cooperation, everywhere in the school environment. We want to see project-oriented learning with integrated curriculum: whatever you're doing; computers, reading, music, history, whatever, it should be integrated. We want to see all of our students using higher-level thinking skills, so that they are stimulated and motivated. And we want them always to be able to understand the objective: is it relevant? Is that what I'm going to *need* to have when I leave this school? What you're giving me now, do I need this?"

Scott hands back to Vivian.

"We did this activity because usually if you ask someone to think about doing something differently, it's very difficult because you stay right within your own parameters. That's why we had you make a perfect world.

"If we can take off the shackles of what we know to do today and, as Dr. Joe would say, get out of the box, maybe we really could come up with some ways to do some of these things. I think they're marvelous ideas. I know we can't make the perfect parent – don't we wish! And we can't necessarily create a perfect home. But we do create the environment in which the children live every day at school. We have total control over it, and if we think in terms of the Japanese, in terms of *kaizin*, then I guess I sorta wonder, what could we create? That's what the systemic initiative is really all about. We are not going to come up with a plan that tells everybody step one, step two, step three. Because we don't know what it is for Kaiser School and Kaiser staff. What we *would* like to do is try to engage you in activities such as these, that get you thinking about what you'd really like to see in your school. What would be *your* perfect world for a school if you could create it? What kind of support would you need from the WRSI team? We do have a grant that gives us sixty-five thousand dollars for the next five years. It's not a lot of money; probably sounds like it but it is not, when you think of trying to do something across the district. We are available as support people, we are available as people who we hope will stir the pot, get your juices flowing, in terms of thinking about teaching and learning, and what these environments should look like. The Kaiser environment, the Willow Run environment. As it relates to the Willow Run vision, that is what we're all about. What we want to do is try to get every person involved."

One of the teachers raises a hand. "We're welcome to come to your meetings, are we not?"

"Yes, you are," Vivian replies. "Right now we're meeting every other Thursday, and our next meeting is this Thursday. You're welcome to come. In the future I'll make sure each administrator knows when our meetings are, so that you can be a part of it."

Scott adds, "I'd just like to say one last thing. I've only been in Willow Run for a short time, but since I've been here there's nobody that can tell me or convince me that all is not possible if we want to do it. I have not seen anything that we have wanted to do, either as a staff or as individual teachers or a department, that we haven't been able to accomplish, somehow."

BELIEVING the following to be true:
- The District is professionally, morally, and ethically accountable to the citizens of our community for the learning that occurs in our schools.
- Because all people can learn, we have the responsibility to see that all Willow Run students successfully achieve the objectives established by the District.
- It is the responsibility of all personnel to create a successful outcome for all Willow Run graduates, including the possession of an endorsed diploma. Our VISION for Willow Run includes developing adaptive life-long learners who:
- have the ability to contribute to and grow with an ever-changing technology based society;

- demonstrate the ability to be effective communicators;
- are flexible lifelong learners;
- are goal oriented, self-directed and accept responsibility;
- demonstrate creative thinking/problem solving;
- demonstrate responsible citizenship; and
- are concerned, caring, compassionate adults.

We, therefore, commit to the following MISSION for our schools:

Willow Run Community Schools believes that all people can learn. Our responsibility is to enable all learners to be successful in the 21st century.

Willow Run Community Schools Vision, adopted Nov. 1992

The WRSI Committee visits each of the district schools, though not every school is as encouraging as Kaiser. At the meeting in Betty Hopkin's classroom at Edmonson, the team members brief Scott, who'd not been able to attend the presentation to Cheney Elementary.

Vivian says, "I found it interesting. Knowing what I know about Cheney, I really felt bad for the staff, because I felt they were quite inhibited and, uh, not as free-thinking as I have known."

"Very cautious."

"Trust level very low," continues Vivian, who had begun her career teaching at Cheney. "I've been on that staff when we used to have people flowing everywhere, every direction, and no one ever said anything about who was there, why they were there. Who cared, you know? It was like, 'Yeah, whoever wants to come, come!' I remember when we used to have visitors at our school on a regular basis. Like Kettering is now, people want to come there. Like Edmonson. And kids didn't stop, teachers didn't stop, folks just came in and did whatever they wanted to do. That's one of the things that I noted. Plus, they're at a level of feeling a need for 'things,' and it makes you wonder what they've been deprived of, that they think they need. For me, that's like when I went to Kettering and I said everybody could have ditto paper, as much as they want, and everybody was like," she gasps. "You'd swear they didn't have ditto paper. You remember that? They couldn't believe they could have the ditto paper any time they wanted." She chuckles. "So I wonder what they don't have, that they *really* think they should have?"

"And things were going to be done *to* them or *for* them," adds Mary.

"Yes," nods Vivian. "I don't think there was anything on that sheet that *they* were going to do. It said to me that, for *that* staff, as we plan future things, we have to really help build a confidence level from within, somehow, and give them information that says that they're able. The good news is, I feel that they have a principal who's already done some things, and I know that, because I know that the first month of school I had people saying to me, 'Gee it's good to be able to laugh again.' " Her voice drops to a conspiratorial whisper. "You go, 'God, you couldn't laugh?' But that was the feeling they had."

Betty taught at Cheney before moving to Edmonson. "Yes!" She laughs now. "I remember all that!"

Scott is intrigued. "So you felt they were more inhibited, as far as . . . ?"

"Much more inhibited than I remembered that staff," says Vivian.

Scott asks, "Compared with the other staffs? Like Kaiser?"

"Oh, just total opposite end of the spectrum," Vivian says. "Remember when I said to Kaiser, 'Do your perfect world,' they just sort of, woo! and everything opened up. I said that to them at Cheney, they couldn't move."

"Is it that they're jaded," Scott asks, "or is it that they're just not excited?"

"I think they're jaded," says Vivian. "I think that there has been a definite effect and, I should close this door, but I'm a pretty honest person . . ." She gets up to shut the door of Betty's classroom. "But I do, I worry about that staff. That's a staff we really are going to take some energy for, but the good news is they have an administrator now that will be working no matter what we do. She's already doing that; she recognizes that there is that need for self-worth, especially on a professional level."

Liza asks about the staff changes at the schools. "So basically at the end of this last year, they took all of the principals in various schools and put them in different schools?"

"Well," cautions Vivian, "I don't want you to think – no, it was not random. Everything was very purposeful in what we did. There was much movement."

Laura Chew and Vivian had been teachers together at Cheney and left at the same time, about eight year ago, Laura to be principal at Kaiser, Vivian principal at Kettering. Just this year Laura has moved back to Cheney to take the principalship there.

Another small comment sets an ominous tone. Earlier in the day Vivian and Mary attended a meeting run by the people in the state Department of Education responsible for the Michigan Educational Assessment Program (MEAP) test – pronounced "Meep."

"The meeting where we were today," says Mary, "they were very clear that MEAP assessment drives curriculum."

"Oh, they must have said it a thousand times," Vivian adds, in a whisper.

Mary echoes what they were told: " 'We're admitting it, and we know it, and we just hope that we selected . . .'" – they didn't say 'We hope' – 'We *know* we have selected the right . . .' my impression was, 'The only saving grace is that we have selected the sort of learning and measurement that we think are good for kids.' "

"Except that's really not the way it's supposed to be," murmurs Vivian.

We don't want to give you too many ideas because we don't want you to think that we know anything. Because we don't! We're learning. And we don't want you to think that we're gonna come up with this *grand* plan that's gonna say, aha!, this is it. So that's why we try not to give too much information.

Vivian Lyte, at WRSI visit to Cheney Elementary

The two large-scale school reform initiatives – Governor Engler's and NSF's – operate with very different interpretations of the schooling they seek to change. Engler applies an economic metaphor, with schooling interpreted as a production process. The goal of Engler's "marketplace" reforms is to improve school "quality" through increasing "efficiency" and "productivity" – measured ultimately in terms of the state's business climate and the needs of industry. The problem is taken to be that production has "broken down," in large part because public schooling is a "monopoly" with no incentives for improvement. The answer, it follows, is removal of "unnecessary bureaucracy" so that schools "compete" in an open market. This requires a measure of "output" to play against the money "input" to the schooling process. The MEAP test is intended to provide this quality index, to give feedback to "consumers" and ensure more efficient production by increasing the "accountability" of teachers, schools, and districts.

The systemic reform efforts, in contrast, seek equality rather than quality. The metaphor here is a political one, with schooling viewed as a "public service," an element of society's infrastructure – like the postal service or the public highway system – that "delivers" learning to students, its citizens. What's needed is "coordination" of this "delivery system" – all components of the system must be "aligned" – like getting the water pipes lined up in the street, or making sure the mail truck meets the plane on time and so gets packages to the mail carrier. Where Engler worries about the supply of workers to global industries, the systemic reformers worry about preparing an informed citizenry for a complex world. What steers their effort is a concern with establishing an appropriate, democratic distribution of goods.

Although the marketplace and systemic school reform initiatives employ quite different interpretive frameworks, both are clearly efforts to *rationalize* the organization and functioning of U.S. public schooling. Each has its coherent logic, but they are largely incompatible, two distinct rationalities at work, the former emphasizing competition and efficiency, the latter coherence and equality. These are the relentless but clashing logics of the economic and political "systems of survival" in our society.[25]

> School is "like a business – but it gets more complicated because you're in the *human* business, and a lot of times we can't even articulate who our customers are. Are they the children? Are they the children's parents? Are they the board? Are they the superintendent? Are they . . . y'know, we could go on and on and on. It's not *nearly* as clear cut and well defined as it would be if we were in business, and if we didn't make a profit we could all lose our jobs."
>
> Janice Brown, Interview, May 24, 1993

But missing from both these interpretations of schooling and school reform is any detailed grasp of the activity of teaching. Marketplace reform presumes that just as business now can seek increased productivity not by telling workers what to do but by holding them accountable and having *them* figure out the best way to organize production, school reform will be accomplished best by holding teachers accountable rather than by telling them how to teach. Teaching is assumed to be analogous to the assembly of automobiles. Systemic reform speaks of "building capacity" to "leverage" local efforts to improve the equity of teaching – providing information and guidance, and the carrots and sticks of small grants – as though teaching is like delivering the mail. In both cases the activity of teaching remains mysterious, an unopened black box. The nature of the production, the means of delivery, these go unexamined, and teaching is obscured by the metaphors and rhetoric of these calls for reform.

In contrast, the local reforms at Kettering and elsewhere in Willow Run recognize the relational and cultural character of teaching and learning. They understood that learning takes place in a living relationship between teacher and student. This relationship is shaped by the community of the classroom, and this in turn by the larger institutions of which each classroom is a part. Mary and her staff seek a whole new culture in their school, changing not just curriculum, not just pedagogy, but the community of the institution. And they are guided by their familiarity with the particular needs and attitudes of the local children.

For example, an indoor lunch recess has begun, and when it is too cold to play outside children can choose among a reading room, an art activity, various games, or a movie.[26] Teachers in first through third grade are using portfolios and observation check sheets, rather than letter grades, to evaluate student progress. The whole school comes together for weekly "gatherings." High school students come to tutor. In the "grandma program," volunteers from the local retirement home work as classroom aides. Children's work, photos, and brightly colored posters fill the walls of the building. Flowers have been planted around the building – the children pull them up, but less then at first. Kettering feels bright, warm, and welcoming.

And the Kettering staff have taken steps to foster their school's professional network – by applying to join the Coalition of Essential Schools – a school-university partnership founded in 1984 by Ted Sizer of Brown University. Most schools in the coalition are high schools, but elementaries have begun to join. Each school develops a plan for reform that reflects its unique circumstances; a simple set of common principles is intended to give focus to these efforts. The principles emphasize personalizing teaching and learning through coaching and guiding, aiming for student mastery and building on students' own experiences, placing decisions about curriculum and pedagogy in the hands of staff and principal, collective planning, family involvement, and viewing students as active participants rather than seeing teachers as deliverers of instructional services.

These local reforms draw resources from the community. Both the reforms at Kettering and the message WRSI delivers around the district draw upon an ethos that is uniquely Willow Run's. The avoidance of "top-down" dictates – in the classroom and outside – and the effort instead to find collective solutions is apparent both at Kettering and in WRSI, but it can only be adequately understood as part of a story that goes back to Willow Run's birth. The community has deep ties to the Willow Run plant, ties that predate General Motors' involvement.

6   Willow Run Is America

The 1940s and 1950s

> To make an educational program suitable to a community requires a basic knowledge of the background and conditions of that community. Usually a community develops slowly from a small beginning and makes adjustments gradually. Willow Run did not follow the normal pattern; rather it was a large community which appeared overnight as a result of a federal housing project. The experiences which come from such a development are likely never to be repeated.
>
> Robert Stevenson, Preface to Marion F. Wilson, *The Story of Willow Run*. Ann Arbor: University of Michigan Press, 1956

> Ford's Willow Run bomber plant may be taken as the symbol of the automobile industry's ability to scale seemingly insurmountable heights. In a cow pasture outside Detroit the world's largest bomber plant was completed in 94 working days.
>
> Rudolf E. Anderson, *The Story of the American Automobile: Highlights and Sidelights*. Washington, D.C.: Public Affairs Press, 1952, p. 85

> Willow Run produced not only 8,685 bombers, but in the words of a Washington housing official, "the worst mess in the whole United States."
>
> Lowell Juilliard Carr and James Edson Stermer, 1952, *Willow Run: A Story of Industrialization and Cultural Inadequacy*. Harper and Brothers, p. 9 (reprinted by Arno Press, 1977)

General Motors has owned and operated the Willow Run complex – the assembly plant and the Hydra-matic plant – since 1953, but this facility had its origins in the ambitions of another one of the Big

109

Three: The Ford Motor Company. The Willow Run community was a child of twentieth-century state-regulated industrial production, born of a union between the wartime demand for complex fighting machines and the efficiency gains of centralized production, and the power of the federal government. The community was created, and then shaped, to meet the needs of large-scale industry, first the military-industrial complex and subsequently the equally massive automobile manufacturing industry.

Anyone who learns the history of Willow Run feels compelled to tell the story of these origins, typically with emphasis on the transition from bucolic tranquillity to industrial commotion. Given the opportunity to summarize local history, even a local planning document of the postwar era waxed poetic.

Near an old Indian trail, called the Sauk-Fox Trail, eight miles east of Ann Arbor there was a favorite camping ground used by Indians over 150 years ago. A stream called Willow Run flowed through this wooded area into the Huron River to the southwest. Today this trail is Michigan Avenue, U.S. Highway 112, and the camping ground the site of Willow Run Village, a community with a history of fast development and change. . . .

World War II changed the face of this quiet rural area. Summer of 1941 saw the construction of the Willow Run bomber plant that was to build nearly 9,000 B-24 Liberator bombers in the next 24 months, and the Willow Run airport of six runways. The bomber plant began hiring workers to meet the employment needs of up to 100,000 workers. From all over the country, from farms and cities the workers came. To meet the urgent demand for nearby housing the Federal Public Housing Administration (FPHA) finally stepped in.

Parkins, Rogers, and Associates, *Master Plan for Willow Village, Washtenaw County, Michigan*. City Planning and Urban Renewal Consultants, 1959

Another recounting of Willow Run's origins can be found in the opening pages of *The Story of Willow Run*, a book written in 1956 for the local school children. Marion Wilson, the author, was asked to write the book by Robert Stevenson, Mary Brandau's father, then assistant superintendent of the Willow Run schools, and later superintendent. Wilson wanted the book to "make kids proud of their parents." "We were very lucky to find her," Stevenson told the *Ypsilanti Press* years later. "It was a labor of love for her. The district owned the book; she never made any money." The story, he added, "will provide an insight into the type of pioneering which existed during and following World War II."

Wilson deftly caught all the major turns in Willow Run's history, and she expressed poignantly the defining relationship of industry and community. She explained how the community has connections to the plant that go beyond mere proximity. She also made the important point that Willow Run was in many respects essentially American. "Willow Run *is* America!" This remains true today, though Willow Run is representative now in ways quite different from those that Wilson pointed to.

"Willow Run," the name. What does it mean?

It's a quiet stream that flows into the Huron River and it's a gracious chapel nearby. It was a place where Indians camped and hunted and where pioneers cleared the forest, built their cabins, settled and farmed the land.

Willow Run was a camp for boys where they learned to farm, to live in the open, to work and love the land.

The name stands for the giant plant first run by Henry Ford, where B-24 bombers were built to help gain victories in World War II; then run by the Kaiser-Frazer Corporation where cars were built and where the C-119, known as the "Flying Boxcar," was built for the U.S. Army; now the great plant where the General Motors Corporation builds hydramatic transmission for its cars.

Willow Run is a fine airport that is known to travelers and pilots around the world.

Willow Run is a community of temporary homes where thousands of the people lived who built the bombers that helped win the war, where thousands of veterans who fought to win the war came to live with their wives and children, so that they could continue war-interrupted educations, the community often being called the "second campus" of the University of Michigan at Ann Arbor.

Willow Run is where every family has a yard where children can play and there are no signs at the rental office saying "No Children Allowed."

Willow Run is a name that sings of pioneers of many kinds, the pioneering people who built the bombers, then built the products of peacetime at the place where people learned to live together in harmony, to go to good schools, to learn to be good citizens of a community of which they could be proud.

Willow Run is not only the place, it is the people, their spirit; the spirit of pioneers.

Willow Run . . . Willow Run is America!

Wilson, *The Story of Willow Run*, pp. 3–15.

The people of Willow Run still have a strong sense of the origins of their community in the war effort – in adversity, urgency, and difficult labor in demanding conditions. The Willow Run plant has provided a geographical center and historical continuity to their identity. Understanding their reaction to GM's decision to close the plant, and understanding what's happening in the community schools, requires a knowledge of this history. This is my telling of the story.[1]

Henry Ford had been acquiring land east of Ypsilanti, around the meandering stream called Willow Run, since the 1920s, primarily for soybean cultivation. (Ford was an enthusiastic proponent of soybeans as a cheap, healthy source of protein and renewable raw materials. He used soybean oil as a base for automobile paints and resins. And bean cultivation and processing created jobs away from the cities, which Ford considered to have an immoral influence. Ford himself sometimes wore a suit, reputedly costing $10,000, woven of soybean fiber.) In 1939 he conducted a boys' camp there – "Camp Willow Run" – to train and discipline the sons of local farmers (some say the camp was for boys whose fathers were killed in World War I) to be "better citizens, better men"[2] by raising and selling vegetables. The boys slept in army tents, were woken for church services at 5:30 A.M., and spent the day working in the fields.

Ford was well into his seventies when war broke out and becoming increasingly eccentric. The Ford Motor Company was riven by internal rivalries and power struggles, Ford refusing to relinquish any authority to his son Edsel. Henry believed that the United States should stay out of the conflict in Europe and was determined that his company should play no role. Edsel, however, was enthusiastic about the company's contributing to the war effort, and he agreed to build Rolls-Royce bomber engines under license. When Henry learned of this contract he insisted that it be canceled, and the UAW and others charged Ford with Nazi sympathies. But at the end of 1940 a group of military and government officials visited Dearborn to ask the company to help build the B-24 bomber – the "Liberator." Henry was unenthusiastic, but Edsel and Charles Sorensen, the manufacturing boss, now vice president of Ford, visited Consolidated Aircraft, in San Diego, which had been given the Liberator contract and wanted subassemblies from Ford.

Consolidated was using antiquated methods of production for the B-24, essentially custom-making each plane, producing one a day. No blueprints were used and major components were custom fit, using tools no more sophisticated than plumbs and levels. Sorensen wrote in his memoirs, "What I saw reminded me of the way we built cars at Ford 35 years earlier." Overnight, in his hotel room, Sorensen sketched out a scheme to produce B-24s, using the assembly-line techniques he had pioneered at Ford, and laid out the floor plan of a plant. He estimated that production of one airplane every hour would require 100,000 workers and a $200 million facility. Consolidated's president suggested instead that Ford simply contract to build a thousand wing sections, but Sorensen told Army officials, "We'll make the complete airplane or nothing." They guaranteed 540 planes a month, when Consolidated was delivering 520 a year.

Henry Ford had little respect for President Franklin Roosevelt, but he was swayed by the president of General Motors, William S. Knudsen, once a Ford employee, who had been appointed commissioner for industrial production of the Office for Emergency Management. Roosevelt tripled the military budget and called for production of 50,000 military aircraft per year; more than were in existence at that time. So in March 1941, Ford received an initial $3.4 million contract to build subassemblies for the B-24 – part of $11 billion awarded nationwide in defense contracts – and that spring construction of the bomber plant began. It was to be sited on the land where Ford had been running Camp Willow Run. Henry was not happy with this location for the new plant; he would shift the stakes that marked the construction site, saying "We're going to grow soybeans there. Build it someplace else."

> Willow Run was where Henry Ford promised to build a better bomber, to build it cheaper and to build it once an hour.
> "War Gave Birth to Willow Run Plant," *Ypsilanti Press*, Jan. 4, 1994

Woodland was felled by workers with bulldozers, saws, and axes, and engineers began to design the tools and equipment needed to build the bomber. Consolidated's methods were completely inappropriate for mass production: a landing-gear pivot, for example, was welded together from about a dozen pieces; each of the hundred welds had to be x-rayed to ensure quality. Ford engineers redesigned the part so that it could be made from just three castings.

> Never before in the history of the world had there been so great and impatient a demand for the materials and weapons of war: 60,000 airplanes for a starter – 100 per cent of the motorized units, which would run into the millions – more than two-fifths of the tanks and tank parts – more than one-third of the machine guns – more than half of the Diesel engines – and one-fourth of all the countless items of military equipment made of metal. This was a production job calling for materials and men sufficient to build the

equivalent of 15 million cars and trucks – about three years' work rolled into one.

Beyond doubt, the greatest triumph of automotive production methods was in placing the key weapons, such as the airplane and the tank, on a mass production basis. The term "know how", coined in the emergency, explains why the automobile industry could tackle the gigantic job and guarantee success. The mechanized war was epitomized in the phrase, "Military Might Moves by Motor."

One thousand automotive plants were mobilized for the crisis. On the production schedule were 300 items that had never seen the inside of an automobile factory – including mess-kits, tent heaters, anti-tank guns, and gas mask components.

Anderson, *The Story of the American Automobile*, p. 85

Such an enterprise required a massive facility. Designed by Ford architect Albert Kahn, and built at a cost that rose from $11 million to $47 million, Willow Run was to be the largest war plant in the world. Kahn called the factory "the longest room ever built"; Charles Lindbergh said it was "a sort of Grand Canyon of the mechanized world"; a Ford executive said it was "the most enormous room in the history of man"; and President Franklin Roosevelt named it "the arsenal of democracy."[3] The plant's central feature was an automobile-style assembly line of the type Ford had pioneered at Dearborn in 1914, but this time three-fifths of a mile long.

Considering its size, the plant was built at an astonishing pace. Ground was broken on April 18, 1941, and the plant was dedicated just two months later. Situated on 446 acres of land, the plant's factory floor space covered 67 acres – 3.5 million square feet, compared with 2.8 million square feet of office space in the Empire State building, and more than the factory space of Boeing, Douglas, and Consolidated combined. It had the largest fluorescent lamp system ever installed. The adjacent airport, required so the Army Air Force could test-fly the bombers and deliver them from the plant, was completed on December 4, 1941, three days before the bombing of Pearl Harbor. The airport, with six runways, the longest 7,366 feet, covered 1,434 acres; the hangers alone occupied 109 acres. The concrete poured here would have built a highway 20 feet wide and 115 miles long. And in summer 1942 the state highway commission constructed expressway I-94 – hundreds of miles of "double super-highway" – to encourage workers to commute from Detroit, Flint, and other cities.

As soon as a section of the plant was completed, manufacturing of parts began. The first workers were Ford employees transferred from automobile production elsewhere, but in December the first new workers were hired, even though a large part of what was to be the assembly line was not yet under the cover of a roof.

Production began in November 1941 but, lacking a complete work-force or all the necessary equipment, it was ten months before the first bomber was completed. In the rest of that year 56 aircraft were produced, although most of these took the form of parts shipped off and assembled by Consolidated and Douglas.

Each completed bomber contained 1,250,000 parts (not counting 700,000 rivets), and 30,000 of these were unique. In comparison, a wartime Ford sedan contained a mere 15,000 parts. The plane, with a crew of 10, weighed 30 tons, had a wingspan of 110 feet, a fuselage 65 feet long and 18 feet high, and four 1,250-horsepower Pratt and Whitney engines, and carried a bomb load of 4 tons with a speed of over 300 m.p.h. and a range of over 1,500 miles. This long range was due to a design that included fuel tanks in the wings, so that the plane could carry around 2,800 gallons of fuel.

Ypsilanti residents bought war bonds in 1942 to pay for the first three bombers and convinced the government to name the first after the city. For an extra dime, buyers of the bonds got a button with the bomber's insignia on it: a winged "V" and the words "Spirit of Ypsilanti." There was a city contest to create the design; it was won by an eleventh-grade student at Ypsilanti High School.

After they were completed, the bombers were handed over to the air force for installation and testing of their armaments. Then they took to the air. The bombers roared overhead, audible throughout Willow Run and the Ypsilanti area at all hours of the day and night.

From the outset, the Ford Motor Company experienced major difficulty finding and keeping enough skilled workers to maintain the breakneck pace of production. In addition to the problem of workers being drafted, turnover averaged 10 percent per week for the three years of production, and daily absenteeism was between 8 and 17 percent. The pace and complexity of bomber production were considered virtually miraculous, but from the start the workers who performed these miracles were disparaged and unwanted. In a 1943 novel set in the plant, author Glendon Swarthout skillfully conveyed the enormity of the factory. The book opened with the words "Willow Run is big in the night. It lies there, L-shaped and a mile long, with a thousand bright eyes of unblinking blue glass. From all directions come roads which twist and turn, their new clean concrete lit mile after mile with festoons of paired lights. In the dim spaces between the lights vehicles roll, dark inside except for burning cigarette ends. Many of the vehicles are huge with heavily-laden bodies" – the "share-a-ride" workers commuting to labor in the plant. Inside is "Immensity. Insane, overpowering immensity. Three-fifths of a mile long of immensity, almost one-fifth of a mile wide of immensity."[4] And inside, too, was an inhuman rationality – "The uprights are numbered, black letters and ciphers stenciled high up in white lead. The numbers march away into infinity, smaller and smaller. A, B, C, D, E, F, G, H, I, J, K-38, K-39, K-40, K-41, 42, 43, 44, 45 . . ." – that contrasts with the almost animate form of the bomber under construction. Chapters begin with statements of its needs: "B-24 must be separated inside." "B-24 needs eyes." "B-24 must be strong." "They are building wings for B-24!" "They are building a body for B-24!" And as the chapter before "Flight" ends, the narrator speaks directly to the bomber: "You have your hearts, B-24, and you have your wings. More care and more man hours have been consumed in your making than have ever been given to one of your kind before. You are made of living and dying and loving and hating and aluminum alloy. You are not yet alive. But they are filling your veins with colorless blood now, for the first time, and they are making your hearts ready to beat."

As Swarthout described it, an informal organization ran through and cut across the rational organization of the assembly line, and the real humanity of the workers contrasted with the apparent life of the machine: the workers sharing a ride to work, splitting rental on a cheap apartment or trailer, and trading tales as they labor – "This place runs on gossip." "Joe The Sweeper" follows his broom around the entire plant, carrying news from one group of workers to the next – and causing one man of the six "share-a-rides" to have a breakdown, another to hit a security guard, and a third to murder the fourth with a high-speed drill bit to the brain ("Pierces the skull – accidentally! Spins six hundred sixty times in ten seconds!").[5] As Swarthout portrayed them, the workers at Willow Run were lazy, shiftless, lecherous, even murderous.

The continued shortage of workers, limited expertise in this kind of production, shortages in supplies, and low morale due to the long commutes and poor housing, led to slow production, and many planes needed modification once the military had taken possession of them. Only about half of the first planes built proved of acceptable quality; aircraft production called for far more frequent design changes than did automobile production – almost 600 in the first year – but the plant was using hard steel dies that couldn't be modified. A study by the military recommended that the government take over the plant.

But the problems were steadily resolved. More workers were recruited from the south, and the war office ordered Ford to hire women. The work may have been tough – nine-hour shifts, 60- and 70-hour weeks at times – but the pay was good. Even a worker in tool inventory received $1.10 an hour – for nine hours a day and all day Saturday – compared with 35 cents an hour working at a dairy store. Typical paychecks could top $100 a week. Servicemen, in comparison, made only about $21 a week. But many of the southern workers became homesick, and the shortages of housing and lack of recreation meant absenteeism was often still high. High wages tempted people to work for a while and return home, coming back only when money ran out. The workforce would remain unstable until finally the provision of temporary housing reduced turnover.

Before the bomber plant, Willow Run was like the rest of Ypsilanti Township: flat, pleasant countryside given mainly to mixed farming, with slow suburban growth along Michigan Avenue, the highway to Detroit. In 1952 Lowell Carr and James Stermer, two sociologists at the University of Michigan, published a study of "the impacts and consequences of unusual population influx into a particular locality in the Detroit hinterland, Willow Run, Michigan."[6] Carr and Stermer reported that there had been a population of 331 in the 420-acre area they focused on – roughly that of the local school district – living in a total of 94 homes. Almost all of these households were supported by nonfarm work. They were close to the urban level in terms of such amenities as inside toilets (51 percent), running water (33 percent), electric light (100 percent), and furnace heat (54 percent). These locals were predominantly Protestant, "but not very churchy," and had been conservative Republicans since the Civil War. It was a semirural neighborhood of "comfortable, sturdy individualists," experiencing some in-migration from the south as a result of slow industrial growth.

Then, in the five years between April 1940 and summer 1945, 10,000 people moved into this small area. These were just a fraction of the more than 250,000 who arrived in the four-county area around Detroit, but an astonishing number nonetheless. Overall, 32,000 people moved into Washtenaw County – a number equal to the population of Ann Arbor at that time. Ypsilanti grew by almost half in a matter of months.

As the plant was constructed rumors had circulated that Ford planned to surround it with a company town and that Alfred Kahn had been asked to start designs. The company neither confirmed nor denied these rumors, but given Ford's notorious paternalism and union busting the UAW would certainly have been horrified at the prospect of Willow Run becoming a Ford company town.[7] In fact, no provision was made by either the Ford Motor Company or the federal government for housing the workers who were needed at Willow Run. Industry in the 1940s felt little responsibility for workers. A bomber-plant executive told a government committee: "Ford Motor Company's business is to build the best bombers in the world, and how our workers live off the job is a community problem, not ours." The Federal Public Housing Administration opened an office in Detroit in March 1942, to address accommodation for workers in the area's war plants, and proposed a permanent housing project located just north of Willow Run. At first the administration requested funds not to build homes for defense workers but to stimulate private builders by insuring mortgages and building an infrastructure of streets, water mains, and sewers. This plan was strongly opposed by Ford, by the Washtenaw County Board of Supervisors, and the real estate interests of Ann Arbor and Ypsilanti. People argued that a housing project was unnecessary; existing housing was adequate. Local businessmen were extremely reluctant to permit construction of permanent housing for fear of causing a postwar housing glut and a shortfall in housing prices. Many saw the government's intentions as "socialistic."

"We welcome any growth that comes with due regard to normal peacetime life but dislike even to think of the effect of the loose aesthetic values almost sure to follow in the wake of an enterprise so gigantic. Ypsilanti is a settled city with a definite character, and we don't want the character to be changed."
Secretary of the Ypsilanti Board of Commerce, quoted in the *Washtenaw Post Tribune*, Apr. 22, 1942. Cited in Roxanne Jayne and Susan Sachs, *Southern White Migration to the North: From Willow Run to Today.* University of Michigan, American Studies class 498, Apr. 25, 1973

The Ford Motor Company put $90 million of taxpayers' money into a plant that would concentrate 42,000 men and women six days a week in the middle of an ex-soybean field 3 miles away from a little town of 12,000, already "full up" and 27 miles from the nearest adequate shopping center.
Carr and Stermer, *Willow Run*, p. 319

So Willow Run began as an industrial plant without an infrastructure. The newcomers had to fend for themselves. Some workers were commuters – driving up to three hours from Detroit and elsewhere – but the plant drew workers from all 48 states in the United States, as well as Canada, Hawaii, Puerto Rico, and Latin America, and these workers needed to live nearby. Ypsilanti, population 12,000, was far too small to provide either the workers, or the accommodation, for a plant designed to employ 100,000. Workers shared beds in local rooming houses, sleeping in shifts. Others lived in tents, tar paper shanties, and trailers along Michigan Avenue. Some even lived in ex-chicken coops and basements. Lots sold for over $100 that had cost $5.00 before the boom.

As Carr and Stermer pointed out, "everything threw the major burdens of the bomber upheaval squarely on the shoulders of the men and women needed so desperately to get the bombers rolling." They concluded that "the industrial culture still has to come to terms with its own dynamism. . . . We have not yet learned how to live with social change."[8]

It took a full year before any accommodation was provided near the plant. In February 1943, the first of 15 dormitories, providing 1,900 rooms for 3,000 to 4,500 single men and women, opened in the area called "Willow Lodge." By that time the plant already employed some 36,000 men and women. A service center was added a year later; until then, the nearest store was three miles away. In March, a trailer camp with communal laundry, toilet, and shower facilities for 960 trailers was opened at "Willow Court" (north of Holmes Road and south of Foster Road).

"Willow Village" opened in July 1943, on land purchased in Superior and Ypsilanti Townships. Costing $20 million, it contained prefabricated housing for 2,500 families: "flat-top" buildings containing 4, 6, or 8 apartments, each with 1, 2, or 3 bedrooms, or even "zero bedroom" apartments that could house a couple without children. By the end of 1943 two other areas of housing were added: West Court and West Lodge, to make six different temporary projects: two with dormitories, one trailer park, a site for private trailers, and two with apartments, housing in all 15,000 people – more than the population of Ypsilanti. Willow Run had indeed become "a big little town out in the country."[9]

Apartments in the Village rented for $32 to $37 per month. Walls were made, literally, of paper. The apartments had iceboxes, coal stoves, and showers, but no bathtubs. The flat-tops were all so similar that even residents got lost. The northern portion of the Village was built first, at a time when planners were skimping on sewer and water connections, and when whites failed to fill these homes, this part of the Village was, in the words of Carr and Stermer, "turned over to Negro occupancy."[10] Rooms at Willow Lodge rented for $5.00 per week, while in Willow Court, the trailer project for childless couples, an apartment cost $6.50 a week.

Two small shopping centers were built, then a laundry, fire and police departments, a motion picture theater with 1,200 seats, and community buildings with cafeteria, barbershop, beauty shop, gym, and post office. Churches were built and Catholics, Protestants, and Jews cooperated in services at Willow Lodge. A full-fledged community had appeared in a matter of months.

> The typical newcomer . . . in 1942 was white, married, in his late twenties or early thirties, with one or two children. His educational background included a year of high school, his wife's about a year more. He was not a floater or a transient. Usually he had given up a good job or a small business back home in order to work at the Run. Not infrequently he still owned a home back where he had come from.
>
> Carr and Stermer, *Willow Run*, p. 41

The members of this community had generally come from small towns and were younger than the local population. Their educational backgrounds were average; their social class ranged from "lower-lower to upper middle-class." A few were African American, but most of the blacks who had moved to the area worked and lived in Detroit. To begin with, half the immigrants came from Michigan. Later on, in 1943 and 1944, as Ford recruited in the Southern Hills, half the new arrivals were from Kentucky, Tennessee, Alabama, and Mississippi.

These Appalachian migrants came from a social structure of extended families, kinship networks, where family loyalty and caring for kin were strong values. Typically warm and hospitable, they valued economic independence, rejecting welfare and holding the individual responsible for poverty. Rather than compete with neighbors for status, achievement, and advancement, they sought to blend with their community. Women were expected to settle down rather than finding a career; the men were to be the breadwinners. Family ties were often maintained during the journey north, and cultural islands were established, as people moved to join relatives who had already found work. Ypsilanti quickly became known as "Ypsitucky" – the city still celebrates Kentucky Day.[11]

The old residents were dismayed at the destruction of their familiar neighborhoods, worried about threats to their health from contaminated water, garbage, and overcrowding, concerned about the changing character of their community, and protective of their children. Most spoke of "the Southern riffraff," the "hillbillies" who were invading. They felt surrounded by strangers, by "foreigners," "undesirables." Some found the newcomers friendly and polite when approached; others felt they took advantage and were "the scum of the earth." Even the efforts of the churches in Willow Run seemed primarily missionary; the newcomers were treated as illiterate, neglected, and impoverished.[12]

> "We're law-abiding people and mind our own business. I wish our neighbors would do the same. There is one family on Harris Road that has no control over its children – three girls and two boys from 7 to 14. Those children threw rocks into our yard last summer, and my husband broke his lawn mower on them. Then they threw green apples into our garden, broke the tomato plants, and ruined the crop. They are regular little vandals, always destroying something. The neighbors have called the police a few times, but it hasn't done any good."
>
> Carr and Stermer, *Willow Run*, p. 241

In reality, the newcomers' poor and off-putting living conditions were misleading; they were the result not of lifestyle or taste but the lack of foresight and planning by officials in charge of housing and the obstructionism of the residents. Old-timers' perceptions notwithstanding, records show a striking absence of crime, delinquency, violence. Indeed, local businesses boomed. But the locals saw moral menace in the new arrivals. At the same time, the old-timers did not see the situation as one of crisis or emergency, as they would a tornado or earthquake. *They* had housing; this fuss would surely all blow over before long.

> Willow Run was, in fact, a sort of moral schizoid: Socially it forced thousands of middle- and upper lower-class people to live under the deprivations of slum and near-slum conditions; economically, however, it produced a boom area without a boom town's embellishments of organized vice and proliferating liquor joints.
>
> Carr and Stermer, *Willow Run*, p. 242

The Village was its own world. People lived in close proximity, all linked in some way to the bomber plant, sharing communal facilities and common recreation, making do with very little. This, coupled with the family networks and kinship values of the southerners, fostered practices of sharing, helping out, and making do. People from the Village clung together when they went out for travel or entertainment, because Ypsilanti was unfriendly, and "Ann Arbor had mixed feelings about us. We were a different group, not accepted in society."[13] Thrown together, rejected and derided by old-timers, the newcomers became close friends. An ethos of sharing, equality, and mutual assistance grew.

Most of all, villagers put up with the scorn of city residents, and the division created then lingers on today, in city-township politics. "They looked at us like we were poor, white trash, and called us that," said Vivian Stumbo, who came from Kentucky to Michigan when she was 17. "We went to town often, but they didn't like us down there. They liked our money. They wanted us to come and spend our money, then get out of town."

Jim Kise, "A Timeless Bond Called the Village,"
Ypsilanti Press Special Supplement, Aug. 14, 1991, p. 9

"The old village was very, very large and almost exclusively – all the people who lived there had come up from the South," said [Jim] Roberts [born in a three-bedroom unit in Willow Village, one of seven siblings]. "It was very difficult to live there as a kid because there were 10,000 of you. We were the classic war babies. . . ."

"People there had a different way of living," he said. "And nobody looked down on anybody because nobody had anything to look down on anybody for."

"All the kids were together," he said. "There was none of this keeping up with Joneses because everybody had the same thing."

Jo Collins Mathis, "I Thought Everyone . . . Grew Up in the Village,"
Ypsilanti Press Special Supplement, Aug. 14, 1991, pp. 31, 33

It didn't take much to talk Hazel Roberts [Jim's mother] into leaving Kentucky to work at the Willow Run Bomber Plant back in 1942. But nothing could make her leave Ypsilanti when the [bomber] plant closed down.

"I love it here," said Roberts, an animated, personable woman who talks with a Southern drawl. "This is home."

For Roberts, 75, life in Weeksbury, Ky. had been rough prior to September 1942.

She was tired of living in mining towns, for one thing. Then one day her husband disappeared, leaving her with two children, the oldest of whom was two years and two days old. Forced to find a job to support her children, the best she could come up with was a 12-hour-a-day job for $15 a week at a variety store. It wasn't enough. . . .

When she learned she could make several times what she was earning in the variety store, Roberts left her children with her parents and got on a train bound for Detroit with her brother, standing all the way.

Getting a job at the plant was a cinch.

"All you had to do was just show up – unless you couldn't pass the physical," she said. "At that time, it was considered big money. When I got the job, the first thing I asked the foreman was how long did I have to work before I got a leave of absence.

"He said, 'Well, you just got started. What do you want with a leave of absence?' I said, 'I have two children I want to bring up here.' I was sending money home to my dad and as well as I can remember, I was sending $50 home every week. It was a big thing to know that you could save some money: I had never been able to do that."

Roberts said some of the local residents were prejudiced against Southerners.

"They called us hillbillies and still do," she said. "But I laughed at it. I didn't have that much of a problem with the people when I came up here.

"I've always been a person who never sees a stranger and I think nothing of walking up and starting a conversation with somebody I never saw before," she said. "Sometimes they'd stand back and look at me, but very soon I made friends and got acquainted. I didn't have much of a problem, but I did see people who did."

She said that while some of the Northerners resented the Southerners, the feeling was sometimes mutual.

"Some of the people from the South had the same feelings about the people from the North," she said. "As well as the northern people calling us hillbillies, the southern people call them, 'those NORTHERNERS!' They'd walk in a store and expect to find the same things in stores down South, which they didn't have up here because people didn't eat like we did."

Jo Collins Mathis, "Family Recalls Living in the Village,"
Ypsilanti Press Special Supplement, Aug. 14, 1991, pp. 30–31

The schools gradually adapted to the special needs of this new community. A single school served the Willow Run area until the bomber plant arrived – Spencer School, a single-room log cabin built in 1834. In 1932, when Michigan Avenue was enlarged, the district replaced it with a two-room brick structure with a basement. Carr and Stermer note that, "For a rural district, Spencer ranked as progressive: On the eve of the bomber boom its school was a modern demonstration unit cooperating with Michigan State Normal College in Ypsilanti" – now Eastern Michigan University – "in the training of rural teachers."[14]

In the slow suburbanization before the plant, new pupils arrived at a rate of about 10 a year; enrollment grew from 40 in June 1936 to 78 in June 1940. Then, children of the workers who arrived to build the bomber plant swelled enrollment at Spencer. The basement was converted to teaching but the district made no other plans; the school board's view was that the workers would soon be leaving.

When it became obvious that Spencer was too small some felt that it was the government's responsibility to pay for expansion, others that it was Ford's. Issuing bonds would place the burden on local real estate owners, and none of the newcomers – mostly "trailerites" at this point – fell into that category. A minimalist plan was adopted: to extend the existing building with four rooms and a principal's office. The federal government would pay three-quarters of the cost. Such a building would house 30 teachers and handle 210 children; after sixth grade, students would be sent to high school in Ypsilanti.

The school reopened in September 1942 with 300 students, and it had 410 by December. In spring 1943 the federal government proposed that the Willow Run area either consolidate with Ypsilanti's school district or create its own. Residents of the Spencer District voted against the former option, and on July 22, 1943, School District #1, Fractional, Ypsilanti Township, Willow Run, Michigan was created. The term "fractional" referred to the fact that the new school district lay in both Ypsilanti and Superior Townships. The first superintendent of schools was appointed in July 1943, and three new schools (Ross, Foster, and Simmonds) were opened by November. Spencer School was included in the new school system, to the consternation of the original residents.

> Just as Henry Ford started from scratch to build one of the world's largest bomber factories, educators in Willow Run started from scratch to build a school system big enough to handle the dramatic influx of employee's children.
> Mark Hugger, "Willow Run Schools Still Thrive,"
> *Ypsilanti Press Special Supplement*, Aug. 14, 1991, p. 11

The new school buildings were of temporary construction, like the rest of the Village, though they were well engineered. State financial aid was based on the 335 pupils registered in the district in May 1943; although by January 1945 enrollment had reached 1,854, the aid was not augmented. The schools faced shortages of such basics as books, chalk, and chalkboards. In addition, student attendance was irregular and turnover was astronomical.

The district employed 54 teachers from kindergarten to eighth grade, plus 6 nursery-school teachers. Many of these teachers were older, married women, long established in the community. Robert

Stevenson describes their charges as lonely, strangers to one another, well-behaved, and polite. "These were kids that needed an opportunity, and we gave it to them. A lot of our students went on to get good educations and took very responsible roles in the community."[15]

Stevenson now lives close to Willow Run, having retired from his work in charge of schooling for children of the military in Europe and in the Far East. Talking with him in his living room I feel I'm moving deeper into the circuits of human connection that span space and time in this community.

Stevenson began his teaching career at age 18 in a rural school in upstate Michigan, during the Depression. When he came to Willow Run he'd already had 10 years of teaching experience, though he was only 28 years old. He began as an eighth-grade teacher in the new Foster School, then became principal and later assistant superintendent. "Of course what was unusual about Willow Run was the fact that one year you have three hundred kids, the next year you have over two thousand. The problem was mostly keeping the students feeling a little bit secure; there was a lot of anxiety. We were very fortunate, we had many teachers . . . [who] came back into teaching that had raised families.[16]

"The teaching staff could have raised a lot of complaints, I suppose, about the way that they were given children that weren't up to grade level. But they were more inclined to accept the kids as they were. And they needed that, because they were uprooted. Some of them were not only uprooted but they were kind of homesick.

"What I found, working as a principal and living in the community, was that for a lot of the people that came in, that had moved around, they had experienced things that they wanted more of, rather than going back. The parents that I was acquainted with really fell into two classes. One was 'We're here, and we're making good money,' better than they ever had anticipated. Their goal was to go back and buy a piece of property, wherever they came from. There was others that could see that there was more opportunity for their *children* if they didn't go back. Here they were near a university, there was Cleary College, and a lot of these children or students were capable. I kind of admire some of these families that stayed so their children could have better education. And they did. When I was superintendent one of my students was on the board of education. Or I'd go into a bank and one of the vice presidents would be. . . . They contributed. I think that was the distinction, the people that could see opportunity, and the people that had goals like go back and buy another five acres or do something.

"There was a lot of homesick people, particularly if their kinfolks weren't up here. But in many cases, one family would come up and then another family would come up and the first thing you know, they had brothers and others and they felt more established and they stayed. Though a lot of them went back as quickly as they could, as their jobs disappeared. The other thing was that they were making money that they'd never expected to have, but there was no way of spending money – you couldn't buy anything. I mean, you could buy food, if you had the ration points and all that, but it wasn't the case you'd go out and buy a car. You couldn't buy a car. There was money, that some of 'em spent I suppose the way they felt – but a lot of it, they couldn't invest it in things. 'Cause there wasn't things." He chuckles. "But some of them tried, they spent money on their children. Some would come to school with jewelry that you normally wouldn't see. And the merchants in Ypsilanti had a heyday!" He laughs again. "They could sell *anything*, because there was a lot of people and money and not much to buy."

Output at the Willow Run plant rose to 31 planes in January 1943, to 190 in June, 365 in December, and in March 1944 a bomber rolled off the line once an hour (actually every 63 minutes; 453 aircraft in 468 working hours). Consolidated Aircraft had produced only 1 plane a day under optimal conditions. Furthermore, the price of a delivered bomber dropped from $238,000 in 1942 to $137,000 in 1944. In August 1943, the U.S. Treasury awarded Bull's Eye flags to plant workers: more than 90 percent were granting a 10 percent payroll deduction for war bonds and stamps. Total production of 8,685 planes was completed on June 28, 1945: 44 months of continuous production. The last plane was named after Henry Ford, but he made it known that he wanted it named instead after the workers who had built it, so they erased Ford's name and autographed the bomber's nose.

By spring 1945 the workforce at the plant had dropped from its peak of 42,000 to 16,000. A thousand families moved from the Village in June 1945, and many of them moved back to the South. Half the students in the Willow Run schools left before the end of the school year. The people remaining were moved into apartments in the central Village; by December fewer than 600 families remained: the boomtown had become a ghost town.

But in January 1946 Willow Run received fresh life. Redesignated "Temporary Veterans Housing," the Village became home for returning veterans, especially those attending college under the G.I. Bill. Over a thousand of the apartments in Willow Village were assigned to veterans who were now students at the University of Michigan, about 10 miles away. Single students were housed in the West Lodge dormitories.

At the end of the war in Europe, May 1945, only 1,406 pupils were enrolled in the district, compared with over 2,000 during the heyday of the bomber factory. But as Willow Village was opened to veterans and their families enrollment increased immediately and reached 3,833 in May 1955. Additional facilities were again needed. In September 1947, Ross School was converted to a junior high, and five years later, in the fall of 1952, Edmonson Junior High opened. In the fall of 1955, Willow Run High School opened. Students no longer needed to transfer to Ypsilanti to complete their education.

Ford announced they had no postwar plans for the facility. Why the decision was made not to continue airplane production is unclear and the subject of some speculation, but the newly formed Kaiser-Frazer automobile company leased the Willow Run plant from the government and then in 1946 purchased it. The news that Henry Kaiser, aluminum magnate, and Joseph Frazer would be building automobiles brought tremendous excitement, both locally and nationally. The "partnership of two industrial Jasons bringing forth automobiles representative of their stature appealed strongly to the public."[17] Willow Run Airport was sold for one dollar to the University of Michigan, which converted it for passenger use; it became the main airport for Detroit. The University later sold it to Wayne County, which still operates it as a commercial facility.

News that the Kaiser and Frazer cars were to be built in the huge Willow Run plant magnified prospects of a new boom for automobiles. The first stock issue of 1,700,000 shares at $10 was over-subscribed six times. A second stock issue of 1,800,000 was placed on sale at $20.25 per share and it, too, was over-subscribed. The public had raised $53,450,000 in cash to put the Kaiser-Frazer cars on the market and placed thousands of orders for them without knowing the sales price or having seen them.

Nothing like this had ever happened before. No automobile business had ever been started with such a quick sale of its stock, and only the proverbial optimism of America for assurance. When the first new cars were finally shown at the Waldorf-Astoria Hotel in New York, a crowd lined up outside two abreast for seven hours in a blizzard to see them.

Anderson, *The Story of the American Automobile*, p. 294

Kaiser-Frazer contributed to the development of the district by constructing hundreds of single-family houses at West Willow, close to the facility, by fall of 1946. Veterans working for Kaiser-Frazer rented housing in the Village. And the company had good relations with their workers: the UAW announced a one-year pact with Kaiser-Frazer at the same time, January 1946, they were on strike against other producers, including the Big Three.

> There is a state law making it mandatory that any person, to be eligible for election to a school board in Michigan, must own property. This meant that, in 1948, the members of the school board were all property owners living in that section of the school district which is outside the Village, even though over 75 per cent of the children registered in the Willow Run Public Schools were residents of the Village. The Resident Council did not think it fair that the Village was not represented on the school board, so the council organized a group of interested residents into a "Better Schools Committee." . . . What the Better Schools Committee did to get fair representation on the school board makes one realize that a great many things are possible under existing laws, if a study is made to find the way.
>
> Wilson, *The Story of Willow Run*, pp. 115–116, 119

Kaiser-Frazer produced almost 150,000 automobiles in 1947, at prices around $2,500, and built cargo planes under contract to the Air Force during the Korean War but, with the Big Three mounting stiff opposition, the company had only two profitable years. After consistently losing money, they closed the Willow Run plant in 1953 – and some people thought this would be the end of Willow Run. But General Motors' transmission plant in the Detroit suburb of Livonia had been destroyed by fire, and GM bought the facility for $26 million to convert it to production of the Hydra-matic automatic transmission. Once again Willow Run was the site of dramatic activity: "In just 12 weeks, the company rebuilt the entire assembly line and installed it at Willow Run."[18]

Production of transmissions continues in the old Willow Run bomber plant to this day. General Motors has operated the Willow Run facility continuously since 1953 and, in doing so, has contributed to the creation of a new middle class of well-paid industrial workers. Michigan auto workers have been the highest paid industrial workers in the country.

> "If you wanted a good job those days, you went to the factory. In the early 60s, it was booming. Young kids could come out of school and get a good job and move out of the home and pursue the American dream." – Jerry Clifton, UAW Local bargaining chairman.
>
> Russell Grantham, "Union Leader Battles Odds: UAW Local Chairman Keeps Up Morale, Seeks Role for Plant," *Ann Arbor News*, May 13, 1992, C1, C6

> Robin dropped out of Willow Run High School and began working at the
> plant in 1978, when she was 18. It was a time when a job in the auto industry
> represented good pay without the need for a high school diploma.
>
> Owen Eshenroder, "Waiting in a Shadow: Sleep's Not Easy as Couple
> Ponders Life Beyond Willow Run," *Ann Arbor News*, May 11, 1992, C1, C4

In 1954 the Ypsilanti Township Board took action to acquire Willow
Village from the U.S. government. The housing had been built to last
only 5 years and now, 10 years later, the government ordered it evacu-
ated and torn down. To prevent eviction of the 2,500 resident families,
the township bought 537 acres of land containing 3,003 housing units,
plus 139 acres of vacant land, for $325,000, with options on another 965
acres and the business district, agreeing to demolish the temporary
structures when they were no longer needed. Superior Township agreed
to waive rights on the portion of the land on its side of the township
line. Private redevelopment began, and throughout the next several
years the temporary buildings were demolished. Willow Village was
torn down in 1957 – in its place is the Green Oaks Golf Course – but
new subdivisions built in the late fifties provided replacement housing.
The "Village people" stayed around after the war and shaped a township
political structure that still often resists having anything to do with the
city of Ypsilanti. When the township asked to be annexed to the city the
request was at first rejected, and this humiliation, 30 years ago, still
stings in Willow Run.

The memory of the bomber plant, too, is still alive in the Willow Run
schools and in the community at large. Every year, in August, Ypsilanti
holds its Heritage Festival, and the *Ypsilanti Press* publishes a special pull-
out featuring the festival. In 1991, on the fiftieth anniversary of the
United States' entry into World War II (and before any hint of the plant
closing), the special focused on "the war and the bomber plant." "Much
of what Ypsilanti is today is tied directly to the industry spawned during
World War II, including the Willow Run bomber plant and the people
who came to town to work there." This is "the bomber Ypsilanti built."[19]

And the Yankee Air Force Museum, housed in the one remaining
hanger from those the Army Air Force built at Willow Run, is searching
for a B-24 to "bring home" and add to their collection. Of the 18,000 B-
24s built only about 11 remain, and of these only 3 still fly. Many of the
rest were recycled: as the *Ypsilanti Press* pointed out, one bomber contained enough aluminum to make 55,000 coffee percolators. In August
1995, the Museum celebrated the bomber's fiftieth anniversary. Workers

in the plant and crew of the aircraft were invited to the reunion; guided tours of the museum during the day were followed by a buffet dinner and dance – $100 a head – with celebrity speakers, and music by the Glenn Miller Orchestra. Actor Jimmy Stewart, a B-24 pilot during the war, sent his regrets at being unable to attend due to poor health; a letter describing some of his war experiences was read at the dinner.

Even at the General Motors Hydra-matic plant, newcomers and visitors are shown a video that recounts the wartime history of the Willow Run facility and told of "our" history, though it was Ford that operated the plant then. And mementos can be found throughout the Willow Run Community Schools. A framed print of the B-24 bomber is one of the souvenirs retirees may choose, laid out in a glass-fronted display case at the entry to the school district administration building – old Spencer School. The same print – a blueprint of the entire plane, showing the details of its structure – hangs at the end of the building's main corridor. A reproduction of the map of Willow Village from Wilson's book is casually propped up on a filing cabinet in a meeting room. The cover of the high school's student handbook shows the B-24 blueprint again. The high school's football team is the Bombers, and the Flyers are the basketball team.

The people of Willow Run are proud, independent, and hardworking. The kind of work many of them have been engaged in for years now at the Willow Run plant – hands-on, manual labor, often difficult, even grueling – is not just what they *do*, it defines who they *are*. The loss of these jobs – the threatened loss of this *kind* of work – leaves them betrayed, abandoned, confused, and torn. It cuts to the center of their identity, and it stabs at the heart of their community. For surely, Willow Run *is* the plant?

The danger is that the material rewards for this kind of work can make one forget one's roots. In early December I pile the students from one of my courses into a university minivan for a tour of the GM plant. The plant is no longer simply "Hydra-matic" – in 1990 GM merged its transmission and engine divisions into "Powertrain": the coordinated power-generating and delivery system of an auto. The entire division has 60,000 employees in 26 factories – 5,500 hourly and 1,000 salaried employees work at Willow Run.

The GM Powertrain operation apparently fills the entire building – all 110 football fields worth. The scale is breathtaking. We can't see the far wall of the building; workers peddling by on tricycles vanish into the distance. Basic features of the bomber plant still exist: underfoot are the original wood block floors, and hanging overhead are thousands upon thousands of fluorescent light fixtures, now lacking their tubes. The plant is filled with a rich, nauseating oily smell, not overpowering but ubiquitous, and with vibrations from the 4,000-pound press, rhythmically stamping out components for torque converters. Perched high atop a machine is a Christmas tree made of steel wool, with a Styrofoam-cup angel sitting on the top.

Dick Gibson, a business manager in charge of production of the 4T40, is our tour guide. He shows us two assembly lines and some of their associated component manufacturing sites. The 3T40, the oldest transmission GM sells, has been in production since 1979. The first digit indicates the number of speeds; T means "transverse" (L would mean "longitudinal," that is, rear-wheel drive); and the second figure is the r.p.m. in thousands. In 1996 the 3T40 is "going out of business" though there may still be some third world demand for it. The new 4T40 is going into production sometime next year, and its manufacturing locations, many sporting computer displays, are being set up.

The assembly work is stressful: there's the physical strain of the work and absenteeism because of problems at home; some workers are on edge when they get to work. There are three shifts at the plant, and people are working six or seven days a week. Some parts are made at a rate of 8,800 per day, because of the "excess need for cars" – "everyone's buying," says Dick. Right now one of the lines is down and Dick needs to get the grinder back on line. It processes 8,000 parts a day and he has two day's worth to put through it. Having a three-day stockpile of parts reduced the pressure; now the float is only hours. When you have one hour to get a machine working that provides a key component for the line, "that's called stress." Weekends he's often up at 4:30 A.M. to go to work. "My wife works for GM too – she just doesn't know it!" He's 49, looking much older.

Dick arrived at Willow Run in 1979, after Frigidaire, a GM subsidiary, was sold. His parents had worked, and met, at the Frigidaire plant. He had gone to college on an athletic scholarship but dropped out ("probably the best thing that happened to me"), enrolled in the military before he could be drafted, and went to Vietnam. On his return he finished college and went to work at Frigidaire. He worked on the line but had been steadily promoted until he transferred to GM to work on production of the 3T40.

Dick describes the "old view" of production, focused on quantity not quality, with "breakdown maintenance" rather than "planned maintenance" and an attitude that could be summarized as "when the boss says do, you do," rather than permitting judgments about the needs of the job. "We recognize the input of people now," he says. "I listen to my people: that's the key. The Japanese haven't nothing on us. We've got the brain power; we know how to do it. We just forgot where we came from."

There is an arc and poetry to his rhetoric, as he presents a single moral message in several ways. Success provides a false sense of security and expectation, and a forgetfulness of what has made that success possible. Like the Buffalo Bills – who are doing extremely badly this year after winning the pennant last year – when you become accustomed to winning you can lapse and fall behind. "We have to wake up. 'Ye in front place, remember where you came from, you may get back there.' "

When he worked at Frigidaire they manufactured a refrigerator every 15 seconds, with a 15-second interval on the line, and he worked in "the pit," but when people spoke of the "blue-collar blues" he thought that was "bullshit – pardon my French." People working on the line in his day had wanted something better for their kids, had viewed success as going to college, so that to end up where mom and dad had worked was considered failure. Those attitudes and expectations, though well intended, had turned young people away from work at plants like Willow Run. "The job is hard enough, but it's not very hard. We get well paid," he tells us. Many line workers now are people with college degrees, even teachers who quit because the work here pays better – $45,000 a year, up to $60,000 or $70,000 with overtime.

GM is now "engineering-poor," trying to recruit engineers but unable to find enough. Salaried workers, says Dick, should be "adaptable." The company hires college people "but they need perspective on the floor" – decisions like whether to reduce the number of bodies from 20 to 10 call for practical experience. Hourly workers now need at least high school, and soon a college degree will be required. Dick says, somewhat sheepishly, "we still go for GPA." They no longer rise from the line to become salaried employees. Ninety-nine percent of salaried employees need a college education: there are "not many like me left."

And on the new 4T40, workers will be staffing machine centers for four transfer lines, feeding parts on a just-in-time basis to the assembly line. The team will be responsible for both training in the new production and assembly methods *and* maintaining the current production schedule. They must continue to make a quality product and engage in teaching and learning. "We need to plan that," Dick notes. William Edwards Deming's ideas are behind these changes. Dick adds that although

Deming was very smart, "he puts you to sleep" in his workshops. "But read his book," he advises.

"But what he says is common sense." We need to get "back to basics. We forgot what our roots were." Japanese industry is going to experience its own "industrial revolution," he insists, using the term to signify something like a workers' revolt. The United States lost its way but now is finding its feet.

7   Crossing to the New Economy

November 1993–April 1994

Top executives from major Michigan companies and business groups did some heavyweight lobbying Wednesday for Gov. John Engler's school plan.

They said their message for lawmakers was simple: The state's education system is broken and needs dramatic repairs to boost its quality.

And they promised to back a tax package if lawmakers take bold quality steps and contain costs. . . .

John Lobbia, the president, chairman, and chief executive officer of the Detroit Edison Co., said he'd be willing to put back every dollar now in the school system if it was totally rebuilt to focus on quality.

"Unfortunately, I don't think that's going to happen," he said. . . .

Alfred Glancy, chairman of Detroit Renaissance and the chairman, president, and CEO of MCN Corp., said the problem was easy to describe.

"The system is not delivering for the state of Michigan," he said. "We need structural reform, not just nice words. We must have education reform in this state.

"This is a golden opportunity and we must seize it and take advantage of it for the betterment of the state and all its residents. . . ."

The executives said their companies find today's high school graduates lack the basic math and reading skills needed for entry-level jobs. Lobbia said Detroit Edison once had to look at only three applicants to find someone qualified to become an apprenticeship lineman, but now has to check 10. He added that it's a national problem and causing the United States to lose ground in world economic competition. "Even our best schools don't compare with the top 50 percent in other countries."

Much of the debate over the North American Free Trade Agreement focuses on the possible loss of American jobs, but unless the nation improves its schools "we're not going to have to worry about NAFTAs because we won't be able to compete," he said.

Associated Press, "Business Pushes for Education Quality," *Ypsilanti Press*, Nov. 11, 1993, 5A

134

Willow Run Community Schools Superintendent Youssef Yomtoob is not sitting by quietly as Gov. John Engler and the Legislature determine how the state's 563 public school districts will be financed in the 1994–95 school year.

Yomtoob has spent at least one day a week in Lansing talking with legislators and plans to continue his weekly visits as long as his schedule allows it.

"I feel guilty either way," Yomtoob told the Board of Education Thursday. "I have work to do here but if I'm not there they don't know what we think."

Juanita C. Smith, "Anticipation: Willow Run's Yomtoob Leery of State Finance Reform," *Ypsilanti Press*, Nov. 5, 1993, 5A

Michiganders wake on Christmas morning to headlines announcing the final legislative votes approving the school finance and quality bills. The House cast its last vote midday Christmas eve, the Senate a few hours later, after deliberations lasting over 24 hours. Engler declares his pride that they have "assured funding for schools and locked in quality reform." The school aid bill approves a $10.2 billion spending package. Through November and December the Michigan House and Senate had continued to develop legislation that would fundamentally alter the operation of the state's public schools. A bipartisan "backup" school finance plan – the Statutory Plan – was unveiled on November 19. It will go into effect if Engler's Ballot Plan – Proposal A – fails. Proposal A would fund Michigan's public schools mainly by raising the state sales tax, while the Statutory Plan would increase income tax.[1] The measure to have a public vote to decide between Proposal A and the Statutory Plan met difficulties, but "the governor made a lot of calls and played Santa Claus," according to the senate minority leader. And "like Santa Claus, we're watching who's naughty or nice."[2]

"I'm very proud of the Legislature. It's been a long arduous process," said [Gov. John Engler.] "What we've done today is historic. We've assured funding for schools and locked in quality reform."

Associated Press, "Lawmakers Pass Plan for Schools," *Ypsilanti Press*, Dec. 25, 1993, 1A

One Willow Run teacher tells me that what "scares the living daylights" out of her about the property tax changes is that "we've lost local control of our schools! We're gonna do what the state says we have to do to get the money. 'Cause *they're* gonna collect the money. And we're not going to see it – the power goes with the money." She fears some reformers are lying, saying they want to reform public schools when they're actually keen to privatize education, so only an affluent elite will attend the better schools.

Most attention is on the finance reform plans, but the school quality reform measures – the school code bill – are the real meat. Public Acts 335, 336, and 339 make important changes to Public Act 25, the "Quality Package" of 1990. A state "academic core curriculum" will be established – schools must adopt by September 1997 specific course work in math, science, social sciences, and communication arts. Ypsilanti representative Democrat Kirk Profit describes this as "equity in the academic curriculum," providing equality of educational opportunity. But Republicans feel it will prove costly and reduce local flexibility and innovation.[3] PA 25's model core curriculum had not been mandated, partly because the Michigan constitution requires the state to provide the funds for any mandates imposed on local government. The new core curriculum has been narrowed, reportedly in response to concerns of business and industry, who saw the model core as unfocused, and of conservative religious groups who perceived values education.

The core curriculum can include no discussion of attitudes, beliefs, or value systems "not essential in the legal, economic and social structure of our society and to the personal and social responsibility of citizens of our society." Schools must, however, teach sexual abstinence.

The number of hours of classroom instruction will rise from 900 to 1080 per year by the year 2000, with districts choosing whether to do this by extending the school day or the school year (though districts are advised to adopt a school year of 210 days). Fourth- and seventh-grade students will be given special tutoring if they cannot read at their grade level, and graduation to junior high will be prevented until students read at the sixth-grade level (special education students, children with learning disabilities, and foreign-born students are exempted).

Both charter schools – "Public School Academies" – and a "schools of choice" program, which would permit districts to accept students living outside their boundaries, are voted in. Democrats accepted a charter school proposal apparently believing that Engler had relinquished the possibility of schools of choice. Engler declared he had not.[4] But he says the charter schools bill alone is more important than the rest of the bills on school quality. "It is central to what we are trying to do." Suburban districts have opposed it, afraid they'll be forced to take less affluent students.[5]

Gov. John Engler heaped praise on house Democratic and Republican leaders for gathering votes for what he calls the most extensive charter school plan in the United States. The House voted 65–34 Monday night, rushing through a key element of a school quality package aimed at overhauling Michigan's education system. Forty-five Republicans and 16 Democrats favored the bill.

The bill would allow the creation of alternative charter schools supported by public funds. Charter schools could be formed by certified teachers, school districts, community colleges or public universities.

"What we have done today is provide for some excellent opportunities, not previously available in this area," said state Rep. Kirk Profit, D-Ypsilanti Township. "We've done it all within the public school context. We have expressly prohibited mixing church and state. We've taken some assets in this area, and given them special opportunities to provide for our children, opportunities we haven't had because of the lack of property wealth in this area."

"These reforms give Michigan the most extensive, expansive charter school bill in the country," Engler said. "The Michigan House took a major step forward in our effort to put a world-class education within the reach of every child. It means more choices and more options for Michigan's students, parents and teachers."

Under the charter school concept, a public school could be converted to a charter school if it were supported by 75 percent of the teachers and 75 percent of parents of pupils enrolled in the building.

The Coalition for Better Schools, a group of business and education advocates, said the House vote could open the doors for change in schools.

"I see enormous possibilities for creativity," said coalition member Katherine DeGrow, co-president of the Michigan Board of Education. "Imagine teachers organizing and operating the schools they've always wanted. That has to be an exciting professional opportunity. . . ."

Conservative Republicans failed repeatedly in attempts to amend the bill to allow entities other than teachers and schools to apply for charter school status. Republican William Bryant of Grosse Pointe Farms, a designer of the bipartisan school package, said teachers and educational institutions would be the best leaders of the alternative institutions.

"They are already in the business of education," Bryant said. "People trust that they will not go out of their way to develop a charter school that is inappropriate."

Associated Press, "House Approves Charter Schools," *Ypsilanti Press*, Nov. 30, 1993, 7A

"John Engler's approach is fundamentally hostile to public education. Michigan must not start down this slippery slope," [Howard Wolpe, a candidate for the 1994 Democratic nomination for governor] said.

"Nothing would be more damaging to public education than to divert desperately needed resources away from our neighborhood public schools into 'charter schools' for a privileged few."
Associated Press, "Wolpe Slams Engler Plan," *Ypsilanti Press*, Nov. 30, 1993, 7A

By 1997 there will be a new High School Proficiency Test (HSPT). In addition, high school students who pass the MEAP in math, reading, and science will receive a "state endorsed diploma" – with the warranty that any graduate who an employer finds academically deficient within two years of graduation will receive remedial instruction.

Another year is about to go into the history books, and it has been – to say the least – an eventful one.

At the international level, Russian President Boris Yeltsin continued his dramatic struggle to bring a free market democracy to his nation. He survived a standoff with a reactionary parliament, only to see a new threat rise in the growing power of a reactionary, nationalist demagogue.

At the national level, a new president took office, and immediately began to shake a few things up, and he has gone right on doing that through the rest of the year. President Clinton's first year has been a roller coaster ride of debate about issues and about him personally.

At the state level, the governor and the Legislature finally took dramatic steps to do something about the school property tax and school funding inequities in the state. They abolished property taxes for schools and then reinvented school finance. How that process finally winds up remains to be seen, since parts of what state lawmakers want to do will have to be approved by Michigan voters.

And in our own community, 1993 saw the end of the long struggle to keep the General Motors Willow Run Assembly Plant open. Sadly, the plant was closed, but if anything, its demise brought new resolve in the community to find new businesses and develop new partnerships to ensure our economic prosperity.
Editorial, "Happy New Year," *Ypsilanti Press*, Dec. 31, 1993, 6A

The weather in Michigan is never boring. January brings lows of 25 degrees below zero and wind chills of minus 55 degrees – colder than Siberia – followed by a spell of freezing mist and freezing rain that shuts schools, closes even ice rinks, and causes power-outages, crashed and stranded cars, frostbite, and a boost in sales of ice-fishing bait. In this year's State of the State address Engler speaks of historical changes achieved and of efforts to "strengthen the family of Michigan" by building a "strong foundation" upon "four cornerstones" – good jobs, great schools, safe neighborhoods, and a better quality of life. "Each of us here in this chamber, working alone, has the ability to climb mountains. There's no doubt about that. But working together, with all Michigan families, we can move mountains! AND WE WILL!" The state economy has rebounded, Engler declares. "Michigan is leading the national recovery" with the lowest unemployment rate in 15 years – 7 percent – and the reason, he asserts, is tax cuts.

"Tonight let me begin by saying thank you – thank you to the men and women of this legislature who have worked together to solve problems that have plagued Michigan for a generation – problems that some said could never be solved.

Together, we have faced no greater challenge and achieved no greater victory for Michigan families.

The skeptics said: 'Mission Impossible.' We said: 'Our kids deserve better!'

This evening, I applaud you: 'Congratulations on a job well done. . . .'

Thanks to your actions last year, Michigan children will benefit from historic reforms of our schools and the way we pay for them.

We invested in our kids with: The biggest improvement in equity in a generation. An additional $230 million for teaching at-risk children. And we nearly doubled spending for pre-school programs. These actions will help every kid move to the head of the class!

On the reform side, we made even greater strides:

An extra hour a day in school for every child. Tough, world-class performance standards. Cost containment through greater financial accountability, with more to come this year. Detailed information to parents through a building-by-building school report.

And greater local control. Let me repeat that: greater local control. Even though state government is paying a bigger share of the school bill, we're sending a bigger measure of control back to parents on the local level. Because I trust parents, not Washington or Lansing, to do what's best for children. School boards won't have to spend all their time being millage committees. Instead, I expect they will become quality committees, working with parents and teachers to make every school better. Because when we put quality first, our children will be the best!

But the most important breakthrough last year was the passage of the nation's most far-reaching charter school legislation. I thank each and every one of you who voted for this measure. . . . With charter schools, I predict nothing less than a renaissance of public education in Michigan. Charter schools will unlock the creativity and excitement for learning that is too often crushed by mountains of bureaucratic regulations and paperwork in our public schools.

By the end of the century, I believe Michigan schools will be the envy of the world."

Gov. John Engler, State of the State Address, Jan. 18, 1994[6]

Engler makes a strong appeal to voters to opt for Proposal A. "It is, quite frankly, a stark choice between setting Michigan back or moving Michigan forward." Failure to choose Proposal A, he warns, would be "a disaster" – property, income, and business taxes would rise again, as would unemployment.[7] The playing field on which Willow Run's strategies for reform are being enacted is tilting dramatically.

> "Classic Gov. Engler. His style is to paint a picture of a beast. If you don't vote for me, then the beast will get you." – State Rep. Kirk Profit, D-Ypsilanti.
> "Engler Pumps Sales Tax Hike," *Ann Arbor News*, Jan. 19, 1994, D4

The national economy is in flux too. Now the U.S. Commerce Department maintains the recession ended in 1991 and declares the economy, which limped in 1992 and 1993, will pick up this year. U.S. industrial production has apparently risen for five months in a row, the biggest jump in a year. But the labor market is still slack, and managers and professionals are being hired at a higher rate than blue-collar workers – though slower than in previous recoveries – probably because so many were squeezed out during the recession. In Robert Reich's interpretation, "Long-term demand is shifting in favor of people with greater skills."[8]

GM has "turned the corner." Nationwide sales jump 18.1 percent in the first quarter of the 1994 model year and a profit is predicted this year. Smith attributes the stronger financial situation to cost cutting, the company's revamping, and the strong yen.[9] GM is working to consolidate vehicle platforms, increase common parts, improve designs, and reduce capacity, and aims to equal Ford's 25 hours for vehicle assembly by 1996. A slew of new models is being introduced, and 2,000 engineers will be hired. The new UAW contract gives GM more flexibility shifting workers among plants, which will increase efficiency. Worker productivity has already jumped 12 percent.[10]

The debate over NAFTA continues. Proponents say jobs will be created in the long run, while opponents say manufacturing companies will move to Mexico to take advantage of cheap labor. Ross Perot describes a "big sucking sound."[11] Clinton has said a million jobs will be created, but many people believe he will not push NAFTA since he has been promoting side agreements on behalf of labor and environmentalists. Speaking in Detroit, Robert Reich says there is "a legitimate dispute" about the issue.[12] George Bush, also visiting Michigan to promote NAFTA, is more vivid. "We must not let the demagogues, the fear mongers, scare the workers of America that jobs will go South," he says. But Bush's views don't carry much clout around here.[13] To blue-collar workers NAFTA epitomizes their worst fears about the changing world economy.[14]

> If there is an emotional heart to the movement against the North American Free Trade Agreement, it may be here [Flint, Michigan], among the auto workers who fear that the agreement is one more devastating blow to a way of life.
> Robin Toner, "In Auto-Making Country, Trade Accord is the Enemy," *New York Times*, Sept. 14, 1993, A18

> "This debate comes down to one simple question: Whose side are you on?" declared [David Bonier, House whip], who represents a blue-collar district outside Detroit. "Are you on the side of the Fortune 500? Or are you on the side of the unfortunate 500,000 who will lose their jobs if NAFTA passes."
> David E. Rosenbaum, "Clinton Musters a Majority for Trade Pact in the House After a Long Hunt for Votes. Political Stakes High in Hard Day of Lobbying on 3-Nation Accord," *New York Times*, Nov. 18, 1993, A1, A14

The Ypsilanti Township Board of Trustees proposes a resolution of opposition to the bill. Supervisor Prater says he attributes the closing of Willow Run in part to the promise of NAFTA and other U.S. government-approved incentives for manufacturing to move to Mexico. "I think it will hurt us, and I think it has hurt us," Prater says. "Money does chase cheap labor."[15]

> Bill Clinton pressed on, growing more rather than less committed as the days passed. Abandoned by two of the three top Democratic leaders in the House, opposed by usually reliable Democrats in the trade unions and by some important leaders of minority groups and environmental organizations, he kept shoving more and more chips into the pot on an issue that few Americans really understood. . . .
> In political terms, it was the most important achievement of his Presidency.
> R. W. Apple Jr., "A High-Stakes Gamble That Paid Off," *New York Times*, Nov. 18, 1993, A1, A14

In a WRSI meeting in January the discussion starts with our visit to Holmes Elementary, before Scott brings it around to the state's new dictates on curriculum.

"So Holmes was traditional?" Vivian asks, told about the needs that staff had identified. They complained they did not feel "empowered" or "supported" by the administration.

Vivian is "totally blown away" by this, in part because this school had organized last year to prevent a staff member being cut. "I will have to go to them at some point and ask them, what is their definition of support? Because if it's not doing what we've been doing, then we need to know what it is. You know that's the kind of thing we have to keep going back and asking staffs for. I guess part of what we have to figure out is, what are the processes that staff use to communicate their need? How do they *identify* what they need?"

By this time most of you will have heard about WRSI, the Willow Run Systemic Initiative Committee. If you haven't, we are a group of Willow Run teachers and administrators (5), and University of Michigan faculty (2), who are working to assist the members of the Willow Run Community engage in conversations about the process of change in schools, and begin to find ways to initiate changes in classrooms, in schools, and in the district. Since August, when five committee members spent two and a half days at a workshop in Lansing, we have met every other week, talked with people at several of the schools in the district, made a presentation to the School Board, and planned for the formation of an advisory board of community members to help in the development of new directions for Willow Run Community Schools.

As we continue to look for ways to support change in Willow Run, we will be asking for help from all of you. The kind of systemic change we hope for cannot be dictated by a small committee, but must come from within; our job is to stimulate discussion, to encourage people to take chances, and to support everyone in their endeavors to find new ways to teach and to help students learn. We will be keeping you informed of our activities, and would like you to let us know what kinds of support you need as you continue the process of change.

Draft for WRSI newsletter, e-mail from Liza Finkel,
Nov. 22, 1993

Betty introduces as an example of this an ongoing discussion over science textbooks in the middle school. The sixth grade has relinquished textbooks to try a project-based curriculum. Seventh- and eighth-grade teachers are making changes too, but were still counting on new textbooks when school started in September. The district had promised modules but these weren't delivered on time; Vivian had thought, mistakenly, that old textbooks were still available.

"I think there's just so much uncertainty and that's what people are afraid of," Betty says.

"There's something else though," Scott adds. "They assume that 'no textbook' means *nothing*."

Betty agrees: "Right, nothing. No supplies, nothing."

Scott explains. "No supplies, not a reference text, not a classroom set for reference material, no books that we can check out to students who need to do something at home. They're thinking, take all the textbooks, throw them in the garbage can, and you start from scratch. Their image, where the textbook doesn't *drive* the curriculum, is throw the textbook in the garbage can and you have nothing in the classroom to start with."

Liza agrees. "The textbook *was* the curriculum before. We need to help people see what to do, or what would be different if they continue to use a textbook."

"That's the scary thing for me," Vivian says. "I had this discussion with the Edmonson staff; I don't even want to deal with the elementary and the high school." She laughs. "I mean the Edmonson staff has been doing all sorts of projects, and activities – and *they're* saying, 'I'm scared to death without a textbook.' Can you imagine what the elementary people are going to say to me?"

She contrasts the situation in science with the Social Studies curriculum, "which we're doing the way it should be done – we're sitting down and we're talking about the curriculum, we're talking about what we do. One of the things we were able to note at the last curriculum meeting is that we went through and talked about all sorts of wonderful objectives that are being taught in the buildings, and nobody talked about the textbook. There was *no* discussion of textbooks. They were talking about units, they were talking about activities, about magazines, you know."

But there's one positive result. "See the good news is that it's got the science department working in totality. So even though I wouldn't have planned to do it this way, it's probably best that it happened this way, because we finally have something that's a catalyst for making that department function as a department instead of, like there's a sixth-grade department and a seventh- and eighth-grade department."

"Can I interject something?" Scott asks, holding up two booklets. One is the executive summary of the *Framework for the High School Sci-*

ence Proficiency Examination,[16] the other is a *New Directions* science teaching unit. He explains that although the new state core curriculum does not mandate specific content or materials, districts are being told that the objectives to be tested in the new HSPT are those in the *Framework*, from which the commercial *Science Units* have been developed. "The *Framework* is coming from these. The state is saying this verbatim. The Middle Cities Science Task Force said this and this" – he waves the two books – "are going to be synonymous. If you aren't teaching these you probably might think about it because you aren't going to do well on the competency test."

"So you still can't *build* a curriculum; you have to *buy* a text which becomes your curriculum," Vivian exclaims. Apparently the work in the middle school will be wasted.

"Which is a bunch of Units," Scott adds.

"Which is *still* not what we're saying is science," Vivian points out.

"So is what's happening at the state level really driving . . . ?" Liza asks.

"Yes," Vivian replies before Liza finishes. "And they intend for it to. This is what everybody outside public education does not understand. When I went to hear our state superintendent he said, almost verbatim – I should have written it in my planner all the way through the rest of the year – but his basic words were, '*You* have local control, but as long as we give the test, *we* have accountability.' So in other words . . ."

"There's no local control," Liza finishes.

"Right," says Vivian. "And if that test is written from that document, then that's what we better buy. It doesn't matter what we think about kids and what they ought to be doing. So once again the school district is made to live a lie, as far as I'm concerned." There are murmurs of agreement. "Because on one hand we're telling teachers, in colleges and other places, that you're empowered, you have some information, you're a professional, you can think, but the state is really saying, don't you dare think. You better do *this.* . . ."

"That's right."

"Doesn't matter what your professional thought is, doesn't matter what research says, or anything else."

"Doesn't matter if your kids are actually better prepared for the world," Scott agrees.

"That's right."

"And the business world," continues Vivian, "has told our illustrious governor in no uncertain terms that he'd better do something with public education and he's on a roll to do it."

"And these are teacher-driven activities," Scott says, thumbing through the Units. "It's not student-driven, it's not written to be student-driven. But if your kids have not gone through the *Framework*'s activities on photosynthesis, when it comes to the photosynthesis questions in the MEAP, then you had better have covered photosynthesis somewhere else. . . ."

"And covered it with the same language," Vivian agrees. "See the problem becomes language on the test. It's not what *information* students are given, all the students are given that information. But if your *language* is not in synch it's like a foreign language to kids.

"The other frustration," she continues, "is we're supposed to be writing a plan. How do you write a plan about systemic change when the state is doing something totally different? They've given you a grant to do something, but everybody else up there is operating on a whole different level?"

"When I see that test I just want to quit," Liza groans. "What's the point of what we're doing if they're going to have this test?"

Mary says, "I know that will be the issue at the next staff meeting cause the staff is. . . . Our MEAPs of course are not very strong – but they're so excited about what we're doing, and this is, this is really different."

"They're diametrically opposed," says Liza.

"They're just really different," Mary agrees. "This is a really good discussion, because I know the staff is really frustrated, they don't know what to do. We're really struggling with . . . we know we're doing the right thing, but we're not putting out good MEAP scores. They're just asking, 'Well what do you want? What do you want me to do?' "

```
Message: 30148273
Posted: 2:51pm EST, Tue Jan 18/94
Subject: some thoughts on yesterday's meeting
To: WRSI
From: Liza Finkel

Notes from WRSI meeting 1/17/94
The following notes are not in the form of official minutes
(whatever that means!) but are my recollections of what we
talked about yesterday. Think of them as food for thought!
   The meeting started with comments from the presentation at
Holmes School. . . .
   Some other important ideas/issues came up:
- Teachers seem to feel that if they don't get a textbook that
means they will have NO resources at all.
- Teachers feel that not having a textbook is the equivalent
to not having a curriculum.
```

- For teachers to know what resources they will need (for a year) they will have to develop a year long curriculum. When do they have time to do that? And how do they develop the skills to do that? (there are some teachers who have a sense of what a student driven curriculum looks like, but many do not). How do we support this sort of effort?

- Even though we claim that we are asking teachers to design their own curricula, and that we will support such efforts, the state testing policies (including endorsing a particular curriculum) makes us "live a lie".

My own initial reaction to all of this is that we (the WRSI team) have to do two things:

- More carefully define what we think teachers ought to be doing. (And communicate that to the teachers.)

- Figure out how to support teachers as they develop curriculum which will allow them to teach this way. I think we can safely assume that the teachers are going to need a lot of help - what are we going to do about that?

What do the rest of you think?
Liza

Message: 30235688 (modified), Reply to: 30148273, 15 lines
Posted: 8:33am EST, Thu Jan 20/94
Subject: some thoughts on yesterday's meeting
To: Liza Finkel, WRSI
From: Vivian Lyte

Liza,
Thanks for capturing the essence of our discussion.
I believe you've asked the sixty-four thousand dollar question. What is that we expect of teachers and how can we support them?

If we believe that student learning should be facilitated and not directed then we must have that same belief system for teachers and others. Then the question is what are the questions that we must raise in order to have teacher and staff think more deeply about what it is they are doing, why they do what they do, what are some things they could do differently, and where can and should they go for more information and assistance.

Just a little of what's on my mind. (smile)
Vivian

In early February the WRSI team travels to Lansing for a workshop on Teaching, Learning, and Curriculum Alignment, organized by the State Department of Education. There are teams representing perhaps 13 school districts; of these 5 are also recipients of funds for systemic change, though the same people are typically not involved in both activities. Willow Run, where a single committee is involved in both TLC and systemic reform, is the exception. There is surprisingly little opportunity for interaction among the teams. Each reports briefly on "change in the last six months" but what they describe is not referred to again.

The topic of this meeting, the last of a series of five, is assessment. Speakers present assessment tasks that are embedded in instructional activities, and standardized and commercially available science and math tests that can be scored both holistically and analytically. "Is this the new MEAP test?" asks one participant. The presenter offers to let Department staff answer this question, but they decline – it's not clear whether or not the state is endorsing these assessment materials. Someone voices the sentiment that we are "fighting another level of bureaucracy" in the new MEAP test, which "has much emphasis placed on it," creating a "dilemma."

We are talked at most of the day, in a patronizing fashion. The half hour for "team planning" at the end of the day is taken up with "worksheets": forms to detail our plans, accomplishments, and so forth – it feels like busy work. Each team has to specify a date when we'll be ready for a site visit from the Department. "We've got to see if you're really doing what you say you're doing!" one of the organizers jokes to Vivian. She decides to leave the date blank. "Let him play phone tag with me! Is that passive aggressive or what?"

At the next WRSI meeting I ask whether anyone feels any better, now we've heard the state talking about assessment, than they did when we discussed the way state-level emphasis on the MEAP is blocking local change. People look at me as though I'm an idiot. Vivian explains that if a district like Willow Run complained about the effects of the MEAP it would simply be assumed that they were getting poor scores on the test.

"I think their intention was good, to provide examples of available materials," says Liza. "However, someone needs to give them better advice about what the materials are. There was no common story. Are all these assessment materials equally good? Or we should use our wonderful judgment to pick one?"

Scott adds, with heavy irony, "She should have had the person come in whose materials they're taking the test from, and say 'Buy this because this is what the test is going to be from!' That would have been the best thing they could have done."

Based on respondents' descriptions, the Willow Run schools are the base of a community created out of two townships lying outside a larger city. There is no central "city center" in the Willow Run district itself. Several respondents described the school's role in establishing and supporting a sense of community among residents in the area. Respondents agreed that the Willow Run schools were noted for a uniquely caring, friendly, and supportive climate. The staff and administration were described as open and well organized by respondents from the community and business.

The district was perceived by many respondents as growing in reputation both within and outside the district. This phenomenon was attributed in part to the innovative professional partnerships and initiatives between the school and other agencies, as well as its [sic] inclusive, multi-culturally-supportive programs. . . .

Based on the thoughts and observations expressed by participants in the focus groups, Willow Run has laid a strong foundation for systemic change in mathematics and science education over the past few years. The commitment of the school board and administration, and the positive, supportive environment that they have promoted, are key components for realizing systemic change; efforts have been initiated that have given school personnel both a sense of success and a realistic knowledge of the task at hand. . . .

Finally, we would like to congratulate you for the broad-based efforts underway in Willow Run. We would also caution you not to be satisfied with unconnected innovations or "change for change's sake." Here we have no recommendations to give, but simply encouragement to continue to go beyond simple innovation to true systemic reform.

MSSI Evaluation Team, *Willow Run Community Schools Focus Group Report*, Western Michigan University, Kalamazoo, Michigan, Dec. 1993, pp. 2, 4, 5

We've just received a document titled "Valuing Report" – feedback from Focus Group meetings run by visiting MSSI staff. Vivian muses over the last paragraph. "'Congratulations.' I don't think that was appropriate. We don't want your congratulations! See I'm terrible like that; I don't need your approval, so don't give it to me. 'Change for change's sake.' I wasn't real sure – we did talk in our group about many of the things that have been done in Willow Run." She laughs. "Maybe they picked up on, we do a lot of things. They're cautioning us about continuing that practice of doing a lot of things."

"They say, 'We have no recommendations to give,' " I point out.

"I guess I didn't expect them to give us recommendations either," Vivian replies.

A trip to the Early Childhood Development Center provides the occasion for conversation about the needs of staff and those of children. Afterward, Vivian speaks in a deliberate tone that causes us all to listen.

"What they don't understand is, that's the way they talk to the community, the community could care *less* about our needs. Not that they're not important, but they want to hear about what we're doing for their kids.

"To me, that's what we have to do, if we're going to be able to make a difference in this system. The reason educators are not listened to right now, at the state department or anywhere else, is because we have spent all of our time talking about *our* needs. We have not been talking about kids. And we've not cared about what happens with them. If we don't do anything else, for *me*, with systemic initiative, we have to change the attitudes of staffs, to understand that their basic responsibility is to think about the kid first. If we did those things we *could* subvert the system, because we could go to our parents and have a level of trust and say, 'Look what the state department. . . .' In Grosse Pointe, in Cranbook, I bet you they're saying, 'We don't care what the state department's doing.'[17] I bet you they don't even think about the MEAP. But that's because they have a proven track record that they care about kids and what they know and what they're learning. Until we get there, nobody cares what we think about the MEAP; they're going to think we think that about the MEAP because we don't do well on it." The others agree. "That's really what we have to do, and not just we in Willow Run – I'm talking about really most education."

Liza agrees. "But I think there is a whole other issue, that the culture of being a teacher works against all the things we're talking about here. What is supported in school is individual teachers going into their individual rooms and teaching their own individual thing with their own individual kids. And somehow to get us to think, to have a different relationship with the community, we have to come out of our rooms and work together with other teachers and people in the community. Working against the culture of teaching is incredibly difficult."

"You can say that again," Vivian laughs.

"And you have to think of it that way," Liza continues, "and not think that people are too stubborn, or too lazy. . . . It's just not supported, that kind of interaction. First, on a purely practical level, who has time? It's a huge problem – at all levels, financial, emotional, psychological, personal, we do not support the kind of interaction that we are all here saying has to happen, or the relationship with the community that we say is necessary. How do we do that? I don't know."

Challenging American educators to move away from pure academics and towards applied skills, President Clinton said today that one of his Administration's top goals would be to help the nation's schools prepare students for work.

"In the 19th Century, at most, young Americans needed a high school education to make their way," Mr. Clinton told 1,500 educators at a luncheon during the American Council on Education's annual conference. "It was good enough if they could read well and understand basic numbers. In the 21st Century, our people will have to keep learning all their lives. . . ."

The President's remarks, just two days before the House plans to take up the $10 billion Elementary and Secondary Education Act, dovetailed with those made in recent days by the Secretaries of Labor and Education. At various times, in various venues, each has underscored the need for radical educational reforms that will help reorient schools [to] prepare the next generation to compete in the global economy. . . .

To accomplish that, [Clinton] said, "we have an opportunity to do something that Americans have resisted for too long – which is to merge instead of keep divided our notion of vocational education and academic education."

Catherine S. Manegold, "Clinton Tells Educators Youths Are Not Getting Practical Skills for Jobs," *New York Times*, Feb. 23, 1994, B12

The WRSI committee began with a small core but attendance is open to all and at each meeting the group is a little different. Tonight, March 7, Vivian brings the newcomers up to speed. She makes it informal, downplaying her role:

"I probably need to do my spiel about what we're all about. I can't remember what I said last time. Anybody want to do that? What are we all about? Do you have that tape?"

"Systems," someone prompts her.

"Yeah, we're about the system, and we have a five-year grant, for sixty-five thousand dollars a year, which isn't a lot of money when you realize that we're supposed to have two teachers released as part of that, half time, to support other staff. This year is a planning year for us, and we've had some unique experiences with the state department, but we're in a data-gathering kind of stage. Our whole agenda is to help the district achieve the Vision that we've all agreed to, at least those people who were here. That Vision is, let's see, two years old? We see our role as facilitating the discussion as well as – staff might ask for assistance and then we might help facilitate what it is that they're trying to do, in the building, to achieve our Vision. What else can I say? Anybody want to add anything?"

"Started out," she continues, "the grant was written to facilitate improvements in the science and math area, and we had some discussion and decided that good teaching and learning is across curriculum, and so we didn't limit ourselves to that. Although, that is a major focus for us. As part of the grant we're supposed to have an advisory team, and so we're planning a Town Meeting with our community to gather some information from them, in terms of their ideas about what we could do to achieve that Vision, as well as provide an opportunity for people to self-select to the advisory board. So that's what we're in the process of doing, planning our Town Meeting, which is this Saturday. If you can come that's great, if not we understand, since it's short notice."

Change is imminent in the Willow Run Community Schools.

The district was one of 24 throughout the state to receive funding under the Michigan Statewide Systemic Initiative.

The Willow Run Systemic Initiative team is working to rebuild the district from the ground up.

Director of Curriculum Vivian Lyte said about 20 people, including teachers and experts from the University of Michigan, are on the team that meets biweekly to redesign the way teachers teach and students learn. . . .

"The whole process of systemic initiative is to get people talking about teaching, learning and how we help our students achieve Willow Run's vision," said Lyte.

One way the group will get people talking is through a town meeting from 9 a.m. to noon Saturday at the Willow Run High School cafeteria, 235 Spencer Lane.

Juanita C. Smith, "Change Coming to WR Schools," *Ypsilanti Press*, Mar. 11, 1994, 1A

"Does the town have an agenda? Why is it called a Town Meeting?"

"Because we're inviting the town," Vivian explains.

"Do they have an agenda?"

"They may. And if it comes up in the follow-up and in the discussion, then we will address – we will listen. We're not going to *address* anything. But we will *listen*. Because the message to them is the same – that we're not here to tell people *anything*, but we are here to say, 'Let's work together, let's go down this path today.' We did talk about the fact that there may be some things come up, and we'll just have to listen. If we can't do that then we shouldn't do this."

WRSI meeting, Feb. 21, 1993

March 12 is indeed our first Town Meeting. Invitations have gone out to students, their families, local businesses, churches, and other groups. The high school cafeteria is filled with displays from each school's science fair, and there's a copy of the district's vision statement on each table. The meeting starts with an ice breaker to introduce people and get them thinking about change, followed by a slide show illustrating where the district is, a "Visioning" activity, a video of "paradigm pioneers," and a discussion of the planned Community Coalition.

The U.S. auto industry is now operating at over 100 percent capacity for the first time since records have been kept.[18] Shortages and "monstrous" demand bring waiting lists and drive prices over the sticker price. There is reluctance to expand production by bringing new plants on line, but GM is keeping open 13 of the 27 plants slated to be shut down or sold, and keeping on 25,000 workers who would otherwise have moved or lost their jobs. It is also, for the first time in 10 years, looking to hire temporary workers, having exhausted the pool of laid off workers.[19]

New figures show a combined profit in 1993 of $7.4 billion for the Big Three, a sharp contrast with the combined loss of $9 billion in 1991. GM alone netted $2.5 billion. Analysts attribute this change to painful restructuring more than to the recovering national economy or cyclical auto sales.[20] Now GM reports a 66 percent increase in profits in 1994's first quarter: $853 million, after a $758 million charge described as for benefits for former employees.[21]

An *Ypsilanti Press* editorial lauds these results. "The positive numbers do not mean the struggle is over, but what they do say is that the U.S. auto industry can remain dominant in the world, but only if we all keep in mind that that dominance is grounded in innovation and hard work."[22]

However GM still has an unfunded pension liability of $22 billion and is being urged not to raise its stock dividend.[23] There are some concerns that the Federal Reserve may take these figures as a sign of inflation that will need to be warded off.[24] Imports have dropped to only 15 percent of the market, with the yen high against the dollar, but Japanese auto manufacturers are working to regain the market share they've lost in the last two years.

And in March, workers at the GM Willow Run Powertrain Division plant threaten to strike, but local and national UAW negotiators reach an agreement with GM that includes job guarantees until 1996. The company is rumored to be planning to shift production of one transmission to another plant, cutting 1,500 jobs. The local has been negotiating its contract since the national contract was settled last September. Outsourcing, safety, and health have apparently been issues, but other details are not made public.[25] "For the last 20 years management has been showing disrespect to the workers," says one local union official.[26]

But Engler is calling Michigan "the job-creating engine of the new Jobs Belt."[27] Michigan's exports have risen this year to around $25 billion per year, some claim due to NAFTA.[28] Unemployment in the state is now 5.7 percent, the lowest in 20 years. It is the service sector that shows the largest jobs gains.

Nearly one out of three workers in the world's labor force either has no job or is earning too little to live decently, the International Labor Organization reports.

Despite a decline in joblessness in the United States, the U.N. organization with 169 member countries calls the situation "the worst global employment crisis since the Great Depression of the 1930s."

President Clinton has invited officials of six other major industrial countries – Japan, Germany, Britain, France, Italy and Canada – to a two-day meeting March 14–15 in Detroit on ways to create new jobs. . . .

"Practically half of the 35 million unemployed workers in Western Europe have been off the employment rolls for a year or more," Michael Hansenne, the ILO director general, said in a statement.

Associated Press, "1 of 3 in World Out of Work – Report," *Ypsilanti Press*, Mar. 7, 1994, 1A, 4A

When recession pushed up unemployment in all the major industrial democracies a few years ago, the conventional wisdom was that the upturn in the business cycle would solve most of the problem. But now that the upturn has arrived in the United States, and the worst of the recession is over in Europe, new high-wage jobs remain scarce in both places, and many governments are beginning to fear that the shortage may be permanent. . . .

In today's highly integrated global marketplace, [Robert Reich] said, economies can grow in size, company profits can soar, a stock market can rise, and yet many people can be unemployed or underemployed – because capital and technology are now so mobile that they do not always create good jobs in their own backyard. Add to that the emphasis on corporate cutbacks and a lot of people have been left stranded. . . .

That sensitivity is the driving force behind the jobs conference being convened by the Clinton Administration in Detroit on Monday, bringing together finance and labor ministers from the Group of Seven industrial democracies. . . .

"Seen from Europe, unemployment is the biggest security problem facing the Western world today, and the G-7 is simply acknowledging that," Dominique Moisi, deputy director of the French Institute for International Relations, said. "Because if we don't find answers to that problem, our entire system will collapse on itself."

Thomas L. Friedman, "World's Big Economies Turn to the Jobs Issue," *New York Times*, Mar. 14, 1994, C1, C4

United States:

Plenty of bad jobs. Over the past two decades, the United States has created many more jobs than Western Europe – 35 million compared with 8 million – but the bulk of the new jobs are low paying, widening the gap between the lowest- and highest-paid workers.

Falling pay. Of the major economies, only the United States has seen real wages fall over the last decade. Total compensation for the average American worker in manufacturing is $16 an hour, less than two-thirds of the $26 an hour a typical German worker gets.

First to streamline. American industry has been cutting payrolls and closing inefficient operations on a large scale for more than a year, a process European companies have just begun. America's lower unemployment rate makes short-term dislocation easier to tolerate.

Thomas L. Friedman, "Job Woes in the Group of Seven: An Overview,"
New York Times, Mar. 14, 1994, C4

Every once in a while, a pupil gets to go on a field trip and hear a sometimes interesting, sometimes not so interesting, speech by a politician.

When the politician happens to be the president of the United States, the speech is usually interesting, or so six Edmonson Middle School pupils learned Monday. . . .

The Edmonson staff tried to secure 130 tickets for eighth-grade pupils to attend the [G7 Jobs] summit [but obtained only nine]. . . .

"We want to let our kids know there is a future for them," said [teacher Lavanda] Weathers. "Things are changing and there is definitely a future in the job market."

"The thing that impressed me about the president's speech was that it never dawned on me as an educator how intertangled we are with the European economy," said Weathers. "The jobs we are preparing our pupils for here they may very well find over there."

The students said their experience at the conference led them to consider working in a global economy, perhaps even finding a job overseas, something they hadn't considered before.

"I figure there would be more jobs (in Europe)," said [14 year-old Tracey] Foley.

"I would make a better living outside the U.S.," said [14 year-old Mike] Basham.

Juanita C. Smith, "Edmonson Pupils Travel to Detroit to Hear President Clinton's Speech," *Ypsilanti Press*, Mar. 15, 1994, 1A, 4A

The news about the U.S. transition to a global economy appears good. But Europe is struggling with the transition. Wages and benefits in Europe have continued to rise since the mid 1970s – by about 40 percent –

but unemployment has also increased dramatically. In Western Europe about 11 percent of the workforce is now out of work. The U.S. unemployment rate is much lower – 6.5 percent[29] – but most of the newly created jobs here are lower paying than the jobs that have vanished. Wages for non–college-educated workers in the United States have fallen 15 to 20 percent since the 1980s.[30] The U.S. workforce faces a much more flexible, mobile labor market than does the European worker.[31]

Detroit is selected as the venue for the next meeting of finance ministers from the Group of Seven. The White House says the choice of Detroit "will send a message that we intend to confront the challenge of job creation and unemployment, not retreat to the economic structures of yesterday."[32]

Michigan's tax system looks profoundly different today, following overwhelming voter approval Tuesday of the state's first sales tax hike since 1960.

In a stunningly lopsided special election, voters approved Proposal A by 70 percent to 30 percent, with 94 percent of precincts counted. The proposal claimed a majority in virtually every county in the state.

In Detroit, however, voters rejected the proposal nearly 2 to 1, by 63 percent to 37 percent with all precincts counted.

Passage of the school tax shift snaps a string of five straight losses on ballot proposals to increase the state's 4-percent sales tax. Proposal A bumps the tax to 6 cents on the dollar.

Mark Hornbeck and Charles Cain, "A: OK. Voters Overwhelmingly Back Sales Tax Hike to Fund Schools in What Governor Calls 'a Great Victory,' "
Detroit News, Mar. 16, 1994, 1A

In the nation's most dramatic shift in a century in the way public schools are financed, Michigan will begin using sales and other taxes, not property taxes, to pay for its 3,286 schools.

William Celis 3d, "Michigan Votes for Revolution in Financing Its Public Schools," *New York Times*, Mar. 17, 1994, A1, A9

This week citizens of Michigan voted courageously to toss out decades of tradition in public school financing. It is the first statewide, voluntary shift away from property taxes, as a rising national chorus of disgruntled homeowners and civil rights activists seek more equitable ways to provide one of society's most basic services.

Education in America has traditionally been seen as a local concern. Hence the reliance on property taxes, which are also less vulnerable to economic fluctuations, to finance school systems.

> But property assessments within and among states diverge wildly. Across the country, the amount of money spent on schools based on the taxes derived from those assessments are unconscionably unequal. In Michigan, for example, the poorest districts spend about $3,000 per pupil, while the richest spend $10,000. . . .
>
> The public schools have given generations of Americans a chance to fight their way up from poverty. If America is to live up to its promise of equal opportunity, this glaring inequity in education must be addressed. The fact that Michigan voters have voluntarily, and so overwhelmingly, tried to make school financing fairer should make other states sit up and take notice.
>
> Editorial, "Fairer Schooling for Michigan," *New York Times*,
> Mar. 18, 1994, A10

The public vote on Proposal A in March gives the go-ahead to Engler's finance reforms. It means that each school district in Michigan is guaranteed a "basic foundation allowance" of $5,000 per pupil. This doesn't mean that all Michigan's school districts are now on a level playing field, but the effect will be to gradually raise the funding for districts now under $5,000, and to allow districts spending $6,500 or more to raise local taxes to maintain their spending. The lowest-spending districts will be brought up to $4,200 immediately.[33]

Engler and House Republicans, arguing that costs must be controlled because Proposal A limits income for public schools, propose legislation that would fine teachers a day's pay and unions $5,000 for each day of a strike (already illegal in Michigan), allow school boards to bid health insurance, and increase local control of school policies and plans. The MEA calls this "union busting."[34] Republicans say the bill will give the administration more negotiating power to control costs; Democrats say it simply attacks teachers and their union. Seven thousand people march in Lansing to protest, but the bill is passed in late April.[35]

> A Republican plan led by Gov. John Engler to control education costs is nothing more than an attack on teachers and their biggest union, a head of the Michigan Education Association said Monday.
>
> Associated Press, "Teachers Union Rips GOP Plan," *Ypsilanti Press*,
> Apr. 12, 1994, 8A

Meanwhile the last few matters remaining from the litigation between GM and Ypsilanti Township are being resolved. The Supreme Court has returned several issues to Judge Shelton's court, including the charge that GM unjustly enriched itself through the tax breaks it received. GM chief executive Jack Smith says, "We weren't happy with the way Willow Run played out. The lawsuit and the haranguing hurt us and cost us a lot of money."[36] On April 13 the township and GM agree to cooperate to seek reuse of the plant and maintain jobs at the Powertrain division next door. GM will clean the assembly plant to state and federal environmental standards and explore selling the plant. The township will provide 12-year tax abatements on the new investment – and this time put the agreement in writing.

Wednesday, the township and automaker went back to court to formalize an agreement under which the final issue was dismissed.

The agreement includes promises to seek reuse of the closed plant, and GM said it would begin this year to invest $80 million in new equipment for two projects at its Powertrain plant. . . .

The lawsuit moved community-corporate relations to a new level. Now that it is over, Ypsilanti Township and the companies that are located there can use the knowledge that has been gained to forge stronger, more forthright relationships than have existed in the past.

Editorial, "The End," *Ypsilanti Press*, Apr. 17, 1994, 6A

"At its core, the law is about nothing if it is not about the impact that our decisions have on human lives, and I have a more hopeful and optimistic view of human relationships than that expressed in the Court of Appeals panel's decision." Judge Donald Shelton.

John Mulcahy, "Judge Discusses GM Ruling: The Interview,"
Ypsilanti Press, Apr. 24, 1994, 1A, 8A

---

8   End-of-Year Report Cards

May–June 1994

The school year is coming to an end – and so is the first year of WRSI. Our thoughts turn from the impact of "quality reforms" to MSSI's end-of-year reporting requirements. May and June bring a series of frustrating meetings. At a typical one, the major item on the agenda is the evaluation plan for year one, due to MSSI on June 1. As Scott hands out copies of the grant proposal and the *Designing Evaluations* document from February's Biennial Meeting, Vivian warns newcomers that we have lengthy meetings. We've already written our plan for two of the five Common Outcomes: tonight we're addressing Community Coalition Building and Systemic Reform.

Overview of Process. District Teams will identify key indicators – tangible evidence – of success at the end of five years based on their outcomes for each area (Mathematics and Science Education, Community Coalition Building, Underrepresented Groups, Systemic Reform, and Other). They will then identify indicators for the first year for each of the objectives in each of the areas of the Strategic Plan. Dividing the work by area among team members, smaller groups or individuals will then design an evaluation process for one area based on the indicators. Each area group will report to the whole team their evaluation plan for that area and revisions will be made in accordance with suggestions from the whole team. Finally, the district team will examine in each area whether the first year objectives/indicators are on target toward the five year outcomes.

Designing Evaluations for Strategic Plans, MSSI Biennial Meeting, Feb. 1994

"Remember those Focus District Common Outcomes we dealt with and we argued about and we complained about?" says Scott. "For Underrepresented Groups we've written a statement saying we aren't going to deal with it the way they want things dealt with, and there's our rationale behind it," he explains.

The rationale reads: "The Willow Run Mission Statement includes all students. Therefore, we believe setting the expectation for all staff that we are responsible for the learning of all students addresses these objectives. Setting separate objectives for underrepresented groups, we feel, reinforces and perpetuates the current paradigm."

This community is not without its racial tensions – indeed, in 1971 the high school principal was literally tarred and feathered when he attempted a reconciliation between blacks and whites in a conflict sparked by federal desegregation.[1] But the district's way of dealing with the issue of race has a certain consistency. The five elementary schools vary widely in their balance of African American and white students. In 1988, shortly before Dr. Yomtoob's arrival, the board tried unsuccessfully to pair Cheney Elementary (then 61 percent African American) with Holmes (15 percent). Yomtoob's approach was different: to provide Cheney with resources, like the district's first computer lab and a gifted and talented program. This approach has not eliminated discrepancies in the academic achievement of African American and white students, but Yomtoob will say later, "Busing doesn't work. . . . Instead we have to change the system. And we have to make sure there are enough resources."[2] Students do describe some tension in the middle school as they come together from the various elementaries, but they also describe an absence of racial conflict in the high school.

We settle down to figure out the reporting requirements of the MSSI charts, and recast what we've done and intend to do in the bureaucratic language of "Outcomes, Objectives, Indicators, and Process." Scott reads each Outcome, then we remind ourselves of what we did to meet the First-Year Objectives, then brainstorm possible Indicators. What are the indicators of success for "fact-finding"? Establishing a data base? "We're really playing their game," says Mary. We begin to get silly, joking about Dream Topping, misspelling "steak-holders." We're all bored with this, but Scott keeps us going diligently.

And one benefit of this process is that people realize the district has already accomplished a lot and start to examine what's been done in new ways. The Science Fair, for example, built family involvement. And the district has a community partnership with Ford Motor Company that provides classroom speakers, job shadowing, one-on-one apprenticeships, and a summer work program in Ford's plant. In the high school the Renaissance Program gives students recognition "for getting it right" – for good grades, improvement, coming to school, being on time. Ypsi businesses, including Bank One, Society Bank, and McDonalds, support the program by offering discounts. And a student who gets A grades all through high school is awarded a scholarship to Eastern Michigan University, or other local colleges.

"Does somebody read these?" someone asks of the charts.

"Yeah. Unfortunately. From a very biased point of view, too."

"Let's move on to Year Two," Mary smiles. "I'm ready! We've done a good job this year. We've worked hard."

"We have accomplished a lot," Vivian agrees. "The wheels are turning."

At the next meeting we continue with the Year-One Evaluation Plan, still "squeezing things into boxes." Again humor helps us get through a time-consuming and thankless task.

"How about we put a little more meat on that?" Vivian responds to one suggestion. Laughter builds through the room; this evening's dinner is vegetarian lasagna, and Scott strongly prefers a meat dish.

"Don't say meat!" Betty chuckles.

"Put a bit more cheese under the Indicators!"

"She said that on purpose," Scott groans.

"No!" protests Vivian.

"I think it was," Scott comes back, "I think it was Freudian!"

Finally we can move on to our Year-Two plans, using the same format.

"Year One was supposed to be Research and Study, Year Two was supposed to be Plan Development, and then Year Three Plan Implementation, Year Four Integration into the System," Vivian reminds us, reading from the district's original proposal. "'School and program personnel work to coordinate school staff, enabling them to seek examples of projects which match targeted curriculum objectives.' 'Projects' meaning project-based science.

"I was telling Scott," she adds, "that I really have come to a level of awareness that if you don't give people *some* information, what is it you're trying to systematically do? Not that I want to *endorse* something, necessarily, but we have to at least plan opportunities for people to see and hear about good teaching and learning. We're trying to push a concept when folk don't even know what it is." Perhaps U of M faculty working on project-based science and project-driven inquiry could plan some sessions for teachers.

"So. What we need to do is go back to page one" – she means the summary of Common Outcomes – "and start over, looking at the outcome and thinking how we want to implement that," to build a plan "not around a particular subject, but more the concept of teaching and learning."

Mary arrives, with a question that's pertinent to this discussion. She's just had a long conversation about what happens when students take a sample MEAP test in the middle of the year. Does the teacher then throw out their plans and teach what the students don't know?

"That's how project-driven teaching is different, 'cause you do a needs assessment – finding out what the students already know, so you know which direction to go."

"It's actually harder, because you have to be so familiar with what is expected. . . ."

"You have to be totally flexible."

"Yes, because they can change where you're going any time."

"Looking at this," Scott says slowly, "you're looking at roads that go like this" – he stretches his hands wide apart – "which is why we've been frustrated with the MEAP and the state. The road we want to go is this direction, and the road the MEAP is going is this direction. Pre- and post-tests really don't work the same if you're going to teach for the MEAP as they do if you're going to teach problem-driven inquiry." In the second case it's information that guides what to teach next; in the first, whatever the pre-test indicates, you'll still simply teach all the objectives.

"Those are your objectives no matter what," Vivian agrees.

"While if you're in problem-driven, that can weave."

"I just realized what's wrong with this plan," Vivian says with a laugh. "It doesn't say who's going to do it when. It'll never get done!"

There's nothing in the MSSI form that allows us to list what we're going to do to accomplish the objectives, or who's responsible!

"Wouldn't we want to think in terms of framing the objectives in student outcome language?" Laura Chew, who's just arrived, suggests. "Then all of the rest of this is our strategies."

Laura reads Outcome Three: "'Teachers will possess the skills and knowledge needed to develop and conduct instruction that effectively promotes engagement in and understanding of science and mathematics for all students.' So it's a student outcome we're looking at. And so there's a staff development on that student outcome to provide teachers with skills and knowledge needed to develop and conduct the instruction that will promote that outcome for students."

"Correct," says Vivian.

"And then, I guess what maybe throws somebody looking at this to start with is everything that's listed underneath that are really strategies, not objectives."

"You're probably very right," Vivian agrees. "But you didn't go to Lansing with us. You would have been a delight to have with us, actually. Because your use of the words leaves people going, 'Yeah!' "

"We can't change a word of this, is that what you're telling me?"

"Well, for us it would be okay, but when I send it to them I'm gonna send it the way that they want it, because they have made it perfectly clear they're not as flexible as they want systemic change to be."

Laura asks if we can change the wording in Outcome Three.

"Oh no no! We're not changing the wording in number three!" Vivian exclaims.

"That was fought about," Scott agrees, "This is their thing. These outcomes were argued about for two days!"

"And they didn't listen to a word we said," Mary adds. "Not a word."

"Okay," Laura says, "I'm not going to argue the point that it has to say that, but can somebody just tell me why?"

"Honestly?" Vivian asks. "We were working with a group of people, even despite the fact that they were teaching systemic change, who were very dogmatic."

"It was amazing," Mary says.

"My favorite kind of people!" Laura laughs.

"It was put up on an overhead . . ." Mary starts.

"They said, 'What do you want to change?'" Scott continues. "We shouted it out, we changed it, we erased it . . ."

"For two days!" Mary adds.

". . . we reworded it . . ."

"Eloquently!"

". . . and then we got it back in the mail, exactly like it was!" There's much laughter.

"They said they're in here for systemic change," Vivian says, "and they want the change bottom-up, and then they started talking top-down. And they have not stopped from day one."

"That's how most of the groups *are* working," Scott points out.

"Right," Vivian agrees. "And the other groups are working in the same fashion, so therefore, guess who's sticking out like a sore thumb?"

Should we write one version for the district, then, and another for the state? Laura suggests we write a report for our community and staff framed in terms of student outcomes, because this is a model we're trying to introduce. Scott types as Laura suggests wording:

"'All students will demonstrate understanding of science and math concepts. Teacher training will focus on skills and knowledge that will assist them to develop and conduct instruction to promote student understandings. And ultimately student demonstration.'

"And then what's listed under First-Year Objectives makes perfect sense as the number one strategy: that staff are given opportunities to attend training to learn about options that would help them develop and implement strategies. . . . I mean, that is just how it works.

"And your evaluation tool always has to be some kind of demonstrable student outcome. But I haven't been at all these different training sessions so maybe I'm way off. Whatever the input to staff might be, the outcome still has to be demonstrated by students, not by staff. Because we all know that a whole variety of teaching styles and strategies can impact positively on student outcomes. Or we would have canned everything. And we don't, we encourage teachers to diversify and find all those different strategies that reach each child. The student outcome is the important thing."

"And then you go to your assessment," Mary picks this up. "Have we decided that the outcome is MEAP performance, which the state has decided, or can it be by using different . . . ? Your assessment instrument might be an artifact, a demonstration. . . ."

"We can evaluate whether we've done what we said we were going to do in terms of giving the staff training," Laura responds, "but that doesn't actually measure the student outcomes. MEAP scores could be one indicator. It could also be participation in Science Fairs, or student generated projects. . . . We're having a Family Biology Night at Cheney School next week, and 150 kids are going to display a project they did – that could be an indicator. Every child in the school is keeping a science journal. All staff attended a three-hour training session after school, which Vivian arranged, and they all agreed and committed to work in conjunction with a support person from the outside helping the children develop some understanding of biology concepts."

Scott is thinking hard. "I guess my sticking point is, again, assessment. How are we assessing whether these students are understanding?"

Vivian answers. "There has to be some level of understanding for a student to create an artifact about what they've learned. The artifacts they've been creating for their projects are coming out of an understanding. The artifact displays some part of the learning they did – it represents the observing, the thinking. . . . The tiles the students at Kettering did – there had to be a level of understanding for them to make a decision about what to put on the tile, and how to represent it."

"An artifact is a demonstration. A student will demonstrate understanding by producing an object or artifact. Or a play, or a skit, or a poem," Laura adds. "I bet you're sorry I came now!"

"Absolutely not!" says Vivian.

"No," Scott says too, "because this gives us another perspective. I was not thinking that deeply at all, because this form doesn't inspire you to do so."

"Even though we're trying to finish this for the state, I hope we're really thinking about what we want to do next year," Vivian says. "What we give staff should be how we want to live life. We already made that decision, a long time ago, that the state really is secondary to what we're doing. We hope we'll be able to satisfy them enough to want to give us the money for the rest of the five years, but our main goal is to make sure we're satisfying the needs of where we are in Willow Run."

It's striking how everyone comes to life once we step out of the boxes on the MSSI form. People share projects and events in their schools and plan ways for colleagues to visit, share, and learn. The new Media Center will provide the opportunity to videotape and build a library of special projects and local models of instruction. We could show kindergartners what their elementary school will be like.

An interesting debate develops over the appropriate measures of success, one that uncovers some differing assumptions about goals. Scott argues that focusing entirely on student outcomes sets up teachers for failure, since student achievement may occur only down the line. Teachers seeing no change in their students will go back to their old ways. He proposes instead we use measures of the process, of the teachers' change – and in particular he'd like to see some evaluation of the extent to which people move from being a "lecture-teacher" to having a more "student-driven" classroom.

Vivian and Laura disagree with him. Laura points out that changes for teachers are often intangible and that changes in their classroom instruction may also not occur immediately after they attend a workshop.

"People have had misunderstandings that if you just go to a workshop, automatically the kids do better and you're better and you're a good teacher and that proves it because you went. But it doesn't! It doesn't change anything if you never talk to a colleague about what you saw . . ." Laura says.

"Or if you don't use it in a way that's meaningful to the students," Vivian agrees. And this has implications for our objectives. "If you don't write it in such a way that people expect something to show in their students, they may or may not make that transition."

"But if you say that your children will be different – and that's what this says – and you don't share with them that there's a process through which this happens. . . ."

"You know what you've forgotten, Scott?" says Vivian. "That's a five-year goal. And we went out to the staff and told them, 'You're gonna go up, and you're gonna go down. And you're gonna fall, and you're gonna get back up.' And what we said is, 'That's okay.' " Vivian adds that already things are being done to protect teachers against failure and to highlight awareness that student achievement will not improve for a while, and may even drop at first when new kinds of teaching are tried.

"Exactly. And at this point, in this process, student change is not an indicator of success," Scott persists.

"We must have, and we will have, some student changes," Vivian insists. "We won't have all that we want to have, but we will have changes. Without a shadow of a doubt – and I can tell you that because I truly believe in the Hawthorne theory:[3] if you do anything – anything – change will occur." She laughs.

"'I'm looking," Scott hypothesizes, "at a teacher that has thirty desks in a row, and lectures, and that's how they run their classroom. That's their classroom management and their instructional method. The teacher goes to a conference. . . . Now if the teacher continues to be a lecture-teacher and does not incorporate some of what they picked up, even if their thinking changes but they don't change the way they do anything, it's not going to affect kids. If we want to get to student-driven classrooms, if that's our ultimate goal, where students are learning because they want to learn, because they want the information, where students are driving the way the classroom runs, then that teacher is not going to get there unless they change their method of instruction. That is very measurable."

Vivian counters that change is often slow and hidden until it suddenly bursts forth. "It's like the student that you work with and work with, and you think you're going nowhere, and all of a sudden they come in and say . . . , and you go, where did that come from? We went all around the district. We didn't talk to any teachers necessarily about *what* they were doing, we talked about the Vision. And the Vision was about who? Our students.

"And we talked about *kaizin.* That was partly so that folks understood that they were to make continuous progress toward the student outcomes, but there should be a recognition that just because you didn't get there today, does not mean you're a failure. If we're going to have a safe environment where people feel like taking risks, then what we have to *allow* is when a teacher tries something new and is not successful, there's somebody right there saying, 'What do you mean, not successful?' "

People quit not because they fail, but because they don't get support; because they work in a system where "you either get it or you don't. And that's what we're trying to change. For kids, for staff, for community, it's not an 'either you get it or you don't,' it's a 'let's keep working towards this goal.' "

Laura isn't convinced that student-driven instruction is the way to go. "I know teachers that can have kids sitting at individual desks in rows and still accomplish *incredible* things. We're trying to *open up* the thinking, instead of saying everyone's got to be in a group, or everyone's got to be in a desk. It could be anything."

"That's what looking at the outcome gets you," Vivian agrees.

"Well, we are running out of time," Vivian notes. "Some people need to go to a millage meeting, some people need to process film, some people need to go say goodbye to their child who's leaving."

"I'm sorry we had . . ." Scott begins.

"No, that was a great point that you made," Laura insists.

"We need these discussions," Vivian says. She sighs. "Well, I'm not sure what to say about getting the state a plan. I'm about ready to say Scott and I will do what we did before and just put something together that they can trash. We have the beginnings. But we really need to keep the discussions going, in terms of what we really want to do. Because we really do want to make a difference in Willow Run, and we want to make a difference for kids."

Message: 35617627, 30 lines
Posted: 7:32pm EDT, Mon May 23/94
To: WRSI
From: D. Scott Heister

```
This is information about "Family biology Night" that is hap-
pening at Cheney Elementary School, those at the last WRSI
meeting, it is what Laura was discussing. It is on May 26 from
5-7PM anyone who is able should get out and support their ef-
forts . . .
It sounds like they are haveing a good time doing science :)
   This is the program that is being partnered with the Hands
on Museum in A2. Let's make an effort to support them. If any-
one goes out there, take some slide film with you and we can
begin work on next years video spectacular!!!
   Last Wed. we met, as most of you know . . . had some very
good conversation and, thanks to Laura and others, revisited
the fact that sometimes the hoops the state makes us jump
through hinder us more than help us! But, we will continue
moving forward . . .
   Vivian and I will jump thought the necc. hoops to get the
second year plan in on time . . .
   Those going to Makinaw, look forward to seeing you
there . . .
   Anyone who did not see the Sunday edition of the A2 News,
you should pick up a copy, the Run got some good positive
press, much of it focused on UM and the WRSI
Grant . . . Hopefully this will help in the districts efforts
to get a millage passed!!
   Will get back to you with copies of the second year plan as
soon as we get it put together . . .
scott
```

Students too are looking back on their past year, and looking forward to the next. I meet with some of Mrs. Page's first graders.[4] They have become able to look back with confidence on their initial anxieties.

"What was it like coming to Kettering at the beginning of this year?" I ask a group of girls.

"*Good!*" they yell together. "But I was a little bit scared," adds one. "Me too," agrees another.

"What were you scared about?" I ask.

"The big people, the big people." "I was scared of the class." "I was too." "I was scared of the whole school." "I was scared of the big school." "I was scared of the big people here."

Is it still scary? "NO!" they all exclaim. "It's fun!" "It is."

What have they learned over the year?

"Lots of work," says one.

"*Lots* of work," agrees another.

"I studied my name, I studied my ABCs."

"Yup, and we studied our numbers."

"Reading."

"And math."

"We write in our journals."

"Yup, and we sound out the words."

They are very aware of everyone's progress through the reading assignments, represented by the bears on the Reading Train, and proud of how few books they have to be tested on before they're done.

"Shanelle needs to read, um, *Out Came the Sun*. And *Make a Wish*."

"Can you believe Daniel's on *Make a Wish*?"

"Yes I can, I hear him read."

"He's not on *Make a Wish*, he's on *Morning Bells*."

"Whoever's the farthest goes to second grade," says one.

Does that mean there will be some students who don't go to second grade next year? "Yeah." Who will they be? "The ones that don't know the words."

"You still get to go to second grade," Shanelle disagrees.

"Uh uh, Shanelle, you've got to work really hard."

"And the people that usually get their name on the board don't get to go either."

"Yes they do, yes they do. They still get to go. It doesn't matter if they're bad or not. It just matters they've, that they have to get their words."

Their sense of their future is as yet largely disconnected from what they're doing in school, based more on those they admire – parents and teachers – and on fantasy. What will they do when they get older? "I'm going to buy myself a convertible." "I'm buying myself a jeep." "I want to buy, I want to buy me a pink car." "I'm going to get a job."

What kind of job do they think they'll get? "I want to be a teacher." "A doctor too," adds another. "I want to work at Toys-R-Us." "I'm going to work where my mom's working. She works on science." "A bluish-green convertible. And I might, I might be a teacher or soccer player."

Can they explain what work is like? "Work is when you, when you have to do a paper." "Or a coloring sheet, like that, that's not really work because it's fun." Why do kids do work? "So they can learn."

In Mrs. Page's classes, when you do bees or gorillas, is that work? There a mixed chorus of "no's" and "yes's." "Not really," says one, "that's really fun." "It's just learning about an animal." "It's not even hard." "It's not hard."

I ask if there's anything they'd like to change about the school.

"The teachers, they are mean sometimes." "The teachers can change to be nicer."

"And no more work!" "Yeah, NO MORE WORK!!" Suddenly they are gleefully chanting: "NO MORE WORK!! NO MORE WORK!!" "Eight pages a day!" "I know, she gives us . . . for the night, she gives us like nineteen." "No, she gives us like twenty-four!" "We have about fifteen words a day to learn." "NO MORE WORK!! NO MORE WORK!!"

The unfamiliar opportunity to step outside the bounds of the classroom permits a shift from competitive individual comparison to action in unison. Two attitudes show themselves. In one the classroom is play, the teacher is fine, school is enjoyed and valued. In the other – "No more work!" – school is work, imposed on them. These may reflect the mixture in Joyce's pedagogy of traditional seat work and new group projects. But the second surely stems also from something deeper, a lingering cultural understanding that work is unfair. These children bring from their families a complex attitude toward work: it is unpleasant, something imposed by others, but a fact of life and a source of adult possessions and status. Perhaps Joyce hasn't yet made the leap to an entirely project-based, student-centered classroom because the kids themselves are not ready for it.

I board a school bus with Kettering's fifth-grade students the morning of May 11, a month before they will graduate. We're off to Edmonson Middle School, where in anticipation of next year an open house is arranged for the elementary students. Mrs. Ryles's bus is a tight ship: she insists that the students are going to be the object of attention and interest at Edmonson and so they must behave.

Kettering has two fifth-grade teachers, Sharon Ryles and Hazel Stangis. Janice Brown has described Mrs. Ryles to me. "This is a teacher with a lot of years of experience and very disciplined, very organized, very much an authoritarian style of teaching, with very firm ideas about what her kids should walk out of the classroom with at the end of the year in order to be ready for middle school. . . . Sharon will listen, but she's going to go ahead and do it her own way. . . . If she feels that this is what it's going to take to get them to finish something, then she'll keep them in the classroom and make them finish. There's no other teacher in the building that would do that." If a first-grade teacher like Mrs. Page appeals to a certain charisma and to her traditional standing in her students' family history, a fifth-grade teacher can trade on her wisdom: her knowledgeable grasp of the circumstances in which the students now find themselves. Some of Sharon's past students drop by to visit after the middle school gets out; they tell her she was their "best teacher ever."

Mrs. Ryles has been drawing her students' attention to their budding careers in middle school since the beginning of the year, when establishing her authority in the classroom and justifying her discipline and sanctions. On the first day of school she gave a spelling test – beginning with simple words like "at," "did," "of," "your," and ending with words like "health," "several," "noticed," "questions," and "transistor" – to see where she needed to place her new students, and tell them where she wants them to be by the end of the year. Anywhere from 5 to 11 was a fine score, she reassured them, but if they copied, she warned, they might get placed in a harder level and fail, and "I don't want anybody to fail. People, do *not* let anyone look at your paper. I know you want to help your buddies, but put your hand over your paper." She makes it clear she knows her charges' impulses and understands their motivation, and that she knows better than they do the broader consequences of their actions.

Sharon tells them her expectations are high – "I expect one hundred and fifty percent of you. Some say I expect one hundred percent, but I expect more than that." Everyone can make good grades, she emphasizes, if they have the "mind set," and fostering this is important to her. She'll teach them study skills, so they can "start early." She gives homework every day except Friday ("I figure you want to enjoy your weekends"). She evinces concern for them, for their fair treatment, for their futures. She can also be strict, but her sternness is always leavened with humor.

"You have three minutes to go to the rest room, get a drink, and get back. And believe me, it's enough time. It's not to socialize. And that means, 'Hey girl, look at this, guess who I like, look what I'm wearing.' "

She often reminds her students of their status in the elementary school. "I really don't like to wait a long time for your attention. In kindergarten, you know how they count to ten? And in first grade they count to five? Well, my number is *one!* So if someone is talking to you then you give them a look. And if they still don't stop, give them a nudge. I don't want ya to break a rib or anything!" She points out that different teachers have different rules – and that Edmonson teachers will have unexpected demands.

When we reach Edmonson, seventh-grade "tour guides," young African American women, form us into small groups and take us to meet a sixth-grade teacher. We are led first to a classroom with the door locked and the lights out. On the door is posted a note: "Do not disturb except in emergency." I have the fanciful image of a teacher cowering inside in the dark, unable to face the arrival of the dreaded fifth graders.

Many of the African American boys have close cropped hair, some with shaved designs. The white boys tend to have hair very short on the sides but the tops longer, sometimes gelled up, with tails at the back. Many of the boys wear athletic shirts, pants, or jeans. Most of the white girls have long straight hair, perhaps caught up in a ponytail but without much more attention. The African American girls have a variety of styles: one has cornrowed hair, another has her hair frizzed and caught back, a third has a ponytail.

Mrs. Ryles's concern that her students have the right "mind set" for the rigors of "junior high" (as she continues to call it, perhaps to sound more imposing) seems not misplaced when we find a sixth-grade teacher who will welcome us to Edmonson. "You do not talk when the teacher is talking or any other adult!" she insists, soon after introducing herself, when a Kettering student exchanges a comment with a friend. On the wall behind her, posted over the chalkboard, are several "positive thoughts." One reads: "I will do as my teacher says, even if I don't want to, as long as it is good and right." Who decides whether what the teacher says is good and right, I wonder?

She sketches a list of topics students can anticipate studying with her in the fall. In social studies they will learn about cultures ("What's that?" she asks the students. "Different ways people do things," one replies), longitude and latitude, state capitals, and other topics I can't jot down in time. "We're trying to build study skills into our social studies," Sharon tells her.

"What's wrong?" she asks one boy, a student from Cheney. I can't see his face, but she must have seen something in his expression. "I feel sick!" he moans, and he's taken from the classroom.

She sketches topics in science, and then in language arts, and explains that students will often be working in groups, so they will be able to talk together and often sit with their friends. But she warns that "some people talk too much" and have to be moved. "You're very courteous, though; I may not have that problem."

Edmonson's 700 students have five minutes to get through these corridors from one class to the next, principal Mr. Anglin tells us as we are gathered together, staff and students from the elementaries and staff from Edmonson, in the Media Center, our next stop. The school's tardy policy is different from what they're used to: a "passing time" is allowed of only five minutes. He begins, though, with some statistics on the faculty: 40 teachers, 24 of whom teach the core curriculum. In addition the school has 2 counselors, a nurse, a psychologist, a social worker, a learning center teacher, a media specialist and a media clerk, three secretaries, and three security personnel, who we might have seen in the corridors, he tells us, carrying walkie-talkies.

Mr. Anglin explains that students are encouraged to participate in sports, clubs, and after-school activities, because that's "the other half of your education"; it helps with "socialization" and "personal growth and development." "You have a right to a fine education," he says, including the right to attend school in an orderly environment, and to reach the highest level of achievement they are capable of. He runs quickly through the areas in the core curriculum and in electives, and speaks of the school's "outstanding breakfast and lunch program," though there is a "snack bar selling what they call junk food, if you're unwilling to participate in the lunch program."

Edmonson has a "closed campus" policy: students cannot leave the school building between their arrival at 8:10 A.M. and their departure at 2:40 P.M. without permission from the office. He explains the attendance policy: more than 15 absences will trigger contact with parents and possibly a truancy finding. "I know each of you loves school *so* well!" he adds with irony. Finally, he tells the young people he hopes they enjoy their tour of the building, welcomes them to Edmonson, and says he looks forward to seeing them the following year.

After this overview from Mr. Anglin, and brief introductory words from a half dozen members of his staff, we are led once more to and fro in the building's corridors to visit the wood shop, the cafeteria, the band room, one of three Computer Centers, and then back to the Media Center. The contrast between the two technologies of cellulose and silicon is striking: the Computer Center houses about 30 machines, along with printers, scanners, overhead projection equipment, CD ROM drives – even a digital camera. Most of the students in the room are busy working with graphics software, manipulating scanned photographic images. The woodshop, in contrast, is bare and echoing. Its acoustics are bad, admits the teacher who greets us there, and so he insists the students be quiet. He rummages in a storage closet to show the children some of the products they will produce in the shop: a key-hanger made of flat stock cut, of course, in the shape of a key, and a gum dispenser, comprising a wooden box upon which the teacher asks us to imagine a large glass gumball container. A few items lay on the benches, held in primitive clamps. Three drill presses line the back wall; a few schematic drawings hang on a bulletin board, but other than that the room seems empty. It is evident that Edmonson has been putting its resources into more modern technology.

Even the more successful fifth graders – Britt, Jamila, Latoya, and Billy – tell me they expect to be scared when they start at Edmonson.[5] "We'll be the little kids again," says Jamila. "I'm kinda scared about the work too," Britt adds. "That school is so big I'm gonna get lost," says Jamila. These children accept the necessity of schooling, but they object to work that is too hard, too easy, or just busy work. Mrs. Ryles might give them hard work, but it's for their benefit. "I like being in Mrs. Ryles's classroom because she's strict on us, and some teachers they're too easy on you." Britt agrees. "She'll challenge us with all the work we get." They hardly ever get recess, but this too is to get them ready for Edmonson next year. "That's what she said," explains Billy. "I'm trying to prepare you guys for next year."

Britt is probably the tallest girl in the class, with long, straight fair hair. She and Billy are white, Jamila and Latoya are African American. Jamila is short, with a serious expression. Each has vaulting ambitions: a professional football player, a lawyer, a doctor – "one of them dietologists" – "I really want to be the president: the first black lady president." No longer do they simply aspire to be like a relative. They all expect to go to college – to the U of M, to Harvard or Howard – and to leave Willow Run, for New York, California, Washington, DC, even a foreign country.

And they all see schooling as important. "I wish my mom was a teacher," says Billy, "and they could just teach you at home, so you didn't have to wait for directions and stuff. But I think school's okay. I mean you've got to get an education to do stuff you want to, if you want money." "Because they're coming out with new techniques" – perhaps Latoya means technologies – "higher." "And you want to keep up," Jamila agrees. "And if you get fired from your job," Latoya continues, "you'll have another place to go to." Knowing about computers is important, Jamila says, telling of her grandmother, born in 1935, who knew nothing about them until Jamila told her. "She was used to just, doing work, what they used to do in the olden days."

What kind of work is their schooling preparing them for? "The world that's coming up with us," Jamila says. "And math and fractions and stuff," Britt says. "All these different techniques," Jamila says.

"Every year everything is changing. Like every year, or every minute, or something, a baby is born, so we'll know about that stuff." " 'Cause you have to learn a lot, in order to get a job," Britt explains. "If you don't know anything you can't do a job well." "Today it's *hard* to get a job," agrees Jamila. "It's not so easy. Even McDonalds they say you have to have at least a high school diploma." "Nobody's going to get anywhere if they don't go to school," says Britt.

A Free Press computer analysis shows that performance on the state's mandatory academic exams is tied to the amount of family poverty in a district: as poverty increased, test performance declined. And students in high-poverty districts lagged far behind their more well-off counterparts. . . .

"Somehow, we have to demystify this notion that high scores say anything about the quality of schools. They don't," said Valerie Lee, a University of Michigan researcher who specializes in equity issues. Instead, Lee and others said, test performance is more a reflection of community wealth. "Social class and achievement is one of those enduring relationships."

Poor children have always been in Michigan schools, but educators and researchers alike believe they are facing greater challenges and doing worse than before. . . .

Today, poor children are bombarded with images of how the other half lives. They see it on television, in the movies, at the malls. The power and immediacy of those images can breed despair. Parents who have tried and failed to make it financially know what their children are up against. Often, they just give up.

Joan Richardson, "MEAP: The Learning Gap. The Means to Achieve,"
Detroit Free Press, May 27, 1994, 17A, 20A

A commission created by President Clinton has concluded that the American workplace cannot become truly efficient and globally competitive until the hostility between labor and management – particularly when unions try to organize a company – is greatly reduced. . . .

Labor and management usually give in to big change only during periods of crisis, the last one being the Great Depression. The labor law that emerged then drew some provisions from a similar, detailed study of the workplace by a Presidential commission. There has been no such study in the intervening decades, and now the question is whether there is enough of a crisis – as there was in the 1930's – to again force change.

Louis Uchitelle, "A Call for Easing Labor-Management Tension,"
New York Times, May 30, 1994, sec. 1, pp. 33, 34

9   Rest and Relaxation?

Summer 1994

```
To:    WRSI Team
From:  D. Scott Heister
Re:    Mission Point Conference Summary;
Date:  July 27, 1994

Summer vacation? When? Well, I hope you are enjoying your
summer, vacation or not. If you have not done so by now, you
are ordered to take at least a little time off to play. Heaven
knows we all worked hard enough over the past year to deserve
a little rest and relaxation. . . .
    It seems that MSSI is beginning to listen, at least in
part, as there were actually a few of the breakout sessions
that were interactive. We also had a fair amount of time to
meet as a team and do some reflecting on the first year and
plan for the coming year. . . .
```

Friday went down in history as the hottest June 17 ever recorded. The previous record was 95 degrees set in 1921, and by noon, the temperature was already tied and would continue to rise into the mid- to upper 90s – reaching 98 by 5 p.m.

> Karen Dugas and Juanita C. Smith, "Record-Set." *Ypsilanti Press*,
> June 18, 1994, 3A

The millage election publicized at Kettering's graduation ceremony – the first to follow passage of Proposal A – is a success. Voters approved a local tax of 18 mills on nonhomestead (commercial, industrial, and rental) property by a healthy margin: 431 in favor, 289 against.[1] Under Proposal A, a district must levy this tax to receive the full amount of the state foundation grant. Yomtoob proposed an additional 1.4 "enhancement" mills,

175

for maintenance and computer software, but the board turned this down, not wanting to put "an increased burden on our residents."[2]

"Whooo! I was sweating this one," Superintendent Yomtoob is quoted in the paper. "We feel good about our community, this is good support. Even though this thing was very hard to explain, our people had faith in us."

Not all dire predictions come true, as is shown by the employment gains made in Washtenaw County during the past few years.

That is particularly encouraging now, nearly a year after the General Motors Corp. Willow Run Assembly plant closed, idling 2,400 active workers.

When the closing was announced in spring 1992, the city posted an unemployment level of 11.4 percent; the township's unemployment level was 9.6 percent. . . .

Two years later, thanks to a rebounding domestic auto industry, nearly all of the idled workers have found positions at other regional assembly plants, and some auto plants are hiring a significant number of new employees for the first time in 15 years.

That has helped lower the city's unemployment to 5.1 percent, while Ypsilanti Township unemployment stands at 4.3 percent. . . .

[But] while the Ypsilanti area is fortunate to gain economic vigor in this manner, it would be prudent for everyone to remain concerned about the issue.

Resting easy because of this turnaround would not be a smart response.

Editorial, "Jobs," *Ypsilanti Press*, June 21, 1994, 6A

Since last Labor Day, the economy has generated more than 2.5 million jobs for Americans. But despite this progress, long-term trends are splitting the old middle class into three new groups: an underclass largely trapped in center cities, increasingly isolated from the core economy; an overclass, those in a position to ride the waves of change; and in between, the largest group, an anxious class, most of whom hold jobs but are justifiably uneasy about their own standing and fearful for their children's futures.

Robert Reich, "The Fracturing of the Middle Class," *New York Times*, Aug. 31, 1994, A13

The future is rapidly arriving, but it's unclear whether the glass is filling or emptying. Economic forecasts now predict growth will slow to below 2 percent by 1995, and then climb a little. Unemployment is expected to rise to 6.4 percent by the end of 1995, then level off and drop.[3] Reports also show a rise in three-job households, with "wage erosion" the cause.[4] Five percent of Americans now must work two jobs to make ends meet.

In contrast, GM just had its best quarter ever, earning $1.92 billion, and Ford and Chrysler also reported records. Productivity gains have combined with increased sales and rising prices. In May GM contributed a mix of cash and stock totaling $10 billion to its pension fund.[5] But GM's profit margin is still only 2.7 percent, short of its goal of 5 percent – GM makes an average of $650 on every vehicle sold worldwide, while Ford makes $945 and Chrysler makes $1,360[6] – so the company is intensifying its efforts to cut costs by "outsourcing" parts production. This strategy meets strong opposition: in August workers at a parts-making complex strike for three days and bring 13 assembly plants to a grinding halt.[7]

> General Motors and the UAW settled a three-day strike at an Indiana parts plant Thursday, but not before 13 assembly plants ran out of components and had to shut down, idling 42,850 workers. . . .
> The key dispute between GM and UAW Local 663 was GM's plan to stop making bumper fascias at the plant and buy them from an independent supplier who could make them more cheaply. . . .
> Alan L. Adler, "Strike Ends at GM Parts Plant," *Detroit Free Press*,
> Aug. 26, 1994, 1E

Continuing inefficiencies for the Big Three are giving the Japanese an opportunity – in June the American manufacturers' market share drops 2.8 percent. A typical GM plant takes several months to retool, whereas Honda's plant in Ohio made the switch in one weekend.[8]

> In the reshuffling of workers, work places and lives following the Willow Run assembly plant closing, probably no group has felt more uprooted than those who went to work in Texas and then came back to Michigan. . . .
> Though the workers took their plant seniority with them, giving them some choice of jobs in the Arlington plant, some also found themselves unable to cope with what they considered outdated working conditions and the distance from home. . . .
> John Mulcahy, "End of the Line: GM Gypsies," *Ann Arbor News*,
> Aug. 15, 1994, A1, A8

Reports from Arlington aren't impressive. An *Ann Arbor News* special calls the Willow Run workers transplanted to Texas "pioneers driven by economic forces beyond their power." Over 400 workers and their families have moved, "changing jobs and communities for the first time in decades, or for the first time ever." Some are unhappy, others enjoy the plentiful overtime in the Arlington plant: GM hasn't taken up that union local's offer to go to three shifts, but absenteeism, job-related injuries, and staff turnover have all risen sharply in the past two years, due to labor shortages and the feverish pace of work. The Arlington plant now has one of GM's highest defect rates.[9]

The Ypsilanti Press today announced that the paper is closing, ending 90 years of publishing a daily newspaper in Washtenaw County's second-largest city.

Wayne Studer, publisher of the newspaper . . . said the closing resulted from adverse business conditions in the Ypsilanti area, particularly the closing of General Motors Corp.'s Willow Run assembly plant.

Studer said he was told of the decision 48 hours ago. "I'm still shaking," he said. Studer said he informed his staff of the closing at 8:30 a.m. "They were very shocked, devastated and disappointed," said Studer, who joined the newspaper in 1990.

"Ypsilanti Press Abruptly Ends Publication Today," *Ann Arbor News,* 27 June 1994, A1

And I'm shocked after receiving the news that the School of Education will not be renewing my contract. I'm "not contributing" to the Educational Studies program. My case is the first in what will turn out to be a decimation of its junior faculty by the University of Michigan's School of Education; of 12 junior faculty only 2 will be tenured. Suddenly I have firsthand experience of what it means to lose one's job without warning. The vertigo, anger, outrage, depression, disorientation, sense of loss, and grieving. The feeling of injustice. Awkward relations with co-workers. Confusion about what to do next. Breathless anxiety as one tries to think clearly about a future that's suddenly ambiguous and uncertain and frightening. I have a one-year "terminal" reappointment; next year is going to be tough. I throw myself into my work, following Kettering's graduates to Willow Run's middle school.

10   Caught in the Middle

August–November 1994

> Middle grade students are unique. No other grade span encompasses such a wide range of intellectual, physical, psychological, and social development, and educators must be sensitive to the entire spectrum of these young people's capabilities. For many students the middle grades represent the last chance to develop a sense of academic purpose and personal commitment to educational goals. Those who fail at the middle grade level often drop out of school and may never again have the opportunity to develop to their fullest potential.
> *Caught in the Middle*, California State Department of Education, 1987, p. v

It is 7:30 A.M. on August 31, 1994, and the sun is just peeping through an overcast sky above the rooftop of Edmonson Middle School. The morning is cool – 52 degrees, according to my car radio – and promises a mild and pleasant day – at least as far as weather is concerned. It is, once again, the first day of a school year.

Willow Run High School is clearly visible, the next building to the northeast – I've just come from there. Students begin to appear, strolling down Forest Avenue to the high school and then, a little later, to the middle school. They walk casually in groups of four or five, carrying no books, no bags. Students collect outside the school. The boys have freshly cut hair, very short, often crew cut, sometimes a cigarette tucked behind the ear.

The middle school offers an opportunity to discover how what I've seen at Kettering plays out at a new level of schooling, with a new organization – academic departments, electives, multiple teachers – and students now grappling with the physical, biological, and social claims of puberty and the dawning possibilities of adolescence. The transition to a new school, together with the beginning of a new year, promises once more

179

to highlight the taken-for-granted background against which teaching and learning are accomplished.

Edmonson was built in 1953–1954 as a combined elementary and junior high school, named after a dean of the University of Michigan's School of Education. Now housing sixth, seventh, and eighth grades, its current enrollment is around 720, 40 percent white and 55 percent African American. The average class size is between 25 and 28.

Just inside the sixth-grade entrance is a handwritten poster of school rules – "We will be polite and respectful of people and property; We will come to class on time daily, prepared to participate with only classroom materials; We will practice safe behaviors in the hallways, cafeteria, and on school grounds." The day will bring many more rules.

Edmonson's principal, Mel Anglin, is in the sixth-grade office, talking in a very gentle manner with an African American girl from seventh or eighth grade. Inside the school all is calm.

At 7:54 a bell rings to usher the new sixth graders in. The first task of the day is to distribute schedules, computer-printed half-pages. Three locations have been established around the school; the sixth grade is to go to the Small Gym. Assistant principal Ms. Lorri MacDonald, in the corridor with a walkie-talkie, directs the children, who file tentatively into the gym and line its walls, quiet and anxious. Some are accompanied by a parent, usually a mother, but most are alone.

The first formal contact of the day begins. Tables are pulled to the center of the gym and Ms. MacDonald calls out: "Okay, everybody, listen up!" The tables span the alphabet of last names. As the students start to move forward she calls, "Don't anybody move until I'm done! It doesn't do any good to push and grab. We're gonna have adults all over the place to direct you."

A woman standing nearby watches me taking notes and asks whether I'm from the press. She is the parent of a new sixth grader and a member of the school board, of nine years' tenure. Her daughter has been very scared at the prospect of attending the middle school; all the rules in the school handbook have frightened her. The new arrivals don't know what things like "in-school detentions" are, she says, but she sees a need for a clear discipline policy. There have been weapons incidents in both the middle and high schools; a high school student was dismissed, but it turned out the middle school had no policy for dealing with such an event.

By 8:10 children are finding their way into Mrs. Thompson's classroom.[1] All Edmonson classrooms are the same size and shape, with a low bookcase running the length of the room under two narrow windows, a TV looking down from high in one corner, and a large cupboard next to the door. Two walls have chalkboards, and the others bulletin boards. Mrs. Thompson's room seems modest, tidy, and functional, not yet inhabited – a generic classroom, conveying only a few hints of her personality. Around the door is an ocean frieze; at the back of the room are three computers. The walls are comparatively bare – I expect they will get filled over the year – but there are some posters (Parts of a Book; Parts of a Flowering Plant; literary genres), some slogans ("Reading Feeds the Mind"; "What is popular is not always right; What is right is not always popular"; "Attitude is Everything"), a monthly calendar, and a political map of the United States. On the shelves are dictionaries and a globe. The desks, with built-in chairs so that no tipping or tilting is possible, are arranged in pairs, in four rows. Some of the students are happily socializing; others sit alone, quiet and shy.

Each sixth-grade student is assigned to a team of two teachers. There are four teams, and I'm visiting the Thompson-Perkins – the "ToPs" – team. Jamila and Britt from Kettering are in this class. This is Mrs. Thompson's first full year at Edmonson, and it will be a busy one. Her team partner, Mrs. Perkins, has just had a baby so Mrs. Thompson will be working with a substitute – Ms. Sanders – until November. Mrs. Thompson is pregnant herself, and will leave to have her own baby soon after that. All this is going to require some organizing but Mrs. Thompson, whose blonde hair is cut short, a reminder of her days as a competitive swimmer, describes herself as a "strict" teacher for whom rules and discipline are important. Her introduction today sets the tone: she is concise, organized, direct, and brooks no interruptions.

"Morning!" she calls out. Then, again, "Good morning! Much better!" as the students respond.

First day is an introduction to the routines of school. "If you will, please take a look at your schedule," she begins, and explains how to read the paper. There may be errors – "Computers are not people, but there are people that work on computers and we all make mistakes. Don't all of a sudden go into a panic."

She gives an overview of their day. Each morning begins with announcements from 8:10 to 8:20, then the students spend their first two hours studying Reading and Science with Mrs. Thompson. (Each class period is called an "hour" though it lasts only 45 minutes.) Third hour is an elective where the students attend gym, the computer lab, study skills class, and so on, depending on what their parents have selected. They take lunch from 10:50 to 11:20, then two hours with Mrs. Sanders for Language Arts and Math. For sixth hour they return to Mrs. Thompson. Seventh hour is a second elective: woodshop, gym, home-alone, or talk time. School ends at 2:40: the buses leave shortly afterward. But today is a half day across the district: first period is extended to 8:43; seventh ends at 11:05. This half day will give them a feel for their teachers and classes.

"One of my very, very steadfast rules," Mrs. Thompson interjects, is that students not talk while she is speaking. "When you have the floor, I will respect that; when I have the floor, you do the same." The children can sit where they wish this week, but as Mrs. Thompson gets to know them she will rearrange the seating.

The assistant principal drops by, and Mrs. Thompson explains that she "deals with any kind of problem issues that you run into, or if we have a problem behaviorally in our classroom. She's also very helpful if you need assistance, or if someone is bothering you." "All these somber faces!" exclaims Ms. MacDonald.

Mrs. Thompson has learned she has to be quick on her feet to keep control without a lot of hassle, otherwise her day will be miserable and she won't get much accomplished. She won't let things slide. She knows students see her as "firm" and a lot don't like her style, but to be herself, to be a teacher, she needs not to have to deal with the "little things," the behavior issues. She won't tolerate a lot of noise, or side talking, and she demands a little more respect from students than some of her colleagues. She doesn't intend to be mean, but these are things she had when she was growing up, and she feels students need to try them a bit more. "They need to understand, and a lot of them don't, there's a difference in how you talk to your friends versus how you talk to an adult." She'd like to relate to them on a more personal level, and let them know she's human, real, but that takes a while; it is hard to do that and hope they will still have respect. So – unlike in Mrs. Page's first-grade classroom – the relationship between adult and the young people here is thoroughly impersonal. Mrs. Thompson establishes her authority not through any connection to the children's past or their future, but through her role in the institution.

Mrs. Thompson must take attendance every period. When she calls the roll for the first time she asks each student what name they like to be known by, but adds, "I don't do nicknames; that's for your friends. I'm a professional; you're a professional student in my classroom; we're kinda on a professional basis.

"I make two different kinds of phone calls home – positive and constructive. Constructive means there's something we need to work on in the classroom. If you do really well on a test, I report that too. Your parents need to know how you're doing."

The students line up to sharpen their pencils, quiet and subdued.

Edmonson is laid out as a jumble of rooms along long, narrow corridors – concrete blocks painted off-white. ("It's too small!" Jordan had exclaimed back in Kettering after the field trip last spring, when Sharon asked for impressions of the school. He's taller than she is and was able to touch the ceiling of Edmonson's corridors.) It is a disorienting layout: the corridors are indistinguishable to new arrivals, and no signs are posted to guide the visitor or uninitiated. Painting each wing a different color would help. In the transition from one class to the next a large number of students must travel relatively long distances in a short time; the result is that organization and management of these transitions becomes a dominant consideration in the daily life of the school. This emphasis is increased today because each class period is shortened and students have only three minutes to get from one class to the next, monitored by security guards with walkie-talkies. Mrs. Thompson explains that during "passing time" they can get a drink or visit the rest room or their locker.

"It's also to socialize with your friends," she tells them. "It is not meant to roam the halls, for running, shouting, or screaming in the hallway. It is not a recess time. It is a social time, it's your time, but it's not an outdoor, loud voice, recess time." If they've got a long way to go to their next class it's not very much time, she warns. And after the first couple of weeks, "we do have a tardy policy." She instructs them in the significance of the bells rung to mark the end of each hour – the one-minute "warning bell" and the "tardy bell." The second, she says, means something different to every teacher. To Mrs. Thompson it means you're in your seat, with pencils sharpened and materials ready, or she'll mark you late. "There are consequences." Three tardies, "I make a phone call." Four, an hour detention after school.

This first day, as the kids swarm down packed corridors to the next class, they spin the combination dials on the lockers they're passing, as though they might open.

And so to Ms. Sanders for fourth hour. Math and English posters brighten the walls (a multiplication table; geometric shapes; fractions;

parts of a letter; punctuation marks), and the chairs and desks are arranged in a horseshoe. Posters proclaim uplifting slogans ("Never settle for less than your best"; "Homework counts"; "Knowledge is Power"; "I know I'm somebody, 'cause GOD don't make no JUNK"; "Attitude is the mind's paintbrush. It can color any situation"). A girl reads one aloud: "I believe in me." The poster of school rules has two extra – "No swearing, rude gestures, teasing, or put downs allowed; Keep hands, feet, and personal belongings to yourself."

Ms. Sanders explains the double period and her rules: her tardy policy (in your seat, not just in the room); one person speaks at a time – "that's the courteous thing to do." "There will be more rules tomorrow!" she warns. But Ms. Sanders is notably less strict than Mrs. Thompson. She even tolerates students talking, quietly, while she's speaking to the class. The children begin to loosen up, talking more, asking questions, and they test her limits playfully. "Can we beat people up?" They joke and tease each other. "This class is going to be fun," says one.

"Everyday, do we sit where we want to?" asks one student. Ms. Sanders says they pick the seat, she'll make a chart, "and that seat will be yours for the rest of the year." They shouldn't sit just with their best friend, "but someone who'll be able to help you out with assignments, because a lot of assignments we'll be working with a partner. The two of you can help each other. Find somebody smart. That shouldn't be tough in this class," she adds.

"Are we allowed to chew gum?" No.

Like Mrs. Thompson, Ms. Sanders places emphasis on conduct in her introduction to the classroom. "What we need to remember when you come in tomorrow – if you're not in your seat by the time the bell rings, what are you? Tardy. That's all you need to know."

The bell rings for the start of fifth period. "That wasn't two hours, was it?" asks someone. "We have to go back to our other class?" Ms. Sanders explains the scheduling again, then has them fill out an address card.

Both teachers emphasize that when the bell rings at the end of class, students can't move until they've been dismissed. "That bell does not dismiss you! Who does?" "You!" the students call in unison. Then, once released, they *run* to the door.

"Are you done talking? My eyes can see all the way to the back of the room!" We're back in Mrs. Thompson's room for sixth hour.

"I didn't mean for first and second hour to sound real solemn," Mrs. Thompson tells the students, "and I didn't even cover half the rules that we have! Let me tell you folks, sixth grade is a big responsibility. But I really think you can handle it."

Soon they won't be sitting in rows, she says, they'll be working in groups. "We can get into our learning and our fun stuff," she explains. But what starts as an incentive turns into an imperative. "Five minutes out there is not your only social time; we do a lot of talking in here. We do a lot of group work where you *have* to talk. Sometimes you don't feel like talking but you're going to have to really communicate with one another. You're going to work with every person in this classroom, not just your buddies. Do we get a choice of who we want to work with out there? When we go to a job do we say, 'I don't want to work with that person, can I please be moved?' No. Sometimes maybe, but we can't always do that." In groups, she insists, they'll get some fun things done. They won't be listening to her talk hour after hour, just taking notes. "I'd get sick of myself if I had to listen to myself all hour long."

From the moment the new students arrive at Edmonson, the staff's primary concern is discipline, maintaining order, and ensuring appropriate consequences when students misbehave. This climate is tangible after only a short time in the building, but it can be understood only in its historical context.

On the face of it the concern is irrational and excessive, but there's a certain logic to it as the response to a series of events. Over a period of about a decade Edmonson acquired a reputation as an unruly, undisciplined, and even dangerous school. Teachers became increasingly dissatisfied with this and with the lack of persistence in various initiatives for change. When in the late 1980s a group called the Michigan Partnership for Education proposed "Professional Development Schools" – partnerships with a business or university – one of Edmonson's counselors wrote to the dean of the University of Michigan's School of Education to suggest such a partnership. The teaching faculty were particularly unhappy with the longtime principal and thought they might lead her toward improvements for the school.

As a PDS, Edmonson undertook a series of reforms of school organization, instructional practice, and curriculum. But the school board still came under pressure from the community and some faculty who insisted that school discipline and management were poor and the school unsafe. Then, in March 1992 an incident occurred which further focused attention on discipline – the sexual assault of a 15-year-old female student by another Edmonson student on a school bus. Parents expressed outrage, anger, and fear at the event, and frustration at what they considered the superintendent's delay announcing it. Although Yomtoob described it as an isolated incident, there was a general perception that Edmonson students were out of control. Parental outcry was followed quickly by removal of the school's principal.

The first replacement, hired from outside the district, lasted only a year – an indication of the extent of the problems the school posed. The next person to take the job had experience as principal of Cheney Elementary and, earlier, as assistant principal at the high school. Mr. Anglin is known as an effective, well-organized manager. He acknowledges that management was his primary concern last year, his first at the school, even above achievement. But in his view it's no longer so great a concern, as clear rules and regulations have become known and respected by the students. A student advisory committee has been established, about 50 students identified as troublemakers were suspended, rules were redefined and tightened, and the closed campus policy was introduced. The children used to hate the teachers, he tells me, and hated the security staff most of all – and vice versa. But Mr. Anglin, himself African American, draws a parallel with Cheney, whose principalship he relinquished to take this job. That school is 80 percent black and, he says, from the outside looks like trouble. But dark clouds often bring no rain.[2]

The concern with order makes sense, then, viewed in its historical context, as an effort to deal with a situation that had got out of hand. Mrs. Thompson considers the principal firm but fair in his discipline of both students and staff, and supportive of what she is doing, though she sees him less often than his assistants. Unfortunately, in its daily running the school seems to have forgotten its history – misbehavior is viewed as something inevitable from children in the throes of puberty. The pervasive account is that middle school children are "bundles of hormones," with whom reasoned explanation is futile. Biological changes do have, of course, an impact on adolescents' behavior, but this is also an age when young people begin to establish increasing independence from adult authority, and when relationships with peers are highly important.[3] At Edmonson, however, assertions of independence are interpreted as insubordination, and every effort is made to minimize and contain students' time together outside the classroom.

Each teacher adapts to the school's pervasive atmosphere in their own way, but in the ToPs classrooms the emphasis is on "behaving."

Very quickly a moral order is laid down in which the teacher is the fundamental authority in the classroom, and children are encouraged to police one another. Very soon, the students are telling each other to shut up when Mrs. Thompson pointedly waits for silence. She uses sanctions to invoke peer pressure at passing time – "Some people have a long way to go – you're not being respectful of them." Often, as in many other school districts, it's the African American boys who bear the brunt of the imposed order. They in particular are the kids seen as having "attitude," as disrespectful and "bad."

Vivian notes that individual teachers at Edmonson work very hard with African American students to build pride in their history and heritage, though there has been no schoolwide effort along these lines. When it comes to the tricky and delicate matter of race relations, people in Willow Run, and in the schools, have the advantage that black and white have been in contact for a long time. The district has been racially mixed for decades, and black and white teachers have been thrown together, over and over, in teams and on committees, trying to make the schools run. Willow Run hired excellent African American teachers when other districts in the county would not. Later they lost some, when other districts scrambled to meet quotas. There are many cross-race friendships among teachers in Edmonson.

Yet the outside view is that this district is "black." In TV news reports Willow Run is described as "close to Detroit": words people here consider coded.

Thursday, the second day of school, is a full day – six and a half hours, from 8:10 to 2:40. A major task this morning is locker assignment. Mrs. Thompson issues numbers and combinations, which she advises students to write down – "It's gonna get lost!" – and not to share, "even if it's your best friend." Problems with their lockers are no excuse for being late to class; they "need to know exactly where it's at, and open it quickly." She shepherds them down the corridor for a practice run. The lockers are tall and narrow, in two tiers, as old as the building. This is the only private space the children will be allowed. "It's gonna be crowded," she tells them, as each finds the right locker and they cluster around. "This is how it's gonna be." Following her instructions, they try the combinations. "A jammed locker is not an excuse to be tardy for class," Mrs. Thompson reminds them.

Back in class she goes over directions for the combination locks one more time on the board. Some children have yet to succeed, but "That's okay." At the break they go back and try again. "I'm quitting!" one grumbles. "Stupid locker!"

Jamila looks around her and says to me, "It looks like a penitentiary, with these windows, the corridors, the lockers."

Today is also the first lunch for these students. As I slip into the lunch-room, the administrators are preparing for the rush. They're figuring that, since they're starting off fresh with these sixth graders, the kids can be told to move their chairs, to clean up their area – there are no bad habits to break.

The entire grade, over 200 students, has 30 minutes, plus two 5-minute passing times, to get from their elective room to the lunchroom, line up to get in, line up for food, find a table, eat, clean up, and get to the next class. After they've eaten, they're not allowed to leave – or even stand – until the bell rings. Each group is dismissed once its table is clean. There's no time outside; no chance to let off steam. It's barely controlled chaos, voices echoing off the concrete walls. "We need a megaphone," says one administrator. "They're doing wonderful," a sea-soned kitchen aide tells me. Any misbehavior here is surely due to the circumstances, not the children's character.

Vivian was once called to Edmonson because the lunchroom was reported to be "out of control." She found that the children were merely banging in unison on the lunchroom tables. She describes the middle school as the site of a power struggle, which ironically fifth-grade students are prepared for by their elementary teachers, and which seniors look back on with scorn.

In her view, those middle school teachers who come to work and shut their doors and go home at the end of the day are the ones who are ready for change. The teachers who are involved in the struggle enjoy it, and are not the people with whom change will start. Vivian would start to change the middle school not with the kids, but with the adults. For example, she would insist that teachers deal with problems for which, at present, they give students referrals to the principal's office. "You got a problem?" she'd tell them, "You deal with it!"

The kids are smart, says Vivian: they know what they have to do to get out of school. When Vivian was at the middle school "playing prin-cipal" there was a rule that a student who got three referrals was ex-pelled. When students were sent to her she'd ask them what they'd done, and why. They'd look blank. One of them said to her, "We're not supposed to talk about that. You're just supposed to kick me out."

The kids at Edmonson who knew her from Kettering would whisper to their peers "Look out for her, she's crazy!" because Vivian would not follow the rules for punishment. Instead she would hug the kids – and they'd wriggle away but feel good about it. To her it is the children's emotional needs that are important, and rules and disciplinary procedures should take back stage when they prevent a teacher from knowing a child as a person and giving them the attention and support they need.

The class visits the Science Lab, equipped with gas and water stations and 16 computers. It looks clean and new; the kids are subdued and nervous. On the way back to Mrs. Thompson's room we stop at the lockers to practice again. Jamila succeeds, exclaiming "I did it!" and gives me a high five. (Two weeks later she'll boast to me again, "I can open my locker!")

There's a chart on the board in both Mrs. Thompson's and Ms. Sanders' rooms – two long rows divided into five boxes, one for each day of the week. It shows the points earned each day in the two homeroom classes – the currency of an incentive system.

"The way we're going to work rewards is this," Mrs. Thompson explains. "Each box represents a week. For that week you start out with a base of 100 points. That point system can go up or down, based on you as a class. If an individual is having a continuous behavior problem, or a continuous listening problem, or a continuous talking problem, I'm not going to make the rest of the class suffer. But, if you're chewing gum – this is a gum-free zone – you take the class down 10 points." The chart is up there all the time for them to see and compare themselves with the other class. At the end of the semester the teachers total the points. "Whichever total is highest gets the reward party. We had a video party, pizza party last year. Granted this is a long wait, but we do a big reward. . . . Sound good? What's it based on?"

"Behavior," in a subdued tone.

"It's your reward, it's based on what you do."

Edmonson is a large school with an unusual organization; it has not yet gone beyond being a sixth-grade elementary school joined to a seventh- and eighth-grade junior high school. The sixth-grade's separation is due in part to the layout of the building, in part because those teachers have an elementary education background. Four years ago almost all of the sixth-grade classes were self-contained, each teacher taking the same children all day, while the seventh- and eighth-grade classes were completely departmentalized. The sixth-grade teachers have a chairperson, while the seventh and eighth grades have a department head for each of the four subject areas – mathematics, science, social studies, language arts – plus one for special education and, this year, one for teachers of electives.

In the eyes of some, this organization produced not just weakness in the school's leadership but virtually a conspiracy against the principal. Rather than considering themselves a community, a learning organization, with interdependent parts and a common aim, some staff refused to cooperate, often by "suboptimizing," following the letter of their union contract. There was little trust within the school. Once Edmonson became a PDS some staff kept their distance with a "this too shall pass" attitude, but others, especially those who disliked the administration, were willing to engage, volunteering to serve on the steering committee, meeting after school on their own time.

In the past two years three department heads have been replaced, though there's been skepticism about whether the superintendent is serious about supporting change, really involving staff and giving them authority. The school has moved to a seven-period day: five for instruction, one for individual planning, and one for team planning. Several good things have come out of the latter, used with varying degrees of commitment and skill over the last couple of years. It permits discussion and reflection about students and instructional programs. The sixth grade especially has made significant changes, implementing team teaching and core classes lasting two or three periods, so that it is now part homeroom, part departmentalized. Mr. Anglin wants to encourage teaming and implement a student advisory system where each teacher has a group of 20 or so students they meet with every day. But the Edmonson administration has kept its distance from other reforms in the district, and from WRSI.

In the opinion of Professor Stuart Rankin, director of the PDS collaboration, Edmonson has begun to deal with the symptoms of its problems, if not their causes. Efforts have been made to show students that misbehavior has consequences. But as Stu puts it, "If you have excellent teaching you don't really have very many discipline management problems, you can deal with them as you go along, and teachers realize they don't have to send kids to the office. But on the other hand if kids do things and nothing happens, and teachers feel that they have no backing and no support in trying to manage the kids in the hallways or in their classrooms, then there's trouble." He adds that now "I think that teachers feel a little more support and a little more consistency in treatment of misbehavior."[4]

Prof. Rankin would like to see Edmonson a place where "kids become *empowered*, which means they develop the knowledge and understanding to make reasonable and sensible decisions on their own behalf, they develop the skills and abilities to carry out those decisions, and they develop the disposition to do it, because they see it as important to their own lives and to their society and community, and they want to be contributing and responsible people." Rankin has coauthored a textbook on thinking skills and meta-cognition, and he's researched creativity, but he's been careful not to impose his views of good teaching on the PDS collaboration. He acknowledges that a lot of progress is still to be made. "This business of changing institutions," he says, "it's not child's play."

Willow Run's Edmonson Middle School is on the rebound, bouncing back from its reputation as a "tough" school.

A districtwide effort, incorporating the help of administration, staff, parents and the community is under way at the school.

Former Cheney Elementary School Principal Mel Anglin took the helm of Edmonson this fall, bringing with him a plan to improve the school.

Administration and teachers worked together to develop new student schedules that bring the school more in line with the "middle school philosophy" district officials have been aiming for.

The University of Michigan staff forged a partnership with Edmonson to update the curriculum offerings. In the second year of the program, the team is working to revise the school's math offerings. Last year, the group tackled the science curriculum.

And after-school clubs are popping up all over the place to keep students interested in learning as well as keep them off the streets.

Still, with all that going on, the school is battling a reputation for being a "tough school . . ."

Juanita C. Smith, "Edmonson Sheds 'Tough' Image," *Ypsilanti Press*,
Mar. 27, 1994, 1A

One element in Edmonson's reforms is a shift in the science curriculum to the more "constructivist" approach of project-based inquiry, but the strategy differs from Kettering's. The sixth grade is using a commercial package, *The Great Ocean Rescue*, that includes a videodisk and information booklets for the students. Its goal is that "Students become research scientists who perform and learn to design experiments, collect and analyze data, interpret maps, graphs, and charts, draw appropriate conclusions from data, and generate possible solutions to the problem."

Mrs. Thompson introduces the science projects in the second week of school, rearranging the classroom desks into clusters. She tells the students she's going to put them in groups, and "you're going to have four different professions. You're each going to have a different job." Although the whole class will go on the same mission together, each child in the group will get a different booklet with information relevant to what they'll need to know, and need to do, to help the group. Their roles will be marine biologist, oceanographer, environmental scientist, and geologist. The video player is connected to the computer, and it will explain the mission, then randomly pick which group will go first. Their job is to "solve the mission."

For instance, in one mission "you're going to catch these criminals that are dumping pollutants, and you're going to figure out where they're dumping, you're going to run different tests to try and locate where they're at. It's not going to tell you where they're at, you as a group have different clues." Every test they run costs money, and they have to keep costs down.

"Working with a group is going to be – not necessarily difficult, but might be new for some of you. Hopefully – Shawna, sit up please – we shouldn't have a problem. Now, if your group is struggling and you're having some really, really hard problems, you need to let me know *immediately*. Do not sit there for ten, fifteen minutes, struggling to try and come to a consensus. What's a consensus?"

"A decision," Will suggests.

"A decision. What else do you think a consensus is?"

"To finish it?" tries Jamila.

"Maybe it's a final decision, or a decision that just one or two people agree upon, or everyone agrees upon? Something everyone has to agree upon. Sometimes we have to take votes to get a consensus, sometimes we just have to step back and say, 'Okay.' Remember, I said that everyone has opinions, and you bring all those opinions to your group. Just because one person has one opinion and another person has another opinion, does that mean there's a right and wrong? No. Not necessarily. We're going to try and make some guesses but they need to be educational guesses, based on what you've read and what you are bringing to the group as your role."

They've been asked to draw a picture of what they think a scientist looks like. "Let's talk a little bit about what a scientist is." Scientists are organized. "You're a scientist in this classroom – you need to have organization." They're not always in a lab; many work outside – to study dinosaurs, for example. They don't look the same, or dress the same, or use the same tools. But they're all organized. And they share their findings. "If they find out something interesting that they think is going to help their fellow scientists, the group of people who study the same thing, are they going to share?" The students aren't sure. "Most definitely."

Today, September 6, Ms. Sanders has a new seating chart, separating some children, putting troublemakers at the front. She's fracturing alliances, asserting her authority. The children are confused by this, then upset – she had told them they would keep their seats – and there's much banging and yelling as they find their new places. Jamila thumps her book angrily on her new desk. She and Britt are now sitting apart in both rooms. They began sitting together halfway through the first day of school and have been working together ever since. Jamila frequently checks her work with the teacher, or shows the completed product, looking for clarification and recognition, and she often volunteers in class. Ms. Sanders gives her the attention she thrives on ("Very good – that's exactly right!"), while Mrs. Thompson is less likely to. Britt works more quietly, but conscientiously.

"Quiet down folks. Quiet please, so we don't have to start losing points. Next hour, you come in you're going to have to be quieter than this. Otherwise I won't say a word to you, I'll just start taking points off the board. First hour has already lost fifteen points." Someone gasps. "So you guys got a good shot at beating them this week. But remember the rules. If by Friday, fifth hour, you still have 75 points left you get half the hour to use as you wish, for your social hour."

"Cool!"

"You can visit with one another, you may get paper out with markers and colored pencils. If you have enough points by Friday." Someone asks whether, if they get 100 points every day, they can socialize the whole hour. "We can't use the whole hour, because we still have to get some work done. I take away points if you're not in your seat, if I ask you to quiet down and you don't. However, if the tardy bell rings and everybody is sitting like this, with paper and pencil out ready to begin, I'll put 5 points more on the board. So you can *gain* points by doing the things you're supposed to be doing." They shouldn't think that if they drop below 75 points they might as well just mess up.

She hands out spiral-bound notebooks for journal writing. They'll write every day in their journals, for 10 minutes, a couple of paragraphs on different topics. On Friday they'll pick one topic and write for an hour. ("How can you write on it again?" one student asks.) If they don't finish, it's homework over the weekend. Friday's writing, she tells them, is graded for something different each week – spelling, or capitalization, or indentation – and they won't know ahead of time. Full sentences, proper punctuation, indenting paragraphs. Points come not from what they write, but how well they do it. Friday's writing is worth 100 points, 10 points for each of the other days.

Jamila cheers up after completing her writing and showing it to Ms. Sanders – she returns to her seat with a big grin.

Next on the agenda, "Mr. Anglin has some things in the Student Handbook he wants us to go over. Dress code." She reads the rule and points to the board, where she's written "Responsibility, Courtesy, Respect." " 'Responsibility.' Since you're not in elementary school any more, what you do in this school is *your* responsibility. If you come to class and you don't have paper, a pencil, your book, I'm going to write that down. By the third time, I sent a note home and you'll have an after-school detention."

There are expressions of shock at this. "That's stupid!"

" 'Stupid' covers the second rule. 'Courtesy.' 'Stupid' is not courteous. No one in here is stupid; no one in here will be called stupid, not by me, not by any of their classmates. Okay?"

"What will happen if we did say 'stupid'?" Ashley asks. "Detention!" another student calls out, and Ms. Sanders says she's right. "All you have to do is follow the rules and you won't have to worry about detentions."

The students talk excitedly. Ms. Sanders says nothing but she walks to the board and changes their points for the day from 100 to 95. "Oh no!" The kids "shhh!" one another. She reads again: they cannot wear shorts, halter tops, tank tops, mesh shirts, spandex, or shirts with bare midriff. "Although these things are suitable for other leisure activities they are not suitable for school."

"You can't wear *shorts* to school?!" In the summer, she tells them, Mr. Anglin will announce what kinds of shorts are acceptable. More rules: totes and sports bags belong in the locker not the classroom. ("My locker's *way* down!" "What if you can't open it?") Shawna is crushing her pencil. Ms. Sanders reads the Schoolwide Rules . . . "What is safe behavior?" No fighting, no pushing, no kicking, they tell her. There's more noise. She walks to the board again and changes 95 to 90. "We lost our pepperoni!" moans a student.

There is a Washtenaw County sheriff's deputy in the Edmonson main office one morning. The deputy, a well-built young man with a fair crew cut, has caught two boys playing in the boxcars on the railroad tracks. There were three others as well, he adds, but he was only able to catch these two. The boys are sitting there in the office, looking defiant but worried. They are tall and gawky in a way that seems both adolescent and a little malnourished. They have narrow faces, pale skin, and stubby brown hair. The taller and older-looking one has a stud in his left ear. He also has a cut on his leg and is holding one hand with the other: the deputy explains that he cut himself while running away. "How did you find us? Who told on us?" demands this boy. "I know who it was!" The deputy says no one told, he just found them himself, but the boys evidently don't believe him.

The assistant principal comes in, asks the secretary to check whether the two boys are on suspension, and whisks the deputy off to her office. Another, smaller boy has been sitting in the office – he has some blood on his head and says he's feeling dizzy. He tells me "I got conked in the head with a hood ornament," that it's "unfair, not my fault." When I ask him how that happened he shrugs, "I dunno."

He goes to join the two boxcar boys in the room they've now been ushered into. I hear him asking the older boy "How did they catch you? You're a fast runner." "Oh yeah," says the boy, "tripped over my own feet!" "Someone probably phoned in," suggests the younger boy. "I told you to wait to my lunch, then you wouldn't'a got busted, stupid!"

The secretary looks out of the office windows overlooking the corridor outside, and picks up the walkie-talkie. "Security? Security!" "Go ahead?" "We have a couple of girls over at the pay phone. They're eighth-grade students and they shouldn't be out of class using the pay phone." There are indeed two girls giggling together at the phone; a few minutes later one of the security personnel shows up and, after some protest, shepherds them off, presumably back to class.

Marshall has found himself in trouble literally from day one, when Mrs. Thompson warned him "that's the last time!" The next day when he hit and punched the person in front of him, she pantomimed a slap as she sent him out of class. (She slapped her own hand as the door closed, in such a way that several students wondered aloud, "What she do? Slap his hand?")

Today Ms. Sanders sends Marshall, who's African American, to sit at the back of the room. The topic for journal writing is: "The best, most pleasant experience you ever had," but Marshall has nothing to write with. He sits quietly facing the wall, occasionally glancing around, looking bored and demoralized. A little later Ms. Sanders comes round to talk with him. "Where are your materials today?" "In my locker." She hands him a blue sheet of paper, a notice to parents that their child is "unprepared." Headed "ATTENTION," it reads: "We do not feel we should have to continue to take class time away from those students who are prepared and ready to learn. Please discuss the importance of being prepared for class with your child. Thank you for your cooperation."

She gives Marshall a sheet of writing paper and tells him to write why he has no materials, why they're in his locker, and what he is going to do about it. After she's left, curiosity overcoming discretion, I ask Marshall if I can take a look at the blue sheet. He stares at the back wall as though he hasn't heard me. I tactfully withdraw.

As the class continues, Marshall sits tapping his pencil on the desk, traces a line speculatively across the blue sheet, and then stares again at the back wall. A little later he closes his eyes and sits with his elbow on the table and his head resting on his hand. He's evidently awake and paying attention because he looks around when Ms. Sanders happens to call on the other boy in the class whose name is Marshall, but he immediately turns back to the wall when he realizes she's not addressing him.

At the end of the period Ms. Sanders tells me Marshall never brings anything to class from his locker. As she tells me this Marshall, short and heavyset, has stopped to fight playfully with Jamila. I follow a few paces behind him as he leaves the classroom and heads toward the lockers. There's a group of several African American boys there, talking about the Bloods, but Marshall ignores them and sets to work on his combination lock. Having no success he looks around and, seeing me, calls that he'd like some help. I say "Sure," go over, and ask him to show me what he's doing, just as I had on the day the students were assigned their lockers. His problem seems to be that he overshoots the numbers, then turns back. I tell him this will reset the lock and encourage him to try again, but the bell rings for the students to return to class, so I have to open the locker myself, showing him what I'm doing. He grabs his books, looking pleased. I head back to the classroom where I explain to Ms. Sanders that Marshall is going to be tardy but that's because I was helping him with his locker. I make a point of emphasizing that he had tried to open it but hadn't been able to. At that point he ambles in and retakes his seat at the rear of the room.

Shawna has often glanced suspiciously at me in class, and unfortunately if in the corner of my eye I catch a glimpse of her turning to look at me, I involuntarily turn to see what she's doing, so we've often found ourselves staring at each other. She'll pull a face; I'll pull a face. In Ms. Sanders's class she sits in the back row, almost directly in front of me, and today at the start of fifth period she turns, glares at me, and says, "I don't like you." "I can tell you don't," I reply, "but I don't know why." "Because you sit in our class and when we try to sneak stuff by the teacher, you're watching."

I think about this for a moment, then go over and kneel down to be on her level. "I've a couple of things to say," I tell her. "The first is that it's okay for you not to like me; that's your choice." Apparently the boy sitting next to her shows astonishment at this, because her response is to laugh at his reaction. "Then," I add, "if you do anything that the teacher would tell you off for, and I see it, I'm not going to tell you off, and I'm not going to tell the teacher. I'm not a teacher." "Oh!" she said, "so you're like a student?"

Immediately there is a complete change in her attitude. She holds out her hand to shake mine, and then laughs at the way I respond. "Like this!" she explains, teaching me to curve my fingers so they link with hers, and to say "straight up!" and not "cool!" Then she takes it upon herself to teach me to say "What's up, kids!" instead of "Hi!" and explains that I will now be "loco" with the gang. She tells me I should sit with my legs crossed not at the knees, which only girls do, but at the ankles. I should wear jeans, and although my Adidas tennis shoes are "straight up," I should really get myself a pair of high-tops. "What car you got?" she asks, and tells me my Honda is "straight up" too. And she shows me how I should be observing and writing notes – with a stylish tilt to my head.

Shawna, who is slim and energetic, African American, and her friends decide that if I can't cross my legs the right way, I must be "proper" instead of "slang." They ask where I'm from, and one of them laughs at my accent, saying she watches *Are You Being Served*. She accurately imitates characters from the British comedy.

Later on, in sixth period, our eyes meet again and Shawna and I exchange palms-up gestures; then she points at my legs, and I realize with the embarrassment of someone behaving improperly in public that I am sitting again with my legs crossed at the knees. I hastily rearrange them.

At the end of September the class begins a new science mission. Mrs. Thompson plays a video clip that introduces the problem. An automated robot incubator submarine has been caught in a ghost fishing net and is drifting north in warm and shallow waters; they are to identify its most likely location. Mrs. Thompson emphasizes the different tasks for each member of the group and that each will take different notes. She stresses that they must reach their decision as a group. "This is your job," she tells them. She replays the video then gives permission to talk and discuss.

I pull up a chair to group six, Britt, Jamila, Ritch, and David, and ask their permission to sit with them while they work. They make a brave venture into a kind of classroom activity familiar to only two of them.

David is a little guy with blue eyes, vulnerable and sensitive, swimming behind large glasses. Ritch is stocky, with a babyish face and short and spiky hair. He's wearing a Chicago T-shirt.

"The only one that talks about current is D," Britt suggests, looking in her booklet at the choices of possible location.

"It's probably D then," David says.

"Who thinks it's D?" Jamila asks.

"Hold on," says Britt.

Ritch is reading from his booklet. ". . . takes them north."

"That's hurricanes!" Britt exclaims. Ritch is looking at the wrong page.

"D. Who think it's D?" Jamila asks again.

"Jamila!?" says Britt.

"It is D – 'shallow,' " Ritch agrees.

"It might be C or D," Jamila points out.

Britt reads from her booklet. "Mine says . . ."

"I think it's C," announces Jamila.

"Why C?" Britt asks her.

"D," states Ritch.

David says, "It's E."

Mrs. Thompson calls out, "Everybody in your group needs to be talking."

"Jamila!" Britt appeals again.

"Who votes for A, raise your hand," Jamila suggests. She repeats this for the other possible locations. "Okay, we'll try D."

Ritch points to the map on the wall. "Arctic Circle." He gets up to look more closely. "Arctic Ocean."

"What do we put down on the page?" Jamila calls to Mrs. Thompson.

"Explain where and why," she replies.

"Oh, we've got to say where and why," Jamila repeats. She writes 'location – D' on her paper.

"B," says Ritch.

Britt and Jamila correct him together: "D!"

"Why?" Britt asks Jamila.

"Because . . . I'm writing all this," says Jamila. She's copying from her booklet.

"You're not supposed to," says Britt.

"I'm writing all D down," says David. They are all now writing their notes.

Mrs. Thompson comes over. "How's the group doing, David? The whole group together. Did you agree?"

"Shallow ocean; continental shelf," Ritch suggests.

"A very good point," says Mrs. Thompson. "Is everybody else getting that down?"

I ask Britt what happens next, now they've made their choice of the incubator's location. She tells me they just wait until they find out if they're right. They've all agreed on D but they can't explain why.

"What I asked you to do, this time, this mission," Mrs. Thompson calls out, "was to make sure everyone in your group was doing their job. I had to get on a few people myself because people were just sitting there not doing their job.

"You are not to be copying, you are to be communicating. Once you've communicated then you put it in your *own* words in your own notes. You pull the group down when you don't do your job.

"Some of you aren't doing your job. As a team-member, you take a little bit of a risk letting someone know, 'Why aren't you writing that down?' I don't need you to be negative about it, I don't need you to be snotty about it, I'm not saying take an attitude, and get on someone's case – that's my job. You need to be concerned, you need to say, 'Why is your page blank when the rest of us have everything written down?' If you can't keep up with the group or if you don't agree with the group, then you better be stating something to the group, for instance 'I don't agree,' 'I don't understand,' 'Could you explain that to me again.' Those are wonderful words to say to somebody, and I bet anyone in your group will try to explain it to you again.

"I see things happening again where two people are sitting there talking, making all the decisions, and two other people, or three other people, or however many other people, are sitting there and just agreeing. Not doing their job. Just nodding your head saying 'Yeah that sounds good,' is not doing your job. Remember our goal is to spend the least money possible, and if some one person, who's just sitting there nodding their head, holds some key information back from your group because they're not doing their job, that could have been money better spent.

"Do you all understand what I'm saying to you? There's this mission and one more mission left. And if I continue to see people just sitting there you will have extra work. You're not gonna hurt the team that you're in by being taken out of it. That puts extra work on people who are already *doing* the work. But you will have extra work yourself. Everyone understand how to get on somebody when they're not doing their job?" There are murmurs of assent.

"Okay. You need to say, 'Well, why is your page blank? Could you write that down? Get that written down!' It's not a fun matter, it's a serious matter. It's one that affects you, all of you, in your group. And please don't be shocked when you get a group grade, and say 'I did my work, I can't believe how I get that grade Mrs. Thompson, I did my work!' Well, someone in your group evidently didn't do their work. It's very serious."

Mrs. Thompson draws a chart on the board to record each team's decision: their "Where" and "Why." Group one, which reports first, picks choice A as the location of the missing robot sub. The other six groups have picked location D, in the Arctic. Their reasons typically make reference to the direction of the current, the warmth of the water, and its shallow depth.

Jamila is the self-selected spokesperson for group six. She reads her notes, which are a direct copy from her booklet. When the teacher asks her for additional reasons for their choice the other members of her team whisper hints to her. The bell rings before the class can check their decisions against the video and computer, but in sixth hour they return to this activity.

"Okay I can't hear you because we have some rude students talking. I assigned extra assignments last hour to those students that couldn't follow along and do what we were doing. That means you have homework. And we're talking definitions and pages of questions and answers out of your science book which I will hand to you if you can't handle. When a student in this classroom is speaking to the entire classroom *your job is to listen.*"

She selects group one to conduct the test. They've changed their choice to location D. Mrs. Thompson plays the corresponding video clip, and the students groan. "It is not location D, folks." Mrs. Thompson tells them to get back to the drawing board and search for another location. After they've had some time to do this she asks group six to share their findings.

Jamila says, "We picked George's Bay, C, because the ocean current in the waters of George Bay" – she reads – "the temperature of the polar regions and is shallow. And it is southeast. . . ."

"Southeast?!," Ritch interrupts. "You mean north –"

"I mean northeast," Jamila corrects.

"Water is shallow," Mrs. Thompson repeats. "David, what else do you need to add to that?"

David is silent.

"I'm not picking on you," says Mrs. Thompson, "but I need to know that everyone in the group hasn't just listened to someone dictate what they think the answer should be. I need to know that you have come to a group consensus, Ritch. And that you know why. Do you know why, Ritch, that your group chose C?"

"Yes," says Ritch, after a pause.

"Why? We're waiting."

The others whisper to Ritch. He says, "Because . . ."

"Read it if you have to."

". . . the kelp and it was floating here. . . ." Ritch reads from his booklet.

"You're reading from the book," Mrs. Thompson interrupts him. "Read me from your notes, which should be *complete*."

Ritch pauses, then tries again. "The whale – the whale got caught, in the net, that had got cut . . ." He's reading from the notes he made for the group's *first* choice.

"This should be under 'Where,' and 'Why,' " Mrs. Thompson says sternly. "There should be a second portion because we all said D wasn't working. Jamila was helpful in telling us you chose C because the water's shallow, I need to know why else your group just chose C, Ritch."

"Because the whales – the whale got caught, and it was cut up, from the net taking it north, where it is shallow. . . ."

"It was cut up by a what? I didn't hear that part."

"It was cut off, from the ghost net."

"It *is* a ghost net, but what was it cut off from?"

"A propeller."

"A propeller." She writes this on the board. "And so you're telling me, in location C there are currents flowing north?"

"Sure," says Ritch, with some relief. Mrs. Thompson writes again, then turns to the next group.

It's time to check answers again against the computer-controlled video. Group six is becoming discouraged. Jamila has her eyes closed and her hands pressed together, praying C will be the correct choice.

Mrs. Thompson calls on David, then Ritch. Ritch bluffs – none of them have any notes.

Jamila says to Britt, "Next it's your turn." Britt looks nervous.

"I see three people right there in one group who did not do their job," Mrs. Thompson announces to the class. Jamila and David quickly look around, but Mrs. Thompson is talking about group five. She tells the three students in that group she wants to see notes written in the next five minutes or she'll give them extra work. "Josh is not pulling your group along. I will come back to group five."

Group six is splintering in acrimony. Jamila takes off her shoe and hits David with it. He looks close to tears. He scrawls meaninglessly on his paper. Ritch is sucking his thumb. Britt is withdrawn.

Mrs. Thompson steps out of the room to deal with some noisy students in the corridor. Jamila hits David.

"Kiss my butt!" David says. "You shouldn't hit me with your shoe."

"You shouldn't kick my desk."

"I didn't, I was kicking my own," says David. "It was an accident."

"You're doing it to aggravate me," Jamila replies.

I try to distract them by asking what they think of school.

"I hate school," says Ritch, " 'cause of the work."

"I *like* school," says Jamila. "I can't work with *him!*"

A little later, when the bell rings, Jamila exclaims, "We're out of here! Finally!"

To criticize Mrs. Thompson for being a "strict" teacher would be to miss what Edmonson illustrates about the character of schooling, and the difficulty of reform. She's struggling to combine constructivist pedagogy with authoritarian management, and the contradictions between curriculum and control produce a classroom climate in which the conditions for student exploration, risk taking, and discovery fail to materialize.[5] Evaluation has become based on conduct, not learning – and is usually disapproval of misconduct. Schoolwork has become punishment, and escape from it a reward. To work is the children's "job," something they *have* to do, with no further reason provided. Learning is seldom mentioned; tests are simply more work. The points system offers extrinsic reward to replace what the work lacks – but it becomes a transparent instrument for the teacher to retain control. Efforts at teamwork by the students dissolve, in this atmosphere of criticism and reproach, into dissension and recrimination.

All this is a clear demonstration, if one were needed, that reform of the curriculum is not sufficient when it occurs without change in the relation of student and teacher, and in the culture of the classroom. Edmonson is undercutting its own efforts at reform.

Our basic idea [is] that character and mind are attitudes of participative response in social affairs.
> John Dewey, *Democracy and Education*, New York: Free Press, 1916,
> pp. 316–317

The longer I live, the more I realize the impact of attitude on life.
Attitude, to me, is more important than facts.
It is more important than the past,/than education,/than money,/than circumstances,/than failures,/than success,/than what other people think/or say or do.
It is more important than appearance,/giftedness or skill.
It will make or break a company . . . a church . . . a home.
The remarkable thing is we have a choice/every day regarding the attitude we will embrace for that day.
We cannot change our past . . . /We cannot change the fact that people/will act in a certain way.
We cannot change the inevitable.
The only thing we can do is to play on/the one string we have,/and this is our attitude. . . .
I am convinced that life is 10%/what happens to me/and 90% how I react to it.
And so it is with you. . . .
> Charles Swindoll, "Attitude," a poster in Ms. Sanders's classroom[6]

---

at•ti•tude [F, fr. It *attitudine*, fr. *attitudine* aptitude, fr. LL *aptitudin-*, *aptitudo* fitness – more at APTITUDE] **1:** the arrangement of the parts of a body or figure: POSTURE **2a:** a mental position with regard to a fact or state **b:** a feeling or emotion toward a fact or state **3:** position assumed for a specific purpose <a threatening ~> **4:** a ballet position similar to the arabesque in which the raised leg is bent at the knee **5:** the position of an aircraft or spacecraft determined by the relationship between its axes and a reference datum (as the horizon or a particular star) **6:** an organismic state of readiness to respond in a characteristic way to a stimulus (as an object, concept, or situation) **syn** see POSITION
> *Webster's New Collegiate Dictionary*, Merriam-Webster, 1977

Edmonson's disciplinarian school climate and stern teaching turn every-day adolescent challenges to adult authority and preoccupation with peers into misbehavior and "discipline problems." Denied positive recognition from their teacher, the students seek it from its other source in the class-room – their peers.[7] Their attitude of opposition and resistance, their mischief, increasingly brazen and impertinent, is both a rejection of their teacher's authority and a performance for appreciative classmates.

Recognizing these dynamics is important to an understanding of how efforts to reform pedagogy succeed and how they fail. And it is also im-portant because schooling is *always* about children's "attitude" as stu-dents – though this remains invisible when the attitude is one of align-ment with a teacher, rather than against. Schools can require attendance and prescribe rules of conduct, and impose penalties for breaches. Teachers can design the formal and informal curricula through which children and adults now relate to one another as "student" and "teacher." But neither schools nor teachers can determine the *manner* in which children live out this relationship and inhabit the world of the school classroom. Every child adopts a stance in this world – an attitude toward teacher, other students, to self, to different ways of knowing, ev-ident in their posture, bearing, and demeanor. When it gets noticed be-cause it is oppositional, this stance is a child's "attitude."[8]

Attitude is an attempt to reconcile the contradictions of life in the classroom; the costs and benefits of being recognized in the abstract terms of "good student" and "bad student." The abstractions of school – "student," "teacher" – are taken for granted and invisible, but attitude can become salient and problematic.

It is because the school can't *determine* the attitude a child adopts, but can only seek to foster it by defining the ground on which it is adopted, that attitude can become such an issue in the classroom. Ironically, even when it becomes salient, "attitude" is misinterpreted by most Edmon-son teachers and administrators as something "natural," the result of all those pubescent hormones, rather than as a response to the school's cli-mate and history. Efforts to counter it consequently take the form of more punishment; at best a blind eye is turned.

A week later, the attitude of recalcitrance and antagonism is growing in both classrooms. In Ms. Sanders's room, Jerry bangs his books down hard and checks to see if she reacts.

"What's a novel anyway?" Britt asks.

"A big old thick book," says Shawna.

Marshall doesn't have his book again today. Ms. Sanders fills out another blue sheet. Next period, Mrs. Thompson sends him out of her room for misbehaving, and he makes faces through the window in the door. Later, while her back is turned, the door opens and Marshall waltzes in, waving his arm and smiling. Then he ducks out again. Later in the year, I'll find Marshall just wandering the corridors during class time. How he's able to do this and not get caught he won't tell.

When Ms. Sanders tells Joey to turn around he interprets her literally and turns *all* the way, with his legs over the back of his chair. She puts his name on the board. When she tells Keisha to read along as she gives directions, Keisha responds "No!" but not loud enough to be heard. Josh belches. When Ms. Sanders corrects Jamal for calling his neighbor a rude word, he objects in a subdued tone, "She called herself that."

At the end of the hour Ms. Sanders complains at the slight progress they've made, and suggests that for next period they "get it together, and come back a different group of people!" But the same tone continues. Ms. Sanders assigns work; Keisha mutters, "This is stupid!" Mrs. Thompson gets the same treatment. Before she comes into her classroom Jerry shouts out, "Raise your hand if you hate Mrs. Thompson!"

By mid-October Mrs. Thompson has rearranged the desks in rows, heightening the sense of constraint and rigor. The students look glum and bored. Even when Mrs. Thompson tells them that scoring 100 percent on three consecutive spelling tests gets them a "spelling coupon" they can use to skip a test, they're subdued. A child caught talking is likely now to stare challengingly back at the teacher.

The class goes to the Science Lab to type letters on the computers. Some finish quickly, using fancy fonts, others are struggling to type, to spell. I talk quietly with some of the kids. Is there anything they don't like?

"Mrs. Thompson. She's way too mean with Jamila, even when she is wild and crazy."

"She's a brat! Her name is . . . , doesn't she look like a . . . ?"

How do they like the school?

"It's boring," Britt replies.

"It fucks!" a boy adds.

The kids see Ms. Sanders as "nice," but the work as senseless and boring. "It's stupid," one girl says to me about a math work sheet. "I won't need it, and I got doctors in my family. I showed them this and they said, 'What!?' " In her class the kids are creatively finding ways not to work. Half the class is talking or just sitting.

They are also ticked that the number of points they need for "social time" on Friday has increased each week. The first week of school they needed 100, now it's 250. "We were quiet all the first hour, why didn't we get any points?" Jamila calls out one afternoon, in an aggrieved tone, when Ms. Sanders says they don't have enough points for social time. Ms. Sanders just calls for silence.

When she gives Joey an extra assignment for misbehaving he drops his head on his desk after she's gone. Then he destroys his pen with his teeth, flicking pieces at the boy next to him, stabbing his reading book. He checks repeatedly to see if Ms. Sanders is noticing – she's pointedly not. At the bell, the children rush to the door.

There's a swim trip to the high school pool tomorrow, but the students don't seem excited. Mrs. Thompson goes over the rules. Snapping people with towels: detention for one solid month. "A month!?" "Yes, we have detention every day." No permission letter: they don't swim; they'll be up in the bleachers, "but you can't talk." "If you swim and you can't follow the rules you're *out* of there. If you're afraid of being splashed, don't even bother to put on a suit."

Mrs. Thompson grabs Jerry. "You need to get rid of the attitude," she says angrily.

"Let go of my arm!"

"Don't tell me what to do! You need to work like sixth grade. Right now we're about third grade."

"There's a lot of grouchy people today!" Jamila whispers.

Don't freak out; Don't wig out; Don't vex, fret, or stew; Don't get all bent out of shape; Don't lose your cool; Don't have a cow; Don't go ballistic; Don't blow a gasket; Don't get your nose out of joint – Get a grip!

Poster on the door of Mrs. Thompson's room

Zero Tolerance for inappropriate behavior for the next 31 days.

Note on the board in Ms. Sanders's room.

Every teacher at Edmonson, despite differences in how they instruct, must adapt to the climate of the school. Not all align with it – attitude is, for staff as well as students, chosen rather than imposed. But to describe other classrooms would be to risk creating the impression that Ms. Sanders and Mrs. Thompson are somehow "bad" teachers, which is not the case.

Q: Why do teachers hate Gov. John Engler so much?

A: Engler views teacher unions as self-serving monopolies with insatiable demands for higher salaries at taxpayer expense. The relationship went from bad to worse last spring with passage of a law to put teeth into the ban on teacher strikes.

After it goes into effect next year, teachers will be fined a day's pay for every day they strike, and their union will be assessed $5,000. School boards will be able to impose their last, best offer if mediation fails and also to contract out non-teaching services without union consent.

The law also allows districts to decide the school calendar, including the length of the day and the start of the year – two items that have been negotiated with teachers for years. . . .

Joan Richardson and Chris Christoff, "Schools Are Big Divide in Governor's Race," *Detroit Free Press*, Oct. 19, 1994, 1A

After eight years of Japanese domination, the U.S. in 1993 had the world's most competitive economy.

But many ordinary Americans, and even some corporate middle managers, might greet that news with a shrug and a "So what?" – or a skeptical obscenity. The price of beating overseas competition has been bitterly high: wave after wave of downsizing layoffs, wage increases limited or foregone, replacement of full-time workers by part-time or temporary hired hands. Even those who have hung on to regular jobs are often too exhausted by long hours of overtime and weekend work to enjoy the extra money they are earning.

George J. Church, "We're #1 – And It Hurts," *Time*, Oct. 24, 1994, pp. 50–56

Despite the growth of the overall economy, the typical American household saw its income decline in 1993, and more than a million Americans fell into poverty, according to figures made public today by the Census Bureau.

Jason DeParle, "Census Report Sees Incomes in Decline and More Poverty," *New York Times*, Oct. 7, 1994, A1, A9

Autoworkers say they are being pushed to the brink of a labor war with General Motors Corp., claiming that demands for more production with fewer people triggered the sabotage of a key Livonia engine plant.

An unknown GM worker, dubbed "Edward Scissorhands" inside the plant, cut the power source to the assembly lines last weekend and then trashed the plant's electrical blueprints. . . .

Workers say the sabotage at the Livonia plant is an extreme example of frayed relations between a rebuilding GM and its United Auto Workers employees. Livonia is one of many GM plants where workers say they are weary from a grueling production schedule. . . .

"Greedy employers," UAW President Owen Bieber said last week in a veiled reference to GM, "as shortsighted as ever, are trying to produce far too much product with far too few people."

GM executives concede their labor relations are strained, but say nothing will change.

"We're in a tough environment now with the UAW," GM North American President G. Richard Wagoner told suppliers he met with this week. "We have no intention to go back to the way things used to be. That was a going-out-of-business strategy."

Keith Naughton and Helen Fogel, "Stress Sparks Labor War,"
Detroit News, Sept. 23, 1994, 1A

The investment community seems convinced John F. Smith Jr., president and chief executive of G.M., has not backtracked on his pledge to make the company as productive as its rivals when he agreed to add 531 permanent employees to the Buick City work force – after eight years of no blue-collar hiring. . . .

One reason G.M. has the worst productivity level in the industry is that many of its models are hard to assemble, compared with its competitors', and include too many parts. That is particularly true of the mid- and full-sized Oldsmobiles and Buicks built at Buick City.

Doron P. Levin, "Market Place. Analysts Seem Willing to Overlook the
New Hiring That Settled a Strike at G.M.," *New York Times*,
Oct. 4, 1994, C6

The kinds of demand the new economy will be making of workers are becoming clearer. In 1993 the U.S. economy became once again the most competitive in the world. A *Time* cover story – "We're #1 and it hurts" – and a full-page *New York Times* article – "It's too much of a good thing, G.M. workers say in protesting overtime" – document how increased productivity has been achieved through downsizing, lowering wages, increasing overtime, and hiring temporary workers with no job security or benefits.[9] If companies are finding value and productivity in workers' on-the-job learning, in creativity, cooperation, and co-responsibility, in "high performance" organizational structures, many are also forcing their employees to work longer hours for lower pay. The average factory work week has expanded to the longest it's been in the 38 years records have been kept by the Bureau of Labor Statistics – 42 hours, including 4.6 hours of overtime.

Despite the new contract that seemed to protect the autoworkers' interests, the Big Three have found ways to squeeze them. Compulsory overtime, for example, has been written into the union contract for years, but only now are the manufacturers putting it to use. GM is requiring 10 hours of overtime, twice the national average for factory workers, strongly encouraging even more voluntary work, and workers are complaining they're being asked to do several people's jobs. GM, now just 14,000 short of its planned 74,000 cut jobs, is loath to hire any permanent workers. And with longer hours come an increased pace of work – GM has speeded up some production lines from 44 to 49 vehicles per hour. Workers say the results are lower quality and more frequent injuries.

Now GM announces its fourth reorganization in 10 years: the merger of four divisions into two, to integrate and streamline design and development. Auto sales – especially pickups and minivans – rose again in September by 7.4 percent. GM reported third-quarter losses of $328 million, but the third quarter is traditionally the least profitable: this time last year GM lost $1.1 billion.[10]

"Do workers get to reap the benefits of the improved efficiencies that they are delivering to employers?" asks an economist interviewed by *Time*. A strike against GM at Flint, Michigan, suggests that the answer is no. The Flint strike is settled only when GM agrees to hire some new permanent workers.

The national unemployment rate is now only 5.9 percent, and jobs are being generated at a rate of around 280,000 a month, but many of these are temporary and low-paid service jobs, so people must moonlight to earn enough to live. And although labor shortages have appeared in several areas, employers are hiring unskilled workers and training them rather than bid up wages to attract skilled workers.[11] Jobs haven't headed south or to the Pacific Rim, but nonetheless downsizing has eliminated many high-paying manufacturing jobs, and with them the blue-collar middle-class lifestyle. In particular, blue-collar, production-line, secure, unionized jobs in manufacturing and construction, available to workers with no more than a high school degree, have vanished. Seventy-five percent of the new jobs are for managers and professionals in the service industries. Many of these are white-collar computer-using jobs.

While corporate profits and executive salaries are soaring, median household income dropped $312 last year and a million more people dropped below the poverty line. The decline has been worst for those without a college education. Workers' wages have dropped an average of 2 percent since 1990; those of managers and supervisors have risen 4 percent.[12] Robert Reich says, "America has the most unequal distribution of income of any industrialized nation in the world. We cannot have a prosperous or stable society if these trends continue."

11 The Change Game

November 1994–June 1995

ATTITUDES
Qualities That Count With Employers

Figures from a Census Bureau survey of 3,000 employers nationwide, conducted in August and September last year.
When you consider hiring a new non-supervisory or production worker, how important are the following in your decision to hire?
(Ranked on a scale of 1 through 5, with 1 being not important or not considered, and 5 being very important.)

FACTOR	RANK
Attitude	4.6
Communication Skills	4.2
Previous work experience	4.0
Recommendations from current employees	3.4
Recommendations from previous employer	3.4
Industry-based credentials certifying skills	3.2
Years of schooling completed	2.9
Score on tests administered as part of interview	2.5
Academic performance (grades)	2.5
Experience or reputation of applicant's school	2.4
Teacher recommendations	2.1

Peter Applebome, "Employers Wary of School System," *New York Times*, Feb. 20, 1995, A1, C8

Marshall Smith and Jennifer O'Day, the architects of systemic reform, imagined that implementing the "common content" of reformed schooling would be an "educational endeavor" involving conversations among parents, teachers, the press, and other members of the public. They were optimistic about the outcome of this conversation: they saw

211

it leading to a more thoughtful media, to a more professional community of teachers, to better informed parents.[1]

Once a common content was agreed upon, and other components aligned, they believed it would be possible to define the educational resources and teaching practices necessary to provide all students with the opportunity to learn. And it might be necessary to define "resource" and "practice" standards that focus on the *input* to education, as well as "performance" standards that focus on its *outcomes*, for only if a school has adequate resources and satisfactory practices can it be justly held accountable for measured student outcomes.

O'Day and Smith acknowledged that debate and controversy are likely to surround attempts to define a common curriculum content, but they treated this as a strength, not a weakness, of their proposal. Given the diversity and inequities of U.S. society, the definition of a common content to school curriculum is bound to be controversial, especially when that content is made the "driving force and linchpin for the entire system." Consequently, O'Day and Smith saw "broad and deep public debate" as essential and productive. They appealed to a sense of liberal justice: schools should be socially neutral toward different conceptions of the good life, respecting and furthering a variety of cultures and traditions. Schools should foster dialogue, encourage tolerance, and foster a critical attitude. Cultural claims would be excluded which are "unsupported by evidence through rational appraisal, such as claims of particular historical occurrences or creationism."[2]

Smith and O'Day considered the kind of performance-based accountability model Engler is promoting, where feedback from outcome measures is used to induce self-correction, "closing the barn door after the horse is stolen," because poor and minority schools don't have the resources to make necessary changes, and waiting for evidence of failure is waiting too long, too late. Such schools don't lack *will*, they lack *capacity*. They don't have a fair opportunity to meet the standards. In particular, Smith and O'Day rejected any idea of holding individual teachers accountable for their students' performance, because education is a collective enterprise.[3]

Something like the conversation Smith and O'Day envisioned has begun in Willow Run, but the quality reforms quickly preempt it, and the Michigan Statewide Systemic Initiative's tendency to get bureaucratic undermines it. On October 14, Vivian, Scott, Betty, and Craig report back to WRSI about the latest MSSI meeting in Traverse City.

MSSI staff appear to be making an effort to be more collaborative. "I think part of it is, when you're trying to do something different," Vivian considers, "it's hard to let go and know that it will happen. There is this fear that at the end of the five years nothing will have happened, and then we will look like – whatever. I keep saying, 'And so if nothing happens, what does that mean?' It won't be because effort wasn't there, because people didn't try. That's a part of what's wrong with education, it's like, if you are not successful that is taken as failure. It should be taken as, you haven't found the clue yet, keep looking. But that's not the way things operate, and it's not the way NSF operates, as we know. We know within the first year people had their grants taken away. That's the other pressure I'm sure is operating at the state level, recognition that the grant can be taken, so they keep doing these things to make sure we're on track."

The Traverse City meeting included a superintendents' session, in the belief that for reform to work the superintendent must embrace it. "They really insisted Dr. Joe be there," Vivian explained. "I kept saying, 'Leave us alone, we know we're okay.' They kept saying, 'People need to know what you're doing. You guys get your picture in the paper, you're doing all these things, we don't know what you're doing.' I said, 'Maybe part of what we're doing is that the board and the superintendent don't tell us what to do. They say, "Okay, you can make those decisions," and we just keep them informed. Maybe we really don't need our superintendent.' "

But MSSI phoned Dr. Joe and he flew up – on the night of a board meeting, too. Apparently there were "a few tense moments in the room" as Dr. Joe stated his view that districts had really begun to open up and try different things "only," as Vivian glossed what she'd been told, "to have this Christmas Package shoved at you, and have all this, 'You must do by . . .' stuff again." Several people approached Vivian afterward "saying what a great boss we have, that he would be so outspoken. I said, 'Well, we'll probably be one of those districts gets audited pretty soon!' " And "everybody wanted a bear!"

"Last year when we went to Mackinac Island we made a little bit of a shift," Vivian tells newcomers. "We recognized that while we would hope that educators really are free-thinking and could deal with the openness, what we're really finding is educators on the whole – not necessarily everybody – tend to be, 'Tell me step one, step two.' Everybody wants to know, 'What is it that you want us to do?' That's what we kept hearing all last year. 'Well, you're not telling us anything.' " So while at Mackinac the committee decided to highlight practices in science and math that move in the right direction – approaches like project-based science and the Hands On Museum project. Not things teachers *have* to do, but guidance for those who need it.

Scott gives us a synopsis of a presentation he and Betty gave at Traverse City on the new MEAP science test. The new test still draws its topics from the *MEGOSE;* these objectives will continue to be tested. But the *format* of the test is very different, and the changes will occur very soon, next fall. For two years each school can choose an "area-specific assessment" they wish to be tested on, "to give us a chance to try and build a curriculum" to suit this "new test-taking method." After that, testing will be "Framework-wide."

Scott emphasizes, "In a short period of time we need to get across to staff the importance of choosing what they're going to study." And "the most important thing about this whole new MEAP is the format of the test."

He passes out examples of the three new kinds of problems on the new MEAP. All deal with "using," "constructing," and "reflecting on" scientific knowledge – the same format that organizes the *MEGOSE*. But they make radically new demands of students.

We try a "cluster problem." It presents "a real world context (an event, a situation or an object)" and asks both multiple choice and short essay questions. A diagram shows the "desert food web" of termite, Joshua tree, yucca moth, screech owl, and so on. We puzzle over the essay question for several minutes: "List three kinds of evidence that biologists might have used to help determine that the night lizard is eaten by the screech owl." "It's a heavy reading test," Mary remarks. The next question is "more ethereal – has nothing to do with the picture at all." "Discuss how the organisms in this food web are supported by the non-living parts of the desert environment. Be specific in the ways in which air, water, sunlight, sand, soil, and rocks support the organisms in the food web." "They're open-ended questions that don't have a lot to do with what you're looking at. Students have to figure out, infer, draw on prior knowledge."

Scott has trouble getting our attention back from the cluster problem. "I feel like I'm teaching in my classroom! It's been a long day already." We apologize.

"I appreciate your efforts," Linda, from Cheney, tells him. "And I'm overwhelmed."

In a "text criticism" problem, students read a passage and respond. "It has nothing to do with trying to search for answers," Scott explains.

"You read the question, you read the article, and you try and interpret from past knowledge and from what it told you, to try and answer these questions. And write responses again. It's not only writing, it's reading, it's very heavily reading based, and it's very heavily thinking in a new open-ended manner. There is no one right answer. We have to get away from a 'one correct answer' type response."

The third kind of problem is an "investigation cluster." At the start of the year every class does an investigation, a lab, following directions and using materials distributed by the MEAP office. In the test, students answer questions about what they found.

Scott says, "The point I wanted to make at Traverse City was, looking at this test, let's think about instructional atmosphere. Can we continue with a traditional atmosphere within a classroom setting where the teacher is talking, the student is writing . . . ?"

"No, the student is checking," Vivian corrects him.

"Or maybe writing down, copying down, not thinking. If we continue that, when they get to this question six, what are they going to do? Last year we gave two pilots of this. The State Department called up on Friday, said 'Can you do this Monday' – there was no prep time. We gave it in a nontraditional setting where the kids are not lectured to, they're taken through a problem-driven or problem-based science course, and then we gave it to a traditional science class. The problem-based science class, the students, about 80 percent scored in the top range. In the traditional course, 20 percent scored in the top range. The kids either didn't answer, or they put 'I don't know,' or they doodled. Those were the types of responses they gave, not even semi-thoughtful responses.

"Regardless of what we might want to believe," he continues, "MEAP drives the curriculum. We're teaching what's on the MEAP, so we can do well for the MEAP. If this MEAP is changing, what's an instructional framework going to look like in order for students to be successful? The teacher's job changes. The teacher is no longer standing and talking, and disseminating information. The teacher becomes a facilitator, or a coach, or a classroom administrator."

Not all the teachers around the table are overwhelmed. "Teachers get excited about this kind of thing," says one of the newer teachers. "The test *needs* to change, because the way teachers are starting to teach now. . . ." says another.

"Hopefully," Scott agrees, "this will drive things in a positive manner. The thing that's disturbing is the timeline on all of this."

Units have been developed, he reports, for the three areas to be tested next year, but Vivian insists we shouldn't be concerned about materials and curriculum right now – what's important first is that all staff understand the format of the test. And that this affects *all* grades, not just those in which the MEAP is given. Vivian reminds us that her efforts to get curriculum writers this summer were without success. "We need to make sure there's a balance so everything gets covered." We don't want every grade covering dinosaurs! "We're gonna have to revamp so it's real clear where the areas fall. And then get the materials." The district is looking at these Curriculum Units, though Vivian is horrified that while the state has used public money for writing the materials, districts are now being charged $150 for each Unit. But "we don't have a choice but to make the material available."

"Scott," she continues, "I understand we always say that MEAP drives curriculum. That is not the case this time. We just didn't follow what was out. That book" – the *MEGOSE* – "has been out for how many years? And I know I sent it to every building at least twice and I've only been in the curriculum office two years. That's very frustrating for me. We can't say MEAP is driving us, we have to say we're behind. We've had this information and we've not done much with it. That test is built off of the state curriculum. We blame them for a lot of things, but what folk need to know is they're really building assessments off those curriculums and if we're not taking a look at it, we're gonna be behind the eight ball again."

Scott says, "We now have a body – us – to try to make sure this gets out to staff."

"We need to begin a discussion," Vivian continues. "What are some things we can do as classroom teachers that will make a difference for kids who will need to write, and read?" For example, "you don't have to correct a paper, you just have to set up an opportunity for your students to write at least fifteen minutes a day.

"We need each person – and I think we have every building represented, that's what we were shooting for – to take this back and as quickly as you can begin the discussion about the differences. This is just the beginning; it's not going to go away. They're going to test, test, test, test, test us and they're going to change the format because there has been some feeling that there has not been in-depth learning on the part of our kids. With the methodology we've been using. Is that real, is it not fair? – I don't know. It's the reality. We don't listen folks, unless they test us. Until they test us we don't hear it. Unfortunately that's really the way life is."

Scott adds, "Staffs need to understand where this is going as soon as possible, so we have the best opportunity for our kids to do well next fall. If we wait – the longer we wait to choose where we're going to have an area-specific assessment, the longer we wait to tell people what's going to be tested, the more we're going to be hurt."

While WRSI has found ways of working with – or around – MSSI's tendency to get "top-down" and bureaucratic, the Governor's new "quality package" is an unexpected delivery of imperatives. Mandates in effect, if not in appearance. The committee works to make the best of a difficult situation, in a manner I've come to respect – communication and community building to help people cope, to voice frustration, to empower, give permission, and model solutions. The emphasis is on what's positive in the new tests: their direction, their goal. The fact that all this is happening much too fast, and that having the test drive instruction puts the cart before the horse, cannot be our focus.

This attitude takes its toll, though. Back in August Vivian confessed she's close to quitting. She hates to talk out of both sides of her mouth, and the state is making conflicting demands, telling people what to do while encouraging "systemic change." Vivian doesn't want to pass along these conflicting messages to her staff.

The MEAP is a high-stakes test and it is pervasive – it's come up in virtually every conversation I've ever had with administrators or teachers from Michigan school districts. One respondent at the state level said that "the most at-risk districts are the most tyrannized by the MEAP." A respondent at the local level said: "We are terrified both of the MEAP and the accreditation process. . . ."

So close is the relationship between MSSI and the Curriculum Development Unit, that the latter is reportedly referred to as "the unfunded component" of SSI. . . .

I interviewed one of the curriculum unit representatives who seemed nonplussed by my question about coordination between MSSI and the frameworks. "It's not a question of coordination; we're one and the same thing; it's completely integrated." Another respondent said "we (MSSI) are the process and they (the curriculum unit) are the content."

Nancy Brigham, *NSF Statewide Systemic Initiative Monitoring Report. Report of Site Visits to Michigan 1993–1994*. Cambridge: Abt Associates. Nov. 1994, pp. 2–4

MEAP is certainly influencing the choice of curriculum, of "content." Last year, staff were surveyed to see how what they are teaching relates to the state curriculum. That information has been collated and it shows holes in the curriculum. Vivian plans to visit each building. "I'm going to want to know from staff what their comfort level would be in a different Unit, and determine what the needs are for that," she tells us at the November 10 WRSI meeting.

"Hopefully we will be able to begin to build a more systemic curriculum for the elementary level. Which then will get us to: what are the tools that we need to implement the kind of curriculum that's going to have students be able to deal with the science objectives and core academic curriculum?" Vivian can show staff a districtwide picture of what they are doing. This information should help each building in its choice of the "area-specific assessment," based on what they're doing right now, and on what they think they're best at.

"Some of the people on my staff are wondering, once we make a decision, will there be materials, inservices . . . ?" asks a teacher.

"If there's something out there that people think will enhance what they're doing – I'm not going to say *I'll* buy it, but certainly there's money in a building budget that should support the work that people need to do, and if there are workshops out there we have professional development money, that's what it's for, those are some of the goals we said we were working towards, why not use the money for that? However, on top of all that you need to know that what I have *finally* ordered – it was really hard to order this stuff, Scott – are the Units that were written to go along with the MEAP.

"When we talk about the holes – when you come and talk to us at the building are you talking globally, like for the long range?" Mary asks.

"I'm talking the long range," Vivian replies. "That's why I hate talking about this MEAP because we need to be thinking on two planes. Right now the building has to be thinking in two places, because next year and the year after that we're taking a test that kids need to have information for, and then the building also has to be thinking about three years from now, *all* of this body of information is going to be pretty important information for the kids. I'm on *one* plane, I'm on long range, and so when I come, I'm looking down the line, overall, what we need to do for curriculum, for the students."

Scott asks, "Are we going to have inservice on these Units before we give them out wholesale? If they're used as nice little activities, it will fail. I mean it is wonderful material, and it saves you tremendous amounts of work, but if you don't know how to use it you're wasting an awful lot of time."

Superintendent Yomtoob has stopped in and is listening to this discussion. "You don't mind my interruption?" he asks.

"Hey," Vivian says, "I love your interruptions."

Dr. Joe clears his throat. "Let me make a suggestion for the committee to consider. I don't know how much time we have left that we could use in terms of a service systemwide, we've got to find that out. Maybe there is half a day somewhere. I'd be willing to recommend to the board a plan for the remainder of this year. Let's say each Unit takes four or five hours, we close the school an afternoon and stay until we finish the Unit. Whatever it takes: three and a half hours, four hours. My preference would be to close the school half a day, for an entire school, and have enough people to service everyone. I'd be happy to look at some recommendation like that. Without question, we're going to fail if we don't inservice people. I know modern math: good idea, not enough inservice, it backfired and we got a generation of people who never learned mathematics. So inservice is very, very appropriate. Put something together. We're sharing the responsibility: the school district is giving two and a half hours, the staff is giving one hour, two hours, in addition to whatever regular time we have. Make sense? Possibility?"

"I have to look to the staff," says Vivian, " 'cause that's who's got to buy in."

"Let's think about this," the superintendent continues. "Whatever we want to do we want to do it right, and let's put our heads together and see what it takes, if we do it as a team, jointly, so board will feel comfortable, teachers feel comfortable. But you're absolutely right, without inservice it won't be any good. If we make a systemic program. . . . I think this is systemic, isn't that what you do?" he finishes with a grin.

"That's what this is," Vivian grants.

"Somebody got some paper we can throw?" grins Scott.

Vivian asks how school staff have responded to the news of the new MEAP. Reactions have apparently been mixed.

"Everybody was really excited about it," says a teacher from Cheney Elementary, "and we decided that a lot of teachers already had classrooms that were doing a lot of those things. We talked for the whole afternoon, but we haven't talked since, and it never tied together at the end because so many ideas were flying back and forth. We never had closure to it. But people were interested and felt good about the direction. I thought everybody was going to fall down dead on the floor, but they didn't, they were excited about it."

Why this receptive attitude? "Maybe because they know it's there and we're going to keep hearing about it. I think, too, that they might have some input into it really helps. That they can make the decision what our kids do best, at the moment. I was amazed."

"Maybe," Scott suggests, "it's more along the lines of where we think we should be going with education. I've always been frustrated knowing I had to teach to a multiple-choice test that had no real-life meaning." There are grunts of agreement, "So it made me frustrated always teaching to this other MEAP, whereas I'm more excited about teaching to this. . . ."

"It's more meaningful."

"Yes, it's more meaningful material."

But Craig says, in a calm and insistent voice, "Well, Kaiser staff is completely blown away. And they still haven't gotten up. They're going to need a lot of nurturing, they're going to need a lot of inservicing; they're going to need to change most of their teaching efforts, because they're more comfortable with a multiple-choice approach rather than an essay approach, so they are still lying dead on the ground. They hate systemic initiative, they know it's going to go away, and all you have to do at Kaiser School is lower the class size . . ."

"And wait!" Mary finishes for him, with a laugh.

"So I came back to them with, 'Well, remember at Traverse City, if you lower your class size what are you going to do different? How are you going to teach differently to address MEAP?' They couldn't give me any answer. Not one of them. They are *furious* with the new MEAP test, they are not teaching the way that they should be teaching; they're going to need a lot of nurturing."

The teacher from Cheney says, "I think our staff too was blown away by the essay, because our kids need a lot of work in writing and reading, but I think they thought it was a good thing that teachers can start to teach to that kind of thought-process. It will take a lot of work . . ."

"Oh yeah, oh yeah!" Vivian agrees.

". . . but I think they thought it was a good thing. Teachers are going to teach to the test no matter what, so what kind of test do we want to be teaching to? One that involves a thought-process."

"I'm relieved to hear about the Units coming," Mary says, "because we worked with U of M for two years, and now they're no longer with us and we're trying to develop our own Units around the theme of environment. We know we have these core curriculums, we know we have these expectations of science, we know we have the MEAP – I almost think we're frozen. We don't know what to do. We've had thematic unit meetings and – Vivian has been in our building; we love themes – we sat there and nobody could come up with an idea for a theme. I mean, how to bring it together. That has never happened in the seven years we have done themes – never. So I really am anxious. Give us another start, give us another push. They sat there and they looked, 'One more thing. How do I fit it in; problem-based science, problem-based inquiry; I'm developing my own Unit; we have a theme – how do I put it together?"

"I think that we have to understand," Vivian says, "that 'Christmas Package' – I'm still floored that people decided to call it a 'Christmas Package' like it's some kind of gift – there are so many changes, *so many* changes, that have been heaped upon the school system. It is over-whelming, and it is frustrating, and it is exciting. It's all those things, so all those reactions are normal. What we have to do is hear them, recog-nize them, and talk about ways to address them. I'm glad Scott said what he did because I probably would have just frustrated more people if I'd just sent those Units out. We need to think about what kinds of things we can do to support staff."

"The MEAP isn't going to go away!" Mary says.

"Truly the open-ended expectations on this new testing process are fueling this fear," Laura ponders. "Now if people can get a handle on that. The people who seem most comfortable with it in our building are the people who picked up on the key piece, that kids need to write. They need to write, and they need to write, and they need to write. And kids *are* writing. As they write to describe things and as they develop flu-ency with writing, and as that becomes an issue and a focus, there's less fear because maybe they're not as tied to a workbook, and to end-of-the-chapter questions."

"I think the fact that Units are coming is going to help," Craig says, "and that Vivian is going to have discussions on all this stuff will help, but teachers are just so threatened that the way that they're teaching is not okay, and . . . 'How in the world am I going to change my style of teaching when I'm having a hard time controlling this group anyway?' "

"The thing that needs to be really looked at," Scott says, "doing any kind of instructional change, and that we need to be aware of, is that kids, almost as much as teachers, need to be retrained. When a kid comes into a classroom and they've been used to sitting here, with pen-cil in hand, looking at the chalkboard, listening to the teacher, sitting in rows, not thinking, not deeply understanding things, and still succeed-ing at a high level – I mean, answering the questions in the back of the book, filling out the worksheets. . . . If you want to quiet a class down, in any classroom, hand out a ditto. Tell 'em to be quiet, sit down, and hand out a ditto."

"The drug of choice!" Laura agrees.

"Should we talk about this when we present these Units?" Vivian asks.

"I don't know," Scott admits. "In most of these meetings that I've gone to that's the one key element that everyone leaves out. Nobody talks about the kids."

"How can we fill that void? Recognizing that folks are going to get inservice on the purpose of the Unit, but not the management. What can we be doing proactively, maybe even right now?"

Laura continues, "Before we get to the point of recognizing that the kids are going to have problems with this, a problem that many *teachers* seem to have, aside from letting go of the safety and security of a textbook, is the safety and security of being in control of that classroom, and letting go of that control is a real big issue for those people."

"And being in control is having those kids be quiet."

"It takes me, with ninth graders, a good month to get them trained in how to think differently and how to work differently," Scott says.

"You're still not dealing with my basic question, that Laura is trying to articulate in a different way," Vivian says.

"What I'm trying to say," Laura says, "is that you, Scott, *want* to let go of the control, and put the children in charge of their own learning. You understand that it takes some work to get the children to do that. But there are people who are operating at a level where they don't even believe the paradigm that children can, or *should*, be in charge of their own learning." Vivian joins in with the "should." "And that is really the crux of the issue."

"But I think that's where we have to use this new MEAP," Scott begins. Other people are getting excited, cutting in to speak their piece.

"But that's still my question, Scott," Vivian says. "Is giving them this inservice going to give them the tools to . . . ?"

"Not *this* inservice," says Scott. "It will give them the tools maybe to utilize. . . ."

"Okay," Vivian says. "But, then that's my question. What are things that we need to be thinking about, and working with?"

"We have to get them to buy in," Scott says, "to the fact that changing classroom structure. . . ."

"How?"

"How do you do that?"

"What are some things . . . ?"

"If we want our kids," Scott continues, "ultimately, to learn how to work cooperatively, in groups, so that we can teach them in a new way, we have to be able to model to our peers how to teach in that kind of situation, because a lot of 'em don't, they have to be in control."

"I agree," says Vivian, "but while I think that the modeling is important, and I think the inservices are important, I also think that if folks have an opportunity to vent, to throw up their hands to scream, and yell, and then come back to the reality of, 'I've still got to do this, now what are my steps?' that we can begin to get from staff, 'I need this, I need that.' Because everybody's going to need something different. Scott's in a place, Linda's in a place. . . . As much as I hate it, and I said when I took this position I wasn't going to do it, I'm falling into the same trap as everybody else that gets these positions, and that's, everybody gets the same medicine. That's not going to work. I guess *I'm* sitting here still with the 'how,' and I think part of the 'how' is to somehow get conversations going in all the buildings around these issues, and have *staff* talk about the fact that, in order to get kids to be able to write on the MEAP, say, 'We gotta get kids to write.' And have *staff* say, that if students are going to have to do cooperative group projects, 'I guess I gotta put 'em in groups.' And then have them say, 'But I don't know how to do that. Where do I go to get that? Who can help me?' We give people plenty of time to be frustrated, but we never give them time to work through to the next step! And the next step is to say, 'Okay, now that I've done this, now that I'm frustrated, what am I going to do?!' We have to help people understand that what you want to control is the fact that things can happen. You want to control the environment for activities to occur, but not what actually is going on from moment to moment. Big difference."

"And there's one more thing that hasn't been said," Laura adds. "As we incorporate the new ideas, however we do it, the 'how' piece and the talking, people I think have to be given *permission* to let go of some other things. They really are waiting for permission. Some people are real ready to do it, and to receive the permission that says you don't *have* to finish every page in that workbook. You don't even have to *do* that workbook. There are people who really would be willing to look at and embrace something new, if they could drop off something else. I think the Units will provide enough structure to give some safety and security."

"See," Vivian responds, "I can see these Units being just another thing that people feel like they've *got* to do. And that's why you heard me say, somehow, even when we get these Units, we've got to make sure that we keep saying to people, 'You don't have to do this as it says on this paper. It is another tool.' Problem is, we can't get people to hear the word 'tool' with everything that we give them. They keep hearing it as a 'must do' instead of 'tool.' Everything that we have – those," she gestures at the Units, "are *tools* to learning, and those I think are the words that we have to begin to use more with teachers, and more with kids. We have a lot of *tools* that we can use, and then we have to make some decisions about, 'Which one of these tools do I use today? And in which *way* am I going to use this tool?' As we present the Units, I want us to present them as tools, and information, that teachers will make some professional decisions about. Maybe that will help us with this permission, and loosening up, and thoughts about, 'I can make decisions; I do make decisions; I'm capable of making decisions!' "

"'And my students do too!'" Laura adds, with a laugh.

"As you go back and have this discussion about the science I think we have to be very careful about what we're saying and how we're saying it. We want to choose our words very carefully, we want to empower teachers as we say it. We don't want to give them *too* many words to hang on to, 'But you said . . . !' cause that's what's gonna happen. As you're talking I really want you to think about how you're answering whatever questions they have, so it comes across that they have to make decisions for themselves. I don't think we have to give them all the answers. That's the first step in empowerment: 'Yeah, that's a good question. So what are we gonna do?' We can only empower as we encourage *them* to make decisions and encourage them to allow their students to make decisions. The more we can get teachers thinking about the decisions they actually *do* make, then they'll make more, because they make plenty of them."

"I think that's where the MEAP can come in as a positive," Scott suggests, "because we can at least invite the conversation that, if kids are going to be successful taking this, what skills do they need, and what are we doing in our classrooms to make sure they have those skills?

"And we need to carry around our mission and vision statement. We really do. Maybe I'm wrong, but I really believe that most people feel they had some say in that, at some level, and there's no *real* disagreement with it. Even if they *don't* feel they had any say in it, they can't look at it and say – most people don't look at that and say, 'Oh that's a crock.' Most people really do believe that students should have these things. I continually say, 'Tell me how what you're doing gets at this?' Most people with kids sitting in rows really can't answer that question. What that vision and those outcomes say is that students are going to be talking to each other, and they are going to be asking questions, and not necessarily looking at the back of the book, and checking off answers. Those two things go hand in hand."

When I visit Kettering now, Mary insists on brewing coffee for me – and it infuriates me that, while I started my work intending to be helpful outside the ivory tower, instead it's me who now needs support. When I attend WRSI meetings I feel stripped of my professional identity. I sit feeling almost naked, a concrete individual, no longer able to be an abstraction – professor, researcher. But in Willow Run this kind of thing isn't unusual. Now I experience firsthand the ethos of caring and sharing in this community. I recognize how laying off or relocating workers destroys commitments people have made to their workplace and work. Unlike the equipment with which they are equated, people become engrossed in their projects, schemes of activity that stretch forward into the future and make life sensible and meaningful. It is a sad irony that as teachers are seeking ways of increasing students' engagement in academic work, business is ignoring or even destroying workers' engagement in theirs. Job loss brings a keener sense of the imperatives – the embodied needs and values – of the system in which one lives. It makes one a different person; a different *kind* of person. The shock and bewilderment, the betrayal, force one to recognize that one's participation in a social order is not freely chosen but is contingent on the authority, power, and will of others. One's attitude changes.

> On Thursday I went to the schools and ended up spending 13 hours in the district, observing, interviewing, then attending a WRSI meeting and the first Advisory Council meeting.... But ... I'm moving in two directions, and feeling extreme guilt as a result. . . . I feel I'm moving closer to the heart of Willow Run, both culturally and intellectually. My research is premised on the conviction that one has to care about what one studies: one has to become practically engaged in and literally concerned and caring about it. I've known for a while that I'm in some way in love with WR; it gives me a sense of place and even of home that Ann Arbor and the University don't provide. And as I've come to know the people in the schools, both adults and children, there has been a growing sense of familiarity and trust that amounts to an intimacy of human contact as well as an intellectual familiarity. . . .
> And at the same time I'm preparing to leave, albeit not from my own choosing. And the guilt and pain ... stem from my complicity with this abandonment of the people and place I've become intimate with. And so

> with an abandonment of the part of myself that will inevitably stay here when I leave.
>
> Fieldnotes, Nov. 15, 1994

There'll be another MSSI conference at Midland in February, and seven committee members will attend. Vivian can't go; she's agreed to give a paper at the annual Michigan Testing Conference, on the effects on school districts of the new state law regarding alternative assessments. (Districts are required to "consider" alternatives to tests and grades.) I'm continually impressed by how hard these people work. Scott is on the team for the Washington-Livingston County Science Center, and a consultant for TLC – the Teaching, Learning, Curriculum Alignment group.

"Willow Run got a huge compliment," says Scott. "The Director of TLC said as we were meeting, 'They're the model TLC school in the state!' "

"We're *struggling* to change curriculum, are you kidding?" Vivian laughs.

"She just said, 'There's more going on there; if all of our TLC schools were moving like Willow Run is moving, we would feel wonderful.' "

Scott also has news about the MEAP and HSPT. 'I was at a MEAP meeting yesterday," he reports, "and all the powers that be were there, giving out all this wonderful information."

"Are we really going to do it?" Vivian asks. "You know there's a belief out there it's not going to happen. That the MEAP won't change – too many bugs."

Scott says it will. The new High School Proficiency Test has four areas: math, science, reading, and writing. A fifth, social studies, comes on-line in 1997, though it may be delayed until 1999 since it's based on the new academic core curriculum, which will not be adopted until 1997. The state has ten versions of the HSPT currently being tested, hoping to use seven of them.

"Is it still held up because they're dealing with multiculturalism in it, and they don't want to deal with that?" someone asks of the social studies area.

"Yeah, that's one of the things," Scott says. "And it doesn't look like they're going to deal with some of that."

"But 'We want to be a world force!' " someone adds.

"Without being multicultural!" There's laughter at the absurdity.

The tests will be given September next year, very soon, so they can be scored and reported to the schools before Christmas. ("Now there's a good reason!") The schools must put a plan in place for remediation of every child that fails – it's also now an accreditation requirement that every child be brought up to proficiency in Reading within a year.

Two new fifth- and eighth-grade tests, science and writing, should also come out next year, though field testing isn't yet complete. The MEAP science test for fifth and eighth grades will take students 2 hours; the cost to score them will be $15 per test. And it's estimated the HSPT will take each student a total of 11 hours!

"Their best estimate," Scott says, "is that one half of the kids will be endorsed in 1997, in science. So half the kids will not get an endorsement, *after* all of the retakes. It's that demanding of a test." Standards won't be set until after the first year, so this is only a "best estimate." "How did they put it?" Scott recalls. " 'When you take the test you have a *chance* of passing.' "

"Well, lottery tickets mean a chance too," says Laura.

The state officials came right out and said that the new test is intended to cause changes in instructional technique and alignment of curriculum. Since people teach to the test, give them a test that will cause desired changes. That's the reason why.

"They want instruction to change so that kids are successful on this. Period. When instruction changes, then kids should be more successful on this. They want this to drive instruction. Period. That's the end-all goal, to have the MEAP drive instruction."

"There's one more. They missed one. Make Engler president."

"That must be what they want," Vivian muses, "otherwise they wouldn't give you a curriculum and a test all at the same time. They'd give you the curriculum and give you time to teach it before coming up with the test."

They know some kids are going to be hurt the first couple of years, but their attitude is this is just necessary to bring about change. And students who took the ninth-grade MEAP last year and scored high enough for endorsement will still have to take the High School Proficiency Test.

"Are they going to come and tell these kids face-to-face what's going on?"

And before they sit down for the new science MEAP in September all students must have conducted a science investigation in class.

Betty says, "I think the thing that's most difficult for the kids in eighth grade next year is, if the MEAP starts in mid-September, that investigation has to be done prior to that, which means almost the first, second week of school. You don't even know your kids, you haven't really got the structure of your classroom. . . . You've got to get them in an investigation." The fifth-grade teachers need to learn how to do this, but so do the fourth-grade teachers, so they too can start investigations this year, the year before the test. The presentation Betty and Scott will do on Monday, along with January's inservice, will start to prepare them for this.

"Well," Vivian says firmly, "we have a job to do."

"We are eons ahead of most districts," Scott says, "Because of MSSI and TLC and the involvement we have with those organizations. There are an awful lot of schools that don't even know this is coming."

TO: All WLEA Elementary and Science Teachers
FROM: Your WRSI Team Colleagues: S. Heister, L. Chew, M. Brandau, B. Hopkins, R. Melberg, L. Verhey, C. Waters, R. Williams, M. Packer, S. Rankin, S. Zaremba, S. Schwartz, K. Dillender, L. Hibsky, I. Singer, M. Lambert & M. Becker
DATE: January 16, 1995
RE: SCIENCE OPPORTUNITY ALERT!!!

We are all intensely aware of the changes coming in the new MEAP assessments in science. The new assessment program format seems to require teaching students more about the discovery and learning process as well as content. In response to many of our teachers' concerns, specifically about availability of training, and resource materials, that will adequately prepare students for success on the new Science MEAP, your colleagues on the District WRSI team have taken several steps to provide requested assistance.

First, we have worked with the Curriculum Office to order and obtain the Science Frameworks curriculum, which addresses the different instructional focus for the new MEAP. This program is developed into specific units of inquiry at each grade level to coordinate with the new state testing format expectations. These materials are new, and have been developed by the state to assist interested districts in preparing for the new test. We recognize that our teachers want both information and training, and that we need some additional time for this in an already planned school calendar. We have therefore requested and received permission from Dr. Joe and the Board to hold an inservice on this program for instructional staff, and to release school for an additional half-day at the elementary level. . . .

We hope that you will eagerly seize this important opportunity to expand your knowledge and resources in the interest of working ever more effectively with all of our students in Willow Run! Thank you!

We, the citizens of Michigan, will collaborate with schools and other institutions and organizations dedicated to promoting mathematics and science learning. Our goal is to help *all* students develop the knowledge and skills needed to participate fully as enlightened citizens in economic, social, and civic actions and decision making in an increasingly complex society. The knowledge, skills, and *habits of mind* needed to achieve this goal include:
- Ability to use mathematical and scientific ideas to reason and communicate about personal, occupational, community, and global issues
- Thorough understandings of: mathematical and scientific ideas, connections among ideas, and the application of these ideas
- Use of mathematical and scientific tools

With this knowledge and these skills, our students will be *mathematically powerful* and *scientifically literate*, and able to lead productive lives.

The Vision for Mathematics and Science in Michigan [Final Version], Michigan Statewide Systemic Initiative, May 1995, 2

Experts now say the economic recovery has been going on for four years, since 1991. Because it "started with a whimper instead of a bang," and because wages remain stagnant, the recovery wasn't apparent at first, and many people remain unimpressed. But the federal deficit is down, exports are growing, investment is rising faster than consumer spending, productivity growing an average of 1.5 percent a year (labor costs are steady; people work longer hours), and 200,000 jobs are being created each month.[4]

But there's still profound dissatisfaction with Washington, especially in the industrial Midwest, based on fear of the unknown, skepticism about inflation and unemployment figures, and a perception that Clinton flip-flops on important issues. In this year's national elections the Republicans win majorities in Congress for the first time in 40 years and quickly sign a "Contract with America" that seeks to pass sweeping legislation in the first 100 days. Republicans win 48 seats in the House, the biggest gain since 1946, for a 230–204 majority, and win the Senate for the first time since 1986, 53–47. And for the first time in 24 years a majority of the nation's governors are Republican.[5] Michigan's seat in the U.S. Senate is won by a Republican, Spencer Abraham, after Democrat Donald Riegle retires. That close race had President Clinton making three trips to Michigan on behalf of the Democratic candidate, the last just the day before the election. Michigan now has seven Republican Representatives and nine Democrats.

While the nation had what is being called a sea change in voter allegiance – with Republicans winning majorities in Congress for the first time in 40 years – the Michigan tide flowed both ways. . . .

> The resounding victory by Engler has to be viewed as an endorsement of what happened in his first term.
> "Michigan has become more conservative," said Dan Pero, Engler's campaign manager.
> Dawson Bell, "Mixed Signals for Michigan: Voters Divide on What They Want From Government," *Detroit Free Press*, Nov. 10, 1994, 1A

Governor Engler is reelected solidly, with 61 percent support statewide, though the Ypsilanti area's Democratic senator wins easily and its Democratic representative runs unopposed. Although Detroit newspaper columnists insist the "Englerization of Michigan" is not a landslide, Republicans now control both the state Senate (a slim 56–54 majority) and House (a 22–16 advantage) for the first time in nearly three decades. One consequence of the new Republican control in Michigan is anticipated to be an initiative to repeal the 1970 constitutional ban on funding private schools with public money.

Willow Run is one of four districts that worked with Detroit Edison to hold a Kid Vote during the elections, to encourage young people to feel voting is important and take this perception back to their families. Among the kids, Engler is narrowly beaten by his Democratic challenger.

And now the ten-seat Michigan State Board of Education has a 6–2 Republican majority. (The other four seats are held by two members of the Libertarian Party, and one each from the Natural Law Party and the Workers World Party.) The board is expected to align more closely with Engler's market-oriented school improvement plans.

> An unprecedented mission statement, rich in moral tone and deeply supportive of parental rights and school choice, was the first item adopted Thursday by a Michigan State Board of Education newly dominated by Republicans.
> "We, the Michigan State Board of Education, believe that to teach a child created by God is a noble calling," says the statement, a first in the board's 32 years. "Throughout life, parents are a child's first teachers with the primary right and responsibility for their child's education."
> Joan Richardson, "Education Board Votes Itself a Mission: Its Moral Tone Has Foes Suspicious," *Detroit Free Press*, Jan. 20, 1995, 1B

> Rarely since World War II have the world's most powerful economies surged forward so successfully at one time. And rarely have their citizens been so worried that the good times are about to end before they get a share of the bounty.
> In the United States, economic growth was the best in a decade, yet that did nothing to help Bill Clinton avoid the revenge of the middle class that

led to the first Congress in 40 years controlled entirely by Republicans. In Europe, even though prosperity is returning after a painful recession that sent the jobless rate back into double digits, Helmut Kohl held on to power in Germany only by his fingertips, John Major seems on his last legs in Britain, France is turning inward and Italy has returned to its perpetual state of political chaos.

> David E. Sanger, "Outlook 1995: A Lingering Unease Despite Strong Growth," *New York Times*, Jan. 3, 1995, C1

A particular kind of economic expansion is also taking place. Felix G. Rohatyn, senior partner of Lazard Frères, described it in a speech at Wake Forest University last week:

"The big beneficiaries of our economic expansion have been the owners of financial assets and a new class of highly compensated technicians working for companies where profit-sharing and stock ownership was widely spread.

"What is occurring is a huge transfer of wealth from lower-skilled middle-class American workers to the owners of capital assets and to the new technological aristocracy.

"As a result, the institutional relationship created by the mutual loyalty of employees and employers in most American businesses has been badly frayed. . . . These relationships have been replaced by a combination of fear for the future and a cynicism for the present as a broad proportion of working people see themselves as simply temporary assets to be hired or fired to protect the bottom line and create 'shareholder value.' "

> A. M. Rosenthal, "American Class Struggle," *New York Times*, Mar. 21, 1995, A15

When Henry Ford built his bomber plant and the airport, that was only the beginning of the ways he changed the Willow Creek landscape. Ford also built a storage building that eventually became GM's now-closed Willow Run assembly plant. He built a wastewater treatment plant on the banks of the Willow Creek; nearby he dammed the creek to create Tyler pond. A mile further south, Ford dammed a small gully to form the Sludge Lagoon.

The site now is one of the most toxic in the state. The Michigan Department of Natural Resources gives it a score of 39 out of a possible 48 on its scale of pollution sites. . . . PCBs at the bottom of the lagoon reach 5,000 parts per million. One part per million is considered safe.

> John Mulcahy, "Willow Creek's Future Rests on Paying for Past: After 50 Years of Industrial Use, Toxic Site Requires Costly Cleanup," *Ann Arbor News*, Mar. 19, 1995, A1, A6

I'll be leaving without taking a close look at Willow Run High School. One Friday in November I drop by with some slides for Scott Heister.

It's lunch, but he's in his classroom talking to some parents. Several kids are there too: three or four boys are working on a slide show for the town meeting. They've taken digital photos of their group doing tests on water samples, and they've woven them into a ClarisWorks report on the work.

And a tenth-grade student is working on her biome project, setting up a simulated ocean beach environment in a cardboard box with blue and green cellophane. I ask her what they've learned about biomes, and she explains to me that she's discovered that the different biomes are all interrelated, we need to have all the biomes for things to work. I ask how she discovered this, and she explains in a way that is very rapidly too detailed and complex for me to follow that the nitrogen cycle is linked to the water cycle, and that everything needs water or plants wouldn't grow.

At the end of the year Scott arranges for me to meet with a group of seniors considered high flyers. These students are very aware of changes in teaching at Willow Run High School. "Teaching is changing." It's now "more hands-on," "more interacting with the students." "We all work in groups, they say it teaches you better job skills, 'cause a lot of times in a job they'll assign a group of people to do a certain task." "All those new teachers are bringing in the new way. . . . There's some old teachers that have gone with the change. . . . But there's some teachers that are, y'know, back where you just had to lecture, you'd give out a work sheet, and that was it." Are they learning different things from these new ways of teaching, or learning the old things more efficiently? "I think it's a little bit of both."

Race isn't openly discussed much in Willow Run, but when I ask what the school is like, their first response is that they're proud of its mix.

"Well, it's different compared to a lot of schools in our area because we have more of a mix of races and ethnic backgrounds here, because, you know, fifteen minutes away is Saline, and there's like one black person at their school, and like Ypsi there's not very many."

"Right, or you could go on to the other side of Detroit and there's like one white person at their school, so we're kind of like the halfway point."

How does that work out? "I think it's preparing us for the real world, because when you're in a school where everybody there is the same, you're not really, you're gonna go out and work with people that are of different races." "Your point of view is kind of broader here."

A younger African American woman who arrives late and hasn't heard what the others say answers my question the same way. "Well, uh, let me see. I guess I would say one thing that's different from a lot of the other area schools is, we're somewhat multiculturally diverse, as far as we have like a lot of African American students, we have Caucasian American, Korean American, you know, students, and that's one thing that I find that's different."

Far from needing a personal relation to sustain their professional relation with teachers, these young adults are critical of those teachers who *fail* to live up to the obligations of their abstract position, who inject an improper personal element into their relations with students. The abstractions of schooling are fully accepted by these students and now are defended. They see personal ties as a *failure* of the institution and a source of unfairness. "Some teachers just have favorite students, that they like." "Yeah, and they always do that little extra something for that student they like, and the person who they don't particularly care for it's just like –" "They'll look at them the wrong way, or they'll. . . ." "'Sorry, don't know you,' y'know?"

Is any of this sexist or racist? "Nope. Just who sucks up to who." And "there's a lot of teachers who suck up to the principal." "And get favors in return." "It isn't really fair, but that's how it works, I think. I mean I think that's how life is. The real world. There's politics in the real world." "I mean life isn't fair, for sure."

They take for granted that school work is linked to whom one will become. Aspirations now entail not emulation of admired adults (as did the first graders'), or simply desire for a high-status profession (the fifth graders'), but "doing what you want to do." And listening to these young people one gets a clear sense of the obstacles they've worked to overcome to pursue a career. "My family doesn't really give me much support on stuff like that. They're like, 'Yeah, whatever.' They're kind of sarcastic, I don't know." "My mom can't afford to put me through college, or nothing. So everything I do I'll have to pay for myself." One plans to move to California, open a martial arts club, and save to study computer animation at Berkeley. He's been accepted to Michigan State but "there isn't really any high paying jobs around here that I can see." Another has a scholarship to Yale to study biology, but "I'm gonna try to get another job, for the summer, because I have to pay for like another four thousand dollars for my education." He'll study medicine, then "I'm gonna be a neurosurgeon."

Another is going to Florida Central University to study engineering, then "I'd like to get in with Universal Studios or Disney World, or some entertainment place down there. I have an idea for a roller coaster; it's far-fetched." The last says "I currently work at K-Mart, I've been there for almost a year. Let's see, when I graduate I'll be attending University of Michigan, and I'll major in business administration, and then after I graduate there I'm gonna go on to law school, become a corporate lawyer. I'll go to the University of Michigan's law school, or Howard University's law school."

Even if the auto plants were still open they wouldn't work in one.

"Because I don't like manual labor," says one, to laughter. "Yeah, it's like too hard a work for too little pay. Not that it doesn't pay well, 'cause I have an uncle that's in management, he makes a lot, but it takes a long time to work your way up through there. I used to have the goal of making a lot of money, in a career or whatever, and to get good grades in school to get that career to make all this money. But over the last year I realized that just being happy and doing what you want to do is more important than making a lot of money. But I think I would go to college, so that is part of what I want to do."

"Yeah, I think that's a big thing for me. I just want to enjoy what I'm doing, 'cause if you can't enjoy going to work every day, then the money isn't worth it."

Vivian describes the high school as being, a few years back, a school where students who did well were stigmatized and most students were dismissive of education. The very existence of the group I've spoken with is a sign of a certain kind of success for the school. There are jokes like, "You get the nerd label permanently with something like that," to the Yale scholar, but then, "No one really cares anymore."

"It seems like when you're a senior, all that . . ."

"You're just, you're grouped as seniors."

"All the walls come down, y'know."

The trajectory a young person takes through school will vary with the attitude they adopt. These "high flyers" have accepted the impersonal relations and abstractions of school and come to view society as an objective structure into which they go to seek personal fulfillment. They are eager now to leave home, family, and community. The high school has done its job: the district reports that 60 percent of WRHS students attend college. What about those students not college-bound? "They wish they was going," someone suggests, but I wonder if this is true.

This is a time of leave-taking, of transition. On February 3, 1995, the local public radio, broadcasting from the Eastern Michigan University campus in Ypsilanti, reported that Dr. Joe would be leaving, seven years to the day after becoming superintendent at Willow Run. The school board jokingly threatened to table his motion to resign. He gives roses to each of the board members, saying that his time in Willow Run has been an important part of his life, that they are all now part of his heart. He thanks all the friends he has made. There'll be a temporary acting superintendent until a permanent replacement for Dr. Joe is chosen by July. There have already been 14 applications for the position. I attend the school board meetings at which the final candidates are interviewed, and when I talk with the board members after their decision on the new superintendent, they're proud to realize they've selected the district's first female superintendent.

Vivian Lyte leaves the Willow Run Community Schools shortly after Dr. Joe retires and his replacement arrives, to accept a position at the Washtenaw Intermediate School District offices. Her place on the WRSI committee is taken by Laura Chew.

And by June 2, 1995, I'm in another rust belt city – Pittsburgh. I keep in touch with my friends in Willow Run by phone and e-mail. And I track the broader changes that are reported in the national press.

12 The Future of the Kids Coming Behind Us

June 1995–February 1997

An "economic" model of schooling – subject to the forces of supply and demand, diversity and autonomy, accountability and results – makes much
more sense than the "political" model that we labor under today. In the "political" model, social and political processes conspire to force schools to a
lowest common denominator.

> Louis V. Gerstner Jr., with D. P. Doyle and W. B. Johnson, *Reinventing*
> *Education: Enterpreneurship in America's Public Schools.*
> New York: Penguin, 1995, p. 26

American businesses have been transformed from comfortable and stable rivals into bloodletting gladiators. Airlines, telephone companies, utilities,
common carriers – and Wall Street itself – have been deregulated. Global
competitors threaten the very survival of American manufacturers. In addition, information technologies have radically reduced the transaction time
between suppliers, wholesalers, retailers and customers. Entry barriers such
as preferential access to capital markets have dropped, allowing small companies to grab market share from big ones. . . .

Electronic capitalism has replaced the gentlemanly investment system
that had given "industrial statesmen" the discretion to balance the interests
of shareholders against those of employees and communities. Now, any chief
executive who hesitates before doing everything possible to maximize returns to shareholders risks trouble. . . .

Do not blame corporations and their top executives. They are behaving
exactly as they are organized to behave. If we want them to put greater emphasis on the interests of their workers and communities, society must reorganize them to do so. In this era of smaller government, such steps seem
warranted.

> Robert B. Reich, "How to Avoid These Layoffs?," *New York Times,*
> Jan. 4, 1996, A21

Of 124 million people who were working in May, 8 million – 2.2 million more than a decade ago – moonlighted, or held two or more jobs simultaneously. Of 22 million part-timers, 4.5 million wanted full-time work and could not get it. The number of temporary workers has tripled in a decade to 2.1 million in May. And the average hourly wage, in terms of what people can buy with it, has been falling since 1973.

Peter T. Kilborn, "Even in Good Times, It's Hard Times for Workers," *New York Times*, July 3, 1995, A1

John J. Sweeney, the A.F.L.-C.I.O.'s new president, called yesterday for a new "social compact" between America's corporations and workers, saying he and the labor movement might forgo their rhetoric of confrontation if business adopted what he called a less greedy, more respectful attitude toward the people it employs. . . .

"I want to build bridges between labor and management, so that American business can be more successful and American workers can share in the gains," he said.

Steven Greenhouse, "Labor Chief Asks Business for a New 'Social Compact,'" *New York Times*, Dec. 7, 1995, A10

Worried that the momentum for overhauling American education is slipping away, the nation's governors plan to gather next month for a second discussion of the subject, six years after President George Bush called them together to make radical changes in the country's schools.

The first gathering led to eight ambitious goals that educators now concede will not be met by the target year of 2000. This year's meeting, organizers say, will try to move from broadly defined goals to rigorous, specific standards for student achievement. . . .

"In 1989, President Bush focused the nation's eyes on education, and there was a tremendous feeling we were doing something about education we could be proud of," said Wisconsin's Governor, Tommy G. Thompson, a Republican, who along with Louis V. Gerstner Jr., chairman of the International Business Machines Corporation, was a prime force in organizing the new conference. "Since then, we've lost the focus on education. I see this summit as an opportunity to get it back."

Peter Applebome, "Governors Want New Focus on Education," *New York Times*, Feb. 21, 1996, B7

While permanent layoffs have been symptomatic of most recessions, now they are occurring in the same large numbers even during an economic recovery that has lasted five years and even at companies that are doing well.

In a reversal from the early 80's, workers with at least some college education make up the majority of people whose jobs were eliminated, outnum-
bering those with no more than high school educations.

> Louis Uchitelle and N. R. Kleinfield, "On the Battlefields of Business,
> Millions of Casualties," *New York Times*, Mar. 3, 1996, sec 1, p. 1

How this all plays out is a matter of debate. Some contend that through
these adjustments American companies will recapture their past dominance
in world markets, and once again be in a position to deliver higher income to
most workers. Others predict that creating such fungible workforces will
leave businesses with dispirited and disloyal employees who will be less productive. And many economists and chief executives think the job shuffling
may be a permanent fixture, always with us, as if the nation had caught a
chronic, rasping cough.

> Louis Uchitelle and N. R. Kleinfield, "The Lost Job and the American
> Dream in Reverse," *New York Times*, Mar. 3, 1996, sec. 1, p. 28

Of all the Governors, Mr. Engler is generally mentioned the most as a possible vice-presidential pick. That has caused some resentment among advisers
to the other Republican Governors, who often criticize him as a standout
showboat in an occupation known for its showboats.

But there are reasons why the 47-year-old Governor, who is probably the
most conservative of his three Midwest colleagues, surfaces on all the short
lists: he is an energetic campaigner with significant appeal to blue-collar
workers and has won acclaim for changing the state welfare system and cutting taxes.

Yet Mr. Engler's ambition may have hurt him. Aides to Mr. Dole said they
were more than miffed that Mr. Engler decided to wait until late last week –
months after most other Governors had endorsed Mr. Dole – to make his
move. Mr. Engler said that as head of the Republican Governors Association
he had to stay neutral – but Dole aides said he was simply hedging his bets.

> Richard L. Beske, "4 Midwestern Governors Push for Dole With Eye on
> Their Own Futures," *New York Times*, Mar. 18, 1996, C1, C13

Government and private economists said today that the 13-day-old strike at
two General Motors brake factories here [Dayton, Ohio] has delivered the
worst blow to the Midwest economy since the floods of 1993. . . .

. . . caused by a dispute over job security and safety. . . . The strike's wide-
spread effects have illustrated the continuing economic importance of the
American auto industry, which exceeds that of many industries that have
been receiving more attention lately. During the fourth quarter of last year,

for example, the sales of G.M. were 19 times the sales of the Microsoft Corporation. . . .

[And] the effects have rippled across North America, as 25 of G.M.'s 29 assembly plants, from Ramos Arizpe, Mexico to Oshawa, Ontario, have shut down for lack of brakes.

Keith Bradsher, "G.M. Strike May Be Worst Blow for the Midwest Since '93 Floods," *New York Times*, Mar. 19, 1996, A1, C5

Robert J. Eaton, the chief executive of the Chrysler Corporation, defended companies today against "the ongoing demonization of corporate America by some of our most prominent politicians and news organizations."

Speaking to the Economic Club of Detroit, Mr. Eaton said that the huge layoffs criticized by politicians and the news media were the result of a changing economy and shifts in corporate power structures. Institutional investors who control larger and larger stakes have changed the focus of businesses to increasing profits and dividends.

"Downsizing and layoffs are part of the price of becoming more competitive," Mr. Eaton said. "The price for not doing it, however, is much higher in both economic and human terms." He said that his company's priority was "perpetuating ourselves so that we can serve all our constituencies."

Robyn Meredith, "Executive Defends Downsizing: Chrysler Chief Hails Corporate America," *New York Times*, Mar. 19, 1996, C5

"At the end of the day, if we are not competitive, we will lose those high-paying jobs in the U.S.," said Harry J. Pearce, G.M.'s vice chairman, in an interview last week. "In that scenario, everybody loses."

Union picketers see it differently. "It's about the future of the kids coming behind us," said Howard Lowe, a 49-year-old metal worker with graying hair who walked the picket line last weekend in a red windbreaker and gray trousers. "If we don't take a stand now, they're not going to have jobs."

Keith Bradsher, "Strikers at G.M. Fear Threat to Way of Life," *New York Times*, Mar. 21, 1996, C1, C16

For the first time in a quarter century, Detroit's Big Three auto makers are on a hiring spree. They are replacing a huge bubble of blue-collar workers who are reaching retirement age – people with strong backs who sweated on the production lines to lift their families into the middle class. But most of the new hires will have far more skills and schooling. . . .

The General Motors Corporation, America's biggest company, went an entire decade without hiring a single production-line worker, before finally adding 4,000 in 1995. The once-troubled Chrysler Corporation, the No. 3

auto maker, began hiring again in 1991. Ford, which is No. 2, did little hiring from the early 1980's until mid-1992. Now, the same companies plan to take on more employees in less than seven years than the combined work forces of the Hewlett-Packard Company, the Coca Cola Company and the MCI Communications Corporation. . . .

But the hiring drive is more than just a gateway to middle-class prosperity. . . . It is also shaping up as a golden opportunity for the auto industry to bring on a new breed of worker, for just as tail fins have given way to technology and modern management techniques, production lines – and the skills needed to staff them – have changed drastically.

The Big Three have learned from the foreign car makers that set up shop in the United States. . . . And now that they are hiring again, they are putting quick minds ahead of strong bodies. . . . As a result, the Big Three are putting job applicants through a grueling selection process that emphasizes mental acuity and communication skills. . . .

"Clearly, we are looking for attitudes," said John F. Smith, Jr., chairman and chief executive of G.M.

Robyn Meredith, "New Blood for the Big Three's Plants. This Hiring Spree Is Rewarding Brains, Not Brawn," *New York Times*, Apr. 21, 1996, sec. 3, pp. 1, 10

The man from the United Auto Workers union didn't want to say it on the record. After all, his boys are just beginning to negotiate new contracts with Detroit's Big Three. But, dropping his voice a little, he conceded the obvious. "Of course, we're not going to see an increase in wages and benefits," he acknowledges, a little exasperated that anyone might expect such miracles from a union. "The cost of labor has been going in the opposite direction for the past six years."

The best the UAW can hope to do is to hold the line on pay and benefits, and stem the loss of jobs in Detroit – mainly by persuading auto makers to limit the work that they farm out to non-union shops. The union's weak hand in this month's negotiations, and its concern about losing jobs to outside workers, cuts to the heart of labor's problems these days, not just in Detroit, but nationwide.

Despite five years of economic growth, employees remain anxious about job security. True, the unemployment rate stands at an impressive low 5.6%, but that figure masks an almost equal number of workers who have stopped looking for work or who are working part-time because they cannot find full-time jobs. This "underutilized" group, approaching 10% of the nation's work force, helps explain why the cost of labor hasn't been accelerating rapidly in the current economic expansion, and it also helps explain why labor costs could remain manageable even if the unemployment rate falls to 5% or below. Millions of workers are desperate to find full-time jobs with benefits and some promise of a future.

Maggie Mahar, "Labor's Day," *Barron's*, Sept. 2, 1996, 25–28

"I have a plan, a Call for Action for American Education, based on these 10 principles.

First, a national crusade for education standards – not Federal Government standards, but national standards representing what all of our students must know to succeed in the knowledge economy of the 21st century. Every state and school must shape the curriculum to reflect these standards, and train teachers to lift students up to meet them. To help schools meet the standards and measure their progress, we will lead an effort over the next two years to develop national tests of student achievement in reading and math.

Tonight I issue a challenge to the nation: Every state should adopt high national standards, and by 1999 every state should test every fourth grader in reading and every eighth grader in math to make sure these standards are met."

"Text of President Clinton's State of the Union message to Congress,"
New York Times, Feb. 5, 1997, A14

It should be up to states and local school boards to decide what students need to learn. Education is a local issue. This is the way our parents and communities want it, and that is how it should be. . . . The benefit of [such an] approach is that it allows every state the flexibility to address the individual needs of its children and the communities they live in. States may want to see schools in different cities and towns achieve the same level of academic success, but there are different roads to the same destination.

Tommy G. Thompson [Governor of Wisconsin], "Leave Standards to the States. National Tests Are the Wrong Way to Improve Our Schools,"
New York Times, Feb. 21, 1997, A35

Higher executive turnover is also occurring because a different kind of manager is needed now, according to Hank Conn, a vice president at A. T. Kearney, a large management consulting firm. "You can't tell people what to do anymore, you have to motivate them," he said. "Companies are looking for people that have the soft skills to manage and technological skills and leadership skills. They're looking for much more complete people."

Judith H. Dobrzynski, "Big Demand for Executives Last Year,"
New York Times, Feb. 26, 1997, C2

For months now, the Federal Reserve has been poised to raise interest rates, but has held off. Why?

The answer lies mainly in what the Fed's chairman, Alan Greenspan, describes as a powerful recent force in the American economy: job insecurity. In his testimony to Congress yesterday, he clearly elevated this insecurity to major status in central bank policy. Workers have been too worried about keeping their jobs to push for higher wages, he said, and this has been sufficient to hold down inflation without the added restraint of higher interest rates.

Louis Uchitelle, "Job Insecurity of Workers Is a Big Factor in Fed Policy," *New York Times*, Feb. 27, 1997, C6

"I would like, at the opening of the 140th Session of the Diet, to state my views on the major policy issues before us. . . .

[W]e are now in an era when the world is rapidly becoming integrated and when people, products, capital and information flow freely, and it is clear that the current framework is an obstacle to the vigorous development of our country. As soon as possible, therefore, we must create an economic and social system which can lead the global trend. Changing systems that are deeply rooted in our society will only happen with great difficulty. What is more, these systems are intricately interlinked. That is why I say that we must be bold in taking an integrated approach to resolute implementation of reform in six areas: administrative, fiscal, social security, economic, and financial system reform, as well as educational reform. . . .

I intend to reform our educational system with the aim of creating an educational system in which diverse capacities can be developed and which accords respect to lifelong education that stresses creativity and a spirit of challenge. We must therefore broaden the options available in our educational field, aimed at building a society in which individuals who retain a spirit of inquiry and find their own answers, and who strike the proper balance among knowledge, insight and conscience so that they may endeavor to turn their answers into action, can pursue their own diverse dreams and aspirations."

Summary of the Policy Speech by Japanese Prime Minister Ryutaro Hashimoto to the 140th Session of the National Diet, Jenzo, 1997[1]

13   Quality or Equality?
   The Standardization of Schooling

March 1997

"You know," said Lynn thoughtfully, "the whole secret of those glorious days was something actually quite rare in our world's society – kinship. Our problems were basically the same. Our ages and our goals were basically the same. No one could be selfish and survive. We needed each other. We needed encouragement and sympathy and help. Beyond this, we needed to belong. I think we were like a family, a good family. We did not try to pry, but we were also willing to lend an ear. There was co-operation. No one walked on a garden or newly seeded lawn, no matter how close he might come to missing the school bus. Everyone's problems were very much the same. Everyone looked for a solution for the other fellow as well as for himself."

Marion F. Wilson, *The Story of Willow Run.* Ann Arbor: University of Michigan Press, 1956, p. 88.

"If you go out in our community, our community *is* a community. It's not just people living in different areas. There *is* a community sense."

The speaker is a young African American woman, a tenth-grade student in Scott Heister's class in Willow Run High School. I've dropped by the classroom this morning, unannounced, to get a glimpse of Scott's teaching. I put my nose around the door – and lean further in; I can't see him. "Scott's not here," one of the students tells me. "He's at a conference."

Their teacher is gone, but all around the classroom students are working. It turns out there are four classes, albeit small, in the room. At the front a group of four or five students quiz each other in preparation for a test. At the back a young woman wearing safety glasses sits at a bunsen burner, concentrating on a collection of petri dishes. On the far side are three or four students working at computers, and another small group is talking quietly in the center of the room.

243

I speak with this last group. They all speak up. "We're making up a play to describe how plants work. How they use water and how they function" – "transpiration, internal pressure" – "and all the different aspects of the plant. It's called 'The Water Runs Through It,' and we're trying to make it a little bit more interesting because it's kinda hard to do a play about just a plant, and so we're trying to make it where this little water droplet" – "Known as H_2O" – "gets lost and has to find her way back to the watering can. The way she does it is through the plant, so the plant helps her through the root and stem and xylem and all the different water ways, I guess you could say, through the plant, back to the watering can."

I'm back in Willow Run for a week, early in March 1997. March in Michigan is a struggle between winter and spring; it's the kind of weather I've forgotten but now seems very familiar – a low, broad, dull grey, overcast sky and a chill west wind that cuts through all clothing. The grass is flattened and burned brown from past snows.

Significant changes have occurred in the Willow Run Community Schools since I was last here. The superintendent who was hired in 1995 to replace Dr. Joe was recently terminated by the school board in an atmosphere of mystery, rumor, and anxiety, after being put on leave after only a year, for suspected misuse of district funds.[1] Another interim superintendent has arrived, with the mandate of making up a budget shortfall of around one million dollars.

In 1996 the district applied successfully for continuation funds from MSSI. Focus districts competed for the funds available for the remainder of the five-year funding period: Willow Run received the largest award granted – $41,000 – and since this was lower than their original level of funding the administration made up the difference. The fourth year of MSSI, 1996–1997, directs efforts toward "focusing, scaling up, and sustaining" reform initiatives.

And in the past few years Governor Engler has introduced massive changes in Michigan's public school system. "Lots of changes, good grief!" one of the Willow Run principals exclaims. "Every time you turn around!"

The new MEAP tests in math and science are up and running, and the new social studies MEAP will begin in 1999. The High School Proficiency Test was administered for the first time in the spring of 1996, replacing the tenth-grade MEAP. Proposed in 1991 as a "high stakes" test, to be passed before a student could graduate, the threat of lawsuits has meant that the HSPT leads merely to a state-endorsed high school diploma.

Charter schools – Public School Academies – have been opening, a restricted number authorized by state universities, an unlimited number by community colleges, intermediate school districts, and local school districts. Like all public schools, PSAs are required to participate in the "School Quality Initiative," with its four requirements: an annual education report, a school improvement plan, a core academic curriculum, and accreditation.

In addition, parents can now make choices among public schools. The School Aid bill for 1997 allows students to attend any school within their intermediate school district, unless the district opts not to have "schools of choice." "A local school superintendent who is afraid of losing funding won't be able to hold students hostage anymore," said the governor. "Independence Day has come a couple of weeks early for Michigan's students and their parents." And intermediate school districts can make a local decision to serve parochial and private school students.

Bilingual education is no longer a state requirement. School districts are now obligated merely to provide equal educational opportunities to students with limited English.

Each local school district can now establish its own definition of sex education, and parents are permitted to exclude their children from sex education classes.

And while a school district or Public School Academy can still determine the length of the school year, reductions in state aid will occur unless pupil instruction is a minimum of 180 days, or 900 hours in 1994. These figures increase steadily to 190 days or 1140 hours in 2006.

Legislation banning weapons in schools went into effect in January 1995. Engler is still seeking passage of a bill that would expel any student assaulting school staff.

The Michigan Accreditation Program has been modified: accreditation standards must now include multiple-year progress in MEAP scores. And the new Michigan Test for Teacher Certification is intended to ensure that new teachers have the basic skills and content knowledge to perform effectively. Professional development funds must be targeted toward training directly related to student achievement of the core curriculum objectives of the local district.

The revised state School Code took effect on July 1, 1996, following Engler's 1995 repeal of many provisions of the original Code, in place since 1975. The changes ostensibly broaden school district powers. For example, the state core curriculum is now a model, not a mandate. The MEAP is mandated as one, but not the only, student performance criterion. Portfolios are no longer required though still recognized as a form of "authentic assessment." But in practice things are not this simple.

Engler has also just succeeded in passing the School District Educational Accountability Act, which permits state intervention in districts failing to meet minimum standards of student performance. The governor can declare a district "educationally bankrupt" if for two years in a row less than 80 percent of students achieve state endorsement in any area of the HSPT, or if the dropout rate is higher than 25 percent. Engler states his belief that this legislation will empower teachers, increase accountability, and raise parental involvement.

And he recently issued two executive orders shifting duties from the state Board of Education – no longer under Republican control – to the state superintendent of schools. The state board has sued.

Engler is evidently proud of these changes and can point to some measures of their success. He declares Michigan "the Education State." Michigan, he says, "has a passion for excellence in education."[2] U.S. Secretary of Education Richard Riley just reported that Michigan has the second highest rate of improvement in eighth-grade math test scores. The state's charter school law has been rated third-strongest of the 26 states with such legislation, and the state has the third largest number of charter schools (76) and enrolled students (11,850). More Michigan residents now grade their public schools "A" or "B."

More broadly, the state's unemployment rate has dropped to 4.3 percent, remaining below the national average for a third year, and 500,000 jobs have been created in the past six years. Tax cuts since 1991 total over $8.5 billion, and the state has risen from twenty-third to sixth in the country for new industrial sites and expansion projects. Engler's welfare reforms have reduced the number of welfare recipients to the lowest since 1971. Engler says, "These are great numbers, but the larger point is this: When our schools do an even better job, there will be even fewer families needing welfare."[3]

And in another coup for the governor, President Clinton is scheduled to address a joint session of the Michigan legislature in Lansing this week, something no sitting president has done since Roosevelt in 1907. Governor Engler has offered Michigan as a proving ground for the new national tests that Clinton is calling for, beginning with the 1998 school year. The *Detroit Free Press* calls Engler and Clinton "the odd couple of politics . . . for today anyway."[4]

In short, Engler has accomplished virtually everything that "market-place" reformers have been calling for – increasing schools' accountability and placing them in competition. The whole "total quality" package. One might imagine that professional educators would be delighted at all this, but they most certainly are not. All those I speak with in Willow Run this week, despite their differences on other matters, are united in their unequivocal denunciation of the state's educational reform efforts. In particular, they see the use of the MEAP test – the "quality" indicator for schooling – as underhanded and manipulative, evidence of an agenda very different from the official rhetoric.

Scott Heister regrets having supported Engler in the past. We talk in his classroom at break, with students coming in and out to work on projects, the yearbook, or just to chat with him. "I happen to be one of those rare teachers who's a Republican, who actually voted for him. Even though I'm still a Republican I won't make that mistake again. He is ruining public education in this state, and I don't care who you are, in what state you live, public education needs to exist and needs to flourish in order for this country to go forward.

"I think we need to move; I don't think we're doing a very good job in education. I mean, I don't disagree with Engler in many ways. I disagree with his *methods*, I disagree with setting up an antagonistic system, because then people are not going to be willing to work with you. You can't – excuse the expression – you can't piss on somebody and then expect them to come follow you, and that's what he's doing. He started out by saying, 'I'm going to get public educators because they didn't vote for me in the election,' and he's continuing to do that. Whatever he can do to harm public education he's doing."

School choice also could be a very good thing, Scott feels, but "it will be driven by Engler so that public education will continue to look bad, and Engler will fight to make public education look bad so it won't matter what public institution you're going to. He wants to drive this into privatization; he wants to drive this into charter schools and . . . , so whatever he can do he'll do.

"My sense is the state is losing its public education, because of the decisions that have been made. The administration is making decisions that are anti public education. So education is losing faith, and the educators are losing faith in the administration, they're losing faith in the system."

Vivian Lyte is also very critical of the state's approach to school reform. She and I meet at an Ypsilanti restaurant on a freezing, blustery day. The

MEAP is being used to drive school reform in a detrimental manner, she says. Accreditation and curriculum are examples of this. "You have to understand – that's why it's so hard to tell the story. If you start to talk about the accreditation process people will say, 'I don't see anything wrong with that, there's nothing hard about that.' You have to pull your team together, your team has to come up with three student outcomes, you have to figure out how you're going to measure them, then you have to figure out how you're going to implement these student outcomes – what's wrong with that? It makes sense. Okay, but what we forgot to tell you was that, it's not based on that. It's based on the fact that your kids have to take this *test*, to prove that you've done these things.

"And, guess what, you can decide whatever curriculum you want – we're just going to make you take this test! But we're not going to tell you too much about this test, oh well, but we will tell you that these items come from *this* curriculum, that we've put together – but you don't have to use this curriculum It's not even mandated, it's just a suggested kinda curriculum. And it's written real nebulous, like, K to 3, 4 to 6, 6 to 8, and 9 to 10. Okay? Now people can maybe begin to see the murkiness. But if you're not in there dealing with it, you don't get it all, you don't get the whole picture, because you just get these pieces of things. Half the parents probably don't even understand accreditation. I haven't had a parent come to me yet and say, I'm upset because my child is in a summary interim accredited school. No one's come in and said that. Now they *have* said, tell me how I can help the school with these MEAP scores, they're terrible." But school accreditation is "*only* based on MEAP; it's a facade when they tell you it's based on other stuff."

I ask if she'd like to keep that comment off the record. "No, people say that stuff *on* the record! It doesn't matter, because there's no system to deal with it." She laughs wryly. "It's very murky because we don't mandate anything in the state of Michigan," she says with irony. "My attitude is, gee wizz, if we don't mandate, then give me mandates! This sure feels like a mandate, but there's nothing I can do with it, there's no way I can change it, I can't protest it. Versus if you had a mandate, there's usually a process that you can impact it. You can't impact this kind of system! 'Cause they'll still be messing with you, but it's not official so therefore you can't do anything with it. You can't even tell people that it's happening, because it's not official."

I want to be sure I've understood her. So the appearance is that there is great freedom of choice? "Uhhuh." Freedom of action? "Uhhuh." But in practice everything is driven by a single measure of quality. "Uhhuh." Scored, I add, in a peculiar way.

"But see, even that's designed to protect the state against attack. It has nothing to do with student assessment, it has nothing to do with measurement of progress – nothing! What it has to do with is making sure the cut-off is low enough that the majority of kids are going to get through. Is low enough that the *right* kids will probably get through."

She means the white kids? "White kids, rich kids – in this day and age it's hard to tell which is which. I think it's beginning to be the kids with money enough to get the lawyer." She laughs. "Be they black or white or Asian or whatever."

It's somehow odd to see Laura Chew in the office I've always thought of as Vivian's. Laura tells me emphatically, "I don't think that the tests themselves are bad, I think that the arbitrariness of the state's cut-points and grading methods are highly questionable, and their purposes are very questionable. The tests themselves are not bad; the HSPT is not a bad thing. The teachers at the high school will say that; it is much more congruent with, and reflective of, cumulative knowledge in the core content areas and related to the state standards and so on. It's the grading of the test that is so outrageous. It's so artificial; they have categories of reporting, and if you got a score of thirteen then you're 'Not Proficient,' and if you got a fourteen you're 'Proficient.'

"Our agenda here, and we take it very seriously and very responsibly, is to educate *all* the kids, whatever it takes. We've signed up for that cruise. We take it seriously. However, the governor's purpose, I believe, is very different. I don't think that there's any interest whatsoever in addressing the needs of the underclass. In fact, everything that I have seen indicates to me that there's every intention of creating – and they're doing a damn good job – of increasing the distance between the haves and the have nots. They absolutely do not want to see what they consider to be kids in the underclass succeed. They cannot stand that that can happen.

"I think it's hard for people like us to comprehend that thinking. I really think it's hard – we are not a them-and-us kind of people, and we are just not exclusionary. We're so inclusive that it goes against everything we stand for, everything that we believe in, and it's insulting, and it's shocking, and it's demoralizing, and it's a direct attack on our kids. It is really painful, and we take it very personally."

High school principal Gail Green's dissertation research examined the influence of mandated testing programs that were intended to drive instruction. When does that happen? What's the local response to testing that shows it drives instruction and therefore scores go up? "The bottom line came out, it made no difference whatsoever what happened at the district level, or at the administrative level in the building. Nothing happened with scores until teachers took the results and took the results apart."

Like the other people I speak with, Gail insists, "I am not objecting to testing; I believe we need a variety of ways to assess students, and testing is one of them." Her point is that if these tests – the MEAP and HSPT – are intended to change instruction, they can only do this if teachers are provided with a detailed breakdown of each student's performance on the test items. Without this "item analysis" students remain in the dark about what they did well and what they did badly, and teachers remain in the dark about what they need to be teaching differently.

And teachers cannot get familiar with the HSPT, because all the test material is secure; the test booklets are counted and must be returned to the state in numerical order. "I got that first round of test results back and there was no supporting data whatsoever. I didn't even know how they had constructed the scale scores, or how they had translated into 'Proficient,' 'Novice.' . . ." So Gail figured it out for herself. "I took every kid's scores and entered them on a spreadsheet, and then I ordered them. I knew what the cut score was, which gave me the scale score, which gave me the raw score. I was resentful as could be that I had to do that, but I now know that test backwards and forwards. I really needed to do that, to look at the data that way. And as the staff started looking at it, all of a sudden lightbulbs went off."

Gail tells me the story of Jason. He came out of the first level of testing "Proficient" in science and math, so he had those endorsements. He was "Proficient" in reading, but there's only one endorsement for "communication arts," for the reading and writing tests together, so he wasn't endorsed, though he's a very proficient reader. "Now, Jason scored twenty-seven on the ACT, which puts him in the ninety-second/ninety-third percentile, he scored twelve hundred sixty on the SAT. He is the award winner from the National Merit for Minority Students; he's got a four-year full ride from Dow Chemical, based on everything. 'Not proficient' in writing! Re-tested. Not 'Proficient' yet! His last re-test . . . he's already been accepted to the University of Michigan; he's been accepted at the University of North Carolina; he's waiting to hear from MIT. He called all three institutions, they said, 'Sleep in!' This test is given in two days; Jason missed the first day and I thought he's not going to do it. He came back and said 'I need to make it up, I'm going to take it.' The essay – this is so good, I love this story! – the essay was 'Describe an experience that has changed your life,' guess what Jason wrote on? Taking the test and not getting any answers! I said, not only will the child be proficient in writing, he's going to get an endorsement in psychology! Here is a kid who is *clearly* an achiever!

"But my whole point it, I don't know enough about that assessment to be able to tell you what is wrong. I see no purpose; why would we pour the money that we pour into giving this test? If it is to drive instruction, then the Proficiency Test needs the same kind of supporting that the MEAP does. This is 'gottcha' evaluation."

This response is not unique to Willow Run. A report from MSSI addressing the state policy system's affect on math and science education detects a deep ambivalence among legislators – and in legislation – over the degree to which state policies should promote "top-down" or "grass-roots" moves toward reform. The report notes that "Beneath the political hauling and tugging, there appears to be a fundamental clash of assumptions about how to build *will* or *motivation* for educational improvement. One group appears to assume that to get real improvement, strong outside pressure is essential: state government (working on behalf of parents, employers, and other citizens) must hold schools accountable for quantifiable results. The other group seems to emphasize processes designed to build commitment to improvement from within the school and school district (for example, school improvement planning and site-based decision making)."[5] There is a danger, the authors conclude, that the approach to systemic reform the state has adopted – the "Smith and O'Day" model – "appears to run the risk of over-controlling the system, under-investing in capacity-building, and depressing rather than raising the will to improve."[6]

The report notes "some major problems with simple quantitative thresholds" such as the MEAP cut-points used for school accreditation. "Approximately 80% of the variation in student achievement can be accounted for by socioeconomic status, alone. If this is true, then a school with a great majority of upper middle class students should not get all the credit for high MEAP scores while a school with a majority of low SES students takes the blame for low ones. The question is, what is each *school* contributing to its students' performance?" The authors point out that Michigan's MEAP program is "grossly underfunded" and suggest that much more discussion is needed about appropriate assessment. "After several years of such discussion," they add with irony, "we might even be ready as a state to establish meaningful performance standards for students."[7]

Mary Brandau believes the community will reject the use of these tests. "I think the people are going to come back on the MEAP and say forget it, this is not a good way to measure our kids. When you see Grosse Pointe and Birmingham opting their kids out, not to take it, I think they are going to come back and say don't do this to our children anymore, and put it into perspective." Indeed, the *Ypsi Courier* has printed an editorial condemning "MEAP Madness."

Richard Riley, in his State of American Education address in February, reiterated that "Education is the engine that drives our economy." But it seems the link between education and the economy is not as simple and direct as people have suggested. Many figures show that, viewed as a whole, the American economy is performing extremely well – much better, in fact, than Japan or Germany. Louis V. Gerstner Jr., for example, the chief executive at I.B.M. – the man who complained in 1994 that the nation's schools were failing and threatening to drag the national economy down – had a pay raise in 1996 of 29.4 percent, for a total, including stock options, of $20.2 million.[8] General Motors is still losing market share in the United States and has been slow to put 15 new models into production, but the company is in a much improved financial situation. With cash reserves over $17 billion, its workers' pension plan fully financed, in January GM bought back $2.5 billion of its own stock, and increased the dividend.

> From the dire warnings of educational and national decline in the "Nation at Risk" report in 1983 to President Clinton's full-court press on education as the key to national prosperity, the direct link between schooling and the economy has become part of the conventional wisdom of American education. . . .
>
> But many educators and economists are increasingly skeptical of the notion that better schools mean a more prosperous nation. And as Mr. Clinton's education agenda makes its way through Congress – he promised that education will be the No. 1 priority of his second term – some wonder if overemphasis on the link between schools and jobs can tilt the public's view of education to an unhealthy degree – expecting too much in building the economy and not enough in developing intellects and personalities and ultimately citizens.
>
> Peter Applebome, "Better Schools, Uncertain Results," *New York Times*, Mar. 16, 1997, sec. 4, p. 5

Have U.S. schools improved dramatically in a few years? Or is the effect of schooling on the economy not as direct as has been claimed? The *New York Times* quotes Richard Gibboney, professor of education at the

University of Pennsylvania: "Education does many things, from teaching kids how to read to teaching ethics and responsibility. If you focus too much on the economy, you squeeze out some of those other values. When businessmen get into the educational business, and they are focusing on the kind of workers they need, the curriculum becomes narrow, technical, de-liberal."[9]

Of course the economic picture is more complex than it seems at first glance. Although the Dow Jones Industrial Average topped 7,000 for the first time in spring 1997, and although corporate profits are excellent, the gap between rich and poor is growing larger. And although official unemployment figures are low, these statistics fail to count those who have given up looking for work. In New York City, 4,000 people started lining up before dawn for 700 jobs at a new hotel.[10] And struggles continue between GM and its employees – strikes have reduced profits by an estimated record $1.6 billion. Workers continue to complain of long hours and job cuts.

"But why beat up on schools? You know what my theory is on that?" says Vivian. "For politicians this is a safe topic. How can you lose? They're telling parents, 'You can do something about this, you get in there and make a difference.' That's the safest topic. What are they going to win if they start dealing with social issues? We know what happened in the '60s, people started dealing with social issues and the country went absolutely mad. Who's touching it? You don't even *hear* a conversation."

The economy appears good in Washtenaw County too. The *Ypsi Press* (the title of a new edition of the *Ann Arbor News*) has just published its *Outlook '97* report. The percentage of Washtenaw County residents who see the local economy as "excellent/very good" has risen from 1 percent in 1992 to 21 percent in 1997, and those rating it "good" has risen from 14 percent to 57 percent.[11] The repercussions of the plant closing are milder than many expected because auto sales rebounded and the local economy has turned out to be less dependent on auto manufacture.

> What a difference five years makes. Here we are, coasting along on the wave of a long, sustained period of economic expansion and low unemployment. But back in 1992, it was a different story. We were in the throes of a recession, and the worst seemed yet to come. General Motors Corp. was at that time on the verge of closing its Willow Run assembly plant. There was much apprehension. Many people feared that the loss of the plant would devastate Ypsilanti.
>
> Well, here we are now, five years hence, and we know that didn't happen. As painful as the loss of the Willow Run plant was, Ypsilanti has survived it.

That tells you something about the resiliency of the community and some-
thing about the underlying strength of the local economy.
Editorial, "Community Shows Resiliency in Its Economy," *Ann Arbor News,
Ypsilanti Press Edition,* Mar. 2, 1997, D1

But this good news seems not to have reached the Willow Run community. The numbers tell a story of families leaving the community and
those who remain growing poorer. Since the 1991–1992 school year,
district enrollment has shrunk from 4,303 to 3,608 – a drop of about 16
percent. Across Washtenaw County other districts have experienced increased enrollment, except Ypsilanti, which had a 4 percent drop. Enrollment in Willow Run's free and reduced-price lunch program has
risen to 50.2 percent from 41.7 percent in 1991, compared with a current state average of 26.4 percent (up slightly from 24.7) and a Washtenaw County average of 17.1 percent (up from 15.4). Across the district
enrollment now ranges from 41.3 percent at the High School to 68.1
percent at Kaiser Elementary. During the same period, the district's
graduation rate dropped dramatically to 43.9 percent in 1992–1993 before rising again to 86.2 percent in 1994–1995, and turnover rose to almost 40 percent in 1992–1993 and again in 1994–1995. Students are either moving out or dropping out, rather than graduating.

MEAP tests certainly seem to be everyone's concern in the district right
now. The school board is very concerned that Willow Run's scores are
too low. The state applied new criteria to the science MEAP (in fifth,
eighth, and eleventh grades) and the math MEAP (in eleventh grade),
and the results were shocking negative publicity for Willow Run. On
the old science test in 1994–1995, 83.5 percent of fifth graders had
scored "satisfactory," but this year on the new test only 18.4 percent
scored "proficient." The story was the same for eighth grade (to 6.0
from 42.9 percent) and eleventh grade (to 8.6 from 43.8 percent).[12]
Board president Clifford Smith took a strong line.

"I am extremely disappointed and I want the building administrators to know
that," Smith said at Thursday night's school board meeting. "We want them
to come back with improved scores next year. If they don't, we'll deal with the
situation. It's as simple as that. We will not continue to see this happen . . ."
     "I'm not threatening anybody," Smith said after the meeting. "I'm just
telling people to do their job. You can't come back here year after year with

the same scores. There are no excuses. . . . In private industry, if you have results like this, you wouldn't have a job."

Janet Miller, "Principals Urged: Improve Test Scores," *Ann Arbor News*,
Jan. 17, 1997

At the board meeting this week the building principals are to present reports responding to Smith's concerns. The meeting is at the high school, which is hosting the area basketball meet, and the Willow Run Flyers are playing a semifinal game this evening. Gail Green and several others keep tabs on the score of the game as the board meeting progresses.

This evening there is the first outspoken opposition I've seen at a school board meeting here – first an accusation of nepotism, no names mentioned, from a parent, and then complaints from the teachers' union president that Willow Run's budget cutting is a thinly disguised effort to pressure teachers during a contract negotiation year.

Two educational consultants make a proposal for an expedited search for a new superintendent. The board members look tired; one senses they feel they stumbled after Dr. Joe left and want to get it right this time.

Mr. Anglin and four staff members present the Middle School's "MEAP improvement plan." They describe summer packets on test-tak-ing skills, an academic incentive program, parent orientation, test-skills tutoring sessions, and a "MEAP rally" to kick off the testing. Teachers have been shown examples of low-scoring test items, of frequently cho-sen wrong answers, and disaggregated scores, to help them develop strat-egies for instruction in low-score areas. Staff development is now tied to the annual changes in the MEAP, and the pending social studies test. "We're trying to look at instructional programs through the test."

"I'm glad to see we have a team and a process," responds board mem-ber Claudette Braxton severely.

The elementary school principals are next, introduced by Laura Chew. Laura explains that each elementary has a testing team in place, and she describes how the principals have come together as a team themselves. She presents item analysis data for the test scores. "What I want to emphasize tonight," she says, "is that the percent satisfactory is a little bit deceptive." The way the state reports scores exaggerates dif-ferences between districts. A more careful look at the data shows that Willow Run "mirrors the pattern in the state very closely." For example, in geometry the median score for Willow Run students is 9.0; for the state as a whole it is 9.6, but the "percent satisfactory" is very different.

This point is being made in a number of districts. The new *Ypsilanti Courier* ("Your ONLY Hometown Newspaper") reports "a 25.7 percent difference between the number of Ypsilanti students scoring satisfactory in math and the state average, but less than a 10 percent difference between the number of items Ypsilanti students and their statewide counterparts missed on that section."[13]

The emphasis on teams at the board meeting is a direct reaction to the board's approach of holding principals and teachers individually accountable for their students' test scores, an approach that cuts like a knife through the ethos of collective responsibility and collaborative work that WRSI has been promoting.

Mary says that the newspaper article on the board president's statement omitted the fact that "the president of the board looked every principal in the eye – he looked me in the eye and said, if you cannot manage the testing situation in your building – that you would be let go."

Vivian sums up the results of the board's attitude about MEAP scores: "Everybody feels personally threatened, and I don't know how you do that." The board president's comments were "about the dumbest thing anybody could say," she comments sadly. "And tell me what literature says that you're the most productive person you can be when you feel threatened."

Laura acknowledges that the board's response, though well-intentioned, adds to the complexity of the situation. "The piece that comes from the local level and from the board level is that" – she sighs – "because the state has created this aura of authority around the myth of the value of these tests, it has caused our board to feel that they're getting beat up in public. It's terrible; it's terrible for our kids, it's terrible for our kids' self-images, and our board wants to stand up and protect our kids. They're saying, our kids are just as good, why aren't we having these scores." It's very hard to explain the distortions of the scoring to the board, she adds.

It's ironic that in seeking to escape the negative image of Willow Run, the school board is taking action that may destroy the strengths of the community's identity. The circumstances of Willow Run's origins produced this image, but also forged a collective identity, an ethos, that is a powerful resource to be drawn upon in difficult times. It may be an identity, a way of viewing the world, that doesn't privilege academic learning, that sees it as just one kind of enterprise among many, but its loss would mean the loss of a resource that keeps people in the community going in the face of exploitation and long odds. Such "reform" would surely be a betrayal.

When I ask Scott Heister what's going on in WRSI he immediately talks of four district teachers recently named part-time "curriculum coordinators," their task to identify "gaps" in the instruction students receive. "Their duties at this point are to work on aligning the curriculum," he explains. He's working with them "trying to evaluate what's being taught and what's not being taught. So that we can assure that a student, when they go through here from K to 12, has had the opportunity to learn all of the objectives that are tested on the High School Proficiency Test." He insists that the purpose is not to change the content of what it taught – "we don't want to tell teachers you can't teach dinosaurs" – but to ensure that content is directed toward the appropriate objectives.

"And the second job of those people is then, once it's aligned, to work on a plan of implementation. How do you implement that aligned curriculum? Finding resources for teachers – if a teacher doesn't know how to teach pH and they need to teach it, getting them the information they need, providing them with the in-service if that's what they need, that will allow them to learn that material.

"So that we can make sure that all of our students are learning all of the objectives they're supposed to – have the *opportunity* to learn, before they get to the Proficiency Test. 'Cause right now there are holes. We know that, when they get to us as ninth graders, there isn't time in a year and a half, two years, to be able to teach them all of the objectives. They have to have some knowledge coming in; you cannot take them as ninth graders and start out fresh and try to teach them all the objectives you need to in two years."

If a student doesn't demonstrate skill in, say, fractions, "That doesn't mean it isn't being *taught*, it means it's not being *learned*. We're trying to delineate between teaching and learning. Just because you teach it doesn't mean it's being learned."

So teaching is curriculum, learning is test scores? "Yep. So we are looking at trying to develop an assessment, a pre-test post-test at each grade level, by the time this is all done, and find out what actually – so the teachers have an idea, more than anything, what worked and what didn't. I mean, if you taught all of the objectives you were supposed to, and the students still are not doing well on some of the objectives, it means maybe we need to look at teaching it in a different manner."

One of the new curriculum coordinators is Bev Dundan. Scott is working with Bev at one of the computers when I return to his classroom. They are plotting and graphing MEAP scores in preparation for a meeting Bev will have with the middle school. Kids tested in 1993, in fourth grade, are now in seventh grade. There's 20 percentage points difference between the lines.

"Does it show something to you?" Bev asks Scott, pointing to the graph. "Shows that the kids did better in fourth grade than they do in seventh grade," says Scott. "Well, yeah," Bev replies. A student enters and comes over to check with Scott. "You didn't get much done yesterday," he says. " 'Cause I didn't have a hammer, I had to bring in my *own* hammer," she complains. Her tone turns teasing. "Which I should beat you with!" Scott and Bev laugh. "We have a guest," says Scott, also teasingly, "you're not supposed to speak like that." "More to the point," I warn him, "she's holding a hammer right now."

The test data could be a hammer too. "Can I ask what's your point?" Scott asks Bev. "My point? What *happens?* They're doing so well, they seem to be up so high. Sure, I know the concepts are less involved, but they're still appropriate to grade level." "Okay," replies Scott. "I'm – You know where I'm going." "I *think* I know where you're going; that I would be too critical?" "Pointing fingers." "Yeah. Well that's not what I . . ." "We just need to make sure that we're not doing that, because we don't want to start out looking like we're going for the jugular, yet." "No, and if this indicates that I'm going for the jugular then I won't print it up." "I think as long as you present it that way, to say the reason we're doing this is, we are losing something between fourth grade and seventh grade. Whether we are teaching the wrong objectives – that's not to say we're not teaching."

Scott adds, "The only person who's going to hear it is Mel, and Mel should hear it. Mel needs to hear something." Bev says she wants to track the kids, to see how far back she can go with MEAP data. Is this an overall trend, or exceptional to this group of kids? How much did the test change? "Now let's find the holes in the curriculum that we need to fill. Let's narrow our scope. You and I have talked about this intensely, that we cover so much, and we cover it only at the surface, and generally speaking with paper and pencil. Certainly we use manipulatives to a certain extent, but maybe not the extent that we should. Part of it certainly is attributed to the hormonal hell, the changes that the kids go through. Family changes."

Scott says, "I think a lot of it is content, I really do." Bev agrees. He goes on, "I think it's alignment of what we teach, when we teach it. I think the elementary schools have done a better job of aligning their curriculum in the past than the middle school has. And it shows." Bev nods in agreement. She ejects her disk from the computer, and heads for the door. "Thank you for your time, Scott. Nice meeting you, Martin." "Your bill will be in the mail," Scott calls after her. "Yes, I know, it always is," and she laughs happily.

Some people see the Willow Run Systemic Initiative becoming more "top-down" in character. The committee was recently institutionalized as the formal decision-making body in the community schools. A newsletter – *WRSI News* – was begun because "our meetings have become extremely long and information intensive."[14] A new organizational chart does indeed show a hierarchical, top-down structure, with the superintendent at the apex, the director of curriculum and instruction next in line, followed by the WRSI-Curriculum Committee, the four curriculum coordinators, the building teams, and, as output at the bottom, "Aligned K–12 Curriculum – Increased Student Outcomes."

Vivian was startled how quickly the WRSI committee changed its character after she left. "It changed immediately. First meeting I went back to and all the principals were there, I just about fell out of my seat! I could never get them to even come! The principals were there, but some of them didn't have teachers there. I always had teachers. Even though I didn't have the principals, I always had teachers. So it was like, wait a minute, what's going on?"

When I ask Scott whether WRSI is now more top-down, he replies, "It is and it isn't. It is in the sense that there's a certain direction that the grant has taken to try to get some things organized. In the initial grant, some of the initial goals were to get people motivated and get people to change, to think about change. As that comes about and as you get more and more people doing that, there needs to be some level of organization there to allow for resources to be passed from one place to another, to not duplicate things that we're doing. So to that extent, yeah, it's top-down, but it's top-down from teachers making those decisions. It's top-down from administrative decisions.

"I think WRSI has created huge changes here. It's brought a lot of people on board, and it's brought a lot of people on board because they think and feel that they actually have a say in things. They can come to a meeting and express concern over something, and something gets done. They can come to the meeting and bring a proposal from students or from teachers, and say, 'We would like to have this funded. This is what we would like to see happen.' It's a clearinghouse for a lot of ideas that can branch out, and help a lot of other people get excited. It really has helped people get excited about teaching again. Even people who are good teachers, if they see things not improving and not getting better, tend to put a little bit less into it than they would if they were excited. So I think it's helped generate excitement within the district, and I think it's helped give teachers the feeling that they're empowered.

"It certainly has me, anyway. If I didn't see the district moving, if I didn't see the district growing and moving, if this were a dead-end place, if this were a place that wasn't going forward, I'd leave."

Laura tells me, "The curriculum committee that used to exist here was a committee in name only. People wouldn't come – they paid them, and they still didn't come! They paid them to come, and they were hard pressed to get one rep per building, to stay for an hour. I don't pay 'em and I have several people from all the buildings come and stay for *four* hours. I think we're talking different languages now.

"It's a living committee, people feel empowered, they feel excited, they feel happy, like it's a place that they can share ideas and also obtain resources, and that it's a committee that sanctions risk taking. And provides, I guess, that risk-taking companionship, you know, 'You're not in this alone. You could try this and there won't be anything punitive that happens.' "

But she acknowledges the difficulty of striking the appropriate balance: of motivating and facilitating without dictating.

Mary Brandau sees the WRSI meetings as different, too. Communication is much more one-way. "WRSI is a" – she hesitates – "is an endurance. They meet from 4:00 to 7:30, and you sit and you listen for three and a half hours. Sharing of ideas – not that the ideas they're sharing are not good, but they are such powerful pieces that you can't do it in three hours. Sharing of experience, sharing of conferences, sharing of topics – it's presenter, presenter, presenter, presenter. It feels like an old staff meeting."

The state's reporting of MEAP scores hits Willow Run where it hurts – it threatens to bring back the negative image the district has struggled to escape. The students I speak with in Scott's classroom are well aware of the stereotype outsiders still have of Willow Run.

"There's a lot of positives to Willow Run that a lot of people don't see because they just see our stereotype" – "Everyone thinks it's a bad school" – "I was like, you haven't been there." "And a lot of the people inside the school are so much more positive than what people believe us to be, because they never ever have enough courage to actually come here and see how it is."

Are the stereotypes about the school, or about students, or about people in the community? "It's just everything about Willow Run" – "They think we're real evil" – "They think that there's fights every day, that's what I've been hearing, and I'm just, I'm gonna figure out what it's like, and it wasn't bad when I came here." "They think we're stupid, you know, we're violent." "My aunt, she said her daughter's smarter than me because she goes to Lincoln and I go to Willow Run." "We have a better education I think, because we get educated socially *and* academically; you know we get to learn more about different types of people, and getting along with them, and I think Willow Run is more like the real world."

"Just because we don't have enough money, you know, doesn't mean that we're not as smart and we can't get the best education. We find our ways. And if you know how to survive without as much money you know how to live in the real world, 'cause in the real world you won't always have money; you won't always have people providing the best things for you."

These young people haven't allowed their aspirations to be curtailed by the stereotyping. Do they plan to go to college? "Yeah, most definitely!" "Most of the people here want to go to college and want to make something of their lives." "Yeah, and people don't realize, and so a lot of people from here have to do better than normal, or make it in the paper so they can actually put their school name, you know, and say, this outstanding kid was from Willow Run. And all these people that you read in the newspapers come from Willow Run, and all these records that are being broken and all of these things come from Willow Run. We have to constantly work at trying to overcome the stereotype that has been set for us."

What do they want to do when they finish high school and college? "I want to be a teacher – come back here and be a math teacher. That's why I gotta work on being mean!" She laughs. "Interesting things; I don't know, I love science, science is just like everything to me, but I want to either be an astronomer, meteorologist, or a marine biologist. I haven't decided yet which one. Something that involves science." "I want to be an archaeologist." "I want to be a psychiatrist during the regular school year, I want to help people that way, and then take off the summers to be a archaeologist. And when I retire, open my own school. So I can help people who don't usually get the chance to express their gifts." "I want to be a lawyer." "I'd like to be a architect; sounds interesting to me, like to build my own house and stuff like that." "She's a very good artist. You know she wants to be shy and not talk."

Willow Run's strength still lies in the ethos of sharing and equality that formed in the early days of the Village.

> For generations, the parents of Willow Run have joined with educators to develop a school system of which we can be proud. Our story has so much heart because in Willow Run, along with their parents, we always look at the children as people. We know that every child comes to school with a story, and every family wants that child to have all the tools necessary to write a story for a bright future.
>
> Our business is to join with the family to assemble the optimum conditions for each child in the garden to grow and flourish and become all he or she can become, creating a future, writing a personal story of success. Every child who attends school in Willow Run is unique, and each comes in a very different package – in looks, contents, needs, interests and hopes and dreams.
>
> We think that in Willow Run, the level of personal care that students in our schools experience provides a *qualitative* difference. It is one that can't always be measured by a number, but captures the essence of the shared joy on the teaching and learning journey. . . . Today, in spite of the new challenges, dramatic changes and great difficulties, there is tremendous and growing excitement going on inside what appear to be ordinary brick buildings, and we want to share our stories.
>
> Willow Run Community Schools, *Telling the Story*, Letter to parents, no date

A report from WRSI to MSSI, summarizing what has been learned, while making a nod to the official rhetoric of "capacity-building," describes "a group cultural norm of support" that differs from top-down control.

> *We've learned* that the process of systemic change is an inside-out process. It is first and foremost a process of capacity building – it occurs through creating shared success in risk taking ventures – well selected ventures that create positive outcomes.
>
> *It works best* when built from the group up. It is powerful because in the change process, people learn to let go of control and thus become much more empowered, and feel confident in terms of sharing power and empowering others. This creates a dynamic of shared energy that opens many new synergistic possibilities, and creates a critical mass in favor of continued capacity building.

> *The synergy that is created* creates a scaffold suitable for broad scale capacity building throughout the district. When embarking on this type of change, do not try to maintain a rigid or top down control framework. The strength of the change is that people who are thus empowered are powerfully energized. They want to learn, they want to teach, they believe that we all have a lot to learn.
>
> What doesn't work? Top down initiatives; narrow, "formula" thinking and teaching; judgmental and critical oversight; becoming rule bound and rigid; tight control over process.
>
> MSSI assignment for WRSI Systemic Design Team, Feb. 28, 1997

The students express this clearly too. How would they describe Willow Run to someone who hasn't been here? "We tight! We hang with the cousins!" – "It's more like a family atmosphere than everybody out for themselves. 'Cause I've visited different schools and that's their attitude. I'll ask them, 'Do you know this person?' they're like, 'Do I care?' You know? And if you come to Willow Run everybody – you might not be friendly but you give everybody a chance." "Yeah. Even, you know, like, the geeks or whatever in our school – people are still friendly to them. They're just the same as everyone else – just because they don't dress like them . . ." "They have this little attitude and caste system in other schools – and here everybody has a place to belong. You know, the smart people have a smart group, and the attitude with them is – 'cause I belong to it!" – the student laughs – "but their attitude is, you know, we don't care – we don't want to be popular. We're just the same as everybody else." "We all have our own little areas." "I don't even think there really is a popular group." "It's just – groups. Where people belong. And all the people who don't belong anywhere have their own group too! Yeah, and everybody is good at something. And it's different in other schools, because there is such a definite caste system." "We don't stereotype as much here as other schools do" "Yeah!" "It's just different; it's more like the real world. And that's it!"

But as the district places emphasis on raising students' scores on the MEAP, there is a danger that the reforms in Willow Run are being tilted away from the ethos of grassroots community, toward a more "top-down" approach. It's not hard to understand why. Mandated tests are intended to drive instruction, and they do this both directly and indirectly. The design of the MEAP test reflects Michigan's core curriculum, so it makes sense to adopt this curriculum, even though it is no longer mandated, and take it as a model with which to "align" instruction. But this means telling teachers what to teach and tying their instruction to objectives defined by the state, rather than the needs and interests of the community and its children. Can the district align its curriculum, fill gaps in instruction, and give teachers diagnostic information on their students' test scores and remain a ground-up enterprise?

A window of opportunity is closing. WRSI – under Vivian's guidance – approached reform with a way of understanding both teaching and administration that had its roots in the community – a grassroots approach in which everyone was essentially equal, in which differences in ability, aptitude, and personality were appreciated and tolerated, in which "encouragement and sympathy and help"[15] were the way to accomplish change. From the outset, the WRSI committee members were aware (though perhaps they preferred not to think about it) that the educational system in general, and the governor in particular, were setting about reform very differently – viewing things in terms of individual accountability, top-down instruction, narrow tests of "quality." In early 1997 it is the latter approach that seems to be prevailing.

The two different perspectives are apparent in the way people talk to and about each other. More rarely do they become the explicit topic of discussion. Instead problems are personalized, and action takes the form of exclusion, factions, alignments that are then viewed as special treatment. One teacher describes another as "top-down," as having an agenda, as wanting to be an administrator, while describing themselves as a teacher-leader, who would rather return to the classroom than become an administrator. The recently departed superintendent is seen as top-down by some, as irrational by others. The interim superintendent is viewed as basically decent but as focusing on numbers rather than the culture and climate of the schools. The result is that the district is considered by some to be rudderless.

In such a situation a school like Kettering can become viewed as having received "too much input for little output" – despite now having many valued elements: integrated instruction, common planning time, teachers working in teams, consensus-driven decisions. Kettering is viewed by some as a place that "likes to be different and special. But everybody wants that, and you still need to have a team."

For Mary Brandau, the "last straw" was a neighborhood dinner put on by the schools. "We were all supposed to work and, you know, serve food. I arrived with my husband in our blue jeans, and we're schlepping in the kitchen and we're carrying milk and stirring potatoes and gettin' dirty and workin' in the back serving food." But most of the others arrived all dressed up – in suits, a cashmere sweater outfit; clearly not planning on slinging any hash! "And this is where I have more respect for Laura – Laura arrived dressed, but she served food. She did know to serve the food, to work." A couple of others also came to work, but "actually, probably just less than ten people ran that dinner in terms of hard work. That frightened me; 'cause this was going to be a district effort, big deal, big deal; it's gonna be a district effort – and people didn't *work.* I think they see themselves above it."

Mary is evidently upset when I talk with her. She speaks of her fears for the future, of the events that have brought her to the brink of quitting her job. She speaks of vulnerability and isolation, of fear and anger, of what has disappointed and disheartened her. She speaks of betrayal. "At this point if we become top-down I'll go back in the classroom and teach because that's fine, I can do that, I only have three years, I can buy my retirement, and I can finish. I think it's sort of a shame, we've come so far, but, if that's what needs to happen. . . . It would be very hard for me; my entire career is here, twenty-two years here, and I have been associated with the district since before I was *born.* So. . . . But. . . . I am alone, I am completely an island, in the school system."

She went to lunch with two other teachers who'd left Willow Run. One of them looked at her and said, "Mary, you might want to think about it – Vivian left Willow Run." Mary adds, "And no one has had a stronger Willow Run" – she pauses for the right word – "belief than Vivian. And *she* left."

Governor Engler welcomes President Clinton to Lansing with these words: "Where our children are concerned, our search is not for a strictly Republican solution or a strictly Democratic solution, but an American solution – a solution that unites rich and poor, parents and teachers, principals and employers."[16] But this isn't exactly how his efforts are viewed by others.

Laura tells me, with great scorn, "It's a way to put down kids, and particularly, if you look across the districts, at the Middle Cities districts and the districts across the state that are scoring lower, it's an economic issue, and it's a racial issue. I think it's very punitive, and I think it's very deliberate, and I think it's very tied to politics, and I think that there is absolutely no interest in leveling up education for all. I think there's every reason to believe that there's a desire to have a growing disparity between the haves and the have nots.

"We're facing all this reform," she adds, "in the midst of this dramatic change that's going on everywhere around us, in terms of all kinds of legislation. It's totally contradictory to all those processes. We're schizophrenic."

I ask how she thinks Engler feels about MSSI and NSF. "First of all, he doesn't understand *process*. Secondly, he doesn't *know* he doesn't understand process. Thirdly, if he *did* know, he doesn't *want* to know how to understand process! And I think as we enter the next century process is going to become pretty important in education. There's no longer – if ever there was – a body of information that could be mastered. It no longer exists. So schooling is about learning processes – thinking processes, information-retrieval processes, analyzing processes, synthesizing processes." Engler's model of education is still, you've got to learn the skills? "I do believe that. The MEAP is starting to test some higher order skills, but again I'd have to say that the way it is being used is what's so wrong."

Why, she asks, does the state set the cut-off points *after* the test has been taken, to ensure that only half the children in the state score "Proficient"?

This important question is raised in the minutes of a WRSI meeting. "The state SAYS (at the recent social studies meeting): if too many kids get it right, the item will be taken out. The benchmarks will not be set UNTIL everyone in the state has taken the test. WHAT THEN IS THE STATE GOAL? Make public education look bad???!!! Our mission is that everyone can learn – at their own pace – in their own time." To Laura, and many others, the test has "artificial cut points that have been set to label us have-nots. And no-goods, and not-worth-its."

It seems that for both students and teachers the "badges of ability" that Sennett and Cobb saw at the core of the hidden injuries to self-esteem among working-class children are being reforged and reapplied. Schumpter believed that in a capitalist economy "the ultimate foundation on which the class phenomenon rests consists of individual differences in aptitude" – but he failed to recognize that aptitude is never an objectively measurable natural characteristic.[17] The MEAP test is being used artificially and crudely to define those – children, teacher, and school districts – who have ability and those who lack it.

I ask Vivian if she senses that, intentionally or unintentionally, Engler is being discriminatory. "See I'm not sure that that's his *original* motive. I do think it's coming out in that way on some level. I think there are things they've done that people could draw that conclusion."

What's the social function of that kind of discriminatory attitude? "First of all, it keeps the stereotype in place that white kids are better than black kids. At everything. Except sports and sex." She laughs. "They don't test those yet. And remember we talked about those systems? In order for Caucasian people to keep the power, they gotta keep stereotyping. If you break down the stereotype that African American people aren't really intelligent, then you got to start coming to some different conclusions in some of your situations. That's the biggest problem in this country, we refuse to understand that everything is color. If you understand that then it does not impact you as greatly. But when you try to deny it you do all sorts of dumb things you don't even realize you're *doing*. Because it *is*. I keep thinking, whoever the person was who decided they were going to bring Africans over here, slaves, really was the smartest person on earth. They built a system that you can *not* get rid of. Everything that's done is designed to maintain that system."

But isn't the notion that all children can learn intended to be antidiscriminatory? "Uhhum. And every time we had to write something we had to write a special thing for the black kids. Every time we had to write a report we had to say what we were doing special for black kids. Or special for girls." Her speech is becoming more ethnic. "I don't have a problem with that, but when you do that then you're back to that assumption that they won't learn. 'Because they don't learn, we have to do something special for them.' I just keep trying to make the point, if you *teach* all children, all children will learn. The research bears that out, over and over and over. I keep saying to people, 'How many times do we have to do this expectation research?' It's been done in every form and every way that I know. But nobody deals with that. Nobody looks at somebody when their kids aren't learning and says, 'Are you really expecting all your kids to learn?' They do not! Believe it or not, Martin!" She laughs. And if the governor really thought differently, "then he wouldn't be attacking the *kids* who don't do well. . . . His plan of attack is, 'If you can't do this, we'll take you over.' How does that help the kids?! His plan of attack is to put in big bold headlines, 'Kids in Detroit don't learn!' "

Vivian muses on how similar the schools are she's seen in different parts of the country. Even an Islamic church school – "And guess what? All the kids are sitting in rows, they're looking at the front of the room!" She laughs loudly. "That's what makes it so difficult to change this system of education, because it has a logic of its own. I don't care what you do with it, it just keeps coming back to life!" Even when student teachers are trained in a different approach, "I don't care what you learn, you get in that system, and it's like, put the kids in rows! The system fights change. That's why it's so difficult; if you are part of the system it is so difficult to change because it pulls against the change. That's what I see; it's so powerful, it is almost terrifying to me. That's one thing last year taught me, when I finally did start getting into schools, it was almost scary to realize that you can have a perfectly new teacher. . . ." I finish her sentence – and they do exactly the same thing. "And if you ask them they will tell you, 'No, I wasn't taught that way.' So you say, 'Well, why are you doing it?' They say, 'Well, I dunno!' But the honesty is, they don't want to say, 'I don't have a choice.' We really haven't figured out how to set up, within the system, the right of people to come in and do what they think is best, even with all this local control and all that crap. Site-based management!" she says derisively.

"If they really were trying to improve education, you would have diversity. Part of the problem with education is everybody keeps making it *a* system. With all the diversity in the United States education system, it can't be *a* system, it's got to be a lot of different things to a lot of different people. That's part of the problem in the classroom, because classroom teachers keep trying to come up with *a* thing to do. As long as they keep trying – you've heard me say, everybody's looking for this magic pill. We are never going to do anything that way."

Mary Brandau makes an effort to be positive. "Well I don't know how the story will turn out. It will be okay. I mean the kids will be here. The community will be here. I think it will come out alright in the end. Willow Run will survive. . . ."

And as I walk along the corridor to leave Kettering something happens that makes me think she may be right. I glance into the fifth-grade classroom and see children and their teacher dancing! Mariah Carey again! I introduce myself. Mrs. Fields is new to Kettering; she has taken Sharon Ryles's place. The class had just finished the writing MEAP test – three days of drafting, revising, and editing – and they're dancing because they feel the test went well. Mrs. Fields, African American, "grew up right down the street" and graduated from Kettering in 1985. Initially a political science major at Michigan State University she decided to get a teaching certificate, and after teaching first grade for four years she heard Willow Run was hiring. She attended Kettering's graduation (her husband's nephew was graduating), reintroduced herself to the school board president (she went to school with his son), sent over her resume, and got an interview. "When I walked into the interview my fourth-grade teacher is sitting there, so I'm like, 'Oh my god! This is my job! This is just too perfect!" "It was just I wanted to come back. I just felt like giving back." She wants to teach the kids skills, like fluent writing, that she knows are important for college. "I think it's easy for me because I kinda feel that they are in my same footsteps. So I can say, 'It is not that hard, you can do it.' I feel more in tune with the kids here." She lives in Canton but her parents and in-laws live in Willow Run. "I know the neighborhood. I go to my mom's house – the kids are like, 'I saw you!' They help me chase down my mom's dog." And just like the teachers she remembers she can say, "I know your mother! I know your family and you do not act like that!"

She finds Kettering close-knit, small enough that teachers know most of the kids, and she likes that. She's still adjusting to the school's system – "They have got a lot of more progressive things going on than some of the other schools." There's "a great technology program," "we have a wonderful sports program," and "I think the community is really supportive of the students and I feel good about that too." The kids are the same as they were when she was a student, she says. "I think their attitudes are really good. I do like what they have done here at Kettering. The kids' self-esteem – they really worked a lot on that. So they really do have high self-esteem and things like that. I do like to see that in kids."

They are partying now "because we worked hard" preparing for the English test and the upcoming science MEAP, "and hopefully it will pay off next week." "When they got this test, they opened it and they started cheering! It at least felt good that they felt comfortable with the topic they had to write with." Their topic was 'Something you are good at.' "They were like, 'Oh my god this is easy' And I'm like, 'Yes, yes!'" "When they walked out on day one of their writing they went to the principal, Mrs. Brandau, saying 'It is so easy,' and they were hugging all the teachers on their way out."

14   Coda – June 1999

Is it possible for an educational system to be conducted by a national state and yet the full social ends of the educative process not be restricted, constrained, and corrupted? Internally, the question has to face the tendencies, due to present economic conditions, which split society into classes some of which are made merely tools for the higher culture of others. Externally, the question is concerned with the reconciliation of national loyalty, of patriotism, with superior devotion to the things which unite men in common ends, irrespective of national political boundaries.

> John Dewey, *Democracy and Education*, New York: Free Press, 1916,
> pp. 97–98

In the first place, if we want to compare universal history to the construction of an edifice, we must point out that men are not only the bricks that are used in the construction; they are also the masons who build it and the architects who conceive the plan for it, a plan, moreover, which is progressively elaborated during the construction itself. Furthermore, even as "brick," man is essentially different from a material brick: even the human brick changes during the construction, just as the human mason and architect do. . . . Finally, man is not only the material, the builder, and the architect of the historical edifice. He is also the one *for* whom this edifice is constructed: he lives in it, he *sees* and *understands* it, he *describes* and *criticizes* it.

> Alexandre Kojève, *Introduction to the Reading of Hegel: Lectures on the Phenomenology of Spirit*, translated by James H. Nichols Jr. Ithaca:
> Cornell University Press, 1947/1969, p. 32

Kettering's 1997 fifth-grade writing MEAP scores bore out the good feelings of Mrs. Fields and her students: 73 percent obtained scores of "Proficient," up from 50 percent the previous year. The following year they held steady at 70 percent "Proficient."

270

The reforms in Willow Run's schools – at Kettering, but elsewhere too – rested on an appreciation that learning is embedded in the social relationships and culture of the classroom. Efforts to challenge the children, to have them work together and discover in "hands-on, minds-on" activities, to move away from tracking and ability groups, to move toward integrated instruction and team teaching, to gain the involvement and support of the community, and to make school a safe, clean place where children would feel their diverse talents valued – these were efforts to transform the culture and to redefine the relationship between "teacher" and "student." Learning in school – growing facility, for example, with genres of writing that render a rationally organized universe – is an aspect of deeper changes in the child that take place within the relationship with a teacher, through participation in the classroom practices. What's important for cultivating children's learning and development is not just the cognitive tools, the mediational means, of the classroom, but the relationships in which these tools are put to use. As Mary Brandau told parents at graduation, "You learn best when you experience it, when somebody says you did a good job, when you're frustrated and you have to cope."

The goal was to introduce children to the skills and rewards of "higher-order thinking" – reading for comprehension, solving complex problems, fluent writing – but also to change who they were: to make them "life-long learners" with a taste for learning, respectful of others and themselves. To have each of them feel that "a hero lies in you." School is inevitably involved in the "production of persons." But such a change in attitude cannot be directed, only facilitated. Schools can only create conditions for its possibility, redefining the terms of the exchange between teacher and student, how they recognize one another. It remains up to the children whether they accept or reject these terms.

The Willow Run Systemic Initiative committee brought the same approach to professional development – learning by teachers is no different from learning by students. As Vivian Lyte put it, "If we believe that student learning should be facilitated and not directed then we must have that same belief system for teachers and others." WRSI sought to bring coherence to the various reform efforts across the district, appealing to the common aims of the district's new vision statement, drawing on the story of the community's origins and its ethos, part myth, part reality. Again relationship and culture were central: WRSI sought to change the attitudes of teachers and administrators, fostering risk taking and the exploration of new approaches to pedagogy by building a culture of support and equality, in which failure was understood to be a necessary component of success.

Both here and in the classroom the aim was to avoid being "top-down," in the belief that forms of evaluation that judge "either you got it or you don't" induce fear of failure and reluctance to take risks and prevent learning. And here and in the classroom some of the same issues arose – finding the right balance, for example, between discovery and instruction.

This approach to teaching and learning rejects many elements of the traditional classroom, especially the axis of achievement along which students are sorted. If learning depends on attitude, and attitude in turn is a reply to the recognition a teacher offers students, and if recognition is institutionalized as the categorization of kids as "haves" and "have-nots," then the measurement of learning as an "outcome" of schooling undermines what it seeks to assess. But Willow Run's teachers did not reject tests like the MEAP wholesale. On the contrary, the types of problem the MEAP now poses call forth the intellectual skills they value. But they decry the use to which MEAP scores are put. The way MEAP tests are scored and reported forces a single criterion of worth on every student, teacher, and district, effectively imposing a single solution on every school. The MEAP captured the agenda in Willow Run, threatening to undermine the hard work of reform. The school board's reaction of holding individual principals and teachers accountable, while exactly the kind of move marketplace reforms value, imperiled the building of common culture.

School finance reform gave Governor Engler the opportunity to claim that the playing field for public schools is now level; that differences in "output" are due no longer to differential "input," but instead to varying "efficiencies" among schools and districts – differences in the "quality of the production process" of schooling. Actually, funding differences have not disappeared, though they have diminished somewhat, and the legacy of past funding inequities lingers. More importantly, funding is only one of the resources a school district draws upon; just as important is the cultural capital families endow their children with.

Early in 1998 the *Detroit Free Press* ran a series of articles titled "Testing MEAP." The *Press* found that "factors such as poverty, single-parent households and parental education account for most of the differences between districts on MEAP scores, most markedly in city-suburban areas." "Among city and suburban school districts, more than 62 percent of the differences in scores can be traced to such nonschool factors."[1] In 1996 Willow Run was one of 32 Michigan school districts in which 90 percent of students failed to score "Proficient" on one or more of the portions in the HSPT.[2] But when these MEAP scores were compared with statistical predictions that included the "nonschool factors," Willow Run's scores were "as expected." The paper concluded, "The results of statewide, standardized tests such as the MEAP say more about conditions in the community in which children live than about the quality of the education available to them," and quoted researcher and ex-U.S. Department of Education staff member Diane Ravitch, "If you're not testing what was taught, then you're testing their social class."[3]

The Willow Run community continues to struggle with poverty. Washtenaw County as a whole now has one of the lowest unemployment rates in Michigan and jobs for which there aren't enough skilled applicants, but, says Vivian Lyte, speaking with the perspective that comes from her new position at the Washtenaw County Intermediate School District offices, "Well, that means that nobody really has time to think about all the people who *are* unemployed." The latest census data, from 1995, showed 25 percent of Willow Run's children living in poverty. Now, enrollment in the district's free and reduced-price lunch program hovers just above 50 percent, after peaking at 55 percent in 1995–1996. At Kettering Elementary the rate has risen steadily to 66 percent.

The local reformers' efforts to cultivate a new attitude on the part of Willow Run's children required finding ways to make schooling relevant to working-class kids, born on one side of the divide between manual labor and mental work. The closing of the Willow Run Assembly Plant represented both a threat and an opportunity – the iron hand of the metal-bending industries lifted for a moment. The local reforms were guided partly by an unquestioned conviction that education is inherently beneficial, partly by a working knowledge of what is necessary for these children's survival in the new economy. If the new economy is eliminating the manual/mental divide in the workplace, on the shop floor, the Willow Run reformers were seeking to undo its impact on the lives of the community's children.

But the new economy has introduced a new division – the exploitation that was central to Fordism has not disappeared. And it is here that the values of the Willow Run reformers clash with those of many who call for public school reform.

The local reform efforts were thrown off track by the larger state and federal initiatives. Neither systemic reform nor marketplace reform has an adequate grasp of the character of teaching and learning; neither reform effort has a satisfactory or articulated conception of the psychology of students and teachers or the sociology of school life. Governor Engler's marketplace reforms and the National Science Foundation's state systemic initiative didn't just have different goals from those of the local reformers, they occupied a different reality. In the events in and around Willow Run we witness a struggle to change the terms in which schools operate, a struggle in which two contradictory logics go head to head.

The problems these efforts to rationalize school sought to address are real ones – unequal educational access and opportunity still exist, as do prejudice and incompetence in the classroom. But the costs of rationalization are real too. Formal economic and bureaucratic solutions to public problems tend to displace discussion and debate, to colonize and undermine the informal relations and communities people create.[4] They distort relationships and objectify participants. The economic metaphor tends to reduce citizens to customers, consumers, while the political metaphor tends to make schooling a mere social benefit, a welfare institution, and reduce citizens to mere clients of the state.

There is no final, single answer to the question of how schools change the kind of person a child is. Schools can perpetuate the society of the past or play a part in shaping a new future. Since they were first created, U.S. public schools have been organized and reorganized to assimilate waves of immigrants into a mainstream American way of life, to sort children so each had an education appropriate to their supposedly inborn gifts and powers, to foster the young person's mental, emotional, and physical adjustment to their circumstances. Now the ostensible imperative is that schools ensure achievement for all. Whether or not one values these goals, whether or not one believes that schools have met them well, schools have done different things at different times.

And those who can control the schools can exert a significant influence on the direction social change will take. The decentralization of public schooling in the United States makes it difficult to achieve such control, but this only makes the struggle over the schools more intense. And since the local school district is, at least nominally, where control begins, the struggle concerns the role distant centers of power – state government, business conglomerates, national and multinational industries, the federal government – should play in the day-to-day life of public schools. What degree of autonomy should communities have

in the running of their schools? Both the state and national school reform movements try to alter the relationship between the local and the
remote.

The system of U.S. public schooling is unusually interconnected and
porous. It fosters a variety of connections with local communities and
families, it depends on state and federal agencies for funding and is subject in return to their complex regulations, it is influenced by local and
national economic concerns, and science and religion also have a stake.
So a district such as Willow Run is not alone; it is part of a network of
linkages. The state and national reform efforts spread the roots of this
network, and one consequence is that the Willow Run teachers are no
longer the primary judges of the success or failure of their efforts, or
even the primary determiners of the products of these efforts. One of the
occasions, now, when children must read and write, figure and calculate,
is when they take the MEAP test. Their work, inscriptions on paper, is
sent off to be interpreted and evaluated by distant experts. Back come the
judgments – some children are "Proficient," others are not. And the
teachers and their school are in turn judged "Effective," "Efficient," or
not. Who kids are told they are – and teachers too – is now defined not
just by what happens in Willow Run, but also by what happens in Lansing, in Washington, D.C., on Wall Street, and even in Japan or Russia.

Where are the larger school reform initiatives now? As might be expected of a major government program, the Statewide Systemic Initiative, now its five-year span is ended, having awarded something
like a quarter of a billion dollars, has spawned a raft of reports, assessments, and summaries.[5] The reports' main purpose is to document
the states' different approaches to SSI, but they also emphasize an
unanticipated finding: the educational system has "limited capacity"
to implement change.[6]

One cynical interpretation could be that this attention to "capacity"
is the reformers' escape hatch. The alignment, the raised standards, the
coherence all went as planned, but the system didn't have the "capacity" to respond. Another (not incompatible) interpretation is that the
systemic reform initiative has discovered the people who live in the system. Capacity, the reports say, is not just an individual matter, because
individuals operate in "communities of practice."[7] And "student learning is also influenced by the culture of the school and community."[8]
Both "individual capacity" and "organizational capacity" must be enlarged, they insist. It's a pity the reformers didn't become aware of

these factors before designing their programs; Willow Run teachers and administrators were attending to them from the outset.

The reports also acknowledge that learning isn't just about knowledge and skills. They describe individual capacity as involving "dispositions" (such as "attitudes" toward subject matter, toward students, and toward change) and "views of self" – "the persona they adopt in the classroom." All these dimensions of capacity "are interdependent and interactive."[9] So "the new standards for students require everyone in the educational system . . . to *change* their roles and relationships."[10] Again, Willow Run knew this.

But at least one analysis noted the failure to "walk the talk" that plagued dealings with MSSI:

> The tension between the assertive state role implied by a mandate and the respect for local autonomy indicated by the permission to vary from the State Board's model cropped up repeatedly in our review, sometimes as a conflict between different centers of power, and sometimes as an ambivalence within individual actors who seem torn by conflicting impulses, a desire on the one hand to get tough with an educational system they see as failing to perform and on the other a reluctance to invest more authority and resources in state government as the instrument of reform.
>
> Charles L. Thompson, James P. Spillane, and David K. Cohen, *The State Policy System Affecting Science and Mathematics Education in Michigan*, MSSI Policy and Program Review Component, Michigan Partnership for New Education, 513 Erickson Hall, 1994, p. 17

Governor John Engler won reelection in 1998, having made education the centerpiece of his campaign. Invited in October 1997 to testify to the U.S. House Committee on Education, which came to chat in Muskegon, Michigan, and asked what the federal government's role in education should be, Engler had a one-word reply: "minimal." Washington spends $120 billion each year on federal education programs, but "is there any proof," Engler asked rhetorically, "that all of Washington's involvement is really preparing our children for the work world of the twenty-first century?"

At the same time, Engler said, Michigan is "spending more money on education than ever before, and spending that money more fairly." Proposal A, he claimed, had reduced the ratio of spending by wealthy and poor districts from 3.33 to 1 in 1990 to 2 to 1 now. And, referring to Secretary Riley's 1997 report that Michigan's eighth-grade math scores showed the second-greatest improvement nationally, Engler asserted,

"There is a causal relationship at work. When you address funding, order in the classroom, and giving families more choices, you can expect better performance. We demand it – and are getting it."[11]

And early in 1999 Governor Engler ordered the takeover of the Detroit Public School District.

The original impetus for reforms like Engler's was the perilous condition of the U.S. economy. But in 1999, as I write this, the economy is apparently in great shape. Why has the attack on public schools not abated? Why are statewide standardized tests being implemented by more and more states? It seems that something deeper must be at stake.

The U.S. economy has been growing at an impressive pace, "the healthiest in a generation and the strongest in the world" says President Clinton.[12] Inflation is minimal, unemployment the lowest in 25 years, the federal deficit has been eliminated, and the Dow Jones Industrial Average reaches one all-time peak after another, topping 11,000 in April 1999. And this last year of the millennium is shaping up to be the best year ever for the U.S. auto industry. Five years of strong sales, especially of light trucks, is feeding an expansion. Sales for the first five months of the year reached a record annualized rate of 17.3 million units, and together the Big Three have a 71.9 percent market share.[13]

In most analyses, this "boom" is attributed to the technological revolution of personal computer and Internet, to increased worker productivity, and to the expansion of markets and labor pool made possible by the end of the cold war.[14] Now that laissez-faire, free-market capitalist economies have been adopted by many former eastern bloc nations, as well as Latin American and far eastern countries, capital is global, moving wherever it can find labor and consumers. Labor doesn't have the same mobility – people cannot easily move to where the jobs are. Thus another factor in the new economy is the absence of wage pressure; the job insecurity left by downsizing has workers reluctant to demand better pay.

But things aren't as sweet as they seem. For one thing, GM's notoriously poor labor relations haven't improved. With six strikes by mid-year, 1997 was "the year of strikes" for GM, costing $490 million[15] – the company's attitude was that "such labor trouble, much of it born of past management mistakes, is a price of becoming more competitive."[16] In summer 1998 the United Auto Workers struck a small metal stamping plant in Flint, Michigan, and quickly forced GM to idle almost its entire North American workforce, more than 190,000 workers from Canada to Mexico. The location was symbolic – Flint was birthplace to both the company and the union – and tactical – the plant was a pinch-point in GM's just-in-time flow of parts. The union's immediate goal was to avoid outsourcing, the longer aim to stem the flow of jobs to Mexico.[17] GM took a tough stance and the conflict lasted seven weeks, costing close to $12 billion.[18] And GM still has less than a 30 percent share of the U.S. market (it was 35.7% in 1990) despite spending $21 billion since 1994 improving U.S. plants and planning to spend $28 billion more in the next five years. New facilities won't increase capacity so much as improve flexibility to switch models quickly; they'll use half to two-thirds fewer workers.[19]

On the larger scale, this new global economy is highly unstable. Capital now moves so rapidly from one opportunity to the next that an entire nation can be buoyed or brought to its knees by one brief statement from statesperson or monetary official. Global economic institutions now far outreach the political institutions supposed to regulate them. In Europe, unemployment remains high and productivity low. Russia's economy has collapsed. Asian nations have gone through a boom-and-bust cycle into deep recession, and Japan is paralyzed by a banking crisis and depression. In spring 1997 the chairman of Toyota Motor Corporation penned an Op-Ed piece for the *New York Times*, writing that Japan's "social and economic systems that enabled success . . . are now obsolete" in the new economy.[20]

Post-Fordism evidently generates considerable wealth. The global economy does need workers skilled in the use of technology and the symbol manipulation of smart machines in the computerized workplace. But generating wealth also requires keeping labor productive and cheap. Between 1979 and 1996 a third of all jobs in the U.S. were eliminated – 43 million – and almost 60 percent of these were blue-collar. Most of the replacement jobs are part-time, temporary, labor-intensive, and low-paying positions in which little capital has been invested.[21] And employment has increased in "semiskilled" work that combines skills traditionally considered either blue-collar or white-collar – in areas such as services, construction, and communications, rather than manufacturing.[22] Wages are stagnant, and the distribution of wealth has become increasingly unequal.

A two-tiered job structure is being shaped, with an inner core of permanent workers and an outer ring of temporary workers. This, it seems, is the class structure of post-Fordism – not "middle" and "lower," but "inner" and "outer." The inner-core workers perform skilled assembly and customization; the outer ring are semiskilled, constantly relocated piece workers. The temporaries are disposable, working only when they are needed, lacking benefits like health care and retirement, vacations and sick pay. The inner core get these benefits and a better rate of pay, but find themselves squeezed, working compulsory overtime, some-times unpaid, and with an accelerating pace of work. In either case, workers find they are expected to be "flexible."

Study of industry in Japan, Germany, and the United Kingdom sug-gests that "workplace flexibility" has led to an intensified pace of work and increased stress levels on the shop floor, largely because the goal is to reduce downtime, waiting time, and other delays. Flexible work prac-tices, sharing Fordism's basic goal of controlling and regulating time, generally seem to "undermine rather than enhance the position of workers in industries such as cars."[23]

And now the "cognitive elite" faces competition from equally skilled but less expensive workers in developing countries. Doctors' notes from a Virginia hospital are transcribed in Bangalore by medical transcription-ists with college degrees, paid a tenth of the American rate, and transmit-ted back overnight via the Internet. Already, college graduates are earn-ing less than they would have (adjusted for inflation), a decade ago.[24]

Similarly, university teaching and research is being divided between a stable, elite inner core of tenured, salaried faculty and an outer ring of temporary, itinerant, untenured junior faculty and lecturers, hired by the course, overworked and underpaid, moving from job to job. And "distance-learning" seems likely to eliminate many of the former, as course content is delivered via the World Wide Web.

The new economy demands a workforce who will work varying hours to suit fluctuations in demand, at a higher pace to ensure sustained pro-ductivity and competitiveness, and who can be laid off and rehired as and when necessary. To some it is self-evident that schools should fabri-cate the human "bricks" with which this global economy is being built. In these post-Fordist times, the best bricks have a "flexible" attitude.

One might wonder what possible difference it could make whether schooling is understood as a production process or a system of delivery. But these metaphors have tangible impacts on and consequences for the school district, classrooms, and the lives of teachers and students. Tests like the MEAP become metrics that make what they measure, that cre-ate what they sort. The recognition they impose, as putative measures of "quality," reestablishes the axis of achievement that labels young people "haves" and "have-nots." Who and what a child becomes now depends not only on their face-to-face relationship with teachers, but also, because of the complex networks that mediate these relationships, on abstract rationalities of efficiency and equity. The needs of large-scale industry can, through the power of a state governor and his legislature, come to define who children are – the kinds of human beings they can become. We've been told that the new workplace requires of workers new skills. What we've not been told is that it also requires of them adjustment to a whole new lifestyle: one of uncertainty, of insecurity, of constantly shifting demands. The euphemism: flexibility, signifying adaptability, compliance, and docility. What better way to legitimate this than by convincing young people that they lack the ability to demand anything better?

At the same time, these abstract rationalities don't drop from the sky: they are interpreted, described, and promoted or decried by individuals – John Engler, Marshall Smith, Louis Gerstner . . . – who are positioned with unusual prestige, authority, and influence, but who are just people nonetheless. It is people who, through their actions, together and individually, give life and voice to these logics, for each of us is "the material, the builder, and the architect of the historical edifice." Each of us "lives in it . . . sees and understands it . . . describes and criticizes it." And this means a logic is never simply stamped onto the classroom, nor do children simply conform to the culture of their classroom community. There is always occasion for challenge, for having "an attitude." This means that local agents – Mary, Vivian, Laura, Scott . . . – can have an impact too. Thank goodness, for the struggles in and around the Willow Run Community Schools are struggles for our future.

Notes

Introduction

1 Martin Richards, "Preface and editorial acknowledgement," in *The integration of a child into a social world*, ed. M. P. M. Richards. Cambridge: Cambridge University Press, 1974.

2 Martin Richards, "Introduction," in Richards, ibid., 7.

3 E.g., Judy Dunn and Martin Richards, "Observations on the developing relationship between mother and baby in the neonatal period," in *Interaction in infancy: The Loch Lomond symposium*. London: Academic Press, 1977; Jerome Bruner, "The ontogenesis of speech acts." *Journal of Child Language* 2 (1975): 1–19; David Ingleby, "Ideology and the human sciences." *Human Context* 2 (1970): 159–180; Colwyn Trevarthen, "Behavioral embryology," in *The handbook of perception*, ed. E. C. Carterette and M. P. Friedman. New York: Academic Press, 1973; John Shotter, "Prolegomena to an understanding of play." *Journal for the Theory of Social Behavior* 3 (1973): 47–89.

4 E.g., Martin Packer, "Hermeneutic inquiry in the study of human conduct." *American Psychologist* 40 (1985): 1081–1093; Martin Packer, "The structure of moral action: A hermeneutic study of moral conflict." *Contributions to Human Development* whole number 13 (1985); Martin Packer, "Tracing the hermeneutic circle: Articulating an ontical study of moral conflicts," in *Entering the circle: Hermeneutic investigation in psychology*, ed. M. J. Packer and R. B. Addison. Albany: State University of New York Press, 1989; Martin Packer, "Interpreting stories, interpreting lives: Narrative and action in moral development research," in *Narrative and storytelling: Implications for understanding moral development, New Directions for Child Development*, ed. M. B. Tappan and M. J. Packer. 63–82. 54. 1991; Martin Packer, "Critical interpretive research: An introduction." 1999. Available at <www.duq.edu/liberalarts/gradpsych/ packer.html>

5 Cf. Paul Ricoeur, *Interpretation theory: Discourse and the surplus of meaning*. Fort Worth: Texas Christian University Press, 1976; John B. Thompson, "The methodology of interpretation," in *Ideology and modern culture: Critical social theory in the era of mass communication*, J. B. Thompson. 272–327. Stanford, CA: Stanford University Press, 1990; Packer, "Hermeneutic inquiry in the study of human conduct"; Packer and Addison, eds., *Entering the circle*.

6 E.g., John Shotter, "The social construction of remembering and forgetting," in *Collective remembering*, ed. D. Middleton and D. Edwards. 120–138. London: Sage, 1990; Kenneth J. Gergen, "The social constructionist movement in modern psychology." *American Psychologist* 40 (1985): 266–275; Edward E. Sampson, "A critical constructionist view of psychology and personhood," in *The analysis of psychological theory: Metapsychological perspectives*, ed. H. J. Stam, T. B. Rogers, and K. J. Gergen. 41–59. 1987.

7 Michael Cole, *Cultural psychology: A once and future discipline*. Cambridge, MA: Harvard University Press, 1996.

8 Richard A. Shweder, "Cultural psychology: What is it?" in *Cultural psychology: The Chicago symposia on culture and human development*, ed. J. W. Stigler, R. A. Shweder, and G. Herdt. New York: Cambridge University Press, 1989; Richard S. Shweder and Joan G. Miller, "The social construction of the person: How is it possible?" in *Thinking through cultures: Expeditions in cultural psychology*, ed. Richard S. Shweder. 156–185. Cambridge: Harvard University Press, 1991.

9 James V. Wertsch, ed., *Culture, communication, and cognition*. Cambridge: Cambridge University Press, 1985; James V. Wertsch, *Voices of the mind*. Cambridge, MA: Harvard University Press, 1991.

10 Barbara Rogoff, *Apprenticeship in thinking: Cognitive development in social context*. New York: Oxford University Press, 1991; Barbara Rogoff, "Observing sociocultural activity on three planes: Participatory appropriation, guided participation, and apprenticeship," in *Sociocultural studies of mind*, ed. James V. Wertsch, Pablo del Rio, and Amelia Alvarez. 139–164. New York: Cambridge University Press, 1995.

11 Jean Lave, *Cognition in practice: Mind, mathematics and culture in everyday life*. Cambridge: Cambridge University Press, 1988; Jean Lave and E. Wenger, *Situated learning: Legitimate peripheral participation*. Cambridge: Cambridge University Press, 1991.

12 Sylvia Scribner, "A sociocultural approach to the study of mind," in *Mind and social practice: Selected writings of Sylvia Scribner*, ed. Ethel Tobach, Rachel Joffe Falmagne, Mary Brown Parlee, Laura M. W. Martin, and Aggie Scribner Kapelman. 266–280. New York: Cambridge University Press, 1990/1997, 271.

13 E.g., Roland G. Tharp and Ronald Gallimore, *Rousing minds to life: Teaching, learning, and schooling in social context*. Cambridge: Cambridge University Press, 1988.

14 Rogoff, *Apprenticeship in thinking*.

15 Martin Packer, "The problem of transfer, and the sociocultural critique of schooling." *The Journal of the Learning Sciences*. In press.

16 Hans Joas, "The unhappy marriage of hermeneutics and functionalism," in *Communicative action: Essays on Jurgen Habermas's The Theory of Communicative Action*, ed. Axel Honneth and Hans Joas. 97–118. Cambridge: MIT Press, 1991, 115.

Chapter 1. The Class of 2001

1 A mill is $1 worth of property tax for every $1,000 of a property's state-equalized valuation – usually half the market value.

2 William Celis 3rd, "Administration offers its program to improve the nation's schools," *New York Times,* Apr. 22, 1993.

3 William Celis 3rd, "Uneven progress in decade of school reform," *New York Times,* Apr. 28, 1993.

4 January 1994, State of the State address. Available at <www.state.mi.us/migov/gov/Speeches/>

5 Dialogue in quotation marks is transcribed from audio recordings made at the time, edited (as little as possible) for length and intelligiblity (removing some of the repetitions, hesitations, false starts, and slips that characterize everyday speech). Where I've drawn from field notes rather than recordings the dialogue is summarized, not quoted.Throughout, I have used pseudonyms for the children.

6 The lyrics are from "Hero," by Mariah Carey, on *Music Box.* Columbia Records, 1993.

7 J. T. Darden, R. C. Hill, J. Thomas, and R. Thomas, *Detroit: Race and uneven development.* Philadelphia: Temple University Press, 1987.

Chapter 2. Blue Monday

1 The Willow Run plant had been on an industry analysts' "at risk" list since October 1991, because of slow sales of the Chevy Caprice.

2 Available at <www.state.mi.us/migov/gov/Speeches/>

3 *Frontline,* "The Heartbeat of America," Public Broadcasting Service, Oct. 12, 1993.

4 For Stempel quote, see James V. Higgins, "GM acts to divert financial disaster," *Detroit News,* Feb. 25, 1992, 7A. D. B. Crary and C. Hogan, *Willow Run and related plant closings: Causes and impacts.* Institute for Contemporary and Regional Development, Eastern Michigan University, 1992.

5 Costs for producing small cars are even higher: $9,068 for GM, $6,591 for Ford, and $7,160 for Chrysler. And GM still has an average of five or six workers reporting to each manager, while Honda has 42. "Detroit's Big Chance," *Business Week,* June 29, 1992, 84.

6 Martin Kenney and Richard Florida, *Beyond mass production: The Japanese system and its transfer to the U.S.* New York: Oxford University Press, 1993, 316.

7 Editorial, "Who's to blame for Willow Run?" *Detroit News,* Feb. 25, 1992, 14A.

8 Editorial, "GM closings. The search for scapegoats won't help save jobs," *Detroit Free Press,* Feb. 26, 1992, 6A.

9 Janet Miller and Marjorie Kauth-Karjala, "Willow Run schools brace for the future," *Ypsilanti Press,* Feb. 28, 1992, C1.

10 David Everett and Dawson Bell, "Engler, Michigan congressmen urge GM to tell why," *Detroit Free Press,* Feb. 26, 1992, 9A.

11 David J. Morrow, "Union won't accept pact in Arlington," *Detroit Free Press,* Feb. 26, 1996, 9A.

12 Crary and Hogan, *Willow Run and related plant closings.* Michigan has 33% of the production of the domestic automobile industry: 2.7 million vehicles in 1979, now down to 1.85 million in 1991. GM, Ford, and Chrysler all have their corporate headquarters in Michigan. GM is the state's largest employer, with 300,000 jobs in 1979, reduced to 178,000 in 1991, and GM's production

in Michigan in 1990 exceeded that of Ford, Chrysler, and Mazda (which has opened a plant in Flat Rock) combined. In the 1990 model year, the Willow Run assembly plant produced over 114,000 units, about 11% of GM's total production in Michigan, and 6% of all automobile production in the state. Willow Run is GM's fourth largest production site in the state.

Two-thirds of the people in Michigan live within 30 miles of Detroit, and since at least 1920 the region has been heavily vested in the automobile industry. But the industry has been moving jobs out of the area for several decades, and this trend has increased in recent years. During the 1980s Ford reduced its employment in the state by about one-third, and both GM and Chrysler by about 40%. This is one reason Michigan had much lower economic growth than the rest of the country during the 1980s: 6.5% versus 20%. And in 1992 the state's unemployment rate was 9.1%: one of the highest among the 11 largest states in the country.

The plant provides 8% – around $4,250,000 a year – of Ypsilanti Township's tax base, and a payroll that was $178 million in 1990. It's estimated the county will lose about $200 million in income each year, the state about $370 million the first year, $600 million the next, and $780 million the third year. Property values will also fall, more slowly, causing further damage to the local tax base. The other job cuts and plant closings will reduce state income by $1,950 million in the first year, $2,950 million the next, and $3,500 million in the third, and will reduce property taxes throughout the state by $580 million. A "major fiscal calamity" is predicted.

13 Sara Rimer, "Stempel's out, and fears mount. Closing Willow Run: Sixth article of a series," *New York Times*, Oct. 29, 1992.
14 Editor's note to: Owen Eshenroder, "Special report: Lives on the line. Waiting in a shadow: Sleep's not easy as couple ponders life beyond Willow Run," *Ann Arbor News*, May 11, 1993.
15 Sara Rimer, "American dream put on hold at car plant doomed to shut. Closing Willow Run. First article of a series. Waiting for G.M.'s telegram," *New York Times*, Sept. 7, 1992, A1, A21.
16 James Higgins, "It's new age of manufacturing for auto firms: Higher output, fewer workers," *Detroit News*, Feb. 25, 1992, 7A.
17 Joseph Schumpeter, *Capitalism, socialism and democracy.* New York: Harper, 1947.
18 David Harvey, *The condition of postmodernity.* Oxford: Blackwell, 1990, 106.
19 Ibid., 121 [emphasis removed].
20 Robert Heilbroner, *21st century capitalism.* New York: Norton, 1993.
21 Heilbroner notes this in ibid., 44, 131–133.
22 Jeremy Rifkin, *The end of work: The decline of the global labor force and the dawn of the post-market era.* New York: Putnam, 1995.
23 Peter Collier and David Horowitz, *The Fords: An American epic.* New York: Summit Books, 1987, 63.
24 Harvey, *Postmodernity*, 125–126.
25 Kenney and Florida, *Beyond mass production.*
26 Joseph H. Boyett and Henry P. Conn, *Workplace 2000: The revolution shaping American business.* New York: Penguin, 1992, 326.

27 Robert Pear, "Ranks of U.S. poor reach 35.7 million, the most since '64," *New York Times*, Sept. 4, 1992, 1A; Steven Greenhouse, "Income data show years of erosion for U.S. workers," *New York Times*, Sept. 7, 1992, A1. Consumer debt is another factor, along with the Federal Reserve's refusal to push interest rates any lower. As a result, the jobless rate is expected to rise to 6.9% in 1992 from 6.7% the previous year, before falling somewhat. And the federal deficit is projected to jump to $383 billion in fiscal 1992, up from a record $268.7 billion in 1991. The Bush administration is actually forecasting a higher figure: $399.4 billion.
28 David McHugh, "Bankruptcy filings soar as the economy plunges," *Detroit Free Press*, Feb. 26, 1991, 8A.
29 Schumpeter, *Capitalism*, 84. Modern economists' development of Schumpeter's analyses into "endogenous-growth" theory, as well as their link to Marx's view of economic growth, especially in *Capital*, is described in a recent article: John Cassidy, "The return of Karl Marx: Why Wall Street should be consulting the scourge of capitalism," *New Yorker*, Oct. 20 & 27, 1997, 248–252, 254–256, 259.

Chapter 3. Vehicles of Reform, Drivers of Change

1 National Commission on Excellence in Education, *A nation at risk: The imperative for educational reform: A report to the Nation and the Secretary of Education*. National Commission on Excellence in Education, 1983, pp. 2, 5.
 2 *Progress of education in the United States of America – 1990 through 1994*, U.S. Department of Education. Available at <www.ed.gov/pubs/Prog95/index. html>
 3 Available at <www.ed.gov/pubs/Prog95/index.html>
 4 Available at <www.migov.state.mi.us/speeches/sos1993.html>
 5 *Crossing to the new economy: A citizen vision for a prosperous Michigan and a strategy for getting there*. Michigan Future, Inc., 1992, p. v.
 6 As of this writing, Smith works at the U.S. Department of Education; O'Day is on the faculty of the University of Wisconsin.
 7 Jennifer A. O'Day and Marshall S. Smith, "Systemic reform and educational opportunity," in *Designing coherent educational policy: Improving the system*, ed. Susan H. Fuhrman. 250–312. San Francisco: Jossey-Bass, 1993. Marshall S. Smith and Jennifer O'Day, "Systemic school reform," in *The politics of curriculum and testing: The 1990 yearbook of the Politics of Education Association*, ed. Susan H. Fuhrman and Betty Malen. 233–267. London: Falmer, 1990. Cf. National Science Foundation, *Foundation for the future: The systemic cornerstone*. 1994. NSF publication #94–121.
 8 O'Day and Smith, *Designing coherent educational policy*, 262, original emphasis.
 9 Ibid., 263.
10 Ibid., original emphasis.
11 Ibid., 265.
12 Available at <www.ed.gov/pubs/Prog95/index.html>
13 Russell Grantham and Owen Eshenroder, "Willow Run closing. Michigan will lose 8,000 jobs," *Ann Arbor News*, Feb. 24, 1992, A1.

14 Interview with Glenn Klipp, Nov. 1992.

15 Interview with Martin Packer, Feb. 3, 1995.

16 The phrase comes from Solon T. Kimbill and James E. McClellan Jr., *Education and the new America*. New York: Vintage Books, 1962, 290. The authors celebrate it as the cornerstone of "productive learning" that serves to maintain social order and to renew flagging commitment and "the joy of living" in the citizenry.

17 Paul Willis, *Learning to labor: How working-class kids get working-class jobs*. New York: Columbia University Press, 1977/1981, 56.

18 Cf. Pierre Bourdieu, *Distinction: A social critique of the judgement of taste*. Cambridge, MA: Harvard University Press, 1979/1984.

19 Jean Piaget, *The moral judgment of the child*. New York: Free Press, 1932/1965, 401.

20 *Curriculum and evaluation standards for school mathematics*. Commission on Standards for School Mathematics, National Council of Teachers of Mathematics. Reston, Va.: The Council, 1989.

21 E.g., Honest Open Logical Debate (HOLD) on math reform, 1049 Metro Circle, Palo Alto, CA 94303. Available at <www.ourworld.compuserve.com/homepages/mathman/holdnctm.htm>

22 *Science for all Americans: A Project 2061 report on literacy goals in science, mathematics, and technology*. Washington, D.C.: American Association for the Advancement of Science, 1989, 28.

23 American Association for the Advancement of Science, *Benchmarks for Science Literacy*. Oxford University Press, 1993, p. 9.

24 National Council of Teachers of Mathematics, *Curriculum and evaluation standards*, 72.

25 Michigan Department of Education, *Michigan Essential Goals and Objectives for Science Education (K–12)*, Michigan State Board of Education. 1991, 7.

26 Jim Kise, "Ypsi Twp. to take GM to task on deal," *Ypsilanti Press*, Mar. 24, 1992, 1A.

27 Jeffrey Schmalz, "Licking bruises, car workers are hearing Brown message," *New York Times*, Mar. 13, 1992, A1, 10. In the Maine primary, Tom Harkin also received 5% and Bob Kerry just 3% (D. Drummond Ayres Jr., "Brown and Tsongas divide Democratic spoils in Maine," *New York Times*, Feb. 14, 1992, A1, 16).

28 Schmalz, "Licking bruises," A1.

29 Sara Rimer, "Hard times change many minds. Closing Willow Run: Third article of a series. Taking the anger to the polls," *New York Times*, Oct. 2, 1992, C1, C4.

30 Michigan voted Republican in the past four elections: for Ford against Carter, for Reagan twice, against Carter and then Mondale, and for Bush against Dukakis.

31 Diana Katz and Valarie Basheda, "They feel as if they've been sucker-punched by plant's closing," *Detroit News*, Feb. 25, 1992, 4A.

32 Jim Kise, "Candidates court Flint, find anger," *Ypsilanti Press*, Mar. 15, 1992. 1A.

33 In Ypsi Township Clinton receives 46% of the Democratic vote, Bush 60% of the Republican vote. Other results in the Township: Brown obtained 35% of the Democrat vote, and Tsongas 15%. Among the Republicans, Patrick Buchanan received 30%, and David Duke just 2%.

34 Steve Lohr, "Business executives in a survey start to see signs of turnaround," *New York Times*, Mar. 13, 1992, A1.

35 Jeffrey Schmalz, "President brought down by faltering economy," *New York Times*, Nov. 4, 1992.

36 Sara Rimer, "Stempel's out, and fears mount. Closing Willow Run: Sixth article of a series," *New York Times*, Oct. 29, 1992.

37 Doron P. Levin, "General Motors chairman quits after growing split with board," *New York Times*, Oct. 27, 1992, A1.

38 Juanita C. Smith, "Auto workers mull Stempel's resignation," *Ypsilanti Press*, Oct. 27, 1992, 1A.

39 Helen Fogel, "Willow Run had financial advantages," *Detroit News*, Dec. 12, 1992, 1A, 11A.

40 But local union agreements must be approved by the International UAW, which has declared this will not be done if worker layoffs would result. See note 39.

41 Maryanne George and David Morrow, "Union was key in GM plant decision," *Detroit Free Press*, Dec. 17, 1992, 1A, 4A.

42 Judge Shelton's remarks are transcribed from the *MacNeil-Lehrer News Hour*, Feb. 10, 1993. Judge Shelton also criticizes Michigan's 1974 tax abatement law as poorly written and ineffective, and suggests that America needs to change the way industry and government relate if it is to compete with other less democratic countries: "Such an effort must be national in scope and must be a real partnership, not one in which industry simply views government as a part of its 'business climate' and another opportunity to increase profits" (John Lippert, "GM told to keep Willow Run open," *Detroit Free Press*, Feb. 10, 1993, 6A).

43 Sharon Theimer [Associated Press writer], "Judge rules GM can't close Willow Run," *Ypsilanti Press*, Feb. 10, 1993, 6B. Clifton quote: Associated Press, "GM must keep operating Willow Run," *Michigan Daily*, Feb. 10, 1993, 1. Other quotations transcribed from *Frontline*, Public Broadcasting Service, Oct. 12, 1993. Cf. Lippert, "GM told to keep Willow Run open," 6A.

Chapter 4. America's Birthday: Summer 1993

1 Doron P. Levin, "Court backs G.M. on plant closing," *New York Times*, Aug. 5, 1993.

2 Raymond McMillan and John Mulcahy, "Ruling stuns workers," *Ypsilanti Press*, Aug. 5, 1993, 1A.

3 John Mulcahy, "GM transplants learning new life," *Ypsilanti Press*, Jan. 26, 1993, 1A.

4 Steve Lohr, "Big business in turmoil. Upheavals at I.B.M., Sears, and elsewhere underline fundamental shifts in economy," *New York Times*, Jan. 28, 1993, A1, C6.

5 GM is the largest private purchaser of health care in the country and spent $3.7 billion in 1992 – equivalent to $711 for each automobile built. Ford, saying it spends more on health care than steel, wants workers to contribute and proposes reduced pay and benefits for new hires. (The company can replace retirees with cheaper hires; the union will get new members.) The UAW maintains workers have already contributed to these costs by foregoing wage increases and notes the rate of growth in health care costs is lower in the auto industry than in others. And the union has accepted prescription copayments and a shift from fee-for-service to managed care plans.

6 Doron P. Levin, "Big three tell labor the glass is half empty," *New York Times*, Aug. 2, 1993.

7 James Bennet, "Ford offers union a contract plan," *New York Times*, Aug. 26, 1993; James Bennet, "Union settles on Ford as target in contract talks," *New York Times*, Aug. 31, 1993; Associated Press, "UAW names Ford as bargaining target," *Ypsilanti Press*, Aug. 31, 1993; Calvin Sims, "After the layoffs, checks in the mail," *New York Times*, Nov. 18, 1993, C1, C2.

8 Editorial, "The NAFTA ruling," *Ypsilanti Press*, July 6, 1993, 6A.

9 Associated Press, "Perot rips trade pact," *Ypsilanti Press*, June 7, 1993.

10 Michael F. Addoniazo, C. Phillip Kearney, and Henry J. Prince, "Michigan's highwire act," *Journal of Educational Finance* 20 (1995), 235–269, 237.

11 Figures (1989–1990) from C. Phillip Kearney, 1990, *Primer on Michigan school finance*, 2nd ed. Bureau of Accreditation and School Improvement Studies, School of Education, University of Michigan, Ann Arbor, MI.

12 Editorial, "A lesson in finance," *Ypsilanti Press*, June 24, 1993, 6A.

13 Associated Press," Legislature passes radical property tax plan," *Ypsilanti Press*, July 22, 1993, 1A.

14 Addoniazo, Kearney, and Prince, "Michigan's highwire act," 239.

15 Dave Melchior, "Opinion. A legislative view of the voter's role," *Ypsilanti Press*, July 4, 1993.

16 Andrew Zucker, Patrick Shields, Nancy Adelman, and Judith Powell, *Evaluation of NSF's Statewide Systemic Initiatives (SSI) program: Second-year report. Cross-cutting themes.* Arlington, VA: National Science Foundation. Dec. 1995. Among the 26 states funded by NSF, only 7 make funding of local districts a primary strategy (Zucker et al., 17).

17 Funds are requested for substitute teachers, teacher salaries, training development workshops, instructional programs, contracted consultants, evaluation, and supplies. "New structures and approaches to learning" are described as necessary to increase student proficiency in "high level technical, mathematical and scientific skills," as "unskilled jobs disappear" ("Project Abstract," *Competitive grant application for 1992–93 Models of Effective Learning grants: Mathematics and science initiative*, May 26, 1993). An appendix to the proposal contains results of a survey in 1991 and 1992 of Willow Run's high school graduates' educational aspirations. The number planning no further education rose from 22% to 50%. Those planning to attend a 4-year university dropped from 29% to 21%; those planning to attend a 2-year college from 47% to 24%.

18 There were very few applications to become an "affiliate district," and of the 24 focus districts, 22 are well above the state average for free and reduced-price lunch.

Chapter 5. The Last First Day?

1 Back in 1968, Robert Dreeben recognized these new relationships in the school, how "student" and "teacher" are positions distinct from the persons who occupy them (Robert Dreeben, *On what is learned in school.* Reading: Addison-Wesley, 1968). Dreeben asserted that the school's "prime function is to bring about developmental changes in individuals," and he suggested that "the traditional notion of learning as a function of teaching, of engagement in instructional activities, may be an overly restricted view of what happens during the schooling process" (20). But Dreeben tried to explain what happens when child becomes student in terms of role theory, as the internalization of new norms and values. That approach is unsatisfactory, in part because it tries to explain concrete behavior in terms of something ideal. The task is really to do the opposite: to explain how people become able to play a role successfully and appropriately – to live an ideal – in and with their concrete behavior.

2 Sylvia Scribner, "The cognitive consequences of literacy," in *Mind and social practice: Selected writings of Sylvia Scribner,* ed. Ethel Tobach, Rachel Joffe Falmagne, Mary Brown Parlee, Laura M. W. Martin, and Aggie Scribner Kapelman. 160–189. New York: Cambridge University Press, 1968/1997, 161.

3 Michael Cole and Peg Griffin, "Cultural amplifiers reconsidered," in *The social foundations of language and thought,* ed. D. R. Olson. New York: Norton, 1980.

4 Robert Serpell and Giyoo Hatano, "Education, schooling, and literacy," in *Handbook of cross-cultural psychology. Vol. 2. Basic processes and human development,* ed. John W. Berry, Pierre R. Dasen, and T. S. Saraswarthi. 339–376. Allyn and Bacon, 1997, 344.

5 Scribner, "The cognitive consequences of literacy," 182.

6 Jean-Paul Sartre. *Critique of dialectical reason: Theory of practical ensembles.* Vol. 1. London: Verso, 1960/1991.

7 Sylvia Scribner, "Introduction: The future of literacy in a changing world," in *Mind and social practice.* 229–234. 1987/1997, 232.

8 John Dewey, *Democracy and education.* New York: Free Press, 1916, 292.

9 Charles Taylor, *Sources of the self: The makings of the modern identity.* Cambridge, MA: Harvard University Press, 1989.

10 This episode is analyzed in detail in Martin Packer and David Greco-Brooks, "School as a site for the production of persons," *Journal of Constructivist Psychology* 12 (1999): 133–149.

11 Interview with Martin Packer and Julie Nicholson, May 9, 1994.

12 Talcott Parsons, "The school class as a social system: Some of its functions in American society," *Harvard Educational Review* 29 (1959): 297–318.

13 Shirley Brice Heath, *Ways with words: Language, life, and work in communities and classrooms.* Cambridge: Cambridge University Press, 1983.

14 Brice Heath, ibid., 351–354. Middle-class parents are also more likely to read regularly to their children and encourage basic reading and writing skills.

15 Richard Sennett and Jonathan Cobb, *The hidden injuries of class*. New York: Vintage Books, 1972.

16 R. Rosenthal and L. Jacobson, *Pygmalion in the classroom*. New York: Holt, Rinehart and Winston, 1968.

17 John Mulcahy, "YT going to Supreme Court," *Ypsilanti Press*, Aug. 18, 1993, 1A; John Mulcahy, "Urgent appeal: YT petitions State Supreme Court to keep WR plant open," *Ypsilanti Press*, Aug. 19, 1993, 1A; John Mulcahy, "Workers prepare for plant closing," *Ypsilanti Press*, Sept. 2, 1993, 1A; John Mulcahy, "Struggle ends: Court rejects Willow Run suit; GM can close plant," *Ypsilanti Press*, Sept. 4, 1993, 1A; John Mulcahy, "A furious battle winds up with barely a whimper," *Ypsilanti Press*, Sept. 4, 1993, 1A. Cf. Suzy Warra, "Workers lose more than jobs," *Ypsilanti Press*, Sept. 12, 1993, 1A; Doron P. Levin, "Court backs GM on plant closing," *New York Times*, Aug. 5, 1993, D4.

18 Kim Kozlowski, "Stunned GM workers see cloudy futures," *Ypsilanti Press*, Sept. 4, 1993, 1A.

19 Meanwhile, in Washington, Clinton's Improving American Schools Act will redirect Chapter 1 federal aid from richer to poorer districts, rewarding these schools when they meet higher standards of student performance. Clifford Krauss, "Clinton aims to redirect school aid to the poor from wealthy districts," *New York Times*, Sept. 15, 1993.

20 *Memorandum re: Models of effective learning continuation award*, Michigan Department of Education, July 19, 1994.

21 *MSSI Exchange*, vol. 1, no. 1, Autumn 1993, 6.

22 The summary of common outcomes is thirty-eight lines in length, too long to include here.

23 Michigan State Systemic Initiative Evaluation Team, *Planning for planning*. MSSI Focus Districts – Orientation Meeting, Oct. 6, 7, 8, 1993.

24 The Change Game is a simulation game.

25 Jane Jacobs, *Systems of survival: A dialogue on the moral foundations of commerce and politics*. New York: Random House, 1992.

26 Mary Brandau drew from Richard L. Curwin, *Discipline with dignity*. Association for Supervision and Curriculum Development, 1988.

Chapter 6. Willow Run Is America: The 1940s and 1950s

1 In writing this chapter I have drawn, in addition to sources cited in the chapter, on *Ypsilanti Press Special Supplement*, "13th Annual Ypsilanti Heritage Festival, August 16, 17, & 18," Aug. 14, 1991; Don Sherman and Grace Shackman, "Willow Run's Glory Days," *Ann Arbor Observer*, July 1995, 29–33; John Gunther, *Inside U.S.A.* New York & London: Harper & Brothers, 1947; and Roxanne Jayne and Susan Sachs, *Southern white migration to the North: From Willow Run to today*. University of Michigan, American Studies class 498, Apr. 25, 1973.

2 Marion F. Wilson, *The story of Willow Run*. Ann Arbor: University of Michigan Press, 1956, 19.

3 R. B. A. Bordin, *Washtenaw County: An illustrated history*. Northridge, CA: Windsor, 1988.

4 Glendon F. Swarthout, *Willow Run*. New York: Thomas Y. Crowell, 1943, 13.

5 Ibid., 218.

6 Lowell Juilliard Carr and James Edson Stermer, *Willow Run: A story of industrialization and cultural inadequacy.* New York: Arno Press, 1952/1977.

7 By the 1940s unions had become keen to restrict the power of industry over workers' private lives. In the 1910s Ford Motor Company had a "Sociological Department" that was responsible for visiting workers' homes to examine bankbooks and marriage certificates, suggesting savings, study, and temperance, and distributing a pamphlet of "Rules of Living" that counseled use of soap and water, refraining from spitting on the floor, and, for immigrants, attendance of Ford-run schools to learn English. Ford had seen himself as a shaper of men, forging self-reliance and individualism. But now Sorensen and others who were the powerful figures in the company thought little of worker loyalty, maintaining that men worked for money and the fear of losing their jobs.

8 Carr and Stermer, *Willow Run*, p. 352, emphasis removed.

9 Wilson, *The Story of Willow Run*, 56.

10 Carr and Stermer, *Willow Run*, 77.

11 Jayne and Sachs, *Southern white migration to the North.*

12 Carr and Stermer, *Willow Run*, pp. 239–249.

13 Jim Kise, "A timeless bond called the Village," *Ypsilanti Press Special Supplement*, Aug. 14, 1991, 10.

14 Carr and Stermer, *Willow Run*, p. 293.

15 Mark Hugger, "Willow Run schools still thrive," *Ypsilanti Press Special Supplement*, Aug. 14, 1991, 13.

16 Interview with Martin Packer, Nov. 17, 1994.

17 Rudolf E. Anderson, *The story of the American automobile: Highlights and sidelights.* Washington, D.C.: Public Affairs Press, 1952, p. 294.

18 Jenny Nolan, "Willow Run and the arsenal of democracy," *Detroit News*, <www.detnews.com/history/arsenal/arsenal.htm>. When GM bought the bomber production facility they assigned the building next door, constructed in 1942 to store parts, to the Chevrolet Truck Division. It became Kaiser-Frazier's administration center after the war, and then the Willow Run assembly plant. In 1958 this building was expanded to permit two-plant operation – the Fisher Body Division and Chevrolet Motor Division. In 1971 it was placed under the management of GM's Assembly Division, and in 1974 the two plants were combined. In 1979 an extensive model changeover was made for the front-wheel-drive X-car. And in 1984 the assembly plant became one of 12 facilities in the Buick-Oldsmobile-Cadillac Group, then in 1989 the Chevrolet-Pontiac-GM of Canada Group.

19 And in July 1995 the *Ann Arbor Observer* published a report on the "glory days" of Willow Run, when the factory was "a worldwide symbol of American industrial might."

Chapter 7. Crossing to the New Economy

1 Proposal A would raise the sales tax by 2% to 6%, cut income tax to 4.4% from 4.6%, raise the cigarette tax from 25 cents to 75 cents, eliminate local residential property tax, and levy 18 mills of local property tax on commercial prop-

erty and 6 mills of state taxes on all property. A Keno lottery would raise $100 million annually. Districts would also be permitted to raise 3 mills of local "enhancement" funding with voter approval. The Statutory Plan would raise the income tax to 6% from 4.6%, drop local property taxes to 12 mills and impose a state property tax of 12 mills on nonhomestead property, raise the single business tax to 2.75% from 2.35%, and raise the cigarette tax to 50 cents.

2 "naughty or nice . . .": Associated Press with *Ypsilanti Press* staff report, "Progress made on school funding," *Ypsilanti Press,* Dec. 24, 1993, 1A. "played Santa Claus . . .": Associated Press, "Lawmakers pass plan for schools," *Ypsilanti Press,* Dec. 25, 1993, 1A. Rancor continued to the last minute. Senate Republicans weighed in with a proposal to cut income tax and raise the sales tax; Senate Democrats proposed an alternative ballot plan increasing income taxes; House Democrats called an adjournment, insisting that any agreement must address finance, spending, and quality as a whole (Associated Press, "School finance deal hits snag," *Ypsilanti Press,* Dec. 13, 1993, 1A, 5A).

3 Associated Press, "Sweeping school reforms pass House," *Ypsilanti Press,* Dec. 8, 1993, 1A, 4A. A narrower core curriculum is now required, no longer a model for voluntary adoption, a summary accreditation process (with emphasis on test scores) is introduced, and accreditation is toughened.

4 Associated Press, "School finance deal hits snag," *Ypsilanti Press,* Dec. 13, 1993, 1A, 5A.

5 Associated Press, "Sweeping school reforms pass House," *Ypsilanti Press,* Dec. 8, 1993, 1A, 4A.

6 Available at <www.state.mi.us/migov/gov/Speeches/>. I have reversed the order of the last two sentences.

7 Engler also speaks of "the success of our reforms to break the cycle of dependency called welfare," and he announces new initiatives for mandatory work, job training, or volunteer efforts for welfare recipients. Engler, who in 1991 cut general assistance welfare payments to 83,000 single adults, is proud of toughened child support laws, 22 new prisons, strict mandatory sentences, a police sweep "to keep violent, dangerous and habitual criminals locked up and off our streets," "truth-in-sentencing," and efforts "to maximize use of prisons and jail facilities." Engler publicizes this new "social contract" at the National Governors Association meeting and the National Press Club in Washington (Associated Press, "Engler to pitch welfare reform," *Ypsilanti Press,* Jan. 30, 1994). As the *Ann Arbor News* points out, Engler's tough stance on issues like crime and delinquent fathers closely resembles that of President Clinton, so Democrats will have little basis here for argument with or opposition to Engler's reelection campaign ([No byline], "Engler pumps sales tax hike," *Ann Arbor News,* Jan. 19, 1994, D4).

8 Steven Greenhouse, "Who gets hired? White collars," *New York Times,* Nov. 2, 1993, C1; Robert D. Hershoy Jr., "Industrial production jumps 0.8%. Rise is 5th in a row: Index sets a record," *New York Times,* Nov. 16, 1993, C1, C2.

9 James Bennet, "G.M. profit may top goal for '93. Chief says company has turned corner," *New York Times,* Jan. 31, 1994, C1, C7.

10 Associated Press, "GM to hire 2,000 engineers," *Ypsilanti Press,* Jan. 7, 1994, 5A; James Bennet, "G.M. sees its results improving: Auto maker expects a break-even year," *New York Times,* Nov. 17, 1993, C1, C2; Associated Press, "Big Three exports surge in '93," *Ypsilanti Press,* Jan. 30, 1994, C1.

11 Perot estimates that 5.9 million jobs could be lost. Cf. Samuel Bowles and Mehrene Larudee, "A low-wage game plan," *New York Times*, Nov. 15, 1993, A17.

12 Associated Press, "Reich: NAFTA in dispute," *Ypsilanti Press*, Sept. 28, 1993, 1A, 4A.

13 Associated Press, "Hard sell: Bush campaigns in Michigan for trade agreement," *Ypsilanti Press*, Sept. 28, 1993, 4A.

14 David E. Rosenbaum, "Splintered on trade. 2 unusual political alliances reflect long-term gain and short-term fear," *New York Times*, Sept. 15, 1993, B12. Cf. James Bennet, "Anger, fear but also hope on the assembly line," *New York Times*, Nov. 19, 1993, A10. Despite opposition from trade unions, minority groups, and environmentalists, Clinton built a narrow majority with more Republicans than Democrats. Democrats in the Michigan House failed in their efforts to bring a resolution opposing NAFTA (John Mulcahy, "Anti-NAFTA resolution fails," *Ypsilanti Press*, Nov. 9, 1993, 1A). And in New Jersey an anti-NAFTA rally that 3,000 auto workers were expected to attend drew only 100, suggesting a lack of recognition of the issue (Thomas J. Lueck, "Rally against trade pact fizzles near a G.M. plant," *New York Times*, Nov. 15, 1993, A11).

15 John Mulcahy, "YT trustees to look at NAFTA," *Ypsilanti Press*, Sept. 22, 1993, 3A. Indeed, NAFTA gives the U.S. auto industry privileged access to the growing market in Mexico. The Big Three, along with Volkswagen and Nissan, built more than a million cars there last year. The manufacturers say if NAFTA cuts restrictions on production they will be able to focus in the United States on making big cars, cutting prices, and creating jobs (Anthony dePalma, "An auto sea change in Mexico. Trade pact expected to reshape industry," *New York Times*, Nov. 16, 1993, C1, C5).

16 The *Framework* is distributed by the Michigan Science Teachers Association, March 1993. The MDE asked the MSTA to write a Framework defining the new HSPT, required by PA 118. "The Framework should include the science the students are expected to learn, conditions and considerations of how the exam should be structured and the kinds of test items and evaluation activities that should be written." The basis for the *Framework* was *Science for all Americans (AAAS)*, the *Michigan essential goals and objectives for science education* (1991), and the *Michigan core curriculum outcomes* (1991). The *Framework* defines three new types of question: "independent items" (that "present a brief description of a real world context and pose a single question about it"), "cluster problems" (each of which "presents a real world context . . . and asks a series of questions about it"), and "investigations" (an "actual investigation performed and written up prior to taking the Proficiency Test" and then a subsequent "investigation cluster").

17 Grosse Pointe is a wealthy community just north of Detroit, historically the home of the families of auto executives. Cranbrook is a private school whose students recently became lost while on a school ski trip; Vivian notes that the parents, interviewed on the television news, expressed their complete confidence in the school.

18 The previous record was 92% in 1978. According to the industry, 120% of capacity can be achieved through overtime and other strategies.

19 James Bennet, "Detroit's booming auto sales mean waiting lists for some," *New York Times*, Apr. 18, 1994, A1, C5; Associated Press, "GM hiring workers, keeping plants open," *Ypsilanti Press*, Apr. 18, 1994, 8A.

20 Associated Press, "GM nets $2.5 billion," *Ypsilanti Press*, Feb. 11, 1994, 1A.

21 James Bennet, "G.M.'s profit jumps 66.5% in quarter," *New York Times*, Apr. 29, 1994, C1.

22 Editorial, "A good year," *Ypsilanti Press*, Feb. 13, 1994, 6A.

23 Doron P. Levin, "Market place. Detroit's newly rich auto makers may decide to conserve cash and scrimp on dividends," *New York Times*, Mar. 28, 1994, C4.

24 Doron P. Levin, "Surpassing predictions, vehicle sales jump 19.8%," *New York Times*, Mar. 4, 1994, C4.

25 John Mulcahy, "Strike averted at GM," *Ypsilanti Press*, Mar. 5, 1993, 1A.

26 John Mulcahy, "GM workers brace for strike," *Ypsilanti Press*, Mar. 4, 1994, 1A.

27 Associated Press, "Michigan economy showing strength," *Ypsilanti Press*, May 7, 1994, 1A.

28 "State business expects GATT windfall," *Ann Arbor News*, Nov. 28, 1994.

29 Even so, 3% or 4% was considered the normal and acceptable unemployment rate in the United States during the 1950s and 1960s.

30 Peter Passell, "Economic scene. A challenge to the complacent on the U.S. unemployment rate," *New York Times*, Mar. 31, 1994, C2.

31 Thomas L. Friedman, "World's big economies turn to the jobs issue," *New York Times*, Mar. 14, 1994, C1.

32 Associated Press, "Focal point: Detroit called ideal setting for economic summit," *Ypsilanti Press*, Feb. 9, 1994, 5A. Cf. Richard A. Ryan, "No 'rabbit out of a hat,' but G-7 set a jobs agenda," *Detroit News*, Mar. 16, 1997, 17A.

33 Mark Hornbeck and Charles Cain, "A:OK. Voters overwhelmingly back sales tax hike to fund schools in what governor calls 'a great victory,' " *Detroit News*, Mar. 16, 1994, 1A. Forty-two of Michigan's 527 school districts spend between $7,000 and $11,000 per pupil (Associated Press with *Ypsilanti Press* staff report, "Progress made on school funding," *Ypsilanti Press*, Dec. 24, 1993, 1A, 4A).

Funding for Michigan's public schools had been on average 64% local, 32% state, and 4% federal. Now it will be 19% local, 75% state, and 6% federal. Willow Run's funding will change from 53% state, 43% local, 4% federal (1989–1990 figures) to 86% state, 10% local, 4% federal. Willow Run's revenue per pupil will rise from $5,359 to $5,563. (Ann Arbor's will rise from $7,279 to $7,439; Bloomfield Hills from $10,358 to $10,518.) C. Phillip Kearney, 1994, *Primer on Michigan school finance*, 3rd ed. Educational Studies Program, School of Education, University of Michigan, Ann Arbor, MI.

Willow Run had a $143,000 surplus last year and reserves of $1.8 million, but Yomtoob estimates that $1 million of this may be drawn on this year. Proposal A bases per pupil funding on the prior year's enrollment; if more students arrive the district will have to cut programs or run a deficit. The state has also already begun to transfer responsibility for teachers' retirement costs and Social Security taxes. Eighty-three percent of the Willow Run school's budget is staff-related expenses: 67% salaries and 16% benefits. Including

Social Security and retirement costs would raise that portion to 90%. Also the state's retirement fund is currently $9 billion in debt and the school districts may inherit that debt.

34 Associated Press, "GOP seeks to cap education costs," *Ypsilanti Press*, Mar. 22, 1994, 8A.

35 Associated Press, "Bitter battle: Republican bill would penalize striking teachers," *Ypsilanti Press*, Apr. 14, 1994, 1A; Associated Press, "Teachers protest anti-strike bill," *Ypsilanti Press*, Apr. 20, 1994.

Engler has been helped by Republican 21–16 control of the Senate, and the narrowly divided Republican House, 55–52 with three Democrat vacancies. (The Democrats last controlled the Senate in 1983, but quickly lost. The Republicans were then led by Senator Engler.)

36 Marianne Rzepa, "GM, township try to put bitter past behind them," *Ann Arbor News*, Jan. 9, 1994, C1.

Chapter 8. End-of-Year Report Cards

1 Judith Frutig, "Assaults shut school," *Detroit Free Press*, Feb. 16, 1971; Judith Frutig, "Willow Run puts students on shifts," *Detroit Free Press*, Feb. 20, 1971; Judith Frutig, "Principal seeks race peace, gets tar, feathers," *Detroit Free Press*, Apr. 3, 1971.

2 Janet Miller, "Willow Run avoids desegregation," *Ann Arbor News*, May 30, 1999.

3 The fact that people are more productive when they know that they are being observed and that someone is interested in them is named the Hawthorne effect, after research conducted at Western Electric's Hawthorne plant in Chicago (Fritz J. Roethlisberger and William J. Dickson, *Management and the worker*. Cambridge, MA: Harvard University Press, 1939).

4 Interview with Martin Packer and Julie Nicholson, May 28, 1994.

5 Interview with Martin Packer and Julie Nicholson, May 23, 1994.

Chapter 9. Rest and Relaxation

1 Editorial, "Support," *Ypsilanti Press*, June 15, 1994, 6A; Juanita C. Smith, "Voters approve area millages," *Ypsilanti Press*, June 14, 1994, 1A.

2 Marjorie Kauth-Karjala, "Willow Run rejects bid for enhancement millage," *Ypsilanti Press*, Apr. 29, 1994, 3A.

3 Russell Grantham, "Forecasters: Economy set for slowdown," *Ann Arbor News*, Aug. 16, 1993, A1.

4 Louis Uchitelle, "Survey documents rise of 3-job households," *Ann Arbor News*, Aug. 16, 1993, A1. [Reprinted from the *New York Times*.]

5 James Bennet, "$10 billion for G.M. pensions," *New York Times*, May 12, 1994, C1.

6 James Bennet, "Best quarter ever: G.M. earns $1.92 billion," *New York Times*, July 29, 1994, C1, C2.

7 James Bennet, "Tentative accord reached in strike at G.M. parts plant," *New York Times*, Aug. 26, 1994.

8 Doron P. Levin, "Ford sets higher prices for some 1995 models," *New York Times*, July 7, 1994, C4.
9 Russell Grantham, "End of the line: Texas transplants. Reluctant 'pioneers' forge new lives," *Ann Arbor News*, Aug. 16, 1994, A1, A7.

Chapter 10. Caught in the Middle

1 I have used pseudonyms for the Edmonson teachers. I've tried to be clear that I don't consider individuals at fault for the tone of the middle school's classrooms, but educational researchers are so entrained to blame teachers for instruction they regard with disapproval that this additional step seems necessary to protect the teachers from this interpretation.
2 Interview with Martin Packer, Sept. 21, 1994.
3 Erik H. Erikson, *Childhood and society*. New York: Norton, 1950.
4 Interview with Martin Packer, Oct. 25, 1994.
5 Cf. Linda M. McNeil, *Contradictions of control: School structure and school knowledge*. New York: Routledge, 1986.
6 Swindoll is pastor of the First Evangelical Free Church of Fullerton, California. He is one of the eminent popularizers of new evangelicalism.
7 Cf. Martin Packer and Jesse Goicoechea, "Sociocultural and constructivist theories of learning: Ontology, not just epistemology," *Educational Psychologist*, in press.
8 I have in mind here something similar to what Bourdieu refers to as *habitus*, but Bourdieu's conception is, I think, lacking the important sense of dynamism and agency. Habitus is "embodied disposition," a style or manner in matters of taste and judgments of distinction that is apparent (in a typical Bourdieuian wordplay) in the distinctions people draw in their everyday conduct. "Attitude" is all these things, but it is actively adopted – not deliberately or even consciously, but as a spontaneous mode of engagement in ongoing relationship with other people. And "attitude" is a striving for something, a movement into the future, not simply the product of past experiences (e.g., Pierre Bourdieu, *Distinction: A social critique of the judgement of taste*. 1979/1984. Cambridge, MA: Harvard University Press, 101).
9 Peter T. Kilborn, "It's too much of a good thing, G.M. workers say in protesting overtime: G.M. says it needs extra work to keep up with demand and limit costs," *New York Times*, Nov. 22, 1994, A10; George J. Church, "We're #1 and it hurts," *Time*, Oct. 24, 1994, 50–56.
10 James Bennet, "G.M. merges car design operations," *New York Times*, Oct. 5, 1994, C1; Doron P. Levin, "Auto sales rose last month despite interest rate fears," *New York Times*, Oct. 5, 1994, C1; James Bennet, "G.M. stock falls on report: A $328 million loss in North America," *New York Times*, Oct. 21, 1994, C1.
11 Louis Uchitelle, "Companies hold the line on wages: Few raises despite need for workers," *New York Times*, Oct. 4, 1994, C1, C5.
12 Jason deParle, "Census report sees incomes in decline and more poverty," *New York Times*, Oct. 7, 1994, A1; Sylvia Nasar, "Statistics reveal bulk of new jobs pay over average: Turnaround in the '90s. Managers and professionals dominate hiring, raising overall level of wages," *New York Times*, Nov. 17, 1994, A1.

Chapter 11. The Change Game

1 Marshall S. Smith and Jennifer O'Day, "Systemic school reform," in *The politics of curriculum and testing: The 1990 yearbook of the Politics of Education Association*, ed. Susan H. Fuhrman and Betty Malen. 233–267. London: Falmer, 1990, 268.
2 Ibid., 296.
3 Ibid., 306.
4 Sylvia Nasar, "Recovery is entitled to respect," *New York Times*, Jan. 3, 1995.
5 Newt Gingrich was now House Speaker, Bob Dole now Senate Majority Leader.

Chapter 12. The Future of the Kids Coming Behind Us

1 Available at <www.mofa.go.jp/announce/announce/archive_3/140session.html>

Chapter 13. Quality or Equality? The Standardization of Schooling

1 Tonja Wilson, "Willow Run board faces challenges," *Ypsilanti Courier*, Jan. 20, 1997.
2 *Engler to President: Welcome to the Education State*. Mar. 6, 1997. Available at <www.state.mi.us/migov/gov/pressreleases/199703/clintonp.html>.
3 Ibid.
4 Editorial, "Schoolmates. Clinton, Engler join forces for better education," *Detroit Free Press*, Mar. 6, 1997, 10A.
5 Charles L. Thompson, James P. Spillane, and David K. Cohen, *The state policy system affecting science and mathematics education in Michigan*. MSSI Policy and Program Review Component, Michigan Partnership for New Education, 513 Erickson Hall, 1994, 43.
6 Ibid., 59.
7 Charles L. Thompson and James P. Spillane, *Recommendations from policy and program review component*. Michigan Statewide Systemic Initiative Policy and Program Review Component, 1995, 6.
8 David Cay Johnston, " '96 was a very good year for I.B.M.'s chief executive," *New York Times*, Mar. 19, 1997, D4.
9 Peter Applebome, "Better schools, uncertain returns," *New York Times*, Mar. 16, 1997, sec. 4, p. 5.
10 Rachel L. Swarns, "4,000 hearts full of hope line up for 700 jobs," *New York Times*, Mar. 19, 1997, A1.
11 Marianne Rzepa, "County residents optimistic about area economy," *Ypsilanti Press*, Mar. 2, 1997, 1A.
12 Available at gopher.mde.state.mi.us:70/00/reports/MSR97/W/81150/81150. TXT, and gopher.mde.state.mi.us:70/00/reports/MSR96/W/81150/81150. TXT.
13 David Frickman, "New perspective: Ypsi MEAP scores look better with more analysis," *Ypsilanti Courier*, Feb. 27, 1997, 1.
14 *WRSI News*, Apr. 16, 1996, 1.
15 Marion F. Wilson, *The Story of Willow Run*. Ann Arbor: University of Michigan Press, 1956, 88.

16 *Engler to President: Welcome to the Education State*, Mar. 6, 1997. Available at <www.state.mi.us/migov/gov/pressreleases/199703/clintonp.html>.

17 Joseph A. Schumpeter, *Imperialism and social classes*. New York: Augustus Kelley, 1955/1951, 210.

Chapter 14. Coda – June 1999

1 "Testing MEAP: How we did it," *Detroit Free Press*, Jan. 20, 1998.

2 Poverty and large minority enrollment are common factors among these districts. On the other hand, 22 of the 31 districts received more than the $5,308 basic state foundation grant in per pupil funding.

3 Heather Newman, "Leveling the test's playing field: Experts offer ways," *Detroit Free Press*, Jan. 21, 1998.

4 Jurgen Habermas, *The theory of communicative action. Vol. 1. Reason and the rationalization of society*. Boston: Beacon Press, 1981/1984.

5 The Systemic Reform study was awarded by the U.S. Department of Education's Office of Educational Research and Improvement (OERI) to the Policy Center of the Consortium for Policy Research in Education (CPRE), in conjunction with the National Center for Research on Teacher Learning (NCRTL), as part of 12 OERI-funded studies of school reform.

6 Margaret E. Goertz, R. E. Floden, and Jennifer O'Day, *Studies of education reform: Systemic reform: Vol. 1. Findings and conclusions*. Rutgers, the State University of New Jersey, Center for Policy Research in Education, 1955, 106. The term "capacity" is so new that it is defined: "the power, ability, or faculty for doing some particular thing," according to Goertz, Floden, and O'Day (1995), who cite the *Oxford English Dictionary*. (*Webster's New Collegiate Dictionary* has a more passive definition: "the ability to hold, receive, store, or accommodate; a measure of content; the measured ability to contain; maximum production or output.")

7 The phrase "community of practice" originates in Jean Lave and Etienne Wenger, *Situated learning: Legitimate peripheral participation*. Cambridge: Cambridge University Press, 1991. The phrase is used by Goertz, Floden, and O'Day without attribution.

8 Goertz, Floden, and O'Day, *Studies of education reform*, 110.

9 Ibid., 109.

10 Ibid., 107–110.

11 Available at <www.state.mi.us/migov/Archives/edtestimony.html>

12 Craig Whitney, "French jobless find the world is harsher," *New York Times*, Mar. 19, 1998, A1; David E. Sanger, "U.S., lauding its economy, finds no summit followers," *New York Times*, June 20, 1997, A1, A6.

13 Robyn Meredith, "A boom built on big wheels: Sales of light trucks drive the auto industry's expansion," *New York Times*, June 3, 1999, C1, C20; Robyn Meredith, "Vehicle sales increased by 5.3% in May," *New York Times*, June 3, 1999, C20.

14 William Wolman and Anne Colamosca, *The Judas economy: The triumph of capital and the betrayal of work*. Addison-Wesley, 1997.

15 Robyn Meredith, "Strike closes parts factory in job dispute," *New York Times*, July 24, 1997, A8.

16 Alan L. Adler, "GM, union locals struggle over contracts," *Detroit Free Press*, May 29, 1997. Workers at GM's Saturn plant in Spring Hill, Tennessee, have considered a strike too, dissatisfied with the company's plans to standardize and outsource parts and attach the Saturn label to vehicles built elsewhere (Keith Bradsher, "Labor's peace with G.M. unraveling at Saturn plant," *New York Times*, July 22, 1998, A1).

17 Ted Evanoff and Jennifer Bott, "GM on brink of total shutdown," *Detroit Free Press*, June 12, 1998; Sam Dillon, "A 20-year G.M. parts migration to Mexico," *New York Times*, June 24, 1998, C1.

18 Keith Bradsher, "General Motors and U.A.W. agree on end to strike," *New York Times*, July 29, 1998, A1, C6; Nichole Christian, "G.M. calls strikes illegal and threatens jobless benefits," *New York Times*, June 25, 1998, C6.

19 See note 13.

20 Shoichiro Toyoda, "Dismantle Japan Inc.," *New York Times*, Apr. 17, 1997, A21; Stephanie Storm, "Japan's new 'temp' workers: Rethinking lifetime jobs and their underpinnings," *New York Times*, June 17, 1998, C1.

21 David E. Sanger and Steve Lohr, "A search for answers to avoid the layoffs. The downsizing of America. Last of seven articles: Is there a better way?" *New York Times*, Mar. 9, 1996, 1, 10, 11. Among the companies that announced job cuts were AT&T (123,000); I.B.M. (122,000); General Motors (99,400); Boeing (61,000); Sears, Roebuck (50,000); Digital Equipment (29,800); Lockheed Martin (29,100); Bell-South (21,200); McDonnell Douglas (21,000); Pacific Telesis (19,000); Delta Airlines (18,900); GTE (18,400); Nynex (17,400); Eastman Kodak (16,800) (Louis Uchitelle and N. R. Kleinfield, "On the battlefields of business, millions of casualties," *New York Times*, Mar. 3, 1996, sec. 1, pp. 1, 11). The Big Three are hiring around 170,000 new workers, but these will replace 190,000 leaving through attrition, chiefly retirement. The total U.S. auto-manufacturing workforce was 442,708 in 1996, down 29% from 1985, and even with the new hires will be 23,000 smaller in 2003 – a drop of another 5%.

22 Robert Hershey, "The rise of the working class: Blue-collar jobs gain, but the work changes in tone," *New York Times*, Sept. 3, 1997, C1.

23 J. Tomaney, "The reality of workplace flexibility," *Capital and Class* 40 (1990): 29–60, 54.

24 David E. Sanger and Steve Lohr, "A search for answers to avoid the layoffs. The downsizing of America. Last of seven articles: Is there a better way?" *New York Times*, Mar. 9, 1996, 11.

Index

Note: Some subentries that are related to events are arranged in chronological order.

AAAS (American Association for the Advancement of Science), 59
ability
    badges conferred in schools, 92, 266
    classroom grouping, 93
Accountability Act, School District Educational, 246
accountability in education
    in economic model of schooling, 106–107, 236
    in MSSI, 48
    in quality reform, 3, 96, 139, 144, 212, 246–247, 251, 264
    and Willow Run school board, 256, 272
    in Willow Run vision statement, 103
accreditation
    effects of MEAP, 248
    of Michigan public schools, 44
    reformed, 245, 248
achievement, axis of, 5, 91–93, 271, 280
achievement-motivation, 91
Addoniazo, Michael F., 288n. 10
Adelman, Nancy, 288n. 16
alignment
    driven by MEAP test, 263
    in Statewide Systemic Initiative, 47, 106, 212, 275
    Teaching, Learning, and Curriculum Alignment, 146–147, 226
    in WRCS curriculum, 258–259

America 2000 Excellence in Education Bill, 43
Anglin, Mel (Edmonson principal), 171–172, 180, 186, 255
Ann Arbor, 20
Ann Arbor News, 32, 50, 177, 253
Appalachian migrants to Willow Run, 120–123
Arlington, Texas, GM plant
    chosen over Willow Run plant, 24
    more flexible, 25–26, 67
    production begins, 71
    production problems, 177–178
aspirations, parental, for their children, 55–56
assembly-line production
    at bomber plant, 114
    at Hydra-matic plant, 131–132
    origin at Ford Motor Co., 36
assessment/evaluation, axis of achievement, 91–93, 271
attitude
    African American boys, 187
    as "attitude," 204
    "capacity, " dimension of, 276
    character and mind as, 203
    defined, 203–204
    of Edmonson students, 203–206
    "is everything," 181
    of Kettering students, 54–56, 59–60, 108, 167–169, 173–174, 269

attitude (*cont.*)
  illustrated: Tabatha, 56; boxcar boys,
    195; Marshall, 195–196; Shawna,
    196–197
  and learning, 272, 276
  mediated, objectifying, 83
  parents', 57, 60, 61–62, 271
  and schooling, 5, 93, 204, 271, 273
  staff, 149
  as theoretical concept, 5
  and work, 6, 225, 279–280
  working-class, 55, 92
automobile industry
  and Fordist production, 36
  in Japan, 26, 41, 152, 177
  in Michigan, 20, 23–25, 283n. 12
  in U.S., booming, 152, 277, 293n.
    18
  in U.S., downsizing, 239, 240
  in U.S., problems, 26–28

B-24 bomber (Liberator), 109–117,
    126, 129–130
Barker, Joe, 100
Bell, T. H. (secretary of education), 41
Big Three
  in Michigan, 20, 22
  competed with Kaiser-Frazer, 128
  problems, 26–27, 72, 288n. 5
  doing well, 152, 177, 239–240, 277
  squeezing labor, 209
"Blue Monday," 23
Bourdieu, Pierre, 286n. 18, 296n. 8
Boyett, Joseph H., 284n. 26
Brandau, Mary (Kettering principal)
  daughter of Robert Stevenson, 110
  Kettering graduation, 13–16, 22
  on quality reform, 252, 256, 260,
    264–265, 268, 269
  on roots of reform, 52–54, 56–61
  visits first grade, 84–88
  at WRSI meetings, 17–19, 105–106,
    145, 159–163, 218, 220–221,
Brice Heath, Shirley, 92
Brown, Janice (Kettering principal),
    57, 61, 91, 169
Bruner, Jerome, 6, 281n. 3

Bush, George
  blamed for plant closing, 29, 32
  the "education president," 42–44,
    237
  hated in primaries, 65, 66
  promoting NAFTA, 140–141

capacity
  building in State Systemic Initiative,
    107
  limited in public school system,
    275–276, 298n.6
capitalism. *See* Fordism; post-Fordism
  dynamic character, 34–40
  electronic, 236
  exploitation, 34–35, 55
  instability, 35, 39
  moral injustice, 35, 39
  undermines moral authority, 39
capitalist economies, widely adopted,
    277
Carr, Lowell, 117–123
charter schools ("Public School
    Academies")
  proposed by Engler, 45, 96, 136–139
  bill passed, 136–139
  opening, 245–246
Cheney Elementary School, 21
  provided resources, 159
  reactions to MEAP, 219–220
  WRSI presentation, 104–105,
Chew, Laura (Cheney principal)
  Curriculum Coordinator, 235
  principal of Cheney, 18–19, 29, 105
  on quality reforms, 249, 265–266
  at WRCS board meeting, 255–257
  at WRSI meetings, 161–166,
    221–224
  on WRSI, 260
Chrysler Corporation, 20, 27–29, 46,
    66, 177, 239–240
class, hidden injuries of, 92
class, middle
  distance from necessity, 55
  forms of literacy, 92
  fracturing, 176
  indirect, cognitive relation, 54

class, working
  attitude to middle class, 92
  attitude to practical reasoning,
    54–55
  forms of literacy, 92
  impact of quality reform, 249, 251
  lifestyle under post-Fordism, 273,
    278–279
  middle-class lifestyle under
    Fordism, 36–37
classroom
  abstractions of, 83–84, 234
  as community, 84, 90, 107, 271
  culture of, 5, 84, 90, 181–206, 271
  formation of self and mind, 85–88,
    90, 271
  instructional atmosphere, 215
  moral topography, 5, 87, 187
  recognition from teacher, 5, 88–90,
    189, 204, 271
  routines of, 80–84, 181–185, 271
  traditional, 5, 58, 91–93, 221–222
  traditional, axis of achievement, 5,
    91–93, 271, 280
climate, school
  at Edmonson, 185–186, 188–191,
    194–195, 204, 206
  at Kettering, 94, 107–108
Clinton, William, J.
  in National Governors Association,
    42
  in 1992 primaries, 64–66
  Goals 2000 Act, 12
  on NAFTA, 140–141, 293n. 14
  on vocational education, 150
  Detroit G-7 meeting, 153–154
  on labor-capital relations, 174
  seen as flip-flopping, 229
  Call for Action for American
    Education, 241
  visit to Michigan, 246, 265
  on 1999 economy, 277
Coalition of Essential Schools, 108
Cobb, Jonathan, 266, 290n. 15
Cohen, David K., 276
Colamosca, Anne, 298n. 14
Cole, Michael, 7, 282n. 7, 289n. 3

Collier, Peter, 284n. 23
community of practice, 7, 275, 298n. 7
conceptual systems, 82
Conn, Henry P., 284n. 26
constructivist pedagogy, 58–60, 191,
    202
"Contract with America," 229, 297n. 5
creative destruction, 34–39
cultural amplifiers, 83
cultural psychology, 7
culture
  of the classroom, 5, 84, 90,
    181–206, 271
  as intentional worlds, 7
  as medium for growth, 7
  of reform, 5
  of teaching, 149
curriculum
  core, in quality reform, 44, 95, 136,
    245–246
  driven by assessment, 105–106,
    215–217, 227, 248, 263
  SSI "common content," 47, 97, 160,
    211–212
  reform in WRCS, 107, 142–144,
    150, 191–193, 197–202, 216–217,
    257–258
  WRSI discussion of, 142–147, 218,
    257–258
Curwin, Richard L., 290n. 26

Darden, J. T., 283n. 7
Deming, William Edwards, 26,
    132–133
Depression, Great, 37, 38, 39
Detroit Free Press, 28–30, 246, 272
Detroit News, 28–30, 33, 65
Detroit public schools, takeover of, 277
development, children's
  culturally and historically situated, 8
  not just cognitive change, 8
  made, not caused, 6
  "new look" to study of, 6–7
  as production of persons, 8, 271
  and society, 1
  studied in school, 4
Dewey, John, 10, 203, 270, 289n. 8

division of labor, under Fordism, 4, 54–55, 273
downsizing
    in economic transformation, 71, 238, 239, 278, 299n. 21
Dreeben, Robert, 289n. 1
Dundan, Bev, 258–259
Dunn, Judy, 6, 281n. 2

economic metaphor for schooling, 106–107, 236, 274, 279
economy, European, 154–155, 230–231
economy, global
    highly unstable, 278
    and schools, 150
    transformation of production, 33, 154
economy, Michigan
    and geography, 19–20
    problems, 25, 28, 30–31
    recovering, 139, 153, 246
    and schools, 46
economy, U.S. *See also* capitalism; downsizing; Fordism; job loss; post-Fordism; unemployment
    severe recession, 6, 37–40, 285n. 27
    roiling, 71
    recovering, 140, 154–155, 176, 229, 252–253, 277
    structural transformation, 22, 230–231, 236–242
    demands on workers, 207, 208–210, 231, 277–279
    and schools, 10, 17–18, 41–42, 252–253
economy, Washtenaw County, 253
economy, Willow Run, 21, 31, 254, 273
Edmonson Middle School, 21, 51, 127
    administration, 171–172, 180, 182, 186, 195, 255
    concern with order, 186–187
    clash between curriculum and control, 202–206
    climate, 185–186, 188–191, 194–195, 202–204, 206
    curriculum reform, 142–144, 191–193, 197–202

    history of, 185–186, 189–191
    image, 185–186, 191
    Lyte, Vivian on, 187, 188–189
    open house, 169–173
    Professional Development School, 185, 190–191
    sixth grade, 180–185, 187–189, 191–202, 204–206
    students' attitude, 203–206
Education, Department of, Michigan, 48, 97, 105, 146–147, 149, 215
Education, Department of, U.S., 42, 43, 49, 273
Education Summit
    1988, 42
    1996, 237
elections
    presidential, 1992, 64–66
    governor, 1994, 13, 230
    House/Senate, 1994, 229–230
    governor, 1998, 276
Emlaw, Michael (WISD superintendent), 46
Engler, John (governor of Michigan)
    on Michigan economy, 13, 139, 153
    and plant closing, 29, 32, 63
    political career, 44, 65, 227, 230, 239, 276
    school finance reform, 73–76, 96, 134–140, 156, 272, 276. *See also* finance, school
    school quality reform, 3, 13, 24–25, 95–96, 134–140, 217, 244–247, 265, 266, 272, 277. *See also* quality education reform
    viewed by teachers, 207, 247, 265–267
environment, for learning, 100
Erikson, Erik E., 296n. 3
equity
    concern in SSI, 47
    and school finance reform, 49–50, 155–156, 272, 276
ethos
    drawn on by WRSI, 108, 256, 262, 271

of Willow Run, 9, 54, 108, 130, 148, 225, 271, 243–244, 262–263
of Willow Village, 121–123, 243

Fields, Mrs. (Kettering fifth-grade teacher), 268–269, 270
finance, school
foundation grant, 11, 96, 156, 175
in Michigan, property tax eliminated, 73–76
Proposal A, 96, 135–136, 139–140, 155–156, 291n. 1, 292n. 2, 294n. 33
Statutory Plan, 135, 291n. 1
of U.S. public schools, 49–50
vouchers, 75
in Willow Run schools 11, 73, 75, 166, 175, 282n. 1
Finkel, Liza (University of Michigan professor), 17–19, 104, 143–147, 149
flexibility, attitude of, 6, 279–280
flexible production
at Hydra-matic plant, 131
post-Fordism, 37
Floden, R. E., 298n. 6
Florida, Richard, 283n. 6
focus districts, in MSSI, 158, 244
Ford Motor Company, 20, 27–29, 66, 177
Highland Park plant, 36
picked as UAW target, 72
Willow Run Community Schools partner, 159–160
and Willow Run plant, 110–118, 120, 124, 127, 240
Ford, Edsel, 112
Ford Elementary School, 21
Ford, Henry, 36, 112–113, 126
Fordism
and auto industry, 36
and exploitation, 55, 273
class structure in, 54–55
countering costs and consequences, 60
division of labor, 4, 54–55, 273
mode of production, 2, 36–37, 279

foundation grant
proposed by Engler, 11, 96,
implemented, 156,
and millage, 175
Framework for the High School Science Proficiency Examination, 143–146, 293n. 16
Frazer, Joseph, 127

Gallimore, Ronald, 282n. 14
General Motors Corporation (GM), 20
token of larger economic shift, 6
purchase of WR plant, 109, 128, 291n. 18
economic problems, 6, 26–28
closing WR plant, 22, 23–34, 67
agile production plans, 34
sued by Ypsilanti Township, 63–64, 68–69, 70–71, 94–95, 156–157
Stempel fired, 66–67
finances improving, 71, 140, 152, 177, 252
squeezing workers, 207, 208–209
conflict with workers, 72, 277–288, 299n. 16
GM gypsies, 32
Gergen, Kenneth J., 282n. 6
Gerstner, Louis V. Jr. (IBM chairman), 10, 16, 17, 236, 237, 252, 280
Gibboney, Richard, 252–253
Gibson, Dick (General Motors plant manager), 131–133
Goals 2000: Educate America Act, 12
Goertz, Margaret E., 298n. 6
Goicoechea, Jesse, 296n. 7
governor's State of the State Address, Michigan
1992, 24
1993, 44
1994, 13, 139, 292n. 7
Greco-Brooks, David, 289n. 10
Green, Gail (WRHS principal), 249–251, 255
Griffin, Peg, 289n. 3
guided participation, 7

Habermas, Jurgen, 298n. 4
habitus, 296n. 8
hands-on, minds-on activities
  at Kettering Elementary School, 53,
    57–60, 90
  Willow Run High School students,
    271
Harvey, David, 34, 284n. 18
Hatano, Giyoo, 289n. 4
Hawthorne effect, 165, 295n. 3
Heath, Shirley Brice, 289nn. 13, 14
Heilbroner, Robert, 284nn. 20, 21
Heister, Scott (high school science
    teacher)
  on curriculum, 258–260
  on quality reform, 247
  reflects on WRSI, 257
  students in his classroom, 243
  at WRSI meetings, 17–19, 142–145,
    147, 158–167, 212, 214–224,
    226–228,
  at WRSI presentation, 101–105
hermeneutic phenomenology, 7
Higgins, James (*Detroit News* writer),
    33–34
High School Proficiency Test (HSPT)
  proposed by Engler, 138
  driving curriculum, 144,
  presented at WRSI, 226–228
  implemented, 244–245
  effects on instruction, 248–251, 257
higher order thinking, 102
  in Kettering reforms, 56–60, 271
  and State Systemic Initiative, 47
Hill, R. C., 283n. 7
history, made not caused, 6, 40, 270,
    280
Holmes Elementary School, 21, 159,
    142
Hopkins, Betty (sixth-grade teacher)
  at WRSI meetings, 17–19, 104–105,
    142–143, 160, 228
Horowitz, David, 284n. 23
Hydra-matic plant (GM Powertrain)
  to remain open, 24
  threat to close, 69
  GM ownership, 109, 128

  tour of, 130–133
  possible strike, 152

identity
  professional, 225
  of student, 80
  of Willow Run community, 130
image
  of bomber plant workers, 116
  of Edmonson, 185–186, 191
  of Willow Run, 51, 60
  of Willow Village, 121–123
  of WRCS, 260–261
inequity
  of economic transformation, 38
  of educational reforms, 247–251,
    265–267
Ingleby, David, 6, 281n. 3
Institute for Contemporary and
    Regional Development, 30–31
instruction
  effects of MEAP, 227–228, 249–251,
    263
  integrated, at Kettering, 53, 57–58,
    90, 271
  WRSI discussion of, 163–166
interests, of business and citizens, 63
interpretive analysis, 7, 8

Jackson, Jesse, 29
Jacobs, Jane, 290n. 25
Jacobson, L., 290n. 16
Japan
  auto industry, 26, 41, 152, 177
  call for systemic reform, 242
  economy, 66, 207, 252, 278, 279
  education, 37, 53
  G-7 meeting, 153
  kaizin, 100–102
  "nothing on us," 132, 133
Joas, Hans, 8, 282n. 16
job loss
  and attitude, 225
  in auto industry, 239, 240
  permanent, 237
  at University of Michigan, 178
  at WR plant, 22, 23–24, 31–32

Kaiser Elementary School, 21
  reactions to MEAP, 220
  student reaction to plant closing, 29
  WRSI presentation, 98–103, 104
Kaiser, Henry, 100, 127
Kaiser-Frazer automobile company,
  127
Kaizin, 37, 100–102, 166
Karr, Cyd (art teacher), 57
Kearney, C. Phillip, 288nn. 10, 11
Kenney, Martin, 283n. 6
Kettering Capers, 88
Kettering, Charles F., 78–79
Kettering Creed, 85, 89
Kettering Elementary School, 21
  fifth-grade fieldtrip, 169–173
  fifth graders interviewed, 173–174
  first grade, 78–94
  first graders interviewed, 167–169
  first-grade MEAP test, 268–269, 270
  graduation, class of 2001, 10–16,
    175
  increasing poverty, 273
  local reform efforts, 4, 52–62
  reactions to MEAP, 220–221
  recognize relational and cultural
    character, 107–108
  students' attitude, 54–56, 59–60,
    108, 167–169, 173–174, 269
  "too much input," 264
Kid Vote 1994, 230
Kimbill, Solon T., 286n. 16
Kojève, Alexandre, 270

labor-capital relations
  Clinton statement, 174
  Sweeney statement, 237
  UAW concessions, 240
Lave, Jean, 7, 282n. 11, 298n. 7
learning
  in action, 7
  and attitude, 272, 276
  fun, 52–55, 91
  not just knowledge and skills, 90, 276
  relational and cultural, 4, 107, 271,
    275
  and symbol systems, 82–83, 90, 271

Lieven, Elena, 6
literacy
  class differences, 92
  skills, 82–84, 271
local control
  Engler statement, 139
  threat to, 75, 135, 241, 274–275
  versus accountability, 144–147
Lyte, Vivian (WRCS Curriculum
    Coordinator)
  on Edmonson, 187, 188–189
  as Kettering principal, 53, 91, 93
  leaving WRCS, 235
  on parents' attitude, 62
  positions in WR, 105
  on quality reform, 247–249, 253,
    266–268
  on unemployment, 273
  at WISD, 273
  on WRCS, 98
  on WRSI, 259
  at WRSI meetings, 17–19, 142–151,
    158–166, 212–224, 226–228, 235
  at WRSI presentations, 100–106

MacDonald, Lorri (Edmonson vice-
    principal), 180, 182, 195
MacNeil-Lehrer News Hour, 68
Magnusson, Shirley (University of
    Michigan professor), 57
manual/mental division, 4, 54–55, 273
"marketplace" reforms, 106, 247
Marx, Karl, 34
math, fuzzy, criticism of NCTM, 58
McClellan, James E. Jr., 286n. 16
McNeil, Linda M., 296n. 5
MEAP (Michigan Educational
    Assessment Program) test
  driving accreditation, 245, 248
  driving curriculum, 105, 218, 263
  driving instruction, 227–228,
    249–251, 263
  and HSPT, 214, 217, 226–228,
    250–251
  single index of quality, 106, 163,
    247, 257, 272
  Kettering fifth grade, 268–269, 270

MEAP (Michigan Educational
    Assessment Program) test (*cont.*)
    making what it measures, 275, 279
    reforms implemented, 217, 244–246
    staff reactions, 161, 219–225, 228,
        247–252, 266
    tests social class, 174, 272–273
    WRCS results, 254–257, 260, 270
mediational means, 7, 271
Melberg, Ray (Kaiser principal), 100
metaphors for schooling, 106–107,
    236, 274, 279
Michigan, 1
    geography of, 19
Michigan Education Association
    (MEA), 78, 156
Michigan Education Warranty, 45,
    95, 138
*Michigan Essential Goals and Objectives
    for Science Education* (*MEGOSE*),
    59, 214, 216
Michigan Future, Inc., 46
Michigan Statewide Systemic Initiative
    (MSSI)
    funded by NSF, 48–49
    MSSI Vision, 48–49, 229
    focus districts in, 76–77, 288n. 16,
        289n. 18
    second-year plans, 97–98
    MSSI Exchange, 97
    reporting requirements, 158–167
    conflicting demands, 167, 217, 276
    clash with "quality
        reforms,"145–146
    MSSI Valuing Document, 148
    tendency to become top-down, 5,
        162–163, 175, 212–213, 217, 251
    Yomtoob and, 213, 219, 228
    evaluated, 251, 276
millage election, 11, 75, 166, 175,
    282n. 1
mind
    as attitude, 203
    created, 82–88
moral concern, in SSI, 47
moral topography of classroom, 5,
    87, 187

MSSI Exchange, 97
MSSI Valuing Document, 148
MSSI Vision
    first draft, 48–49
    final version, 229

NAFTA (North Atlantic Free Trade
    Agreement)
    issue in primaries, 64, 65
    fears of job loss, 72–73, 134
    passes, 140–141
narrative, 8
NASDC (New American Schools
    Development Corporation), 43
Nation at Risk, A, 41–42, 44
National Education Goals, 12, 42–43,
    95
National Education Goals Panel, 43, 44
National Governors Association, 42
National Science Foundation (NSF), 3,
    46–48, 106–107, 213, 274. *See also*
    Statewide Systemic Initiative (SSI)
NCTM (National Council of Teachers
    of Mathematics), 58
NESAC (National Education
    Standards & Assessment
    Council), 43
New Directions Science Units, 144–145
"New Economy," 6, 46
New York Times, 32, 64, 66, 71, 208,
    252, 278

O'Day, Jennifer, 47, 211–212, 285nn.
    6, 7, 297n. 1, 298n. 6

Packer, Martin, 281nn. 4, 5, 282n. 15,
    289n. 10, 296n. 7
Page, Joyce (KES first-grade teacher),
    79–87, 89–91, 93–94, 167
parents
    aspirations for children, 55–56
    attitude toward school, 57, 60,
        61–62, 271
    challenged, 14
    involved in Kettering reforms,
        55–57, 60
    views of schooling, 61–62

Parsons, Talcott, 91, 289n. 12
participation, legitimate peripheral, 7
Perot, Ross, 73, 140, 293n. 11
Piaget, Jean, 286n. 19
political metaphor for schooling,
   106–107, 236, 274, 279
post-Fordism
  class structure in, 278–279
  mode of production, 2, 37, 278–279
poverty
  in KES students, 53
  in Willow Run, 21, 254, 273
Powell, Judith, 288n. 16
Prater, Wesley (township supervisor),
   69, 141
Presidential election, 1992, 64–66,
   287n. 33
Prince, Henry, J., 288n. 10
problem-driven instruction, 215
production of persons, 8, 271
professional development
  inservice on MEAP, 219–225, 228
  quality reform and, 245
  WRSI on, 4, 104, 142, 149,
   164–166, 271–272
Professional Development School,
   185, 190–191
project-based inquiry
project-driven inquiry
  at Edmonson, 191–193, 197–202
  at Kettering, 57–60, 84, 169
  WRSI discussion, 160–161
Proposal A, replacement revenue
   proposal
  proposed by Engler, 96, 291n. 1
  bill passed, 135–136, 292n. 2,
  promoted, 139–140
  public vote approving, 155–156,
   294n. 33
Public Act 25, 44
Pygmalion effect, 93

"quality education reform" in Michigan
  threat to local reforms, 5, 147, 167
  Public Act 25, 1999, 44
  Engler's "fundamental principles,"
   95–96

  bill approved, 135–139
  implemented, 244–246
  academic core curriculum, 95, 136,
  accreditation, 44, 245, 248
  annual report card, 45, 96, 245
  charter schools, 45, 96, 136–139,
   245–246
  economic metaphor, 106–107, 236,
   274, 279
  High School Proficiency Test, 138,
   144, 226–228, 244, 248–251, 257
  higher standards, 95
  Michigan Education Warranty, 45,
   95, 138
  schooling as a production process,
   106–107, 279
  schools of choice, 75, 95, 136, 245,
   247
  changes to MEAP test, 105–106,
   214–217
  longer school year, 136, 245

race
  an issue in reform, 265
  in Willow Run, 159, 187
  Willow Run High School students
   on, 232–233
Rankin, Stuart (University of
   Michigan professor), 190–191
rationalization
  in economic change, 2
  in school reform, 107, 274
  of schooling, 5, 280
Ravitch, Diane, 273
"Reagan Democrats" in Michigan, 65
Reagan, Ronald (U.S. president), 41
recognition, from teacher, 5, 88–90,
   189, 204, 271
reform, school. *See* systemic reform;
   quality education reform
Reich, Robert (secretary of labor), 71,
   153, 140, 176, 210, 236
Renaissance Program, in WRHS,
   160
respect and responsibility
  at Edmonson, 194
  at Kettering, 85–88

report card, annual school
  proposed by Engler 45, 96
  implemented, 245
Richards, Martin P. M., 6, 281nn.1, 2, 3
Ricoeur, Paul, 281n. 5
Rifkin, Jeremy, 284n. 22
Riley, Richard (secretary of education),
  12, 246, 252, 276
Rogoff, Barbara, 7, 282nn. 10, 14
Rosenthal, R., 290n. 16
Ryles, Sharon (Kettering fifth-grade
  teacher), 14–16, 169–171, 173

Sampson, Edward E., 282n. 6
Sanders, Ms. (sixth-grade teacher),
  181, 183–184, 189, 193–196,
  204–206, 296n. 1
Sartre, Jean-Paul, 289n. 6
schooling
  development studied in, 4
  and the economy, 17–18, 41–42, 46,
    252–253
  preparation of citizens, 1, 47, 106
  preparation of workers, 1, 106, 134,
    150, 276
  relevance to working-class children,
    4, 60, 273
  and social change, 1, 274
  transformation of children, 1, 4, 60,
    78–94, 266, 280
  viewed as a delivery system,
    106–107, 279
  viewed as a production process,
    106–107, 279
schools of choice
  proposed by Engler, 75, 136,
  implemented, 245, 247
Schools, U.S. public
  blamed for economic problems,
    17–18, 41–42, 46, 252–253
  character of, 49–50, 274–275
  demands for reform, 1–2, 10, 25,
    41–44, 134
  as monopoly, 96, 106, 207
  struggles over, 1, 274, 280
Schumpeter, Joseph, 34, 39, 284n. 17,
  285n. 29, 298n. 17

Scribner, Sylvia, 7, 282n. 12, 289nn.
  2, 7
Sennett, Richard, 266, 290n. 15
Serpell, Robert, 289n. 4
Shelton, Donald Judge
  to hear YT/GM lawsuit, 63
  rules GM can't close plant, 68,
    287n. 42
  overruled, 70, 156
  order lifted, 94
  reflections, 157
Shields, Patrick, 288n. 16
Shotter, John, 6, 281n. 3, 281n. 6
Shweder, Richard, 7, 282n. 8
Sizer, Theodore, 108
Sloan, Alfred (first president of GM),
  26
"Smith and O'Day Model" of reform,
  251
Smith, Adam, 34–35
Smith, John ("Jack") (GM chief
  executive), 67, 140, 157, 208, 240
Smith, Marshall, 47, 211–212, 280,
  285nn. 6, 7, 297n. 1
Smith, Roger (GM chief executive),
  26–27
socialization, primary and secondary, 80
sociocultural inquiry
  as interpretive, 8
  and narrative, 8
  U.K. version of, 6
Sorensen, Charles
  and assembly line production, 36
  and bomber plant, 112–113
Spencer School, 52, 123–124, 130
Spillane, James P., 276, 297n. 7
Stabenow, Debbie (Michigan state
  senator), 74, 95
standards
  higher, proposed by Engler, 95
  national, 43, 241
  setting takes years, 251
Stangis, Hazel (Kettering fifth-grade
  teacher), 13, 16, 57, 169
state, role of, in SSI, 47–48
State Board of Education, Michigan,
  230, 246

Statewide Systemic Initiative (SSI)
  See also systemic reform; Michigan
    Statewide Systemic Initiative;
    Willow Run Systemic Initiative
  launched by National Science
    Foundation, 3, 46–48
  Smith and O'Day, 47, 211–212,
    285nn. 6, 7, 297n. 1, 298n. 6
  delivery of higher order thinking,
    47
  role of state, 47–48
  finding "common content," 47, 97,
    160, 211–212
  alignment of components, 47, 106,
    212, 275
  capacity of system, 107, 276, 298n. 6
  political metaphor, 106–107, 236,
    274, 279
  as rationalization of schooling, 107,
    274
  teaching and learning
    misunderstood, 5, 107, 271
  evaluated, 275–276, 298nn. 5, 6
Statutory Plan, backup finance
    proposal, 135, 291n. 1
Stempel, Robert (GM chairman)
  restructuring plan, 27
  announces Willow Run plant
    closing, 23, 24, 25, 30
  pleases business community, 33
  forced out, 66–67
Stermer, James, 117–123
Stevenson, Robert, 110, 124–126
Story of Willow Run, The, 110, 243
student-centered pedagogy, 55, 56–60,
    145
student-driven inquiry, 164–166, 169
student outcomes, evaluation of,
    161–167
Swarthout, Glendon, 115–116
Swindoll, Charles, 203, 296n. 6
symbol systems, 82–84, 90
system of schooling. *See also* systemic
    reform
  diversity of solutions, 268
  and economy, 270
  resistance to change, 267–268

schooling as a delivery system,
    106–107, 279
  of U.S. public schools, 49–50
systemic reform, 3, 274. *See also*
    Statewide Systemic Initiative
    (SSI)
  appeal of, 50
  in Willow Run, 100, 148, 149, 150
systems of survival, 107, 274

target districts, in MSSI 48
  See also focus districts, in MSSI
Taylor, Charles, 289n. 9
Taylor, Frederick, 36
teacher, relationship with students,
    88–90, 94, 107, 203, 271
  impersonal character, 80–81, 90,
    170, 182, 233–234
  recognition from, 5, 88–90, 189,
    204, 271
teacher, as coach, 215
teachers, professional development.
    See professional development
teachers' know-how, drawn on in local
    reforms, 52–53
teaching
  mysterious in reforms, 5, 107, 274
  relational and cultural, 4, 107
Teaching, Learning, and Curriculum
    Alignment, 146–147, 226
technology in school, 51, 95, 101
Tharp, Roland G., 282n. 13
Thomas, J., 283n. 7
Thomas, R., 283n. 7
Thompson, Charles L., 276, 297n. 7
Thompson, John B., 281n. 5
Thompson, Mrs. (sixth-grade teacher),
    180–187, 189, 192–193, 195,
    197–202, 205–206, 296n. 1
Thompson, Tommy G. (Governor of
    Wisconsin), 237, 241
Thurston Early Childhood
    Development Center, 21, 149
Time, 208, 209
Tomaney, J., 299n. 23
top-down and bottom-up reform
    and legislators, 251

top-down and bottom-up reform (*cont.*)
  in MSSI, 5, 162–163, 175, 212–213,
    217, 251
  in State Systemic Initiative, 47–48
  in Willow Run, 108, 259–260, 262,
    263–265, 272
Total Quality Management, 26, 100
Town Meeting, 151–152
Trevarthen, Colwyn, 6, 281n. 3

unemployment
  global, 153
  in Michigan, 153
  in U.S., 154–155, 207–209, 240,
    277, 294n. 29
  in Washtenaw County, 176, 273
United Auto Workers (UAW)
  relations with Ford in 1940s, 112,
    118, 291n. 7
  relations with Kaiser-Frazer, 128
  on plant closing announcement,
    29–30
  on YT/GM suit, 63, 70, 71
  on Stempel's firing, 67
  contract with Big Three, 72
  strikes against GM, 177, 238–239,
    277
  on GM's greed, 208
University of Michigan, School of
    Education, 3, 11, 178, 180, 185

vouchers, proposed by Engler, 75

Washtenaw County, 20, 254
Washtenaw County, demographics,
    20–22
Washtenaw County Intermediate
    School District (WISD), 20,
    235, 273
Wenger, Etienne, 282n. 11, 298n. 7
Wertsch, James V., 7, 282n. 9
Western Michigan University, 98
Willis, Paul, 55, 286n. 17
Willow Run
  defined by its school district, 21
  demographics, 21–22
  location, 20

Willow Run Assembly Plant, 109
  as Ford bomber plant, 109–133
  closing announced, 22, 23–25,
  predicted consequences of closing,
    30–32, 283n. 12
  media coverage of announced
    closing, 28–29, 32–34, 68–69
  closed, 70, 273
  consequences of closing, 253–254
Willow Run bomber plant
  housing for workers, 118–123
  mementos in WRCS, 130
  story of, 109–131
  toxic site, 231
  workers disparaged, 115–116
Willow Run Community Schools
    (WRCS), 1. *See also* Cheney;
    Edmonson; Ford; Holmes;
    Kaiser; Kettering; Thurston;
    Willow Run High School
  complemented by TLC, 226
  demographic overview, 21
  described by Vivian Lyte, 98
  described by MSSI, 148
  origins, 124–127
  regions, 99
  role in community, 50
  vision statement, 101, 103–104, 150,
    166, 224, 271
Willow Run High School (WRHS),
    21, 51, 127
  Renaissance Program, 160
  seniors interviewed, 231–234
  Scott Heister's students interviewed,
    243–244, 263
Willow Run school board meeting,
    254–256
Willow Run Systemic Initiative
    (WRSI) committee
  funded by MSSI, 77, 244, 288n. 17
  central members, 17–19
  school presentations, 98–103,
    104–105, 142
  Town Meeting, 151–152
  evaluated, 148, 158–167
  reports to MSSI, 158–167,
    262–263

drawing on WR ethos, 4, 108, 256, 262, 271
becoming top-down?, 259–260, 263–265, 272
on assessing learning, 163
on building confidence, 104, 271–272
on building curriculum, 144–147, 218, 257–258
on culture of teaching, 149
on goals of reform, 164–166
on MEAP, 105–106, 161, 214–217, 218–225, 226–228
on MSSI, 162–163, 167, 175, 212–213, 217
on needs of staff and students, 142, 149
on quality reforms, 218, 226–228, 264
on systemic reform, 100, 102–103, 150
WRSI News, 259
Willow Village, 119–130
Wilson, Marion, 110, 243
Winters, Doug (township attorney), 63
Wolman, William, 298n. 14
work, changes in, 2
workers, inner core, 279
workers, outer ring, 279
"Workplace 2000," 2
World War II, 20, 110, 129
writing, process, 57
WRSI News, 259

Yokich, Steve (UAW vice president), 29
Yomtoob, Youssef ("Dr. Joe") (Superintendent, WRCS)
WRCS reform, 30, 50–52
on WR plant closing, 50–52
visits first grade, 85–86
visits Lansing, 135
and equity, 159
millage election, 175–176
and Edmonson, 186
visits MSSI, 213,
at WRSI meeting, 219, 228
leaving, 234–235
Ypsilanti, city of
Heritage Festival, 129
housing Willow Run plant workers, 31
known as "Ypsitucky," 120
location, 20
public schools, 254
and Willow Run bomber plant, 115
Ypsilanti Courier, 252, 256
Ypsilanti Press
on YT/GM suit, 70, 94
on school finance, 73, 74, 75
on plant closing, 28–29, 71
on NAFTA, 72
special issue on bomber plant, 110, 129
on WRSI, 151
publication ended, 178
Ypsilanti Press (Ann Arbor News), 253
Ypsilanti Township (YT)
before World War II, 117
and Willow Village, 119, 129
and WRCS, 21, 124
suing GM, 63–64, 68–69, 70–71, 94–95, 156–157

Zucker, Andrew, 288n. 16